Flexible Semantics for Reinterpretation Phenomena

CSLI Studies in Computational Linguistics

This series covers all areas of computational linguistics and language technology, with a special emphasis on work which has direct relevance to practical applications, makes formal advances, and incorporates insights into natural language processing from other fields, especially linguistics and psychology. Books in this series describe groundbreaking research or provide an accessible and up-to-date overview of an area for nonspecialists. Also included are works documenting freely available resources for language processing, such as software, grammars, dictionaries, and corpora.

Series edited by Ann Copestake

CSLI Studies in
Computational Linguistics

Flexible Semantics for Reinterpretation Phenomena

Markus Egg

CSLI PUBLICATIONS
Center for the Study of
Language and Information
Stanford, California

Center for the Study of Language and Information
Leland Stanford Junior University
Printed in the United States
09 08 07 06 05 1 2 3 4 5

Library of Congress Cataloging-in-Publication Data

Egg, Markus.
Flexible semantics for reinterpretation phenomena / by Markus Egg.

p. cm. – (CSLI studies in computational linguistics)

Includes bibliographical references and index.
ISBN 1-57586-502-5 (pbk. : alk. paper)
ISBN 1-57586-501-7 (cloth : alk. paper)

1. Semantics—Data processing. 2. Colloquial language.
3. Computational linguistics. I. Title.
II. Series: Studies in computational linguistics (Stanford, Calif.)

P325.5D38E38 2005
401′.43′0285–dc22 2005023300
CIP

∞ The acid-free paper used in this book meets the minimum requirements of the American National Standard for Information Sciences—Permanence of Paper for Printed Library Materials, ANSI Z39.48-1984.

CSLI was founded in 1983 by researchers from Stanford University, SRI International, and Xerox PARC to further the research and development of integrated theories of language, information, and computation. CSLI headquarters and CSLI Publications are located on the campus of Stanford University.

CSLI Publications reports new developments in the study of language, information, and computation. Please visit our web site at
http://cslipublications.stanford.edu/
for comments on this and other titles, as well as for changes and corrections by the author and publisher.

Contents

Introduction vii

1 Previous Work 1

2 Representing and Deriving Meaning 65

3 Type Coercion 99

4 Landing Site Coercion 141

5 The Duration Principle 189

6 Conclusion 219

Glossary 223

References 229

Index 237

Introduction

This chapter lays the ground for the investigation of reinterpretation in the form of a brief introduction to the phenomenon. The goals and the structure of the book will then be outlined.

0.1 The phenomenon of reinterpretation

Under the heading of *reinterpretation* two hitherto unrelated linguistic topics are brought together, viz., *metonymy* and *aspectual coercion*.

Metonymy is known traditionally as a figure of speech in which an expression does not refer in the usual way. E.g., one can use *hand* to refer to workmen or sailors, or *blade* to refer to a sword. But the new referent is linked to the referent of the literal interpretation of the expression in a salient way: For the cited examples, the relation is one between a whole and its parts. (This special case of metaphor is also known as *synecdoche*.) However, metonymy is not restricted to literary texts, hence, a comprehensive account of ordinary linguistic behaviour must be capable of handling the phenomenon as well.

Aspectual coercion typically shows up when constituents of a verbal projection exert conflicting requirements on the way in which a state of affairs is presented. E.g., durative adverbials like *for two hours* indicate the duration of a state of affairs that does not yet have boundaries. By measuring its duration they introduce boundaries for it. Consequently, they can only modify verbs (or verbal projections) that present a state of affairs as having no inherent boundaries, for instance as with *rain* or *sing*. Thus, *rain for two hours* is well-formed.

In contrast, *play a song* presents a state of affairs as having boundaries (viz., the first and the last note of the song), hence, *play a song for two hours* is not well-formed in a literal expression. But if we reinterpret *play a song* iteratively, it refers to a state of affairs (the repetition of the playing of the song) that has no inherent boundaries. This makes *play a song for two hours* well-formed in the interpretation that introduces a two-hour-long repetition of the playing of the song.

The goal of this book is to describe these two phenomena as instances of the more general phenomenon of reinterpretation. The analysis that is developed in this book describes reinterpretation as the (monotonic) augmentation of the semantics of an expression in order to derive its full meaning. Reinterpretation is pragmatically motivated, characteristically, by the attempt to avoid an impending semantic mismatch of the constituents of an utterance.

This view on reinterpretation necessitates some comments on the expression 'reinterpretation': It not only refers to certain phenomena of natural language, it also suggests an analysis of these phenomena in terms of nonmonotonic, destructive processes that act upon a fully specified semantic representation of an expression and replace at least part of its original interpretation. But since the expression 'reinterpretation' is well established, I will retain its use. However, the reader is asked to bear in mind that my use of this expression does not subscribe to the explanation of the phenomenon it suggests.

0.1.1 A first pattern of reinterpretation: Type coercion

Consider first some examples for expressions that are in need of reinterpretation, called *reinterpretation candidates*. In metonymic expressions, reinterpretation is motivated by sortal selection restrictions that verbs exert on their subcategorised arguments. Sentences that are acceptable only after reinterpretation (but not in a literal interpretation) are marked by a 'hash' (#) sign:

(1) # Amélie labelled the wine

In (1), the verb selects for objects that denote *things*, but the object refers to a *substance*. If this distinction is modelled in terms of sorts, care must be taken to avoid a mismatch for (1), since the respective sorts SUBST(ance) and THING would be disjoint. This impending mismatch is resolved by augmenting the meaning of (1) with the help of conceptual knowledge that beverages typically have *containers*. The resulting interpretation of (1) is that Amélie labelled the containers of the wine. Since containers are things, this respects the selection restriction of the verb.

But reinterpretation need not involve such a semantic mismatch within an expression. It may also be motivated by the attempt to fit in an utterance with nonlinguistic conceptual knowledge. Consider e.g. (2). Its semantically well-formed literal reading 'all tenors occupy the top shelf' is incompatible with our knowledge about the stability of shelves. If, however, (2) is reinterpreted, e.g., in the context of a CD store, one can use a reinterpretation operator that introduces the notion of a recording. I.e., we can take (2) to mean that all *recordings* of tenors are on the top shelf:

(2) # All tenors are on the top shelf

This pattern of reinterpretation is familiar from the literature. It has been christened *type coercion* by Moens and Steedman (1986, 1988) and can be characterised as follows: To make an argument (the semantics of a subcategorised or modified expression) compatible with the functor that is applied to it (the semantics of the corresponding subcategoriser or modifier),[1] an operator intervenes between functor and argument. If F stands for the functor, A for the argument, and Op for the additional material, the schema of type coercion is $F(Op(A))$.

Type coercion is recurrent in the nominal as well as in the verbal domain. It is expounded in Moens and Steedman (1986, 1988) and Pulman (1997) for the aspectual domain and in the work of Dölling (1992, 1995) and Pustejovsky (1995), for the nominal domain. Type coercion is not the only pattern of reinterpretation. In section 0.1.5 I will present a second reinterpretation pattern called *landing site coercion*.

0.1.2 The pragmatic motivation of reinterpretation

But from the viewpoint of both hearer and speaker, reinterpretation is no matter of course. Why do hearers bother at all to make sense of expressions that have no literal reading? Why are reinterpretation candidates acceptable to hearers and not rejected with reference to the fact that the utterance is either not semantically well-formed or incompatible with conceptual knowledge? From the speaker's perspective, why do speakers choose an indirect way of expressing themselves in terms of reinterpretation candidates instead of verbalising every part of the information they want to communicate?

This willingness of the hearer to accept, and of the speaker to produce reinterpretation candidates is pragmatically based. Thus, reinterpretation follows from the rules of rational linguistic behaviour, which are described in the form of *conversational maxims* (Grice, 1975).

For the hearer, the fundamental motivation of accepting reinterpretation candidates is his firm belief that the speaker follows the conversational maxims even when he utters an expression that does not make sense in a literal reading. In particular, the hearer imputes compliance to the *cooperative principle* to the speaker. I.e., he regards all utterances of the speaker as adequate to the conversation and is thus extremely hesitant to assume that the speaker utters nonsense. This presupposition of the cooperativeness of the speaker secures acceptance of reinterpretation candidates, since it enforces a 'charitable' view of their seeming defects (semantic ill-formedness or in-

[1] The sole exception to this rule are verbs and their NP arguments: Here the semantic contribution of the subcategorising element (the verb) emerges as the argument, while the subcategorised NPs provide a functor in their semantics.

compatibility with conceptual knowledge). They are not taken as signs for the ill-formedness of an utterance by the hearer, but instead are interpreted as signalling reinterpretation candidates.

On the part of the speaker, reinterpretation optimises the trade-off between *contrary* requests in conversational maxims. These maxims emerge on a more fine-grained level of pragmatics, which breaks down the cooperative principle into several conversational maxims. The maxim of *manner*, which requests perspicuity of utterances, requires an utterance to be maximally succinct and clear at the same time. However, often succinctness can only be obtained at the cost of a certain obscurity and ambiguity, and vice versa.

Reinterpretation enables the speaker to comply to both requests simultaneously: On the one hand, it allows considerably succinct utterances, since only parts of the meaning of the utterances have to be put into words (e.g., the reference to the containers of the wine can be omitted in (1)). On the other hand, speakers use reinterpretation when conceptual knowledge immediately supplies that part of the meaning of the utterances that is not verbalised. Thus, the utterances do not suffer from obscurity and ambiguity in spite of their brevity.

0.1.3 Semantic mismatches in reinterpretation candidates

In the following, I will discuss reinterpretation for expressions that exhibit semantic mismatches between their immediate constituents (called *m-expressions*). The proposed account of these reinterpretation candidates extends to those cases where reinterpretation is triggered by incompatibility of an expression with conceptual knowledge.

For m-expressions, reinterpretation seems to introduce a certain amount of flexibility: Selection restrictions of linguistic expressions for certain semantic properties of the expressions which they modify or subcategorise for seem to be not hard and fast, but to express only tendencies that can easily be violated. This was illustrated for the nominal domain with the m-expression (1) above.

The area of aspectual semantics is another domain that is fraught with reinterpretation possibilities. Any semanticist who has ever tried to introduce novices to aspectual semantics is aware of this fact, because it complicates the introduction considerably: In many cases, when he adduces sentences as negative evidence for proposed aspectual regularities, his audience will question the validity of this evidence, as it is possible to understand these sentences somehow – albeit in a somewhat marginal way or only if one constructs a more or less odd context in which it would be possible to utter the sentence felicitously.

Consider for instance the m-expression (3), which features the case of reinterpretation in the aspectual domain that was mentioned at the beginning of the introduction:

(3) # Amélie played the sonata for ten days

This sentence is acceptable (in an interpretation where Amélie played the sonata repeatedly), although the aspectual selection restriction of the durative adverbial *for ten days* seems to be violated. In a preliminary description that simplifies the exact spellout of the syntax and semantics of (3), one can describe this seeming violation of the selection restriction in terms of the aspectual property of *boundedness*.

Bounded expressions introduce states of affairs with inherent boundaries. E.g., *Amélie played the sonata* is bounded, because for the playing of a sonata it is constitutive that it has a beginning and an end (the first and the last note). In contrast, *Amélie played the piano* is unbounded, since the states of affairs it introduces are not characterised by such boundaries. I.e., a state of affairs may count as Amélie's playing the piano regardless of whether it has a beginning or an end. (See section 1.6 for a formal definition of boundedness.) The durative adverbial can modify only *unbounded* expressions, but in (3), it modifies a bounded one. The impending conflict is avoided by interpreting the modified expression iteratively, which returns an unbounded expression.

In sum, reinterpretation is motivated by the fact that reinterpretation candidates in a literal interpretation would be semantically ill-formed or in conflict with conceptual knowledge. For (1) and (3), the selection restriction of a modifying or subcategorising subconstituent would be violated. (2), though well-formed, would be in conflict with conceptual knowledge. But reinterpretation avoids these conflicts, which would otherwise have rendered the semantic representation of reinterpretation candidates ill-formed or incompatible with conceptual knowledge. I consider these *impending semantic conflicts* to be the first characteristic of reinterpretation.

However, in my description of data like (1) and (3), I assume that there are selection restrictions that can be violated. Otherwise, one could not characterise reinterpretation as involving an impending semantic mismatch between the constituents of an expression. Thus, one might disapprove of my description in terms of a semantic mismatch and instead account for the data by *relaxing* selection restrictions so that they are no longer violable. For instance, one could make them more general or model them in terms of defeasible regularities.

But such an account would disregard the fact that reinterpretation candidates have *no literal reading*. If their semantics were derived compositionally, one would expect such a reading. For all reinterpretation candidates, deviance from the literal reading proceeds in the same manner: The interpretation involves semantic material over and above that which is contributed by the constituents of the expression.

Reconsider the examples (3) and (1): (3) does not simply express the fact that Amélie played the sonata and that it took her ten days to do so. Rather, the interpretation of this example involves the notion of an *iteration* (i.e., she played the sonata repeatedly). But this iteration is not expressed in the semantics of any constituent of (3). Similarly, the notion of *container* that is part of our understanding of (1) (Amélie labelled the containers of the wine, not the wine itself) is not introduced in the semantics of any constituent of (1).

This additional material is introduced to *buffer* the semantic mismatches in the reinterpretation candidate. The iterative operator maps bounded propositions onto unbounded ones, the notion of container mediates in (1) between the verb semantics, a relation between persons and things, and the object NP semantics, which specifies the second argument of this relation as a substance.

If selection restrictions of subcategorisers and modifiers were too relaxed to be violated, this buffering could not be motivated at all. Hence, the non-literal readings of reinterpretation candidates corroborate my claim that reinterpretation involves a semantic mismatch between constituents of an expression in that certain selection restrictions are not met. That is, reinterpretation makes possible a more flexible use of language without having to relinquish the restricting power of type-theoretic and sortal restrictions.

The strategy of capturing reinterpretation by relaxing selection restrictions is not only problematic because it neglects the fact that reinterpretation candidates have no literal reading. Another problem that arises immediately for this strategy is that due to this relaxation, one is in danger of losing the power to distinguish between reinterpretation candidates and ill-formed expressions.

Consider, e.g., the treatment of reinterpretation in the Verbmobil system (Wahlster, 2000), a translation system for spontaneous spoken language in the domain of scheduling appointments and travel planning. (4) is a reinterpretation candidate from the Verbmobil database:

(4) # I will pencil you in at 10 am

It exhibits a sortal mismatch between the selection restriction of the verb *pencil in* (to abstract entities) and the sort PER[son] as introduced by the personal pronoun *you*. Since reinterpretation is outside the scope of the Verbmobil system, it captures (4) by weakening the sortal selection restriction of the verb for its object argument to $\top$ (top).

But this is problematic: Intuition tells us that it is the entity that is pencilled in (and not the pencilling in itself) that is to take place at 10 am. I.e., the selection restriction of the PP *at 10 am* would have to be weakened, too, in this strategy (to be compatible with entities of the sort PER[son]), but then plainly inacceptable sentences like (5a) as opposed to (5b) could no longer be ruled out:

(5) a * You were at 10 am

b The meeting was at 10 am

No such problems arise in a reinterpretation account of (5). This illustrates my point that one cannot treat reinterpretation candidates by the mere relaxation of selection restrictions.

In sum, there may be considerable mismatch between the semantic contributions of the constituents of an expression that nevertheless does not render the expression unacceptable but gives rise to reinterpretation. Thus, semantic construction for reinterpretation candidates must fulfill two seemingly contradictory goals. On the one hand, the resulting representations of these candidates comprise potentially conflicting material. Smoothing out these conflicts, e.g., by describing them in terms of defeasible properties cannot explain why reinterpretation candidates have no literal reading. Hence, their semantic representations must bring out these potential conflicts. On the other hand, reinterpretation candidates are acceptable, thus, semantic construction must return a well-formed representation for them. I.e., this conflicting material may not render the resulting semantic representations ill-formed.

0.1.4 Sources for the meaning of reinterpretation candidates

In the preceding subsection I pointed out that reinterpretation candidates include in their meanings material that is not contributed by any of the constituents of the expression. This immediately raises the question of where this material comes from and how it is integrated with the result of semantic construction.

Examples (1) and (3) suggest that we employ extralinguistic conceptual knowledge to mediate between the conflicting properties of the semantically mismatched constituents. This is particularly suggestive for sortal mismatches as in (1): It is part of our conceptual knowledge about beverages that they tend to be found in containers, but this piece of information is not included in the semantics of *wine*.

If we use this knowledge of beverages, we obtain the desired interpretation of (1) by attributing the property of being labelled by Amélie (as contributed by the semantics of (1)) not to the wine but to its containers. There are numerous other instances of this kind of integrating conceptual knowledge into the semantics of reinterpretation candidates; they are presented in great detail in the work of Dölling (1992, 1995).

This view has been challenged recently by Pustejovsky (1995), who claims that part of the knowledge used for the interpretation of sentences like (1) (in particular, knowledge about the origin and the purpose of things) belongs to compositional semantics and is thus available for semantic composition. While this theory may account for many reinterpretation candidates in the nominal domain, (1) shows that it cannnot capture them all: Neither the origin nor the purpose of the wine introduce the notion of container. I will back up my view that reinterpretation involves the inclusion of extralinguistic knowledge into semantic representations of reinterpretation candidates in a detailed discussion of Pustejovsky's theory in chapter 1.

For the aspectual case (3), the method of integrating conceptual knowledge is similar. Here the goal is to turn the bounded *Amélie played the sonata* into an unbounded expression that fits in with the selection restriction of the durative adverbial.

The crucial extralinguistic information for this reinterpretation candidate is the *typical duration* that is associated with the modified expression *Amélie played the sonata.* This duration information, which is eventually based on conceptual knowledge on sonata playings, is somewhat vague: One would associate this expression with a duration of minutes or hours, but not of days or weeks. The typical duration of the modified expression should be compatible with the duration of ten days as introduced in the semantics of the modifier. This suggests a reinterpretation by an operator whose output is not only unbounded, but also associated with a considerably longer typical duration than its input. Therefore the iterative operator is chosen (rather than, e.g., the progressive operator): The typical duration of an iteration of *Amélie played the sonata* (but not the one associated with the progressive of *Amélie played the sonata*) is compatible with a duration of ten days.

If one claims that reinterpretation makes use of material from nonlinguistic knowledge sources, this begs the question of how the derivation of fully-fledged utterance meanings integrates this material with the results of semantic construction for reinterpretation candidates. In particular, is reinterpretation *destructive* in that it must undo results of semantic construction, or does it merely add information in a *monotonic* way?

Here it is important to note that reinterpretation candidates trigger no kind of *garden path effect* whatsoever. While such effects are characteristic for the parsing of syntactic structures, there are also semantic instances, e.g., in the example (6), where the subject NP *the astronomer* primes an astronomical context that leads to a rash resolution of the polysemy in *star*:

(6) The astronomer married a star

Even if these effects may vary in strength, one would expect that at least a weak garden path effect would have to accompany the undoing of results of semantic composition. Thus, the lack of garden path effects in reinterpretation suggests that reinterpretation involves no undoing of this kind. Instead, the integration of the extralinguistic knowledge is *monotonic* and need not undo the results of semantic composition. This, however, means that semantic construction must restrict itself to the semantic parts of full utterance meanings and leave enough space for extralinguistically derived material.

As an illustration of the way this monotonic integration of extralinguistic material works, consider (8a), a very simplistic and schematic representation of the result of semantic construction for the reinterpretation candidate (7). (It serves expository purposes only and will be expounded in detail in chapter 4.)

(7) # Amélie played the sonata for some time

The representation comprises a position between the semantic contributions of the durative adverbial and of *Amélie played the sonata* (indicated by the dots) that is not determined by semantic construction. Information from other sources can determine this position, e.g., as an iterative operator. This determination preserves (8a), the result of the semantic construction for (7), in its entirety. The result of the determination is (8b), which models one of the meanings of (7) that (7) may have after reinterpretation, viz., the proposition that Amélie played the sonata repeatedly for some time:

(8) a $\mathbf{for\_some\_time}(\ldots\mathbf{play}(\mathbf{amélie}, \mathbf{the\_sonata}))$
b $\mathbf{for\_some\_time}(\mathrm{ITER}(\mathbf{play}(\mathbf{amélie}, \mathbf{the\_sonata})))$

The representation (8a) highlights the fact that the proposed account of reinterpretation characterises it as yet another instantiation of the more general phenomenon that the meaning of some expressions can only be determined by the interaction of various knowledge sources. But this entails that the full meaning of reinterpretation candidates is not completely determined by semantic construction; that is, that these expressions are *semantically underspecified*.

(7) exhibits this semantic underspecification of reinterpretation candidates clearly, because even with the help of conceptual knowledge no preference can be derived for one of its readings: Out of context one cannot decide whether *Amélie played the sonata* is to be reinterpreted in terms of the progressive or of the iterative operator, both options not only meet the aspectual requirements of (7) (they turn the bounded *Amélie played the sonata* into an unbounded expression), they also yield readings of equal plausibility.

This shows that the semantic representations of reinterpretation candidates can only specify what the reinterpretation operator must look like in order to mediate successfully between the conflicting requirements of their mismatched constituents. Since there may be several options for the instantiation of this operator, these semantic representations are underspecified.

However, due to the close interaction between linguistic and nonlinguistic knowledge sources, not all examples illustrate this point clearly. Language understanding hardly ever proceeds in zero contexts, in particular, one cannot shut off conceptual knowledge, which often immediately resolves the semantic underspecification that arises through reinterpretation. E.g., nothing in the semantics of (1) bars one from understanding it in the sense of 'Amélie labelled an object that consists of the frozen wine', but conceptual knowledge about the melting point of wine makes one strongly prefer the 'container' reading over this reading.

Similarly, knowledge about the typical duration of sonatas immediately triggers the choice of the iterative operator in the reinterpretation of (3), which differs from (7) in that its adverbial introduces a specific duration. The progressive operator would have been possible as well; it would (roughly) map a bounded expression onto an unbounded one that refers to a *part* of the action referred to in the bounded expression. But then the typical duration associated with the resulting expression would be even shorter than the one of *Amélie played the sonata* itself, i.e., it would be even less compatible with the one introduced by the adverbial. Therefore, this second reinterpretation possibility is ruled out immediately, in fact, I suppose that it would only be noticed by persons who have undergone a certain amount of semantic training.

In summary, with the help of reinterpretation, semantic construction can avoid right from the start impending semantic conflicts between the constituents of an expression. To this end, reinterpretation augments the semantics of an expression with suitable extralinguistic information that buffers the potentially conflicting material in the semantics of the expression. Hence, reinterpretation *cannot be captured in terms of compositional semantics alone*.

0.1.5 Two kinds of reinterpretation

There are reinterpretation candidates that resist an explanation in terms of type coercion, i.e., in terms of an appropriate operator that intervenes between functor and argument. Consider e.g. (9):

(9) # Amélie left for two hours

This example exhibits the same aspectual incompatibility as (3) above. While one could take recourse to type coercion for (9) analogously to the case of (3),[2] the preferred way of mediating between the conflicting aspectual properties of functor and argument is different here. This mediation proceeds in two steps. First, the argument is augmented with additional material that provides an alternative position to which the functor can apply (this position is called a *landing site* for the functor). Second, the functor does not apply to its argument as a whole but only to this newly created landing site. This type of reinterpretation is called *landing site coercion* (LSC).

[2]The resulting interpretation would be that Amélie left *repeatedly* for two hours.

For (9), landing site coercion works in the following way: The argument (the semantics of *Amélie left*) is augmented by an expression that introduces an *aftermath* e' for the eventuality e of Amélie leaving. This aftermath is an *absence* of Amélie ('eventuality' refers to all kinds of states of affairs).

In this expression the property of being an aftermath of e is a potential landing site for a functor. Since the property of being an aftermath of some other eventuality is unbounded, this new landing site fits the aspectual selection restriction of the adverbial, therefore the adverbial semantics applies only to this landing site. The resulting interpretation of (9) is that it is not Amélie's leaving but her subsequent absence that lasted for two hours.

This reinterpretation pattern draws on extralinguistic knowledge just like type coercion. For aspectual LSC, the concept of *nucleus* is crucial: I follow Moens and Steedman and assume that conceptually the flow of eventualities is carved into small portions, called 'nuclei'. Nuclei consist of an eventuality together with associated preparatory eventuality and aftermath. These additional eventualities can be referred to by the operators that are used in LSC.

But landing site coercion is not restricted to the aspectual domain. Examples like *train to London* also instantiate this phenomenon. This expression can be predicated of trains irrespective of their spatiotemporal position; what is specified by the PP is their *destination*. I.e., the PP does not characterise a train as a spatiotemporal entity, which means that it does not act as a modifier of the semantics of *train* as a whole. It only modifies that part of the interpretation of *train* that refers to the train's destination. Since the lexical semantics of *train* does not include reference to a destination, LSC is needed to augment it accordingly.

The abstract schema of LSC is $A \;\&\; a_1(F(a_2))$, where $a_1(a_2)$ is the augmentation of the argument A that introduces the additional landing site a_2 for the functor F ('&' is the generalised conjunction of Rooth and Partee 1982 that conjoins any pair of expressions that have the same type, see p.57). This abstract schema shows that after LSC the functor has scope only over a small part of the argument (a_2) while a large part of the argument (viz., $A \;\&\; a_1$) outscopes the functor. This distinguishes landing site coercion from type coercion, where the functor as a whole has scope over the argument.

In the remainder of this subsection, I present a diagnostic to distinguish type coercion and landing site coercion for reinterpretation candidates that involve intersective modifiers. (Recall that the semantics of the modifier is the functor, the semantics of the modified expression, the argument.) This technique is based on the different abstract schemas for the two kinds of coercion.

The test case is modification of an expression E by an intersective modifier which triggers coercion. If this coercion changes entailments of E, then it must be type coercion. Landing site coercion cannot change such entailments.

Consider, e.g., (7) in its progressive interpretation and (9). In (7), reinterpreting the sentence by type coercion in terms of inserting a progressive operator between functor and argument leads to a loss of entailments. While *Amélie played the sonata* entails that she played all parts of the sonata, this entailment no longer holds for (7) in the chosen interpretation. In contrast, if we assume that the adverbial in (9) refers to the aftermath of Amélie's departure (this aftermath was introduced by landing site coercion), (9) carries all the entailments of *Amélie left*.[3] This criterion provides additional evidence for the claim that *train to London* and similar examples are instances of LSC in the nominal domain: *Train to London* has all the entailments of *train*.

This diagnostic is based on two observations. First, intersective modifiers by themselves do not affect entailments of the expressions they modify, they add information conjunctively. Thus, any loss of entailments in coercion cannot be attributed to such a modifier, it must have been caused by an operator like the progressive operator in (7). Second, an operator has scope over the argument as a whole only in type coercion, and this scope constellation is a precondition for the ability of the operator to trigger the loss of entailments of the argument. Consequently, if coercion caused by intersective modification results in the loss of entailments of an argument, we are dealing with a case of type coercion.

I conclude that reinterpretation does not follow a uniform pattern. There are (at least) two patterns of reinterpretation, type coercion and landing site coercion.

0.1.6 Reinterpretation vs. polysemy and homonymy

In this subsection, I comment on the difference between polysemy and homonymy on the one hand and reinterpretation on the other hand. I adopt the usual definitions of polysemy and homonymy: Polysemy is ambiguity of a single lexical item all of whose readings are synchronically related. Homonymous lexemes share the same form, but are synchronically unrelated.[4]

Polysemy and homonymy are cases of lexically determined semantic underspecification. Consider, e.g., the notorious case of *bank* ('water's edge' or 'financial institution') or the famous polysemous lexeme *school* with its numerous readings (like 'institution', 'building', 'principle', etc.) as discussed in Bierwisch (1983).

If a complex expression comprises a polysemous or homonymous item, it

[3]This example simplifies the analysis of durative adverbials for ease of exposition, see section 4.2.1 for details.

[4]Here I ignore the fact that for some lexemes this identity only holds for the written (*homography*) or spoken forms (*homophony*).

may inherit semantic underspecification from this item. In contrast, there is no such lexical foundation of the semantic underspecification in reinterpretation candidates. I.e., reinterpretation candidates are semantically underspecified, but this does not entail that any of their constituents is itself underspecified. Consider, e.g., (7): None of its constituents is underspecified, in particular, *to play* is not ambiguous between an iterative and a single (one playing eventuality only) reading.

This observation highlights the fact that the semantic underspecification of reinterpretation candidates arises only *in the process of the semantic construction* of smaller units into larger expressions. This underspecification is not introduced by lexical items, which explains why the possible readings of reinterpretation candidates cannot be predetermined in the semantics of the expression but are dependent on factors like conceptual knowledge.

Another difference between polysemy and homonymy as opposed to reinterpretation is that reinterpretation must be *triggered by some kind of impending conflict* for a semantic structure. I.e., reinterpretation arises as an attempt to avoid a potentially dangerous conflict between the semantic contributions of the parts of an expression or between an expression and conceptual knowledge. No such conflict is incumbent in cases of polysemy and homonymy.

These differences separate reinterpretation clearly from homonymy; the distinction between reinterpretation and polysemy is somewhat obfuscated by the fact that diachronically reinterpretations can give rise to polysemy by conventionalisation: I.e., a lexeme may be reinterpreted in specific ways so regularly that its resulting interpretation is reanalysed as a new (synchronically related) reading of the lexeme.

This concludes the introduction to the phenomenon of reinterpretation. In the next section of this chapter, I will briefly outline the goals and the structure of this book and add some acknowledgements.

0.2 Goals and structure of the book

The goal of this book is to present a comprehensive account of the syntactic and semantic aspects of the phenomenon of reinterpretation. This account is to incorporate previous work and to unite the (hitherto mainly unrelated) strands of research on reinterpretation in the nominal and the aspectual domain. I also want to extend the perspective on reinterpretation from the already established domains of metonymy and aspectual type coercion to a more general view of reinterpretation.

I will present a flexible semantic construction that allows the derivation of appropriate semantic representations for reinterpretation candidates on the basis of a simple phrase structure grammar. It is based on an underspecification formalism that allows a thorough formalisation of the phenomenon, in particular, it brings out the semantic underspecification of reinterpretation candidates.

The proposed analyses of the syntax and semantics of reinterpretation are also intended to outline the boundaries of semantic construction for reinterpretation candidates clearly. In this way, I wish to demarcate those aspects of reinterpretation that draw on additional knowledge sources, in particular, sources for conceptual knowledge. From the viewpoint of natural language processing, the goal of this book is to contribute to the definition of a module for the syntactic and semantic processing of reinterpretation candidates. This module can then be integrated with other modules for storing and accessing other kinds of knowledge that is relevant for reinterpretation in order to provide a complete analysis of reinterpretation phenomena.

Finally, I also want to show at least for a tiny segment of conceptual knowledge, viz., information on the typical duration of eventualities, how it interacts with the semantic representations that I assume for reinterpretation candidates. I will offer an analysis of this duration information that accounts for its interaction with the results of semantic construction for reinterpretation candidates.

This book is structured as follows. Chapter 1 discusses in detail previous work on reinterpretation. Apart from giving an overview of this work, I will in this discussion also identify and point out the essentials for an appropriate analysis of reinterpretation. In this chapter I will also introduce the aspectual classification on which my account of aspectual reinterpretation is based.

Chapter 2 is then devoted to the formalisms that are employed in the proposed analysis of reinterpretation in order to derive and represent the meaning of reinterpretation candidates. First, I will present underspecification formalisms, in which I will encode my representation of the semantic underspecification that is incumbent in the semantics of reinterpretation candidates. With the help of such formalisms it is possible to derive partial structures like (8a) as the result of semantic construction and to model the integration of additional, extralinguistic information as in (8b).

The language CLLS, which was designed for the underspecified representation of various kinds of ambiguity, will also be introduced in chapter 2. This language will be used to represent reinterpretation, since reinterpretation crucially involves semantic underspecification. Finally, I will describe a grammar fragment with which to derive the semantic representations for reinterpretation candidates on the basis of a simple phrase structure syntax.

The next two chapters are the core of the presentation of my analysis of reinterpretation. They give detailed analyses of type coercion (chapter 3) and landing site coercion (chapter 4), both in the nominal and the verbal domain. In this chapter, I will take up the problems noted in chapter 1 for the analysis of reinterpretation.

In chapter 5 I will cross the boundary of semantics and expound the *Duration Principle*: Constituents of a larger expression may not introduce conflicting duration information for one single eventuality. Such information characteristically stems from nonlinguistic sources, in particular, from conceptual knowledge, e.g., our knowledge about the typical duration of sonatas. This chapter exemplifies at least for a tiny section of conceptual knowledge – which is notoriously difficult to formalise – how one can integrate both linguistic and extralinguistic knowledge in the determination of the meaning of a reinterpretation candidate. It will be shown that the Duration Principle closely interacts with reinterpretation: On the one hand, it constrains aspectual reinterpretation (although it is not an aspectual regularity in itself), on the other hand, it may itself trigger reinterpretations. Finally, a glossary summarises the abbreviations, technical terms, and key concepts introduced in this book.

Acknowledgements

This book was written as a part of my work in the project CHORUS in the Sonderforschungsbereich (Special Research Division) 378 in Saarbrücken. The influence of this global setting is visible throughout the book. Therefore I would like to thank all (past and present) members of the CHORUS group, in particular Alexander Koller, for continuous discussion of and feedback on the analyses that are presented in this book.

Special thanks are due to Manfred Pinkal, who supervised the thesis out of which this book emerged. He has read and commented extensively on a first version of the book. The book has profited enormously from the purgatory of his thorough criticism. Thanks are also due to an anonymous reviewer from CSLI Publications for his extraordinary diligence and care; his suggestions have greatly improved the book.

Numerous other people have contributed in some way or other to this book, I'd like to mention just two of them here: Hannes Dölling, whose work got me hooked on the topic of reinterpretation, and Michael Kohlhase, who'll always have a formalism for your problems. Parts of the material of this book were presented in different places during the last few years. Thanks to all the audiences for stimulating feedback and discussion.

Finally, I also would like to thank my friends and my family for unfaltering support, stoic endurance of protracted status reports on the progress of the book, and the occasional cheer-up. Nevertheless, I feel that they will be glad to hear that I do not intend to write another book in the near future.

1

Previous Work

In this chapter, I will mainly present previous work on the phenomenon of reinterpretation. The chapter has two goals, to review previous work in the domain of reinterpretation, and to identify important issues and open problems for an analysis of reinterpretation by discussing this work. In this way, I will lay the ground for the presentation of my own analysis in chapters 3 and 4.

These two goals may sometimes exert conflicting restrictions on the structure of the presentation. To resolve these conflicts, the account of previous work is arranged with respect to content: First, I discuss other researchers' work on type coercion, then, those parts of previous work that relate to phenomena of landing site coercion.

Since an analysis of reinterpretation in the aspectual domain needs to be based on a theory of aspectual classification, this chapter includes a brief introduction to aspectuality and an outline of the aspectual classification which underlies my analyses of aspectual reinterpretation.

1.1 Basic notions of aspectuality

This section provides a very brief introduction to aspectuality. Its sole goal is to facilitate the understanding of the subsequent discussion by recapitulating basic notions of aspectuality and by comparing the aspectual classifications that are presupposed in previous work on reinterpretation. These notions of aspectuality will be taken up again in section 1.6, which introduces the aspectual classification assumed in this book.

The group of expressions that can be classified aspectually are verbs and their projections and larger constituents that contain verbal projections on the condition that these constituents do not include tense and sentence mood (except for embedded sentences). I refer to these expressions as *predicates*. An important subgroup of predicates, called *sentence radicals*, comprise for every verb all the constituents it subcategorises for, unless this is ruled out by syntactic subcategorisation.[5] Sentence radicals may also comprise auxiliaries such as the progressive auxiliary and verbal modifiers such as durative adverbials. They are distinguished from full sentences by an uninflected verb form (e.g., *Amélie sing-* or *Max dance- for two hours*).[6]

Aspectual classifications characterise predicates by *tests*, which check the compatibility of predicates with specific linguistic environments in a literal reading (without reinterpretation). E.g., a modification structure where the modifier is a durative adverbial like *for two hours* is a possible environment for *play the piano* but not for *play a sonata*. The results of these tests are then attributed to *properties of predicates* that characterise aspectual classes. One such property is *cumulativity*: If a predicate is valid for two adjacent temporal entities, it also holds for an appropriate sum of these entities. E.g., if *it rained* holds for the period from 8 to 9 o'clock and for the period from 9 to 10 o'clock, it also holds for the period from 8 to 10 o'clock.

In the following, I will distinguish six groups of predicates and show their distribution in the classifications that are assumed in the previous work on type coercion which will be discussed in this chapter.

The first group are *stative* or *state predicates* like *love* or *be in the pub*. They are compatible with both time point PPs like *at six o' clock sharp* and durative adverbials but not with the progressive. (10c) cannot be reinterpreted, hence is unacceptable:

(10) a   Max was in the pub at six o' clock sharp

b   Max was in the pub for 30 minutes

c * Max was being in the pub

The property of stative predicates that distinguishes them from all other aspectual classes is their *divisivity*: Stative predicates that are valid for a temporal entity are valid for all its parts, too. E.g., if Max was in the pub from 8 to 9 o'clock, he was in the pub at every moment within this hour, too. The compatibility of stative predicates with time point PPs is attributed to their divisivity.

Next come *process* or *activity predicates* like *run* or *chatter*. They are compatible with durative adverbials and the progressive, but not with time point PPs, hence, (11a) has no literal reading (it must undergo ingressive reinterpretation):

(11) a # Max ran at six o' clock sharp

---

[5]E.g., sentence radicals may comprise VPs in control constructions like *Max wants to dance*, even though there is no subject NP for *to dance*.

[6]I.e., Smith's (1991) *verb constellations* (verbs together with their arguments, including subjects) are a subgroup of predicates in the sense used in this book.

b Max ran for 30 minutes

c Max was running

These tests show that process predicates are not fully divisive: While it is true that if Max ran from 8 to 9 o'clock, he also ran from 8:15 to 8:20, it is not true that Max ran at every part of this one-hour interval: Eventualities of running minimally comprise one step, but many parts of this one-hour interval are too small to be an entity at which a step can take place. But then it is not true that Max ran at any part of the interval. This holds in particular for its momentaneous parts, therefore process predicates are incompatible with time point PPs. Stative and process predicates, which share the property of *cumulativity* and of (at least partial) divisivity, are both compatible with durative adverbials.

These two aspectual classes occur in most classifications, in particular in those that are relevant for the discussion presented in this book.

There is far less uniformity for the classification of the other predicates. They are often referred to as *event predicates* and share the property of *boundedness* mentioned in the introduction (0.1.3). For expository purposes, I will break down these predicates into four groups.

The first group are *point predicates* like *cough* or *flash*. Point predicates are compatible with time point PPs but not with time frame adverbials like *in two hours*, the perfect, or the progressive.[7] In addition, if they are modified by durative adverbials, they bar a reinterpretation where the adverbial measures the length of the *aftermath* of an eventuality in the extension of the predicate. (This pattern is called *aftermath modification*). Thus, (12e) cannot mean that Max coughed and that the aftermath or poststate of this coughing lasted 30 minutes; only *iterative* reinterpretation is possible, just like for (12d):

(12) a Max coughed at six o' clock sharp

b # Max coughed in 30 minutes

c # Max has coughed

d # Max was coughing

e # Max coughed for 30 minutes

These results are attributed to *punctuality* (point predicates refer to minimal, durationless temporal entities only) and *atelicity* (they introduce no change of state).[8] Punctuality is adduced to explain the compatibility with time point PPs and the incompatibility with time frame adverbials and the progressive. Atelicity is responsible for the incompatibility with the perfect

[7]However, (12c) – as well as (14c) below – can be reinterpreted, e.g., in terms of the *experiental perfect* (see section 3.2.4.)

[8]See chapter 5 for a discussion of the aspectual relevance of punctuality.

and the aftermath modification, since either crucially refers to the aftermath of a change of state.

Next come the group of *immediate change* predicates (point and immediate change predicates constitute the class of *achievements* in Vendler 1967) like *vanish* or *burst*. They are punctual and telic (introduce an aftermath, e.g., for *vanish* the aftermath is absence). Accordingly, they are compatible with time point PPs and the perfect but not with time frame adverbials or the progressive, and allow aftermath modification. I.e., (13e) can mean that Max vanished and the aftermath of his vanishing (his absence) lasted for 30 minutes.

(13) a Max vanished at six o' clock sharp
b # Max vanished in 30 minutes
c Max has vanished
d # Max was vanishing
e # Max vanished for 30 minutes

The third group are neglected in most classifications, members of this group are *run a mile* or *play a sonata*. They are dubbed *quantised predicates* (the term is borrowed from Krifka 1992). These predicates are non-punctual and describe a state of affairs that has boundaries yet does not introduce a change of state. As expected, the test results are exactly the inverse of those for immediate change predicates. In particular, (14e) disallows aftermath modification:

(14) a # Amélie played a sonata at six o' clock sharp
b Amélie played a sonata in 30 minutes
c # Amélie has played a sonata
d Amélie was playing a sonata
e # Amélie played a sonata for 30 minutes

Finally, *extended change predicates* like *build a house* or *go to the pub* are telic and non-punctual. (Vendler's *accomplishments* consist of quantised and extended change predicates) Their test results are the opposite of those for point predicates:

(15) a # Amélie went to the pub at six o' clock sharp
b Amélie went to the pub in 30 minutes
c Amélie has gone to the pub
d Amélie was going to the pub
e # Amélie went to the pub for 30 minutes

These four groups of event predicates follow from a cross-classification of the group of event predicates with respect to punctuality and telicity.

Most aspectual classifications in the literature can be described in terms of these six classes. Diagram (16) summarises the classifications of Vendler (1967), Dowty (1979), Moens and Steedman (1988) (and Pulman 1997), de Swart (1998), and myself (Egg, 1995):

(16)

<table>
<tr><th></th><th>Vendler</th><th>Dowty</th><th>Moens/St.</th><th>de Swart</th><th>Egg</th></tr>
<tr><td>stative predicate</td><td>stative predicate</td><td>stative predicate</td><td>state</td><td>stative predicate</td><td>stative predicate</td></tr>
<tr><td>process predicate</td><td>process predicate</td><td>process predicate</td><td rowspan="2">process</td><td>process predicate</td><td>process predicate</td></tr>
<tr><td>quantised predicate</td><td>accomplishment predicate</td><td></td><td rowspan="4">event predicate</td><td rowspan="2">intergressive predicate</td></tr>
<tr><td>point predicate</td><td>achievement predicate</td><td></td><td>point</td></tr>
<tr><td>ext. change predicate</td><td>accomplishment predicate</td><td>accomplishment predicate</td><td>culminated process</td><td rowspan="2">change predicate</td></tr>
<tr><td>imm. change predicate</td><td>achievement predicate</td><td>achievement predicate</td><td>culmination</td></tr>
</table>

The diagram highlights the gap in Dowty's reconstruction of Vendler's classification. Dowty does not incorporate bounded yet atelic predicates, whereas Vendler regards them as part of his accomplishment and achievement classes. Note also the difference in terminology: Moens and Steedman use expressions like 'point' to refer to point *predicates*. In addition, their 'process' class should not be confused with the class of process predicates, since it also comprises quantised predicates.

1.2 Formal preliminaries

This section briefly recapitulates the formal prerequisites for the discussion of previous work on reinterpretation, viz., types, sorts, functional application, and functional composition.

Types describe the combinatory potential of logical expressions (here, λ-terms). From basic types e ('entity'), s (for eventualities, a special case of entities), and t ('truth value') one can construct complex types: $\langle\alpha,\beta\rangle$ is a type iff ('if and only if') α and β are types. E.g., $\langle s,t\rangle$ is the type of propositions (properties of eventualities). Expressions of type $\langle\alpha,\beta\rangle$ are functors from expressions of type α to expressions of type β.

Functional application means that an expression A of type $\langle\alpha,\beta\rangle$ (the functor) and an expression B of type α (the argument) form an expression $A(B)$ of type β.

Functional composition combines an expression A of type $\langle\beta,\gamma\rangle$ and an expression B of type $\langle\alpha,\beta\rangle$ into a new expression $\lambda\varphi.A(B(\varphi))$ of type $\langle\alpha,\gamma\rangle$, where φ is a variable of type α.

E.g., composing $\lambda x \lambda e.\mathbf{dance}'(x)(e)$ with $\lambda P \lambda e'.\text{PROG}(P)(e')$,[9] where P is a variable of type $\langle s,t \rangle$, returns $\lambda x \lambda e'.\text{PROG}(\lambda e.\mathbf{dance}'(x)(e))(e')$. Functional application then emerges as a special case of functional composition where α is empty.

Sorts model subsets of entities. They often correspond to ontological categories like things or substances. Sorts are informally integrated in the type-theoretic framework as subscripts of types for the purposes of this chapter. E.g., the type $\langle e_{\text{SUBST}}, t \rangle$ characterises properties of substances. Sorts constrain functional application and composition in that the argument must meet the sortal restrictions of the functor. Eventualities are also modelled as entities of a special sort that is disjoint from the sort for entities that are objects or kinds. Eventuality variables are indicated by variables like e, e', or e_1. A formal account of sorts is deferred to section 2.2.4.

Finally, there are three equivalence relations over the set of expressions of the typed λ-calculus, which are used in semantic representations in this book. In their definitions, '$P[x/y]$' means that all free occurrences of x in P are replaced by y.

- α-*equivalence* allows constant renaming of bound variables (α-conversion): $\lambda x.P \equiv \lambda y.P[x/y]$. Here y does not occur free in P, and replacing x with y does not lead to the binding of y within P. As an example, $\lambda e.\mathbf{rain}'(e)$ is α-equivalent to $\lambda e'.\mathbf{rain}'(e')$.
- β-*equivalence* allows the simplification (β-reduction) of functor-argument structures: $[\lambda X.P](Y) \equiv P[X/Y]$, if all free variables in Y remain free in $P[X/Y]$. Thus, $[\lambda x \lambda e.dance'(x)(e)](\mathbf{max}')$ is β-equivalent to the simpler $\lambda e.dance'(\mathbf{max}')(e)$.
- η-*equivalence* holds between expressions P and $\lambda x.P(x)$, if x is not free in P. For instance, $\lambda e.\mathbf{dance}'(\mathbf{max}')(e)$ is η-equivalent to $\mathbf{dance}'(\mathbf{max}')$.

In the following, I will freely use all these kinds of equivalences to make semantic representations more readable.

1.3 Type coercion: Previous approaches

The approaches to type coercion I am going to review are those of Moens and Steedman, Pulman, de Swart, Dölling, and Pustejovsky. Moens and Steedman (Moens, 1987, Moens and Steedman, 1986, 1988) were, to my knowledge, the first researchers to discuss reinterpretation as a topic of its own. They introduced the term *type coercion* – borrowed from the theory of programming languages – into aspectual semantics. Their approach was refined and formalised by Pulman (1997), who supplied a model-theoretic basis for

[9]These two expressions are semantic representations for *dance* and the progressive operator, respectively. See p.94 for the interpretation of PROG.

type coercion and worked out a fragment that assigns semantic representations to reinterpretation candidates on the basis of phrase-structure rules and appropriate interface rules. De Swart (1998) integrates an account of reinterpretation into DRT, with great emphasis on the syntax-semantics interface for reinterpretation candidates. For the nominal domain, Dölling (1992, 1993, 1995, 1998, 1999, 2000) did pioneering work on reinterpretation. He offers a very comprehensive account of nominal reinterpretation and works out its basis in commonsense ontology.

Finally, some researchers claim that at least some potential instances of reinterpretation can be covered in terms of an extended notion of semantic construction. Most prominent among them is Pustejovsky; other analyses of this kind include Naumann and Osswald (1999) and Ramsay (1996). Pustejovsky's (1991, 1993, 1995) basic framework (the *Generative Lexicon*) provides rich lexical structures and composition strategies that allow him to reintegrate at least a part of the reinterpretation phenomena into compositional semantics. Copestake and Briscoe (1995) present a formalisation of some of Pustejovsky's analyses in the grammar and lexicon development environment *LKB* (Linguistic Knowledge Building; Copestake 2002). Lascarides and Copestake (1998) show that some of Pustejovsky's intuitions can be fruitfully integrated in a typed feature structure formalism with default unification that includes pragmatic knowledge.

The discussion of problems and open questions of previous approaches will be deferred to section 1.4, unless a problem is of relevance only for one specific approach. In that case, its discussion follows the presentation of the respective approach.

1.3.1 Moens and Steedman's approach

Moens and Steedman describe aspectual type coercion in terms of finite-state automata. Type coercions are modelled as the transitions between the aspectual classes (which appear as the states of the automata). They apply their aspectual transition network to a specific aspectual classification that distinguishes five aspectual classes. However, as they themselves note, the basic idea of such a transition network does not presuppose any particular underlying aspectual theory. Their classification distinguishes five groups of predicates:

- states: *love, be a student, ...*
- processes: *run, shake, ...*
- culminated processes: *build a house, climb to the top, ...*
- culminations: *fall, die, ...*
- points: *cough, flash, ...*

Nonstative classes are based on a cross-classification of the binary features '$\pm c$[onsequence]' (having an aftermath or poststate, i.e., telicity) and '$\pm p$[unctuality]'. Processes are $-c,-p$, points, $-c,+p$, culminated processes, $+c,-p$, and culminations, $+c,+p$. Boundedness is not relevant in their classification; their process class comprises both unbounded and bounded predicates (e.g., *play the piano* as well as *play a sonata*). (For the feature punctuality, see also section 5.4.1.)

As the basis of aspectual reinterpretation Moens and Steedman postulate a conceptualisation of event structure. They assume that human beings conceptually divide up a course of events into clusters whose members are related by relations like causality. These clusters constitute a tripartite elementary event structure, the *nucleus*. Nuclei consist of a preparatory process (or phase), a culminative event (for expository purposes the original term *culmination* is not used here, since it is also used for an aspectual class), and a consequent state.

Aspectual semantics relates to nuclei in that predicates of different aspectual classes denote eventualities that constitute (im-)proper parts of nuclei.[10] Culminations denote culminative events and abstract away from their preparatory phases and consequent states, culminated processes denote whole nuclei, and processes, preparatory phases. States and points are exceptional here: States are unrelated to the nucleus structure; points denote events without an inner structure.

This allows Moens and Steedman to attribute aspectual reinterpretation to a common denominator: They add or remove parts of a nucleus structure. This characterisation can also be used to delimit the range of possible aspectual reinterpretations. E.g., the reinterpretation in (17) introduces a preparatory phase not yet included in the semantics of the modified predicate *Amélie reach- the top*. This turns the culminative event *Amélie reach- the top* into a culminated process, which then fits the selection restriction of the adverbial *in two hours*:[11]

(17) # Amélie reached the top in two hours

Moens and Steedman's analysis is summarised in their diagram (18). In this picture, labelled arcs indicate changes in meaning that are associated with specific transitions. E.g., the move from points to processes introduces the notion of iterativity:

---

[10] I assume a Davidsonian verb semantics, in which all predicates have an additional argument position in their semantics for an eventuality. (See section 1.6.1 for extended comments on the Davidsonian framework.)

[11] An analysis of this example in terms of landing site coercion (rather than type coercion) is presented in section 4.2.2.

(18)

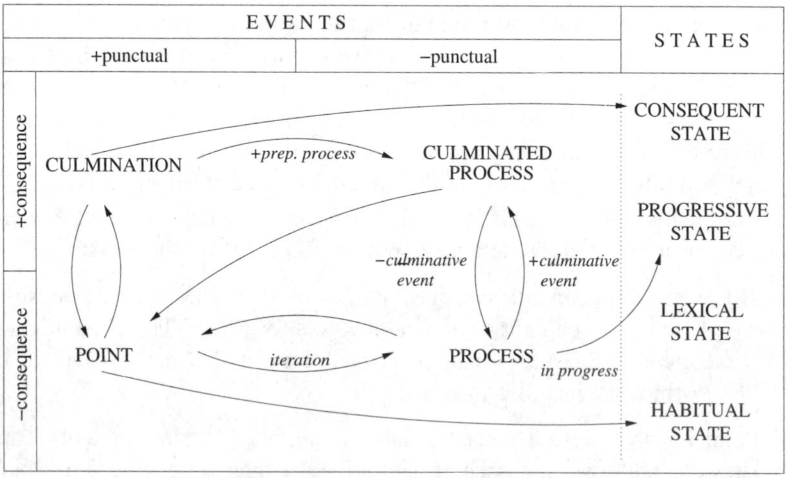

One might consider complementing the range of possible type coercions in (18) with type coercions that affect *states*. This is motivated, e.g., by the observation that they also allow the *experiental perfect*. The experiential perfect of *P* is true if there is at least one eventuality in the extension of *P* in the past, e.g., in (19):

(19) # Have you ever loved a woman?

Moens and Steedman's explanation of this usage of the perfect extends quite naturally to cases like (19). It would involve coercion of the state into a culmination. See section 3.2.4 for an account of the experiential perfect and the type coercions it may trigger.

Although Moens and Steedman do not formalise their analyses of type coercion, their framework seems to embody a distinction between abstract operations of aspectual shift and their potential instantiations. This fits in with my observation that reinterpretation does not directly include an operator into the semantic representation of a reinterpretation candidate. Rather, it introduces *room* for such an operator into this representation, which makes the representation underspecified.

1.3.2 Pulman's approach

Pulman (1997) offers a formal description of type coercion. His description of type coercion is based on the work of Moens and Steedman, but he proposes numerous changes and refinements to their account.[12] Pulman inte-

[12]E.g., he assumes that both culminated processes and culminations include the aftermath of

grates the theory of aspectual type coercion into model-theoretic semantics. At the heart of his formalisation of this theory is a representation of aspectual classes in terms of *sorts* of eventualities (the proposed approach adopts this design choice, see section 2.2.4). The five classes of Moens and Steedman are rendered by the sorts STATE, PROCESS, POINT, ⟨PROCESS,STATE⟩, and ⟨POINT,STATE⟩ (for state, process, point, culminated process, and culmination, respectively; the latter two sorts are composed from the simple sorts, which exhibits the complexity of the eventualities they characterise).

The formalisation explicitly spells out type coercion operators. For instance, the account of the iterative operator (1997, 25) is as follows:

(20) When a predicate P has eventualities of sort POINT in its extension, there is an eventuality e of sort PROCESS for which ITER(P) holds and there are at least two distinct eventualities e' and e'' in the extension of P which are included in e.

Pulman also designs a syntax-semantics interface for reinterpretation candidates that addresses the issue of delimiting the range of positions in which type coercion may take place. Pulman proposes determining these positions in terms of syntactic constituent structure.

He sketches a fragment in which the integration of reinterpretation operators is modelled as an instantiation of metavariables that were previously inserted into semantic representations. This insertion is determined in the interface rules that specify for a syntactic constituent structure how the semantic contributions of its immediate constituents are combined into the semantics of the structure as a whole.

For syntactic constituent structures where reinterpretation may occur, the interface rules insert a metavariable 'coerce' between the semantic contributions of the immediate constituents of the structure. This metavariable can buffer conflicting aspectual properties of these contributions if necessary. At the same time, this insertion of metavariables models the fact that the semantic representations of reinterpretation candidates are underspecified.

Appropriate instantiations of such metavariables model the monotonic integration of extralinguistic information into the semantics of reinterpretation candidates, which characterises reinterpretation. If there is no such aspectual conflict, they can be projected away, i.e., instantiated as the identity mapping $\lambda P.P$.

E.g., Pulman's syntax-semantics interface rule (21) (slightly adapted) builds the semantics of a VP from the semantic contributions of its immediate constituents (an auxiliary and another VP). This rule inserts a metavariable between the semantic contributions of auxiliary and VP ('Tr' is a recursive

---

a culminative event in their semantics.

function that maps syntactic constituents onto their semantics; 'Aux', the category of auxiliaries that includes the progressive and the perfect auxiliary).

Since auxiliaries adjoin syntactically to VPs, rule (21) rephrases functional composition of auxiliary and VP meaning.

(21) $\text{Tr}([_{\text{VP}} \text{ Aux VP}]) = \lambda x.\text{Tr}(\text{Aux})(\texttt{coerce}(\text{Tr}(\text{VP})(x)))$

(21) handles the fact that combining an auxiliary and a VP may give rise to reinterpretation: The progressive auxiliary is incompatible with states; the perfect auxiliary selects for culminations or culminated processes.

(22) shows the (slightly adapted) derivation of the semantics of *be being silly*. Here the semantics of the progressive operator is a function from properties of eventualities to properties of eventualities.

(22) $\text{Tr}(\textit{be- being silly}) =$

$\lambda x.\text{Tr}(\textit{be- -ing})(\texttt{coerce}(\text{Tr}(\textit{silly})(x)))=$

$\lambda x.[\lambda P \lambda e.\text{PROG}(P)(e)](\texttt{coerce}([\lambda y \lambda e'.\textbf{be-silly}'(y)(e')](x))) =$

$\lambda x.\lambda e.\text{PROG}(\texttt{coerce}(\lambda e'.\textbf{be-silly}'(x)(e')))(e)$

Then coerce can be instantiated to a suitable functor from propositions to propositions, most likely, to a maximality operator, see section 3.2.1. (It cannot be projected away, since *be silly* is a state.)

1.3.3 De Swart's approach

De Swart (1998) integrates an analysis of type coercion into the DRT framework (Kamp and Reyle, 1993). The resulting representations of m-expressions are well-formed, since they comprise 'coercion operators' that buffer aspectually conflicting material. These operators are ambiguous; their range of meanings corresponds to the set of reinterpretation operators that can mediate the respective aspectual conflict.

De Swart models aspectual classes with sorts of eventualities: *State predicates* like *be silly* refer to eventualities of sort *s*, *process predicates* like *run*, to eventualities of sort *p*, and *event predicates* (i.e., bounded predicates) like *leave*, to eventualities of sort *e*. Nonstative eventualities are characterised by the type *d* (for 'dynamic').

Consider, e.g., her semantic representation of *be being silly*. Here the mismatch between the progressive operator (whose argument must be nonstative) and its stative argument is buffered by the operator C_{sd} from stative to nonstative predicates. The underspecification of the representation (23) can then be resolved by disambiguating C_{sd}:

(23) 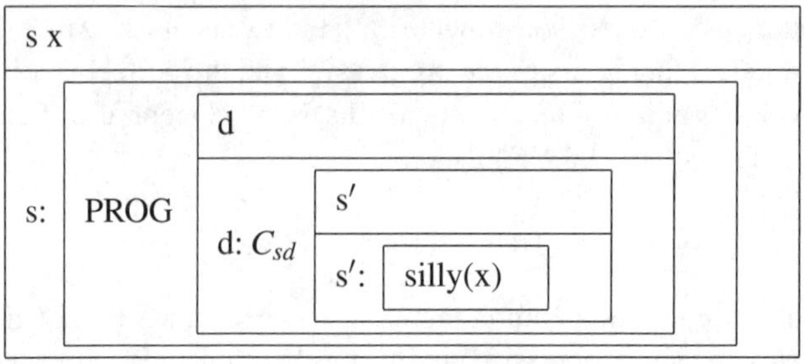

For the derivation of these structures, de Swart proposes syntax-semantics interface rules that associate specific syntactic structures (like the adjunction of an auxiliary to a VP) with reinterpretation potential. In this respect, her interface is similar to that of Pulman. It differs from Pulman in that it checks the expressions that exhibit these syntactic structures for aspectual conflicts between their syntactic constituents. If and only if there is such an aspectual conflict is a reinterpretation operator inserted.

E.g., the rule that constructs the semantics of progressive expressions as in (23) distinguishes two cases, depending on the aspectual class of the semantic contribution of the VP, which must be checked first. (Her analysis is adapted here in that the progressive auxiliary adjoins to a VP and not to a sentence.)

In either case, construction introduces a discourse referent s for the eventuality to which the progressive expression refers and adds '$s : \mathrm{PROG}(K_1)$' as a condition on s. If the semantic contribution of the VP is nonstative, then K_1 is the DRS that models its meaning. In contrast, if the semantic contribution of the VP is stative, the spellout of K_1 is different: A new (non-stative) discourse referent d is introduced in this DRS and the condition '$d : C_{sd}(K_2)$' is added. Here K_2 is the DRS for the meaning of the VP. Thus, (23) is more complex than the semantic representation of a non-m-expression like *be- running*:

(24) 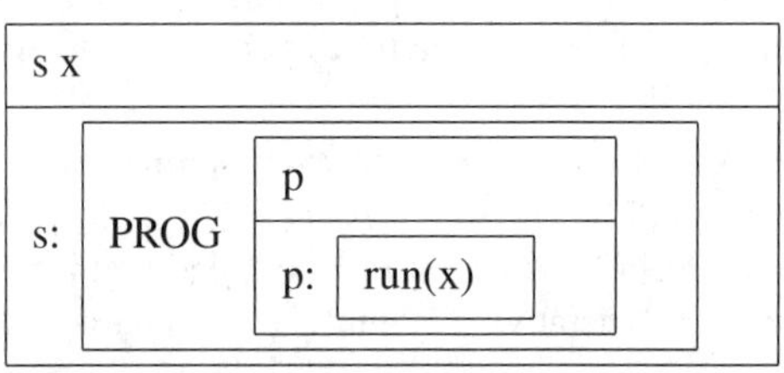

This approach provides a compositional way of constructing the semantic representations of reinterpretation candidates. These representations are underspecified and the integration of extralinguistic information into these representations is modelled as a monotonic process (instantiation of an ambiguous operator).

1.3.4 Dölling's approach

Dölling's work offers an in-depth analysis of type coercion in the nominal domain. His approach[13] focusses on examples like (25):

(25) # A bottle froze

Reinterpretation is necessary for (25) due to a sortal mismatch between a functor and its argument. The functor (the subject NP semantics)[14] is of type $\langle\langle e_{\text{THING}},t\rangle,t\rangle$ (eventuality arguments are neglected here), but the argument (the semantic contribution of the VP) is of the type $\langle e_{\text{SUBST}},t\rangle$. Or, to put it differently: If semantic construction proceeded straightforwardly for (25), one would end up with a representation that cannot be β-reduced in the usual fashion, because after β-reduction one would end up with a binder (here, an existential quantifier) that binds two occurrences of a variable onto which two properties (viz., the restriction of the quantifier, the $\bar{\text{N}}$ semantics and its scope, the VP semantics) impose conflicting sortal restrictions.

To avoid this sortal mismatch, Dölling introduces reinterpretation *templates* that are to be inserted between functor and argument. These templates avoid the impending sortal conflict by introducing an additional entity into the discourse (by means of an existentially bound variable) to which one of these two conflicting properties is applied.

For (25), Dölling's relevant template (**SHIFT4**) is (26a). It maps properties of entities of sort S_1 onto properties of entities of sort S_2. This presupposes a relation $\underline{R}$ between entities for which the second property holds and entities for which the first property holds. ('x:$P(x)$' means that x carries the restriction that $P(x)$.) Dölling regards his templates as type shift operators (similarly to the ones introduced in Partee 1986). These operators are special in that they introduce into semantic representations a free variable $\underline{R}$ whose instantiation calls for extralingustic knowledge. In the following, these templates are adapted to the notation used in this book, e.g., **SHIFT4** emerges as (26b):

(26) a $(\lambda P : P \subseteq S_1)(\lambda x : S_2(x))(\exists y : x\,\underline{R}\,y)[P(y)]$
  b $\lambda P \lambda x_{\text{SORT2}} \exists y_{\text{SORT1}}.\underline{R}(x,y) \wedge P(y)$

If one applies this template to the VP semantics $\lambda x_{\text{SUBST}}.\mathbf{freeze}'(x)$, and then the NP semantics $\lambda P \exists y_{\text{THING}}.\mathbf{bottle}'(y) \wedge P(y)$ to the result of this application, the result is (27), a well-formed semantic representation of (25). Here the incompatible sortal restrictions of **bottle**$'$ and **freeze**$'$ do not lead to

[13] There are different versions of the approach, here, the 1995 version is presented. More recent developments of the theory are discussed where appropriate.

[14] In Dölling's account of type coercion of NP-VP structures, sometimes the NP and sometimes the VP semantics is the functor. In my review of Dölling's analyses, the NP semantics is uniformly the functor. Dölling's theory is also simplified in that common nouns denote properties of objects.

ill-formedness, since they hold for different entities. The paraphrase of (27) is 'there is a bottle and a substance which are somehow related, and the substance froze':

(27) $\exists x_{\text{THING}}.\mathbf{bottle'}(x) \wedge \exists y_{\text{SUBST}}.\underline{R}(x,y) \wedge \mathbf{freeze'}(y)$

Finally, the relation $\underline{R}$ is instantiated with the help of conceptual knowledge, which models integrating extralinguistic information into semantic representations. For (25), conceptual knowledge about liquids and their containers provides the relation **CONT** of *content* between containers and their contents. This yields the desired representation (28) for (25), which says that there is a bottle whose content froze:

(28) $\exists x_{\text{THING}}.\mathbf{bottle'}(x) \wedge \exists y_{\text{SUBST}}.\mathbf{CONT}(x,y) \wedge \mathbf{freeze'}(y)$

The relations that are available for the instantiation of such underspecified relations are eventually to be attributed to ontological relations like 'content of' or 'substance of' that establish relations between entities of quite different sorts. Dölling models these relations as links between items on different branches in a *commonsense ontology*.[15]

For Dölling's approach, the issue of *semantic construction* for reinterpretation candidates is crucial, in particular, the question of how reinterpretation templates are integrated in semantic representations of reinterpretation candidates.

In his earlier papers, he derives the meaning of reinterpretation candidates in the following way: First, the argument is derived, then comes the application of the reinterpretation template that mediates between the argument and the functor that is yet to come. The final step in the derivation then is the application of the functor to the reinterpreted argument. But this begs the question of what motivates the insertion of the reinterpretation templates: The templates are applied to the argument at a step in the derivation where the functor is *not yet known*.

Recently (Dölling, 1999, 2000), reinterpretation is anticipated by inserting an abstract reinterpretation template between any functor-argument pair. Thus, these templates are applied to arguments regardless of the properties of the functor they are to be combined with. In this way, type coercion is modelled monotonically: For reinterpretation candidates, the abstract template is instantiated appropriately; templates that are not necessary for reinterpretation are projected away.

[15] In this respect, Dölling's templates emerge as (extensional) specifications of Sag's (1981) *sense-transfer functions*. One of these functions models type coercion in the nominal domain in that it maps one-place predicate senses (i.e., relations between world-time tuples and individuals) onto other one-place predicate senses.

Dölling's analysis focusses on reinterpretation that involves impending semantic mismatches (typically between constituents of an expression), which are buffered by integrating extralinguistic material. His analysis returns appropriately underspecified semantic representations for reinterpretation candidates: The relations $\underline{R}$ in these representations introduce underspecification. These relations are to be instantiated after semantic construction, which fits in with the observation that this instantiation draws on extralinguistic knowledge and integrates it into semantic representations of reinterpretation candidates.

1.3.5 Pustejovsky's approach

Pustejovsky's approach offers a theory of type coercion that differs from the theories discussed so far in that it regards type coercion – or, at least, many of its instances – as *part of semantic construction*. This view is embedded in his global theory of the *Generative Lexicon*. According to this theory, the lexicon is not a static part of linguistic competence, but, rather, a component of linguistic competence that allows one to generate meanings in a flexible yet compositional way. The theory assumes richly structured semantic lexical entries and rules of semantic composition beyond the standard repertoire of semantic construction. These rules can access and combine this rich structure of the semantic lexical entries in novel ways.

In the Generative Lexicon, semantic lexical entries, in particular those of nouns and verbs, are 'structured meanings'. They provide additional information on several essential properties of their main arguments in the so-called *Qualia Structure* (QS). E.g., the semantics of *novel* comprises in its QS information about the origin of novels (someone writes them; the *agentive* quale) and their purpose (someone reads them; the *telic* quale). These two qualia are formalised as the property of reading or writing x, the main argument in the semantics of *novel*.[16]

Impending semantic conflicts between constituents of an expression can then be avoided by rules of semantic construction that take recourse to this structured meaning. In this way, the derivation of the meanings of expressions that is usually regarded as an instance of reinterpretation can be explicitly integrated and licensed as part of semantic construction. E.g., if the semantics of a verb and one of its arguments does not match, one may derive the semantic representation for the constituent consisting of verb and argument by combining the verb semantics and a suitable quale of the argument. Such operations are still referred to as type coercions, but they emerge as semantics-internal in the GL theory.

[16]The QS comprises two more qualia, called the *constitutive* and the *formal* quale. The former provides information about the constitutive parts of x, the latter gives the distinctive characteristics of x that distinguish it within a larger domain. Since these qualia play no role in Pustejovsky's account of type coercion, they are neglected in the following.

These operations are constrained lexically in that they must refer to information within the semantic structure of the argument (characteristically, within the QS). Since the QS contains only a well-defined set of pieces of information, this considerably constrains the range of these operations. However, I will show below that Pustejovsky's approach still encounters problems of both over- and undergeneration.

This abstract account of the GL theory will now be fleshed out with one of Pustejovsky's prime examples, viz., the interpretation of *begin*.

(29) a Max began to read a novel

b # Max began a novel

While the meaning of (29a) is fixed, there is a certain leeway in the interpretation of (29b). It expresses the fact that Max started an activity that is somehow related to the novel, but the activity is not specified. For (29b), such activities include, e.g., reading or writing the novel. That is, the range of readings of (29b) comprises the meaning of (29a).

Pustejovsky observes that *begin* has two different subcategorisation frames; it occurs as a transitive verb, or as a subject control verb (which subcategorises for an NP and a VP). Nevertheless, in the light of the semantic similarity of sentence pairs like (29a) and (29b) (either one denotes an initial part of a novel-related activity by Max), he claims – and I adopt his claim – that in spite of this syntactic difference, the semantics of both variants of the verb is the same. The verb denotes a relation (called 'begin-relation') between an individual and a property of individuals (a relation between individuals and eventualities). Pustejovsky does not define the begin-relation, but an initial definition[17] might be the following:

(30) $\mathbf{begin}'(x,P)(e)$ holds iff e is an initial part of an eventuality in the extension of $\lambda e'.P(x)(e')$.

Pustejovsky wants to capture this semantic uniformity by one single lexical entry for *begin*, whose second syntactic argument may either be an NP or a VP, but whose semantics is uniformly a relation between an individual and a property of individuals. But this analysis immediately raises the question of how to account for the meaning of examples like (29b), where the verb has a non-event-denoting NP like *a novel* as its second argument. The semantics of this NP is not a property of individuals, i.e., as it stands it does not qualify as the second argument of the begin-relation, hence, there is an impending type mismatch.

[17] The *imperfective paradox* (introduced in the discussion of the semantics of the progressive in Dowty 1979) is neglected here: How can an entity qualify as a proper part of an entity in the extension of a property P if the set denoted by P is empty?

At this point, the rich structure and the generative flexibility of the lexicon are crucial. The semantic entry of *novel* provides information on some 'novel-related activities', which is available for the interpretation of (29b). In addition, the lexicon comprises processes of type coercion like the operators Q_T and Q_A that access telic and agentive information of a noun *N* and make it available – in the form of a property of individuals – at the level of the NP of which *N* is the head noun. The goal of this mapping is to turn the NP semantics into a property that qualifies as a possible second argument of the begin-relation. For (29b), this yields two well-typed semantic representations that correspond to two options for the reinterpretation of (29b), viz., that Max began to read or to write a novel. Accessing the telic or the agentive quale (but not the formal or constitutive quale) in this way returns a property, which matches the selection restriction of the begin-relation.

Regardless of the concrete spellout of this analysis, which will be discussed immediately, this strategy raises the question of the confines of linguistic knowledge as opposed to conceptual knowledge. I do not regard as settled the question of whether it is appropriate to include into the lexicon background knowledge on entities like information about their origin or purpose. Rather, such pieces of information seem to belong to the realm of conceptual knowledge, which should hence not be modelled as part of linguistic knowledge.

Moreover, describing reinterpretation candidates like (29b) in terms of a (nondeterministic) choice of one of a small set of lexically specified reinterpretation options is problematic, because this set is too small to account for the whole range of reinterpretation possibilities, especially for cases where context knowledge influences reinterpretation. (This is the issue of undergeneration which was mentioned above.)

This problem shows up, e.g., in a context in which Max is a professor of literary studies who gives a series of lectures, say, on different specimens of Victorian literature, starting with a epic or two and then moving on to novels. In this context, the reading 'Max began to lecture on a novel' is much more preferable for the sentence (29b) than its 'author' or its 'reader' reading. But Pustejovsky's approach as it stands would be forced to ignore this extralinguistic information and hence fail to account for this reading. This is due to the fact that the GL theory privileges the 'author' and the 'reader' readings of a sentence like (29b) over all other reinterpretation possibilities in that only these two readings can be derived compositionally. Although these two readings are among the preferred ones in an empty context, appropriate contexts may well induce a preference for other readings.

Pustejovsky (1995) does mention the possibility of letting an appropriate quale of the subject NP override a VP-internal interpretation, which might lead to the preferred reading, e.g., in the case of (31):

(31) # The professor of literary studies began the novel

But if the subject is a proper name like in (29b), no such strategy is available for a purely linguistic approach to such reinterpretations.

Lascarides and Copestake (1998) address this undergeneration problem by encoding the information in the Qualia Structure as *default knowledge*. They follow Pustejovsky in assuming that verbs like *begin* determine (in their transitive variant) the property that is their innermost semantic argument with reference to QS information of their object NPs. But as this information is only a default, it does not constrain the range of possible readings to the ones provided by the QS, rather, it models the preferred status of these readings.

However, in the light of the restrictions for reinterpretations as mentioned in Godard and Jayez (1993), one might wonder whether QS is suitable as default values. Their example *bathroom* could be employed here: Although bathrooms have a purpose, *begin the bathroom* has no 'telic' interpretation 'begin to wash oneself' or the like.

The concrete spellout of Pustejovsky's analysis exhibits several problems as well. Consider, e.g., his (1991) derivation of the telic reading of sentence (29b). If one changes this analysis slightly (in the semantic representation of a verb, the subject position should correspond to a λ-abstracted variable of type e) and adopts the semantics of the begin-relation in (30), his analysis of (29b) can be reformulated as (32), where 'Tr' is again a (recursive) function from syntactic expressions to their meanings. Issues of tense and sentence mood are ignored in the analysis:

(32) Tr(*Max began a novel*) =

Tr(*Max*) [Tr(*began a novel*)] =

$\lambda P \lambda e''.P(\mathbf{max}')(e'')$ [Tr(*began*)[Q_T(Tr(*a novel*))]] =

$\lambda P \lambda e''.P(\mathbf{max}')(e'')$[Tr(*began*)[$\lambda x \lambda e.\mathbf{read}'(x,$Tr(*a novel*)$)(e)$]] =

$\lambda P \lambda e''.P(\mathbf{max}')(e'')$ [Tr(*began*)[$\lambda x \lambda e.\mathbf{read}'(x,$
$\lambda P \lambda e' \exists y.\mathbf{novel}'(y) \wedge P(y)(e'))(e)$]] =

$\lambda P \lambda e''.P(\mathbf{max}')(e'')$ [Tr(*began*)[$\lambda x \lambda e \exists y.\mathbf{novel}'(y) \wedge$
$\mathbf{read}_*(x,y)(e)$]] =

$\lambda P \lambda e''.P(\mathbf{max}')(e'')[\lambda P \lambda x \lambda e'.\mathbf{begin}'(x,P)(e')$
$[\lambda x \lambda e' \exists y.\mathbf{novel}'(y) \wedge \mathbf{read}_*(x,y)(e')]] =$

$\lambda P \lambda e''.P(\mathbf{max}')(e'')[\lambda x \lambda e'.\mathbf{begin}'(x,$
$\lambda x \lambda e' \exists y.\mathbf{novel}'(y) \wedge \mathbf{read}_*(x,y)(e'))(e')] =$

$\lambda e''.\mathbf{begin}'(\mathbf{max}', \lambda x \lambda e' \exists y.\mathbf{novel}'(y) \wedge \mathbf{read}_*(x,y)(e'))(e'')$

Thus, the telic reading of (29b) is rendered as the property of eventualities to be the beginning of another eventuality in which Max reads a novel. In (32) NPs have meanings of type $\langle\langle e,\langle s,t\rangle\rangle,\langle s,t\rangle\rangle$. (32) uses a suitable version of the standard meaning postulate for extensional verbs like *read* in the fifth derivation step:

(33) $\forall x \forall \mathscr{P} \forall e.\mathbf{read}'(x,\mathscr{P})(e) \leftrightarrow \mathscr{P}(\lambda y \lambda e'.\mathbf{read}_*(x,y)(e'))(e)$

This derivation of the telic reading of (29b) begs the question of how to explain the insertion of Q_T in the third step of the derivation (32), which seems to be unmotivated: At this early stage of the derivation, one is still busy breaking down the syntactic structure, hence, one cannot access the contributions of the constituents of (29b) yet. But this means that the information on the impending type mismatch between *begin* and its second argument is not yet available. This problem can be handled by an appropriate syntax-semantics interface that introduces a metavariable between the semantic contributions of the verb and of its second syntactic argument regardless of their types. In case of a type conflict between the verb and its argument, the variable can be instantiated by an operator like Q_T or otherwise be projected away (instantiated as the identity mapping $\lambda P.P$).

This strategy would also solve the problem that Pustejovsky's analyses of examples like (29b) yield no underspecified semantic representations but capture the underspecification by a nondeterministic selection of one out of a number of fully specified readings. E.g., in the analysis (32) of (29b) the choice of an fully specified operator like Q_T is obligatory. But this could also be solved by assuming that a metavariable is inserted during the process of semantic construction.

A more serious problem for Pustejovsky's approach is the spellout of Q_T. He defines Q_T as an operator that maps the semantics of a noun onto its telic quale, but in (32) Q_T has the interpretation (34):

(34) $\lambda \mathscr{P} \lambda x \lambda e.\mathbf{read}'(x,\mathscr{P})(e)$

This difference is due to the fact that in (32) Q_T must coerce the semantics of a *whole NP* in terms of the telic quale of its head noun. It is unclear how this could be effected compositionally, perhaps by passing the head noun qualia on to its NP.

Finally, the main problem for Pustejovsky's approach emerges if we regard sentences in which type coercion and quantifier scope ambiguity coocur. E.g., (35) exhibits a sortal mismatch between the sorts SUBST and THING, which triggers reinterpretation, and its NPs are also scopally ambiguous:

(35) # A man froze all the bottles

(35) shows that the semantic underspecification that reinterpretation in-

troduces into the semantics of these expressions is independent of the one introduced by scope ambiguity. One can reinterpret the resulting semantic representations or determine scope relations between their quantifiers without affecting the semantic underspecification that arises from the respective other source.

But this means that a comprehensive approach of reinterpretation must be able to deal with expressions that exhibit quantifier scope ambiguities, too. My claim is that Pustejovsky's analysis of type coercion runs into insurmountable problems with these expressions.

At the heart of these problems is the fact that operators like Q_T mediate a mismatch between the verb and one of its arguments, in (29b), the object NP. Since the analysis inserts the operator *between* the verb and its object NP, it predicts wide scope of *begin* over the quantifier that is introduced in its object NP. But this analysis makes the wrong predictions for (36a) and (36b), variants of (29a) and (29b), where the indefinite determiner of the object is replaced by *every*:

(36) a Max began to read every novel

b # Max began every novel

(36a) and (36b) comprise two scope bearers, viz., the matrix verb and *every novel*, hence, one would expect both sentences to be scopally ambiguous. However, even in its 'reader' (telic) reinterpretation, (36b) lacks one of the two readings of (36a): Only (36a) can refer to an initial part of an eventuality of Max's reading every novel. The entailment of this reading is that at least an initial part of *one* novel was read.

In contrast, both sentences share the reading 'for every novel, Max began to read it'. This reading entails that for each novel, at least an initial part was read. I.e., the universal quantifier from *every novel* is scopally underspecified with respect to the relation **begin**′ in (36a), but has wide scope over this relation in (36b).

Thus, there are two mutually exclusive requirements for the semantic representation of cases like (36b): Giving the NP wide scope over the verb is required to represent the interpretations of the examples correctly, but simultaneously the type coercion in these sentences entails narrow scope of the NP.

At a first glance, it seems as if one could reconciliate these conflicting requirements by complementing Pustejovsky's analysis with an appropriate treatment of quantifier scope, e.g., Logical Form in Generative Grammar (May, 1985) or Cooper Storage (Cooper, 1983). In such approaches the semantic contribution of an NP is divided into two parts, on the one hand a bound variable, and on the other hand the binder of this variable plus the $\bar{\text{N}}$

semantics. This distinction lets parts of the semantic contribution of the NP have different scopes, since only the bound variable must always remain in situ.

This suggests a reconciliation of the conflicting requirements in the following way: The coercion operator applies to the NP semantics in the form of its bound variable, while the other part of the NP semantics (that comprises the variable binder) is not affected by this application. Hence, the scope of this part may well extend over the coercion operator and the verb semantics, which then models the fact that examples like (36b) have only such a wide-scope reading.

However, for a QS account of sentences like (36b), this strategy would not work. If the coercion operator applied only to the bound variable from the NP semantics, the other part of the NP semantics would be outside the scope of the coercion operator. But since this part comprises the Qualia Structure of the head noun, nothing in the scope of the coercion operator could provide the information necessary for the reinterpretation (the agentive or the telic quale of *novel*).

To sum up, Pustejovsky models a number of type coercion cases in terms of compositional semantics – but at a cost: The range of operations in semantic composition is enhanced considerably, and pieces of information are integrated into the semantic lexicon whose privileged status as linguistic knowledge is not undisputed.[18] The proposed analysis of examples like (36b) in section 3.1.1 will take up the issues discussed in this subsection. It handles type coercion and quantifier scope in a way that does not entail conflicting requirements on the semantic representations of these examples.

1.3.6 Further analyses

In this subsection, two approaches are reviewed that are similar to Pustejovsky's in that they suggest a compositional analysis of potential type coercion data. These analyses try to derive the iterative interpretation that emerges for 'point' predicates that are modified by durative adverbials or occur in the progressive. E.g., the following examples refer to iterations of Max's coughing that last two hours or are ongoing:

(37) # Max coughed for two hours

(38) (#) Max was coughing

Naumann and Osswald (1999) and Ramsay (1996) offer compositional analyses of (37) and (38), respectively. Their strategy is to weaken the semantics of durative adverbials and the progressive to make it compatible with

[18] For further reflection on Pustejovsky's framework, see also the discussion in *Linguistic Inquiry* (Fodor and Lepore, 1998, Pustejovsky, 1998).

point predicates.[19]

Naumann and Osswald (1999) assume that all 'relevant' parts (down to a certain lower bound) of the time interval involved in the semantics of a durative adverbial are the time of an eventuality in the extension of the modified predicate *P*. For unbounded *P*, this is compatible with the usual interpretation: The time interval is the temporal extension of a *P*-eventuality. Due to the divisivity of *P* (at least down to a certain lower bound), all relevant parts of the interval involved are the time of a *P*-eventuality, too.

For 'point' predicates P', adverbial and predicate semantics interact differently: All relevant parts of the interval are the time of a P'-eventuality, but these eventualities do not add up to another P'-eventuality whose duration is measured by the adverbial, because P' is bounded. Instead, the adverbial measures the duration of an iteration of P'-eventualities.

This explanation postulates a rather weak reading for durative adverbials to account for a wider range of modification structures with durative adverbials in terms of compositional semantics. But this weakening leads to overgeneration for others of these modification structures.

The iterative interpretation as illustrated in (37) is not restricted to point predicates like *Max cough-*. It appears also with immediate change predicates. E.g., (39) has an iterative reading that refers to a whole series of Max giving up smoking:

(39) # Max quit smoking for two years

The iterative interpretation in both sentences stems from the modification of a 'punctual' predicate by a durative adverbial. Due to this analogy between (37) and (39), the latter should be covered by Naumann and Osswald's (1999) approach as well. But the iterative reading of (39) shows that the restriction of the durative adverbial must be weakened in that not *every* relevant part of the interval involved in the adverbial semantics is the time of an eventuality in the extension of the modified predicate: One needs gaps in between these times, since the modified predicate *Max quit- smoking* introduces a change of state. The gaps provide the time between two such changes during which the preparatory phase of the change of state is reestablished. This is indispensable for a repetition of the change of state. E.g., for (39) Max must take up smoking again before he can quit it once more.

But this weaker semantics of durative adverbials then yields unwanted readings, e.g., for (40) a reading where Max spent only part of the time in the pub. For instance, the presence of Max in the pub between 8:00 and 8:15 and 9:45 and 10:00 would make (40) true:

[19]The brackets around the hash sign in (38) indicate that it need not always undergo reinterpretation. This observation is expounded in section 5.2.

(40) Max was in the pub for two hours

To model data like (38), Ramsay (1996) assigns the progressive operator PROG a weaker meaning than usual:

(41) $\forall t \forall P.\text{PROG}(t,P) \rightarrow \exists E(\forall e(e \in E \rightarrow P(e)) \wedge$
$\exists e_1(e_1 \in E \wedge \exists t_1(t_1 < t \wedge startpt(e_1,t_1))) \wedge$
$\exists e_2(e_2 \in E \wedge \neg \exists t_2(t_2 < t \wedge endpt(e_2,t_2))))$

In prose: The PROG relation holds for a time t and a predicate of eventualities P if there is a set E of P-eventualities such that at least one element of E starts before the beginning of t and at least one element of E ends after the endpoint of t.

According to (41), the progressive interacts differently with 'non-punctual' and 'punctual' predicates. For the former, it yields the standard interpretations of the data, for the latter, the resulting interpretation involves more than one eventuality in the extension of the 'point' predicate.

If P is non-punctual like *rain*, the eventualities e_1 and e_2 may coincide, which gives the standard progressive semantics, where a part of an event (or of its temporal duration) is singled out. But if P is punctual, this possibility is ruled out by its semantics: No element of E can start before and end after t. Thus, E comprises at least two elements, which directly yields an iterative interpretation for (38).

The analysis correctly models the fact that for this reading of (38) to be true it is not necessary that Max coughs at the moment of utterance, it is enough if the moment of utterance is positioned within the (time of) an iteration of Max coughing.

But this weakening of the semantics of PROG leads to unwanted readings for cases like (42): Its truth condition would be that some raining eventuality started before the moment of utterance t_0 and that some raining eventuality will stop after the moment of utterance:

(42) It is raining

This truth condition would falsely predict that (42) is appropriate in contexts where there was rain in the past that started and ended before t_0 and where there will be another occurrence of rain that will start and end after t_0. I.e., according to this truth condition, no rain need be ongoing at t_0, which runs counter to intuitions on (42).

In sum, in trying to account for data like (37) and (38) in terms of a compositional interaction of adverbial/progressive and modified predicate one is in danger of opening a Pandora's box of unwanted readings. Thus, it seems safer to assume fairly strong semantic analyses for durative adverbials and to attribute iterative readings as in (37) and (38) to reinterpretation.

1.4 Type coercion: General problems

This section continues the discussion of previous work on type coercion with comments on issues that are of a more general nature and hence affect several of the previous approaches to type coercion.

1.4.1 Generality of the analysis

The majority of the reinterpretation operators encountered in previous work on reinterpretation are similar in that they all map expressions of type $\langle e,t\rangle$ or $\langle s,t\rangle$ onto expressions of the same type. However, additional reinterpretation operators are needed to account for the whole range of reinterpretation data, in particular, reinterpretation candidates where a verb semantically mismatches with *several* of its NP arguments, e.g., in (43):

(43) # London phoned Brighton

Since I assume that in such cases, too, there is one single reinterpretation, in (43), one that maps the verb semantics from a relation between persons to a relation between geographical locations, reinterpretation operators of more complex types are necessary as well.

It is the simultaneity of mismatches in cases like (43) – not the type of the argument that is to be reinterpreted – that brings about the need for additional reinterpretation operators: One can model reinterpretation options for arguments whose types are more complex than $\langle e,t\rangle$ or $\langle s,t\rangle$ by operators of type $\langle\langle e,t\rangle,\langle e,t\rangle\rangle$ or $\langle\langle s,t\rangle,\langle s,t\rangle\rangle$. This presupposes appropriately designed interface rules; a first example was Pulman's interface rule (21) for the reinterpretation of VPs (here, the semantics of VPs was of type $\langle e,\langle s,t\rangle\rangle$).

In this way, one could also use Dölling's templates for a description of the fact that for verbs with more than one argument, more deeply embedded arguments may lead to a type coercion of the verb, too. E.g., in (44), the semantics of the verb *phone* is reinterpreted as a relation between persons and geographical locations due to the object NP:

(44) # Max phoned London

Written in Pulman's style (and ignoring eventuality arguments and matters of quantifier scope), a suitable interface rule could combine the semantic contributions of verb and object NP in the following way ('Tr' is a function that maps constituents onto their semantic contribution; 'T', a template like Dölling's **SHIFT4**):

(45) $\text{Tr}([_{\text{VP}}\ \text{V NP}]) = \lambda x.\text{Tr(NP)}(T(\lambda y.\text{Tr(V)}(x,y)))$

The VP *phone London* would then get the following semantics, where **SHIFT4** instantiates T and the relation $\underline{R}$ in **SHIFT4** is instantiated as the relation of spatial containment **spCONT**. In prose, (46) stands for the set of persons who phone someone in London:

(46) $\lambda x \exists y.\mathbf{spCONT}(\mathbf{london}', y) \wedge \mathbf{phone}'(x, y)$

With a specific interface rule like (45) for every syntactic structure whose constituents are a verbal projection and an NP subcategorised for by the head of this projection, one could model a semantic mismatch of the verb with n of its arguments by n consecutive coercions of the verb. But this would run counter to the assumption that such simultanous mismatches trigger one single reinterpretation of the verb.

In section 3.1.2 I will offer an analysis of sortal type coercion where a verb semantically mismatches with several of its NP arguments. This analysis retains Dölling's intuitions but overcomes the problems noted in this subsection.

1.4.2 The distinction of semantic and conceptual knowledge

The discussion of reinterpretation phenomena so far presupposes that there is a distinction between (linguistic) semantic knowledge and (extralinguistic) conceptual knowledge. However, this view has not gone unchallenged; Jackendoff (1997) in particular refuses it on the grounds of type coercion data. His argument centres on the claim that for these data, compositional semantic construction in the usual sense is impossible. Jackendoff defines this kind of semantic construction (which he calls *syntactically transparent* [ST] semantic composition) as follows:

- all parts of the meaning of a complex constituent are already present in its syntactic subconstituents[20]
- once the semantic representations for the lexical entries are fixed, the process of semantic construction is guided by syntax alone, neither the internal structure of semantic representations nor pragmatic considerations may influence it

He argues that it is exactly this view of semantic construction that allows one to distinguish semantics proper from conceptual knowledge: As long as conceptual structures in their full complexity are not relevant for the purpose of semantic construction, it is possible to isolate from them a coarse semantic structure that idealises away from the details of the internal structure of concepts.

The next step in his argument is the claim that ST semantic construction is only a special case of a more general – and more involved – pattern of *enriched* semantic composition, where the meaning of a complex constituent may comprise material not present in its subconstituents and where the process of semantic construction is susceptible to the internal structure of seman-

[20]Syntactic rules that license the constituent structure of an expression may also contribute to its semantics, but this does not affect Jackendoff's point.

tic representations and pragmatic considerations. As a proof for this claim he adduces the fact that ST semantic construction cannot derive the full interpretation of type coercion expressions.

However, this step of the argument is only valid if one defines ST semantic composition as strictly as Jackendoff does. But I feel that this definition is too strict for reinterpretation and non-reinterpretation cases alike: Even expressions without any type coercion may comprise context-dependent parts (e.g., deictic elements), which means that their meaning cannot be fully derived by their syntactic and semantic properties. This suggests weakening the first part of his definition to claiming that there is a *part* of the meaning of a constituent that is invariable across contexts, all aspects of which must be present in its syntactic subconstituents or in the syntactic rules that serve to build the constituent.

It is then the task of appropriately designed syntax-semantics interfaces to delimit semantics and conceptual knowledge. The interface must be able to derive exactly that part of the meaning of a constituent that is invariant across contexts; this part follows from its syntactic and semantic properties. In this book, I show that it is indeed possible to do this for type coercion expressions. But then type coercion by itself is not a counterargument to the assumption of ST semantic construction and the distinction of semantic and conceptual knowledge.

This relegates part of the determination of the complete meaning of a type coercion expression to extralinguistic knowledge sources. If one regards semantic constants as pointers into more detailed conceptual structures, there is an immediate link to a much richer amount of knowlege that is directly related to semantics and which can then be used to complement the semantic part of the meaning of a type coercion expression.

That conceptual knowledge guides the full determination of type coercion expression is illustrated by many cases. In particular, semantic information by itself cannot fully determine the range of actually occurring coercions, it can only specify the type-theoretic (including sortal) properties of the coercion operators involved. Jackendoff (1997) shows this for the well-known cases where mass nouns are reinterpreted as thing-denoting expressions and vice versa. Mass nouns *M* may be reinterpreted in the sense of 'fixed quantity of the substance denoted by *M*'. Jackendoff observes that this process is restricted to nouns denoting food and drink, and returns expressions that refer to portions of food and drink that are suitable for one person. Thus, we have *two beers*, but not **three petrols* (in the sense of three tankfuls of petrol). This observation holds even if other interpretations would also be feasible: Even though there is a highly conventionalised way of serving ice cream (scoops), *three ice creams* gets the interpretation 'three portions of ice cream', and not 'three scoops of ice cream'. In a similar fashion, the range of potential reinterpretations for *begin*+NP cases like *begin a book* is constrained by conceptual knowledge (Godard and Jayez, 1993).

But even if one does not regard type coercion as a counterargument to the general applicability of ST semantic composition, one has to address yet another argument by Jackendoff against the attempt to integrate type coercion into compositional semantics. The argument focusses on the cooccurrence of type coercion and anaphora, which, he argues, shows that it is impossible to postpone the full determination of the meaning of a type coercion expression until after semantic construction. Consider, e.g., the two sentences (47) and (48):

(47) (#) Nixon heard himself sing an aria

(48) (#) Nixon saw himself leave the opera-house

(47) allows an interpretation in which the real Nixon heard an opera singer playing the part of himself, but (48) cannot be understood in the sense that this opera singer watched the real Nixon leave the opera-house. But these facts, Jackendoff argues, rule out such a postponement of the coercion processes: Binding is a central syntactic phenomenon, which crucially involves establishing the identity of the referent of the anaphor in terms of the referent of the antecedent. But the identification of these referents involves interpreting the NPs, which includes the coercion process for examples like (47) and (48). I.e., type coercion must have taken place by the time binding is processed, therefore it cannot be postponed until semantic construction is over.

Thus, proponents of an analysis in which type coercion takes place after semantic construction must show that anaphoric binding can be established even if the interpretation of antecedent and anaphor has not yet been completed. And, indeed, in the proposed account it is possible to give a semantic representation of these examples that establishes the anaphoric link in terms of coreference of referents without having to decide on the eventual interpretation of antecedent and anaphor.

As a preliminary step, one has to account for the fact that a simple sentence like (49) has other readings apart from the preferred, literal interpretation. E.g., in the opera context mentioned above, it can refer to an action of the singer playing the part of Nixon:

(49) (#) Nixon left

To get this interpretation of (49), I propose the following semantics for a proper name like *Nixon*, in prose, the set of properties such that some entity

x who is identical to Nixon has them:[21]

(50) $\lambda P \exists x.(\underline{\lambda z.z = \mathbf{nixon}'})(x) \wedge P(x)$

The underlined part of (50) may undergo coercion in examples like (49), in a normal context (without coercion), (50) boils down to the usual representation $\lambda P.P(\mathbf{nixon}')$, the set of properties possessed by Nixon.

In the opera context, however, coercion may take place. The relevant operator maps properties P onto the property of portraying someone with the property P, which is analysed (as a first approximation) as pretending to be identical to someone for whom P holds:

(51) $\lambda P \lambda y.\mathbf{pretend}'(y, \hat{}(\exists z.y = z \wedge P(z)))$

The relation **pretend′** relates an entity x and a property of possible worlds p iff p holds for all worlds compatible with what x pretends.

Coercion can now be modelled by replacing the underlined part in (50) by the result of applying (51) to this same part. The semantic representation for *Nixon* after coercion with (51) is (52), for (49), we obtain (53) after simplification. (53) states that some entity portraying Nixon leaves:

(52) $\lambda P \exists x.\mathbf{pretend}'(x, \hat{}(\exists z.x = z \wedge z = \mathbf{nixon}')) \wedge P(x)$

(53) $\exists x.\mathbf{pretend}'(x, \hat{}(x = \mathbf{nixon}')) \wedge \mathbf{leave}'(x)$

After these preliminaries, we can now turn to the crucial examples (47) and (48). Intuitions about these sentences that must be encoded in their analysis are the following:

- anaphora does not necessarily entail identity of referents in antecedent and anaphor
- but this identity holds in the default interpretation of anaphors, other interpretations have to be forced by an appropriate context[22]
- if the referents of antecedent and anaphor are not identical, there is an identity relation between *some* entity in the anaphor interpretation and the referent of the antecedent

E.g., (47) would be interpreted in the sense of 'Nixon overheard Nixon' in a null context; the reading where *himself* refers to an opera singer portraying Nixon must be forced by the context of the real Nixon attending an opera about himself. But even if there is no coreference between *Nixon* and *himself*, there is an entity in the anaphor interpretation (the person whom the actor impersonates) that is identical to Nixon (the referent of *Nixon*).

[21] Analogous representations are needed for personal pronouns, since they may undergo coercions just like the one illustrated for proper names in (49).

[22] This once again illustrates my claim that not all reinterpretations are triggered by impending incompatibilities between the constituents of an expression.

I will now show for the simpler (54) what a semantic analysis looks like that incorporates the above intuitions on cases that comprise both type coercion and anaphora.

(54) (#) Nixon saw himself

The crucial point of this analysis is that anaphora involves *two* identity relations. One is expressed in the meaning of the anaphor as the property of being identical to some entity x. In the uncoerced case, this property constitutes the restriction of an existential quantification that is introduced by the anaphor. I.e., its meaning is (55), the set of properties of someone who is identical to x (the referent of the antecedent):

(55) $\lambda P \exists y.(\underline{\lambda z.z = x})(y) \wedge P(y)$

The other identity relation is introduced by the anaphoric relation, it establishes strict coreference between this entity x and the referent of the antecedent.

The first identity relation, which is underlined in (55), may undergo coercion in the way defined above, which would alter the restriction of the quantification. Now in a null context no coercion is enforced. But then the anaphor semantically introduces a referent that is identical to the referent of the antecedent. For (54), we get (56), which boils down to (57). In (56), coercable properties are underlined once again. I.e., the intuition that anaphora establishes coreference between the referents of antecedent and anaphor follows immediately in the simple case:

(56) $\exists y.(\underline{\lambda z.z = \mathbf{nixon'}})(y) \wedge \exists x.(\underline{\lambda z.z = y})(x) \wedge \mathbf{see'}(y, x)$

(57) $\mathbf{see'}(\mathbf{nixon'}, \mathbf{nixon'})$

But the property of being identical to the referent of the antecedent can be coerced, if an appropriate context enforces this, e.g., the afore-mentioned opera context. Coercing the second underlined property in (56) by the operator (51) gives (58), the interpretation of (54) in the opera context ('Nixon sees some individual x that portrays Nixon'):

(58) $\exists x.\mathbf{pretend'}(x, \hat{}(x = \mathbf{nixon'})) \wedge \mathbf{see'}(\mathbf{nixon'}, x)$

At this point, Jackendoff's argument breaks down, because it is possible to give an appropriate semantic representation of the problematic data that can establish binding relations without having to determine referents for antecedent and anaphor in advance (in terms of type coercion). I.e., even in these cases one can separate a semantic and a conceptual part of interpretation. What this representation cannot (and is not meant to) explain is the difference between (47) and (48). Here further work is necessary, but whatever the restrictions are that apply here, they can be modelled as processes that restrict the reinterpretation potential of the relevant sentences *after* the semantic effect of binding has been established. See section 3.1.3 for a representation of these semantic representations in terms of the underspecification formalism CLLS.

1.4.3 Syntactic triggers for reinterpretations?

To further delimit the range of possible reinterpretations, Moens and Steedman assume that certain kinds of reinterpretations must be licensed by syntactic triggers. E.g., they state that in English the transition from a process to a (progressive) state is only possible for reinterpretation candidates that comprise a progressive morpheme. They assume that the progressive selects for processes and returns states.

But since the progressive is compatible with culminated processes like *build a house*, this claim presupposes that culminated processes undergo a coercion that 'strips off' their culminative events before they are compatible with the progressive. I.e., this loss of culminative events is not attributed to the progressive, but to a reinterpretation operator, which I will refer to by Pulman's term '**pphase-of**'. (This operator must also be licensed by a progressive morpheme.)

But why stipulate an operator like **pphase-of** if the progressive operator PROG itself can do this 'stripping off', since it introduces *proper parts* of eventualities (this is also the intuition of de Swart 1998)? For eventualities *e* in the extension of culminated processes, this yields the stripping effect in that these parts no longer have to comprise the culminative event of *e*. (See section 2.4.2 for the semantics of the progressive.) This entails that one needs no type coercion to account for the semantics of the progressive of culminated processes.

But as soon as one assumes that PROG itself performs this stripping off, Moens and Steedman's constraint on the transition to progressive states can no longer be upheld: PROG can then act as reinterpretation operator in all type coercion cases where one wants to strip off a culminative event – regardless of the presence of a progressive morpheme.

Consider, e.g., (59). In its preferred reading, Amélie was building a house for a few weeks, she built only a part of the house and did not finish it (this finishing would constitute the missing culminative event):

(59) # Amélie built a house for a few weeks

The modified predicate *Amélie build- a house* belongs to the group of culminated processes. This is illustrated, e.g., by its compatibility with time frame adverbials like *in 20 weeks*, which characterises culminated processes and other bounded predicates. Since durative adverbials are not compatible with culminated processes, reinterpretation is called for.

If PROG can strip off the culminative event for *Amélie build- a house*, the analysis of (59) is straightforward: PROG mediates between the conflicting aspectual properties of modifier and modified predicate by turning the latter into a state. I.e., (59) receives a progressive interpretation, even though there is no progressive morpheme present.

This alternative to Moens and Steedman's treatment of cases like (59) is simpler in that it can do without the operator **pphase-of**. This result undermines to a certain extent the claim that it is generally necessary to delimit possible type coercions, here, coercion into a progressive state, by assuming syntactic triggers for certain transitions in the network.

1.4.4 Delimiting reinterpretation positions

The fourth general issue for any account of type coercion is the question of how to delimit the range of *positions* in semantic representations of reinterpretation candidates where type coercion may take place (I dub these positions *R-positions*). Only by the delimitation of this range can one prevent severe overgeneration of analyses of type coercion.

This issue haunts in particular Dölling's analysis, which anticipates reinterpretation by inserting abstract reinterpretation templates between *any* functor-argument pair. E.g., in (25) one might in principle resolve the sortal mismatch in two ways, by adapting the VP to the $\bar{\text{N}}$ semantics (as shown in (28)), or vice versa. Either strategy would return a well-formed semantic representation, but this does not entail that the representation models a possible reinterpretation.

The alternative coercion of the $\bar{\text{N}}$ semantics into a container-denoting expression could be effected by the template **SHIFT3** (60) which is just like **SHIFT4** except that the arguments of $\underline{R}$ are switched:

(60) $\lambda P \lambda x_{\text{SORT2}} \exists y_{\text{SORT1}} . \underline{R}(y,x) \wedge P(y)$

Integrating this coerced $\bar{\text{N}}$ meaning with the standard meanings of the other constituents and instantiating $\underline{R}$ by **CONT** would return the semantic representation (61) that is equivalent to (28). In this case, overgeneration merely duplicates the analysis.

(61) $\exists x_{\text{SUBST}} . (\exists y_{\text{THING}} . \mathbf{CONT}(y,x) \wedge \mathbf{bottle}'(y)) \wedge \mathbf{freeze}'(x)$

But for (62), a universally quantified variant of (25), an derivation analogous to that of (61) would return a well-formed expression that fails to describe its meaning:

(62) # All the bottles froze

(62) is interpreted as universal quantification over bottles, not over their contents. To derive this meaning, coercion of the VP semantics is called for, which returns the desired representation (63): 'For all bottles, their content is

frozen' (i.e., every bottle must have some content).

Hence, for the derivation of the meaning of (62), the unwanted yet feasible alternative derivation that coerces the $\bar{\text{N}}$ meaning must be ruled out: Coercing this meaning with the help of the template (60) would return the well-formed (64) ('everything that is contained in some bottle is frozen'), where again $\underline{R}$ is instantiated by **CONT**.

(63) $\forall x_{\text{THING}}.\mathbf{bottle}'(x) \rightarrow \exists y_{\text{SUBST}}.\mathbf{CONT}(x,y) \wedge \mathbf{freeze}'(y)$

(64) $\forall y_{\text{SUBST}}.(\exists x_{\text{THING}}.\mathbf{CONT}(x,y) \wedge \mathbf{bottle}'(x)) \rightarrow \mathbf{freeze}'(y)$

To see the difference between these representations, consider a context in which half of the bottles are empty, and the content of the other half is frozen. In this context, (62) in the chosen reinterpretation is false. Since (64) is true in this context, it does not qualify as a representation of (62). In contrast, the correct representation (63) is incompatible with this context.

For more complex cases of type coercion, delimiting R-positions is even more complicated. E.g., (65) exhibits two sortal mismatches, between adjective and noun, and between noun and verb. Adjective and verb introduce properties of persons; the noun introduces a property of groups. Therefore, there are two reinterpretation options: reinterpreting the noun only, or reinterpreting both adjective and verb. The results of the two potential reinterpretations can be glossed as 'most people with red hair who are members of some team fell ill' and 'for most teams whose members have red hair, their members fell ill'.

(65) # Most red-haired teams fell ill

To choose between the two potential reinterpretations, consider the following context: A minority of the red-haired people fell ill that nevertheless constitute the majority of the teams with red-haired members (due to multiple memberships). In this context, (65) is true, but the context is only compatible with the second of the two potential reinterpretations as sketched above. I.e., the quantification in (65) is over teams (whose members have red hair), and not over human beings (whose hair is red and who are members of some team or other). Hence the VP semantics is coerced into a property of groups. This means that in the $\bar{\text{N}}$ semantics the same kind of coercion affects the adjective semantics. I.e., factors like economy (use as few reinterpretations as possible) do not guide the choice of reinterpretation.

These observations suggest complementing Dölling's analysis by constraining R-positions by syntactic constituent structure. That is, one could adopt interface rules in the spirit of Pulman (1997) and de Swart (1998) for the nominal domain, too: R-positions are introduced into semantic representations of reinterpretation candidates only by specific interface rules.

E.g., the rule that combines a determiner and an $\bar{\text{N}}$ into an NP can block reinterpretation by *not* inserting an R-position between the semantic contributions of determiner and $\bar{\text{N}}$, while the rules that adjoin an AP to an $\bar{\text{N}}$ and combine an NP and a VP into a sentence would license it (by such an insertion).

However, syntactic structure by itself does not suffice for the delimiting of R-positions. E.g., the following two sentences share the same constituent structure, viz., an adjunction structure in which an adverbial phrase adjoins to a sentence radical. Nevertheless, aftermath modification is only possible for (66) [= (9)] but not for (67):

(66) # Amélie left for two hours

(67) Amélie left yesterday

The notorious 'ham sandwich' examples (Nunberg, 1977, 1979) also refute a simple correlation of R-positions with syntactic constituent structure. In these examples, assuming an R-position between NP and VP and not assuming one between determiner and $\bar{\text{N}}$ would lead to the wrong result, because in these examples the reverse analysis is to be chosen (coercing the $\bar{\text{N}}$). This can be verified by once more applying the strategy of identifying appropriate reinterpretation options. It turns out that (68) quantifies over customers, not over sandwiches:

(68) # Most ham sandwiches are angry

Thus, even if the majority of the ham sandwiches is eaten by non-angry customers, (68) is true if the majority of ham sandwich eaters is angry. But the only chance to get this reading is to coerce the $\bar{\text{N}}$ semantics into an expression that denotes human beings. This means that the correct analysis of (68) is (69), which is derived in the same way as (64) above (its derivation involves **SHIFT4**; $\underline{R}$ is instantiated by the relation of consuming). See section 3.1.2 for the formal details and the derivation of this analysis. (69) can be paraphrased as follows: 'The cardinality of the set of angry ham sandwich consumers divided by the cardinality of the set of ham sandwich consumers is larger than $\frac{1}{2}$.'

(69) $\text{MOST}(\lambda y_{\text{PERSON}} \exists x_{\text{FOOD}}.\mathbf{consume}'(y,x) \wedge \mathbf{hamsandwich}'(x),$
$\lambda y_{\text{PERSON}}.\mathbf{angry}'(y))$

Such examples abound in technical languages, for instance, in the domains of medicine and music. The following examples exhibit the same pattern of type coercion as (68). Either case involves a reinterpretation that maps properties of musical instruments onto properties of their players:[23]

(70) # Die Oboe schraubt an ihren Klappen
the oboe is screwing on its keys
'the oboe is screwing on his keys'

(71) # Gitarre gesucht, die auch Baß spielt
guitar wanted which also bass plays
'guitar wanted that also plays bass'

These examples show that the strategy of delimiting R-positions in terms of the the underlying syntactic structure is by itself too coarse. Thus, this strategy is used in the proposed analysis only in a lexically constrained form (see in particular sections 3.1.2 and 4.2.1).

De Swart's approach is still more restrictive in that its syntax-semantics interface introduces underspecification (in the form of ambiguous operators) only for m-expressions, and thus avoids assigning seemingly superfluous reinterpretation potential to all other expressions ('non-m-expressions').

However, two observations speak against this strategy of restricting underspecification. First, reinterpretation may be called for even for non-m-expressions if the literal reading is ruled out by *extralinguistic considerations*, as in (72) [= (2)]:

(72) # All tenors are on the top shelf

Thus, it is advisable to anticipate such non-semantically triggered reinterpretation cases by including reinterpretation potential even to examples like (72). See section 3.1.3 for a formal account of some of these reinterpretations.

Non-semantically triggered reinterpretation cases abound in the domain of the *Duration Principle*. This principle does not belong to the realm of semantics and enforces agreement between temporal durations of eventualities that are introduced by different constituents of an expression, e.g., by a verb and an adverbial that modifies it.

(73) # Max played soccer on the beach for three months

Although (73) is not an m-expression, it involves an iterative reinterpretation in a normal context, which mediates between the incompatible duration

[23]The first example was actually uttered by Kristina Striegnitz (a colleague of mine) before a concert while watching the goings-on in the orchestra pit. The second example occurred in the want-ad section of the local newspaper.

German differs from English in that the gender of an anaphoric pronoun whose antecedent is a coerced NP is determined with reference to the uncoerced antecedent. E.g., in (70), the possessive pronoun *ihren* (lit. 'her') exhibits the feminine gender of its antecedent *die Oboe* 'the oboe', even if the coerced NP refers to a male oboe player. In English, the coerced antecedent determines the gender of the pronoun.

information introduced by *play soccer on the beach* (such eventualities typically last at most several hours) and by the adverbial. These reinterpretation cases are discussed in chapter 5.

The second observation is that for some non-m-expressions that are compatible with conceptual knowledge in a literal reading the need to reinterpret them shows up only within *larger texts*. This calls for a semantic analysis that does not rashly preclude any reinterpretation potential on the basis of the fact that there are no semantic mismatches in the expressions themselves. In particular, anaphoric reference may trigger this kind of reinterpretation. The reason for this seems to be that anaphoric reference carries sortal restrictions from the anaphor to its antecedent, even across sentence boundaries, e.g., in (74):

(74) # The ham sandwich is nice. He always gives big tips.

If one would assign no reinterpretation potential to the semantic representation of the first sentence of (74) since there is no semantic mismatch between any of its constituents, one would erroneously predict that no reinterpretation can take place for this sentence.

For the aspectual domain, (75) works analogously. Only the second sentence reveals that reinterpretation takes place in the first sentence, in order to make accessible the preparatory phase of the reaching of the top that is anaphorically referred to in the second sentence:

(75) # Max reached the top. It had taken him four hours to do so.

In sum, de Swart's strategy of delimiting R-positions by a check for semantic mismatches between the constituents of an expression is too restrictive since it erroneously precludes reinterpretation for non-m-expressions. The reinterpretation potential of non-m-expressions is also emphasised by Markert and Hahn (1997, 2002).

1.4.5 Type coercion and anaphoric reference

Fauconnier (1985) points out that type coercion may influence the anaphoric potential of NPs. I.e., the range of potential anaphors for which such an NP could serve as the antecedent may depend on the kind of coercion that affects the NP.

He distinguishes two cases, one in which anaphoric reference to a coerced NP in its literal sense is possible, and one in which it is not. E.g., in (76), the pronoun *it* cannot refer to the omelet, therefore (76) is inacceptable. In contrast, the pronoun *he* in (77) may refer to Plato even though there is type coercion (from authors to their works) in the first sentence of (77):

(76) * The mushroom omelet left without paying. It was inedible.

(77) # Plato is on the top shelf. He is a great author.

Fauconnier also suggests that reference to the discourse referent introduced by the coercion is always possible, e.g., the consumer in (78) and the book in (79). But this would amount to claiming that type coercion always changes the anaphoric potential of an NP.

(78) # The mushroom omelet left without paying. He jumped into a taxi.

(79) # Plato is on the top shelf. It is bound in leather.

He accounts for the difference between the omelet and the Plato cases in terms of 'openness/closedness' of coercion operators (which he calls 'connectors'). Open connectors, he argues, allow either kind of reference, e.g., a connector from authors to their work. But closed connectors bar anaphoric reference to an NP in its literal interpretation, like the connector from food to its consumers. Among the possible explanations for the openness of connectors he mentions familiarity.

To rephrase Fauconnier's data in my terms, type coercion introduces an additional discourse referent into the interpretation of an expression. Now the question is: Can the anaphor refer to the referent of the literal interpretation of the NP, to the other one, or to both? In the omelet sentence, reference to the additional referent is the sole option, but in the Plato sentence, either referent can be referred to.

Now the first thing to note is that there is a third option, viz., that reference to the literal interpretation of the NP is the only possibility. Consider, e.g., (80), where the pronoun *it* refers to the referent of *the wine*, even though this NP appears in a sentence that undergoes type coercion (introducing containers for the wine):

(80) # The wine was labelled. It had a spicy, slightly confected finish.

(81) shows that reference to the newly introduced discourse referent for the wine container is not possible:

(81) *The wine was labelled. It was mouth-blown.

This option lies outside Fauconnier's typology and seems not to fit in the open/closed dichotomy: It is not 'closed', because reference to the referent of the literal interpretation of the NP is possible, but it is not 'open' either, because reference to the newly introduced referent is impossible. Section 3.1.4 offers a different explanation of the data, which explains the data in terms of positions where reinterpretation takes place.

1.4.6 Composition of reinterpretation operators?

The next general issue for analyses of type coercion centres yet again on the problem of overgeneration for analyses of type coercion. But this time, the potential source of overgeneration is not that analyses may predict too many R-positions for a reinterpretation candidate, but that too many reinterpretation operators might be inserted at an R-position.

This issue is highlighted in Moens and Steedman's transition network (18). They assume that one single type coercion may involve more than one transition in the network, i.e., aspectually relevant operators may be composed from several simple operators. But since the network comprises several loops, one can construct complex operators whose input and output is of the same aspectual category. This allows for an infinite number of reinterpretation options.

To give a simple example, culminations can be turned into culminated processes by adding a preparatory phase. But culminated processes can be made into culminations, too (via a detour through the point class). I.e., one might build a complex operator whose parts are three operators, one for the first, and two for the second transition. The input and output aspectual class of this operator would be the same. Consequently, the composition of any number of such complex operators would once again return a feasible reinterpretation operator.

Even if one takes into account that reinterpretation is guided by conceptual knowledge, which constrains the complexity of feasible reinterpretation operators, allowing composed reinterpretation operators considerably heightens the number of reinterpretation possibilities. But this brings with it a certain potential for overgeneration.

Since this is a problem only if one allows type coercion to involve *more than one* reinterpretation operator, one might consider ruling out the composition of reinterpretation operators.

But this ban on the composition of reinterpretation operators would take away a seemingly indispensable factor of the analyses of Moens and Steedman. There are two groups of phenomena for which the possibility of composing reinterpretation operators seems to be crucially important:

First, they assign to some aspectually relevant operators selection restrictions that are so narrow that often two combined reinterpretation processes (whose result is a composed reinterpretation operator) are called for to mediate between these operators and their arguments. Here the ban seems to lead to an *undergeneration problem*. Second, they adduce cases of coercion with *several* aspectual reinterpretations as an argument for composed reinterpretation operators.

The first problem shows up in Moens and Steedman's analysis of the progressive and the iterative. E.g., the progressive is assumed to select for processes exclusively. Consequently, the progressive of a predicate of any other aspectual class must have undergone coercion into a process. Some of these coercions seem to necessitate a composed reinterpretation operator, among them (82):

(82) # Amélie was reaching the top

Moens and Steedman claim that the culmination *Amélie reach- the top* is first coerced into a culminated process (by adding a preparatory phase). This culminated process must then be coerced into a process in order to fit in with the selection restriction of the progressive.

But this second coercion step (which is to strip off the culminative event) could be dropped: There is no need for it, since the semantics of the progressive operator brings about this stripping effect by itself. This calls for a generalisation of the selection restriction of the progressive to make it compatible with culminated processes directly. But then cases like (82) no longer require a composed reinterpretation operator.

For iteration cases, the argumentation is similar. Moens and Steedman assign the iterative operator a very narrow selection restriction for points only. This selection restriction of the iterative is to model the intuition that iteration involves a kind of 'packaging' for the subeventualities that constitute the iteration. Thus, composed reinterpretation operators seem to be necessary in examples like (83):

(83) # Al was running a mile last week. This week he is up to three.

In (83), an iterative reinterpretation of *Al run- a mile* is enforced by the context (the second sentence). According to Moens and Steedman, the culminated process *Al run- a mile* is first coerced into a point to fulfill the selection restriction of the iterative, this point predicate then becomes the input for the iterative operator, which finally returns a process that is compatible with the progressive suffix.

But one might alternatively encode the packaging effect in (83) in the semantics of the iterative operator and allow predicates of any aspectual class as the argument of this operator. This takes away the need to compose reinterpretation operators in cases like (83), which then involves only one iterative reinterpretation operator. Section 2.4.2 will present such a semantic representation for the iterative operator, which models the packaging effect in terms of *maximality*.

In sum, the ban against composing reinterpretation operators does not necessarily lead to an undergeneration problem.

The second group of phenomena where Moens and Steedman explicitly require composed reinterpretation operators are cases like (84) with several aspectual reinterpretations:

(84) # Joe played the 'Minute Waltz' in less than sixty seconds for more than an hour

However, such examples are not proof of the need to compose reinterpretation operators, since each operator is required to mediate between a *different* mismatched pair of expressions, i.e., each operator is used on its own for one specific type coercion case within the sentence.

To see this, consider the derivation of (84) in Moens and Steedman's framework, starting from *Joe play- the 'Minute Waltz'*. They regard this predicate as a process, whose combination with a time frame adverbial like *in less than sixty seconds* calls for coercing the process into a culminated process by a bounding operator. (I would claim that it is directly compatible with time frame adverbials due to its boundedness.) *Joe play- the 'Minute Waltz' in less than sixty seconds* then emerges as a culmination (this is suggested by Moens and Steedman's examples). This culmination fails to meet the selection restriction of its modifier *for more than an hour*. To reconcile the modified expression with its modifier, it is coerced into a process by an iterative operator. (I drop the detour through the point node in the light of the above considerations.) (84), which consists of a durative adverbial and a predicate which it modifies, is then a culminated process. See also Pulman (1997) for a formalisation of the derivation of the meaning of (84).

Pulman provides example (85) to argue for the composition of reinterpretation operators. In (85), there are two iterative operators, which lead to the interpretation that there are iterations of sneezings (one for each morning) that are themselves iterated:

(85) # Joe is sneezing like that every morning now

But rather than assuming two iterative reinterpretation operators for (85), I regard one of them (the one that embeds the other one) as part of the semantics of the frequency adverb *every morning*.

In sum, the existence of numerous reinterpretation operators in one single sentence does not by itself provide an argument for the composition of reinterpretation operators: In the examples discussed, each of the operators was used in isolation, no two of the reinterpretation operators in these examples were composed. Consequently, I will assume that every R-position can be filled by at most one operator.

This ban on composed operators can then explain, e.g., the troublesome example (86) of Moens and Steedman (1986, 1988). As they note, this sentence has no meaning at all. But at a first glance it looks as if (86) could be interpreted as expressing the fact that Red Rum was participating in the race and likely to win for the first few minutes:

(86) * Red Rum won the race for the first few minutes

This potential reading of (86) would call for the composition of two reinterpretation operators. One adds a preparatory phase (for Red Rum's participation in the race) to the culminative event denoted by *Red Rum win- the race*, which returns a culminated process. The other one then strips off the culminative event (the winning), which yields a process predicate that fits the selection restriction of the durative adverbial *for a few minutes*. Moens and Steedman block this reading by claiming that only an explicit progressive form may license the second reinterpretation operator. But as discussed above, one may do without such an operator, and attribute the stripping off effect to a progressive reinterpretation operator (i.e., this operator is available for reinterpretation whenever one wants to get rid of a culminative event, regardless of the presence of a progressive morpheme). But then a composition of the first reinterpretation operator with a progressive operator could lead to the derivation of the unwanted interpretation of (86).

Blocking composed reinterpretation operators directly avoids this unwanted interpretation. The fact that (86) does get this interpretation as soon as one of the two operators is explicitly provided in the expression (by a progressive morpheme) corroborates this explanation of the unacceptability of (86):

(87) # Red Rum was winning the race for the first few minutes

However, this blocking of composed reinterpretation operators applies to the aspectual domain only. Examples like (88) show that composed reinterpretation operators are necessary in the nominal domain:

(88) # Goethe is blue, and Shakespeare is red

(88) can be used in reference to a picture of books, where all books by Goethe have a blue cover, and all books by Shakespeare, a red one. I.e., (88) involves reinterpretation operators that map authors on depictions of their works. These operators are composed of two more basic ones, first, one that maps producers onto their products, then, one that maps entities onto depictions of these entities.

In conclusion, the ban on composed reinterpretation operators bars overgeneration for cases of aspectual reinterpretation: Reinterpretation operations may insert only one operator into an R-position in the semantic representation of a reinterpretation candidate.

1.4.7 Summary of the discussion of type coercion

To conclude the discussion of previous analyses of type coercion I briefly summarise the points that are of relevance for all these analyses.

Excepting Pustejovsky and Markert and Hahn, there is agreement in the literature that reinterpretation is a process in which linguistic and extralinguistic knowledge interact in the determination of the full meaning of an expression. The overall strategy of modelling this interaction lies in weakening the semantic representations of reinterpretation candidates in the syntax-semantics interface to allow for a monotonic integration of extralinguistic information into these representations. This strategy also does justice to the observation that the result of semantic construction for reinterpretation candidates is underspecified.

The issue of delimiting reinterpretation possibilities arises in two different ways: One must delimit both the *material* that is integrated with the semantic representations of reinterpretation candidates and the *positions* within these representations where it is integrated.

For the first kind of delimitation it is assumed that aspectual (but not nominal) type coercion can insert at most one basic operator like a progressive or an iterative operator. I.e., there is no composition of reinterpretation operators from basic operators. In addition, type coercion is ontologically constrained: In the nominal domain, reinterpretation operators are ultimately based on a commonsense ontology; in the aspectual domain, most type coercion operators refer to the nucleus structure of eventualities.

The second kind of delimitation is still an open problem. Reinterpretation potential cannot be restricted to otherwise semantically ill-formed expressions, since reinterpretation may affect semantically well-formed expressions, too. While it seems advisable to base the determination of R-positions on syntactic structures, this strategy by itself is still too coarse: Expressions with the same constituent structure may differ with respect to their reinterpretation potential.

Finally, comprehensive analyses of type coercion must cover type coercion for functor-argument pairs of all types. So far, analyses have concentrated on only a subgroup of type coercion data, in particular, on those that involve coercion of a property of some sort. They should also be able to handle expressions in which type coercion and issues of quantifier scope cooccur.

1.5 Landing site coercion

In this section, I will discuss references to phenomena of landing site coercion (LSC) in previous work on reinterpretation. LSC was identified in the preceding chapter as a second kind of reinterpretation. Other researchers do discuss the kind of expressions that I introduced as instances of LSC, but either deny them the status of a reinterpretation candidate at all (Moens and Steedman, Pustejovsky) or propose analyses that explain them as yet another case of type coercion (Dölling).

1.5.1 An analysis of LSC data in terms of intentionality?

Moens and Steedman explicitly exclude sentences like (89) [= (9)], which were adduced as examples for LSC (in particular, for *aftermath modification*), from the realm of aspectual reinterpretation.

(89) # Amélie left for two hours

Instead, they explain (89) by an ambiguity of *for*. The additional reading of *for* that they assume – in contrast to the standard reading as the head of a durative adverbial – enters in the construction of adverbials that refer to an intended, not to an actual duration. As an argument for this view, they claim that in German and French there are different translations for the two purported readings of *for*: The first reading is translated by *lang*/*pendant*, the second, by *für*/*pour*.

But Pulman (1997) points out that structural ambiguities in one language may well be resolved lexically in another language. I.e., if a language exhibited different translations for expressions like *for*, this would by itself not prove that there is a lexical ambiguity of *for* in English if one could show that there is a structural ambiguity for durative adverbials (whose head is an unambiguous *for*). The structural ambiguity Pulman has in mind arises because the adverbial may pertain to the expression it modifies syntactically as a whole or to that part of this expression that introduces the aftermath or post-state. I.e., the (potential) structural ambiguity in question is exactly the one that is introduced by LSC (see section 4.2.1).

What is more, the German evidence Moens and Steedman adduce for their view is less clear-cut than they suggest. It is true that the German *zwei Stunden lang*, an equivalent to *for two hours*, blocks an interpretation of sentences in terms of aftermath modification. Therefore, (90), an attempt at a translation of (89) into German, fails to preserve the aftermath modification of the original, hence, is not acceptable. However, durative adverbials can be expressed in German by a temporal NP in the accusative case as well, e.g., *zwei Stunden* 'two hours' is another possibility of expressing 'for two hours' in German. But these durative adverbials allow aftermath modification like their English counterparts. (91), the second translation of (89), is thus the exact German analogue of (89):

(90) * Amélie ging zwei Stunden lang weg
Amélie went two hours long away

(91) # Amélie ging zwei Stunden weg
Amélie went two hours away

Hitzeman (1993) adduces further arguments against this intentional interpretation of durative adverbials in sentences like (89). One of her counterexamples is (92):

(92) # The raft submerged for one hour before bobbing up to the surface again

(92) shows that intentionality is not necessary to license aftermath modification. The reading that the raft stayed under water for one hour (as the aftermath of its submersion) is available here, and yet no intention whatsoever is involved.

Finally – in anticipation of the results of chapter 4 – there are cases of LSC that involve the *preparatory phase* of a nucleus structure. These cases cannot be attributed to intentionality in any way. As an example, consider (93) in the interpretation that Max ran *after* 20 minutes:

(93) # Max ran within 20 minutes

In this interpretation, the duration as introduced by the adverbial measures the actual, not the intended duration of an eventuality that *precedes* the eventuality of Max's running. I will argue in section 4.2.2 that (93) is a case of LSC where the argument (the semantics of *Max run-*) is augmented so that it also comprises a part that refers to a preparatory phase of the running. This part provides a new landing site for the functor (the semantics of the adverbial).

In the light of all this evidence, my conclusion is that it is not possible to reduce the data adduced for landing site coercion in the aspectual domain to a notion of intentionality.

1.5.2 An analysis of LSC data in terms of type coercion?

Dölling (1998) analyses aftermath modification as in (94) as *type coercion*, while I present it as a case of aspectual landing site coercion.

(94) # Amélie went to the pub for two hours

The aspectual incompatibility between modifier and modified predicate in (94) is modelled by sorts of eventualities $\pm$BD ('bounded'). The modified predicate introduces a property of bounded eventualities, the modifier contributes **2h**, the property of unbounded eventualities to last for two hours. Dölling's analysis of (94) (minus tense and sentence mood) is (95) ('**GTP**' stands for the property of going to the pub):

(95) $\lambda e_{+\mathrm{BD}}.\mathbf{GTP}'(\mathbf{amélie}')(e) \wedge \exists e'_{-\mathrm{BD}}.\underline{R}(e,e') \wedge \mathbf{2h}(e')$

In prose: (95) expresses the set of bounded eventualities of Amélie's going to the pub which are related by some relation $\underline{R}$ to another, unbounded eventuality that lasts for two hours. This expression distinguishes between the eventualities in the set denoted by *Amélie go- to the pub* and the entities whose duration is measured by *for two hours*.

The relation $\underline{R}$, which relates these eventualities, must be instantiated conceptually. $\underline{R}$ cannot be the identity relation in (94) due to the conflicting sorts +BD and −BD. But instantiating $\underline{R}$ as the relation POST between eventualities and their poststates or aftermaths yields a semantic representation that models the reinterpreted meaning of (94), that Amélie went to the pub and stayed there for two hours.

This representation is derived in close analogy to Dölling's analyses of type coercion in the nominal domain. In both cases, he assumes the same structure that triggers reinterpretation. There is an impending sortal mismatch because two predicates (with incompatible sortal restrictions) are to be applied to occurrences of the same variable through an operator that takes both predicates as arguments.

In the nominal domain, a characteristic constellation that gave rise to type coercion (the semantics of (25)) can be represented as follows. Issues of tense and sentence mood are once more ignored in the analysis.

(96) quantifier semantics:
$\lambda P \lambda Q \exists x.P(x) \wedge Q(x)$

$\bar{\text{N}}$ semantics:
$\lambda x_{\text{THING}}.\mathbf{bottle}'(x)$

VP semantics:
$\lambda x_{\text{SUBST}}.\mathbf{freeze}'(x)$

The constellation for the semantics of (94) has the same structure. The difference lies in the operator that takes the two sortally conflicting properties as arguments (and applies them to occurrences of the same bound variable). The operator that occurs in (94) is MOD, an operator that maps properties of type $\langle e,t \rangle$ onto expressions of type $\langle \langle e,t \rangle, \langle e,t \rangle \rangle$ (the usual type for modifiers). Dölling assumes that expressions like durative adverbials and PPs denote properties of entities. MOD turns them into functions from properties of entities to properties of entities only if they appear as modifiers in the syntax. I.e., for (94), the type coercion takes place within the *functor*, the semantics of the modifier.

(97) MOD semantics:
$\lambda Q \lambda P \lambda e.P(e) \wedge Q(e)$

S semantics:
$\lambda e_{+\text{BD}}.\mathbf{GTP}'(\mathbf{am\acute{e}lie}')(e)$

AdvP semantics:
$\lambda e_{-\text{BD}}.\mathbf{2h}(e)$

The strategy for coping with the impending sortal mismatch in constellations like (96) and (97) is similar: A reinterpretation operator is inserted between the operator and one of the two conflicting properties. This operator introduces an additional entitity into the discourse (in terms of an existentially quantified variable), to which one of the conflicting properties is applied. This avoids a sortal clash and returns a semantically well-formed representation.

To derive (95), the semantic representation of (94), one can once again employ the reinterpretation template **SHIFT4**. Together with a suitable instantiation of $\underline{R}$ it can mediate between an unbounded property of eventualities (e.g., the property of extending over two hours) and a bounded one (like the property of being a going to the pub of Amélie).

(95) is then constructed by applying (98) to the semantics of *Amélie go- to the pub*. (98) was built by applying **SHIFT4** (99) [= (26b)] to the semantics of the durative adverbial ($\lambda e.\mathbf{2h}(e)$), and then applying MOD to the result.

(98) $\lambda P \lambda e.P(e) \wedge \exists e'_{-\mathrm{BD}}.\underline{R}(e,e') \wedge \mathbf{2h}(e')$

(99) $\lambda P \lambda x_{\mathrm{SORT2}} \exists y_{\mathrm{SORT1}}.\underline{R}(x,y) \wedge P(y)$

Now this approach could easily be extended to reinterpretation in the nominal domain. E.g., one could use it to represent the semantics of *train to London* (which was introduced as an instance of LSC in the nominal domain) in terms of (100). In this representation, the meaning of the preposition is rendered by a constant '**to**′'. The free parameter $\underline{R}$ in (100) indicates that it is not yet clear on the semantic level to what the PP pertains.

(100) $\lambda x.\mathbf{train}'(x) \wedge \exists y.\underline{R}(x,y) \wedge \mathbf{to}'(y,\mathbf{london}')$

(100) denotes the set of trains x that stand in the relation $\underline{R}$ to an entity y that is directed towards London. If one instantiates $\underline{R}$ in (100) as a relation between objects and their destination, one gets the desired representation for *train to London*.

But Dölling's analysis of data like (94) raises a number of questions. The first observation is that the insertion of a reinterpretation template within the semantics of the modifier (the functor) crucially presupposes an approach to modification as in Dölling (1998), in which the semantics of a modifier is not yet completely fixed lexically but is composed of a core meaning and operators like **MOD**. Only by composing the semantics of the modifier during semantic construction can one insert the reinterpretation template into the semantics of the modifier. It is an open question whether this analysis can be generalised to other approaches that take a different stand on the semantics of modifiers.

What is more, this approach once more raises the issue of overgeneration: The derivation of the aftermath modification reading of (89) must be excluded for sentences like (101), which has no reading that an aftermath of Max's coughing (whatever it may be) lasted two hours:

(101) # Max coughed for two hours

Here one might exploit the aspectual classification to block such overgenerations. For the examples here, the crucial difference is that between predicates which lexically involve an aftermath, like *Amélie go- to the pub*, and those that do not, like *Max cough-*. One would restrict the domain of the relation POST to eventualities in the extension of the former, but not of the latter group of predicates. I will integrate this line of reasoning into my own analysis of examples like (94) and (101) in section 4.2.1.

However, the most troublesome problem that emerges for Dölling's approach is its failure to generalise. At the core of his approach is the introduction of another eventuality that serves as the landing site for the functor, i.e., for the semantics of the durative adverbial. For (94), we end up with one eventuality of Amélie's going to the pub and another one (the aftermath of her going) that lasts two hours. This presupposes an analysis of durative adverbials as intersective modifiers, which in itself may give rise to problems, as I will discuss in section 4.2.1. But even if one is willing to accept this analysis of durative adverbials and is thus able to analyse data like (94), one loses the intuitive connection between (94) and sentences like the following:

(102) Amélie almost climbed to the top

(103) Amélie climbed to the top again

Both these sentences have readings in which the modifiers, *almost* and *again*, respectively, pertain to the aftermath of eventualities in the extension of the modified predicate, viz., to Amélie's stay on the top. For (102), this yields the interpretation that the aftermath of Amélie's climbing did not occur (while the climbing itself did happen). That is, Amélie climbed towards the top and came close to it, but she was never on the top. Similarly, the relevant reading of (103) is one in which the presupposition of *again* (roughly, that there was a preceding eventuality of the same kind) pertains to Amélie's stay on the top only, but not to her climbing there (i.e., it might have been her first climbing to the top, but not her first stay on the top).

Neither of the two modifiers can be modelled in analogy to Dölling's account of durative adverbials. The problem here is that one cannot simply introduce another eventuality and say that the modifier pertains to it. Thus, these sentences cannot be paraphrased as 'she climbed to the top and the aftermath of this climbing was again/almost'. The modifiers introduce the notions of repetition and similarity of events, respectively. But an eventuality is the repetition of another eventuality, or has a similarity to another eventuality, only *with respect to a certain property*. I.e., the scope of these modifiers must extend over a property of eventualities. Therefore their meaning is modelled as a relation between properties of eventualities and eventualities, which immediately bars an account of the problematic readings of (102) and (103) in terms of type coercion templates and **MOD**.

In sum, Dölling's (1998) analysis of aftermath modification looks very attractive at first glance, but carries with it a number of problems that suggest it does not qualify as an alternative to the LSC account of the data that was introduced in the first chapter.

1.5.3 A compositional analysis of prospective LSC data?

LSC is not restricted to the aspectual domain, it appears in the nominal domain too, for instance in *train to London* and (104):

(104) # fast road

Since the modifier *fast* selects for predicates that denote sets of entities with (im-)proper parts that may undergo some change (typically, a change of location),[24] (104) cannot be interpreted directly. The intuition on the resulting reinterpretation is that rather than coercing the argument predicate *road*, the modifier is applied only to a part of the argument which describes a suitable aspect of the objects denoted by *road*. In an empty context, the preferred interpretation of (104) is one in which *fast* pertains to the purpose of roads, e.g., the interpretation that (104) denotes the set of roads along which one can move fast.

But in a standard analysis of the semantics of nouns like *road*, no such information that may serve as an additional landing site for a modifier is provided in the lexical entries. This begs the question of how to derive this additional information on roads and how to integrate it with the semantics of *road*.

Pustejovsky offers an explanation for these data within semantic composition, which once again crucially involves the *Qualia Structure*. Pustejovsky assumes that *road* provides in its semantic representation (in the *telic* quale) the information on its purpose that is central to our preferred understanding of (104). In addition, he counts *fast* among a group of modifiers that can semantically pertain to only a specific (for *fast*, the telic) quale of the expression which they modify. A special process of semantic composition, called *selective binding*, combines the semantic contributions of modifier and modified expression in this case. This strategy allows the derivation of the preferred interpretation of (104) within compositional semantics, i.e., in Pustejovsky's framework, this expression is not an instance of any kind of reinterpretation.

[24]Because of cases like *fast car* (in the non-reinterpretation reading 'car that is actually moving fast') I do not follow Pustejovsky's assumption that *fast* uniformly selects for event predicates. See section 4.1.2 for a discussion of reinterpretation in cases like *fast car* in which there is no semantic mismatch.

But the possibilities of selective binding for *fast* should be generalised to let it apply to *any* suitably typed quale of its modified expression. This would allow one to derive the semantics of *fast solution* and the like, which refer to entities that are brought about fast (rather than to entities whose purpose is fast).

This account of (104) and the like extends straightforwardly to a related phenomenon, viz., the modification of agentive nouns (*agentive modification* for short, e.g., in *fast typist*). Both phenomena are similar in that in agentive modification, too, the functor may pertain only to a part of the argument. For agentive modification, the relevant part is the one that is contributed by the verb stem, which, e.g., produces the reading 'person who usually types fast' for *fast typist*.

Pustejovsky models the similarity between both phenomena by attributing them both to selective binding in which the modifier *fast* pertains to the telic quale of its modified expression. This means that the lexical entries of agentive nouns have a telic quale that comprises the semantic contribution of the verb stem, which is thus accessible to the modifier. For *fast typist*, the resulting reading is 'person whose purpose it is to type fast'.

But this analysis is in danger of overworking the notion of purpose. E.g., the notion of purpose is inappropriate for nouns like *writer* or *dancer*. Thus, the analysis is built on a somewhat stretched notion of 'telic qualia role'.[25]

Another problem arises if one generalises *fast* in that it may pertain to any suitably typed quale, as was suggested above. This generalisation is motivated by examples like *fast solution*, but once it is adopted, it is unclear how one could block readings like 'typist who was brought about fast' for *fast typist* (whatever this may mean).

Selective binding would have to be licensed by lexically distinguishing those modifiers for which it is an optional strategy of semantic construction. Otherwise, there would be much overgeneration, since modifiers differ with respect to their applicability to only part of the semantics of their modified expression (e.g., *fast* differs from *pretty* in this respect). But nothing in the rule of selective binding itself prevents for instance the interpretation of *pretty typist* as 'typist who types prettily'. This lexical licensing of agentive modification and of data like (104) will also be included in my own account of the phenomenon in section 4.1.1.

But in spite of all these problems for Pustejovsky's account of selective binding, his analysis highlights the structural similarity between (104) and the

[25]This account seems to be more suitable for an analysis of nouns like *fertiliser*. These nouns comprise another nominalisation suffix *-er* (homonymous to the suffix *-er* in agentive nouns like *writer*). Combining this suffix with a verb *V* returns a noun with the meaning 'entity whose purpose is *V*-ing'.

like and agentive modification by attributing both phenomena to alternative attachment sites which arguments provide for their functors. This feature of his analysis will show up in the proposed LSC account of the data as well.

However, while this approach recognises the *similarity* between both phenomena, its main problem is handling their *difference*. They differ in that in agentive modification the part of the argument to which the functor may alternatively pertain is fixed in the compositional semantics. I.e., an example like *fast typist* has a fixed set of context-independent readings: one where the modifier pertains to its argument as a whole ('person who usually types and who is moving fast') and one where it pertains to the verb stem only ('person who usually types fast'). This shows that it is not a reinterpretation candidate.

In contrast, cases like (104) exhibit the wide range of possible interpretations and the context-dependency of interpretation that characterise reinterpretation candidates. E.g., for street-sweepers, *fast road* may well refer to roads in which there is little dirt and which hence allow for fast cleaning. Similarly, for postmen, *fast road* might take a reading like 'road where the delivery of the post does not take long'.

But Pustejovsky's approach treats both phenomena alike. Thus, the restriction on the number of potential readings that is adequate for the description of agentive modification reappears for cases of LSC as well. But predicting LSC cases to have only a fixed number of interpretations is in conflict with the considerable leeway in interpreting expressions like *fast road*. This is a major drawback for Pustejovsky's analysis and iterates the problem noted for his analysis of type coercion cases in section 1.3.5. Once more, the Qualia Structure can only encode default information (Lascarides and Copestake, 1998).

Finally, Pustejovsky also offers an analysis of aspectual LSC cases like (94). This analysis closely resembles the one for agentive modification and LSC in the nominal domain. Predicates that explicitly introduce a change of state have as their telic quale a predicate that characterises the aftermath of this change. E.g., for *go to the pub*, the telic quale refers to a stay in the pub. Selective binding can then allow the semantics of a durative adverbial to pertain to this aftermath predicate just as in the nominal cases discussed above. For (94), this yields the reading in which the adverbial measures the length of the stay in the pub.

However, once again the notion of 'telic quale' is stretched too much. Even if one concedes that the aftermath of a change of state may sometimes be the purpose of the change (e.g., being in the pub may well be the purpose of going to the pub), this relation is not essential to the notion of an aftermath of a change of state. E.g., in an expression like (105) it makes no sense to regard Max's lying on the ground, which is the aftermath of his falling down, as the purpose of falling:

(105) Max fell down

This analysis would also need to be complemented by lexical licensing of selective binding. Otherwise, one could not account for the fact that a sentence like (106) has no interpretation in which the adverbial pertains to the aftermath of Max's leaving:

(106) Max left yesterday

In sum, Pustejovsky's approach covers the relation between LSC and agentive modification only in part. It meets the requirement of modelling the similarity of both phenomena but not the requirement of accounting for their differences. What is more, the account of the data tries to apply the theory of Qualia Structure to quite a large variety of expressions which do not all lend themselves to a straightforward explanation in terms of qualia.

1.5.4 An interface account of LSC data?

Other approaches propose analysing the data in terms of special *interfaces* between syntax and semantics. In particular, one might either assume that this interface relates not to the visible syntactic structure but to another syntactic level. This is the option taken in Generative Grammar. Alternatively, one might stick to a syntax-semantics interface that relates the visible syntactic structure to semantics but assume a much looser relation between syntax and semantics. This alternative is proposed in Autolexical Syntax.

Generative Grammar

The structural ambiguities that emerge in cases of agentive modification and LSC are given an underspecified representation in this book. Thus, even in cases where one syntactic structure corresponds to a whole set of (fully specified) semantic structures, the relation between syntactic and semantic representations is 1:1, since one underspecified semantic structure is enough to describe this set of structures. This approach to the description of structural semantic ambiguity imposes comparatively few conditions on the syntactic analysis with which it is coupled.

Alternatively, one might establish an 1:1 relation between syntax and semantics in cases where one syntactic structure corresponds to several semantic structures by associating each semantic structure with an underlying syntactic structure of its own. I.e., one surface structure may be derived from several underlying syntactic structures, each of which determines a specific semantic structure. Ambiguity arises because the surface structure of an expression does not suffice to identify its underlying syntactic structure, which would be necessary to determine the meaning of the expression. This semantic analysis needs no underspecified semantic representations, but can only be coupled to a highly constrained range of syntactic analyses. E.g., attributing ambiguities arising in cases of modification by *again* to different underlying syntactic structures presupposes a syntactic analysis that licenses boundaries within the confines of words (von Stechow 1996; see section 4.3.1).

Larson (1998) accounts for agentive modification in terms of a suitable underlying syntactic structure. He discusses the example (107) and assigns it the semantic representation (108):

(107) Olga is a beautiful dancer

(108) $\Gamma e[\text{Con}(\textbf{olga}', e) \wedge \textbf{dance}'(\textbf{olga}', e)]\ [\textbf{beautiful}'(e)]$

'Γe' is a generic quantifier over events, 'Con' holds for an individual x and an eventuality e iff e is contextually relevant and contains x. In prose, (108) denotes a quantification over events: Usually, contextually relevant events where Olga dances are beautiful.

The derivation of (108) is based on the syntactic structure (109):

(109)

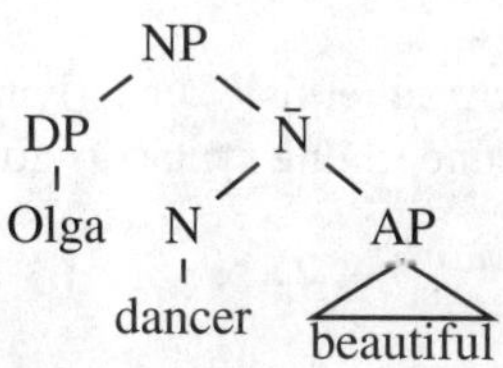

(109) is only a part of the syntax tree Larson assigns to (107), viz., the main part of the complement of *be*. Following Chomsky's (1995) analysis of predicative adjectives, Larson regards *Olga* as the subject of the predicate nominal *dancer*, whence its position in SpecN. It must be raised from this position to receive case and to be brought into agreement with the finite verb and the adjective, for (107), to the specifier position of the Agr_SP. (Agr_S is one of the functional heads that model inflection, it is mnemonic for 'agreement with the subject'.) Attributive adjectives are assigned a postnominal position.

Then (108) is derived from (109) in the style of Diesing's (1992) *Mapping Hypothesis*: According to Diesing, the scope of a strong quantifier is determined by lower material in a syntax tree, its restriction, by higher material. If one assumes that in (109) the scope of the generic quantifier (Γe is part of the semantics of *dancer*) is determined by the AP, and the restriction of the quantifier by the rest of the syntax tree, one obtains (108). I.e., the semantics of *dancer* comprises both $\text{Con}(x, e)$ and $\textbf{dance}'(x, e)$. (*Olga* is an argument of *dancer*, hence, in the derivation of (108) the meaning of *dancer* applies to the meaning of *Olga*.)

But even if one adopts all these preconditions for the derivation of (108), there is still the question of how to derive the semantic representation for (110), which is (111) in Larson's approach. (110) denotes a quantification over events: Usually, contextually relevant events (where Olga is a participant) are eventualities where Olga dances:

(110) Olga is a dancer

(111) $\Gamma e[\text{Con}(\mathbf{olga}', e)]\ [\mathbf{dance}'(\mathbf{olga}', e)]$

(110) would have to be assigned the syntax tree (112):

(112)

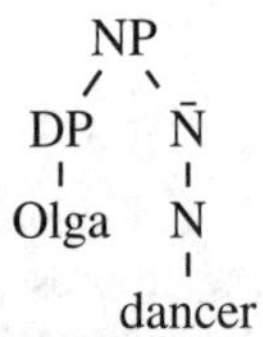

However, it is unclear how one could use the Mapping Hypothesis to derive (111) from (112). In particular, it seems difficult to derive the fact that in this example, the semantics of the noun must provide both the restriction and the scope for the generic quantifier.

Another way of handling cases like *fast typist* in terms of underlying syntactic structures would be to postulate the two underlying syntactic structures (113) for the expression:

(113) a [fast [type -ist]]
b [[fast type] -ist]

These syntactic structures guide the order in which the semantic contributions of adjective, verb, and suffix (114a)-(114c) are combined by functional composition. The exact account of the semantics of the affix is postponed to chapter 4; here, I use as shorthand an operator '**usual**′' (for 'usually') that relates a property P to an individual x if x usually has the property P:

(114) a $\lambda P \lambda x.\mathbf{fast}'(x) \wedge P(x)$
b $\lambda x \lambda e.\mathbf{type}'(x)(e)$
c $\lambda P \lambda x.\mathbf{usual}'(x, P)$

Without further assumptions, the structure (113a) would yield the reading 'set of fast persons who usually type, (113b), the reading 'set of persons who usually type fast, as spelt out in (115a) and (115b):

(115) a $\lambda x.\mathbf{fast}'(x) \wedge \mathbf{usual}'(x, \mathbf{type}')$
b $\lambda x.\mathbf{usual}'(x, \lambda x \lambda e.\mathbf{fast}'(e) \wedge \mathbf{type}'(x)(e))$

This analysis assumes that *fast* may be a property of both persons and eventualities. This begs the question of how to model the semantics of the adjective in a way that covers its use in the characterisation of both mobile entities like cars and racers and immobile entities like eventualities.[26]

An entity x is a member of the extension of **fast′** iff an (im-)proper part of x undergoes a rapid sequence of changes of state, i.e., the frequency of these changes is higher than a (context-dependent) standard of comparison. According to this definition, *fast* may characterise movement: A fast racer is one who undergoes rapid changes of location. In the case of *fast thinker*, there are rapid changes of mental states.

But this kind of approach would encounter a number of problems. The first problem is the distinction of those modifiers that enter into structures like (113b). To prevent overgeneration in cases like *pretty typist*, one would have to introduce some syntactic difference between modifiers like *pretty*, *friendly*, *willing* on the one hand (they do not engage in agentive modification), and modifiers like *fast*, *good* on the other hand (which do give rise to ambiguities because they show up in cases of agentive modification). However, rather than modelling this essentially semantic distinction in terms of syntactic categorisation, I opt for an account of the distinction that brings out its semantic nature.

It is also unclear how such a syntactic approach could be extended to LSC cases: For agentive modification, the syntactic structures are based on the morphology of agentive nouns (stem vs. affix), for LSC, no such morphological basis would be available. But if agentive modification and LSC were treated in a completely different manner, this would ignore their common ground, which will be highlighted in my approach.

In addition, a syntax-based approach to agentive modification would presuppose specific syntactic structures as in (113b). Therefore it is compatible with only a small range of syntactic analyses. In contrast, the analysis of agentive modification and LSC as proposed in this book has the advantage of being very flexible. E.g., *fast typist* can be assigned an underspecified semantic representation on the basis of the simple syntactic analysis (113a). In section 4.3 this flexibility will be illustrated: It will be shown that the proposed approach can be generalised straightforwardly to account for other phenomena that were taken as evidence for a syntax-based approach to structural ambiguity, in particular, the different readings of *again*-sentences (the so-called 'repetitive/restitutive' ambiguity[27]) e.g., in von Stechow (1996).

While this short discussion is not intended to settle once and for all the

[26]Here I assume that eventualities are not mobile themselves, but that their spatiotemporal extension is fixed once and for all.

[27]E.g., in *Max opened a window again* the repetitive reading presupposes that he performed another opening before, the restitutive reading, that the window was open before. See section 4.3.1 for details.

question of which of the approaches fares better on a global perspective, it illustrates my claim that agentive modification and LSC pose important touchstones for analyses of compositional semantics.

Autolexical Syntax

A more radical solution to the syntax-semantics mismatch as encountered in agentive modification is proposed by Sadock (1991). His system of *Autolexical Syntax* analyses language in terms of the interaction of three autonomous linguistic levels or modules (syntax, semantics, and morphology).

Lexical items are arranged into larger units (sentences, well-formed formulae, and words) at all levels. But there is no 1:1-correspondence between the construction steps of different levels. Construction of units may follow a different order whenever the properties of lexical items and the applicable construction rules at a specific level require this. In this way, cases like *fast typist* emerge as non-exceptional phenomena.

There are principles that constrain the difference between the ways in which larger units are constructed at each level. Relevant for the modification of agentive nouns is the *Constructional Integrity Constraint* that allows a lexeme to combine with an expression in one module and with only part of that expression in another module. *Fast typist* could be analysed as an instance of this possibility: Syntactically, the affix *-ist* combines with the $\bar{V}$ constituent *fast type*, but morphologically, it attaches to the head of this constituent. If one assumes that the semantics is read off from the syntactic structure, an interpretation in which the modifier pertains to the verb stem follows immediately.

But this means that one must allow the syntactic (and semantic) combination of any modifier of an agentive noun with the stem of the noun. But then the problems of overgeneration as sketched for examples like *pretty typist* apply here as well.

1.5.5 Summary of the discussion of landing site coercion

This section reviewed references in the literature to reinterpretation data which are regarded as instances of landing site coercion in this book. I pointed out problems that arise from alternative explanations of these data.

It was shown that such prospective LSC cases in the aspectual domain cannot be reduced to a notion of intentionality, as was proposed by Moens and Steedman, since some of these cases involve no intentionality at all. Neither can prospective aspectual LSC data be analysed in terms of type coercion, as suggested by Dölling: This would enforce a special analysis of the semantics of the involved modifiers and lose the common ground between aspectual LSC and phenomena like the repetitive/restitutive ambiguity of *again*-sentences.

For Pustejovsky's approach, it was pointed out that it brings out the common ground between LSC and the modification of agentive nouns (agentive modification), but fares worse when it comes to modelling their differences. The reason for this is once again Pustejovsky's attempt to model reinterpretation in terms of the Qualia Structure: This restricts the range of predicted LSC possibilities too much. In addition, I am worried that the notion of telic quale is somewhat stretched when it is applied to aspectual LSC and agentive modification.

The issue of delimiting the range of R-positions, which was noted for type coercion, recurs for landing site coercion. Fine-grained strategies are called for to identify R-positions for instances of LSC.

In sum, the alternative explanations that are offered in the literature for reinterpretation candidates which are analysed as cases of landing site coercion in this book do not satisfactorily account for them. In chapter 4 I will show how to capture these reinterpretation candidates by an analysis in terms of landing site coercion.

1.6 The aspectual classification

This section will present the aspectual notions that underlie my analyses of aspectual reinterpretation. It will specify the semantics assumed for aspectually relevant expressions (sentence radicals and other predicates), and sketch the system of aspectual classes on which the presentation of the reinterpretation data is based. This section is based on the analyses in Egg (1994, 1995).[28]

Before starting the presentation of my aspectual classification, I emphasise (as do Moens and Steedman) that formal methods of describing reinterpretation do not presuppose the choice of a particular aspectual classification. While I feel that there are good reasons for preferring the presented aspectual classification, the method of description for an account of reinterpretation phenomena could be based on other aspectual classifications as well.

1.6.1 Preliminaries

To formalise aspectual classes I first outline the semantics of those syntactic constituents that are to be classified aspectually (viz., predicates). Following Herweg and others, I concentrate on *sentence radicals*, since these predicates are the expressions that typically enter as immediate constituents in constructions with aspectually relevant subcategorisers or modifiers. In particular, they can be modified by aspectually relevant modifiers like durative and time frame adverbials.

The interpretation of predicates is based on an appropriate semantic analysis of verbs. I adopt a 'Davidsonian' (Davidson, 1967) verb semantics, i.e.,

[28]In Egg (1994, 1995) the term 'aktionsarten' was used to refer to aspect.

verbs are represented as relations with an explicit argument for the state of affairs or *eventuality* involved in the verb semantics. This kind of semantics differs from standard Montague semantics in that it reifies the possible world/time parameter in the interpretation of verbs. E.g., the semantics of an intransitive verb like *dance* is modelled as a relation between individuals x and and eventualities e such that x dances at e, rather than as a set of (dancing) individuals whose extension may vary across possible worlds and times.

I wish to remain agnostic with respect to the ontological status of eventualities. For my discussion of aspectual reinterpretation it is of no matter whether they are regarded as *times*, *situations*, *events*, or, possibly, something else. See, e.g., Bäuerle (1987), Galton (1984), Herweg (1990) or Krifka (1989) for further discussion of this point. As mentioned in section 1.2, eventualities are formalised as individuals with a specific sort EV(entuality). As usual, variables for such individuals are represented within λ-terms by $e, e', e'', \ldots$ (rather than $x_{\mathrm{EV}}, x'_{\mathrm{EV}}, \ldots$).

The Davidsonian verb semantics and the syntactic characterisation of sentence radicals determine the type of their semantics as properties (or sets) of eventualities. These properties will be referred to as *propositions*.

In the Davidsonian approach, the semantics of verbal modification is straightforward. Verbal modifiers are interpreted as functions from propositions to propositions, e.g., the semantics of *on 15 February, 2000* intersects properties of eventualities with the property of having a temporal extension that is an (im-)proper part of 15 February, 2000.

This allows a simple semantic composition for cases of verbal modification in terms of functional application. The semantics of *Max dance-* and of *Max dance- on 15 February, 2000* is given in (116) and (117).

(116) $\lambda e.\mathbf{dance}'(\mathbf{max}')(e)$

(117) $\lambda e.\mathbf{dance}'(\mathbf{max}')(e) \wedge \mathbf{on\text{-}15/02/2000}'(e)$

The result of the application of the modifier semantics reveals that the eventual semantic contribution of verbal modifiers like *on 15 February, 2000* is an additional property of the main eventuality argument (i.e., the one that is filled by a λ-abstracted variable) of the modified sentence radical. This facilitates deductions such as: Every instance of Max's dancing on 15 February, 2000 is also an instance of Max's dancing. See Parsons (1990) and Landman (2000) for an in-depth discussion of this point.

For the approach to aspectual reinterpretation proposed in this book, another advantage of the Davidsonian approach is that the eventuality arguments provide a well-suited handle for the anchoring of the aspectual information, which will be expounded in section 2.2.4.

The aspectual analyses presented will not venture beyond sentence radicals, but I will briefly outline how the propositions they denote are integrated into the meaning of full sentences. First, these propositions are conjoined (by the generalised conjunction[29] of Rooth and Partee 1982) with the proposition that is contributed by the tense morphology, after which the semantics of the sentence mood applies to this conjunction. If one, e.g., assumes that the semantic contribution of the past morpheme is $\lambda e.e < e_0$, the property of preceding the utterance eventuality e_0, one can assign the semantic representations (118) and (119) to a declarative sentence in the past (by existential closure) and to a yes/no question in the past (following Karttunen and Peters 1980), where P is the semantics of the respective sentence radical:

(118) $\exists e.e < e_0 \wedge P(e)$

(119) $\lambda p.\left[p = \lambda e.e < e_0 \wedge P(e)\right] \vee \left[p = \lambda e.\neg(e < e_0 \wedge P(e))\right]$

In prose, the declarative sentence expresses the existence of an eventuality in the extension of P that precedes the utterance eventuality, the yes/no question is the set of propositions which are equal to the conjunction of P with the property of preceding the utterance eventuality or equal to the negation of this conjunction.

Finally, this subsection will be rounded off with definitions for a couple of basic notions that show up in the definitions of aspectual classes in section 1.6.2.

- There is a (transitive, reflexive, and antisymmetric) relation of (im-) proper *part* ('$\sqsubseteq$') between eventualities. As usual, e is a proper part of e' ($e \sqsubset e'$) iff $e \sqsubseteq e'$ and $e \neq e'$.
- The operator '$\sqcup$' maps two eventualities e_1 and e_2 onto their *join*, the smallest eventuality such that e_1 and e_2 are part of it.
- *Overlap* '$\circ$' of x and y is defined as the existence of a common part, i.e., $x \circ y$ iff there is a z such that $z \sqsubseteq x$ and $z \sqsubseteq y$.
- Following Krifka (1998), *adjacency* is defined as follows: Adjacent elements do not overlap, and, if x is adjacent to a y that is part of z, then x is either adjacent to z too, or overlaps z.

After these preliminaries, the underlying aspectual classification will be outlined in the next section.

---

[29] Generalised conjunction '$\sqcap$' conjoins any pair of expressions of the same type whose type 'ends' in t, i.e., expressions that return an expression of type t after n applications ($n \in N_0$). It is defined recursively:

(i) if α and β have the type t, $\alpha \sqcap \beta = \alpha \wedge \beta$

(ii) if α and β have the type $\langle a, b\rangle$, $\alpha \sqcap \beta = \lambda x.\alpha(x) \sqcap \beta(x)$

1.6.2 The classification

The classification that underlies the proposed analysis of aspectual reinterpretation was developed in Egg (1994, 1995) and is presented here in a slightly revised version. It distinguishes four aspectual classes, *stative* predicates (e.g., *be in the pub* or *love*), *process* predicates (e.g., *run* or *eat apples*), *intergressive* predicates (e.g., *play a sonata* or *flash*) and *change* predicates (e.g., *die* or *build a house*). It is based on three properties of predicates, called *interval-based*, *bounded*, and *telic*.

If an *interval-based* predicate holds for an eventuality *e*, it need not hold for all the eventualities that are a part of *e*. E.g., *waltz* is interval-based as it can only apply to eventualities large enough to comprise a series of a certain number of steps. Compare on the other hand *Max be- in the 'Fox and Hounds'*: If this predicate holds for an eventuality *e*, it also holds for all eventualities that are a part of *e*. Often this difference is referred to as 'divisivity' (closedness with respect to a suitable part-of relation), stative predicates are divisive, but interval-based predicates are not. A similar distinction was presented by Taylor (1977) to distinguish stative and process predicates.

This distinction is important because it determines whether a predicate is compatible with the progressive (only nonstative predicates are) and with time point PPs (stative predicates are, but see section 5.2.2). Therefore, rather than disregarding the difference between stative and process predicates with respect to interval-basedness (like Galton 1984 and Herweg 1991a), I consider it to be the main factor that distinguishes both aspectual classes.

This criterion would need refinement if one assumed an aspectual class of *punctual* predicates, e.g., *flash* or *cough*. These predicates would be defined as having in their extension only eventualities that are extremely short or have no inner structure. Thus, such predicates would trivially fail the criterion of interval-basedness, although they should not be classified as stative predicates. However, the criterion as it stands suffices since I consider punctuality to be a phenomenon that is outside the realm of aspectual semantics. See section 1.6.4 below and section 5.4 for a detailed argumentation for this viewpoint on punctuality.[30]

The property of *boundedness* is defined as follows: Proper parts of elements of the extension of a predicate cannot likewise fall under that predicate. This property distinguishes, e.g., the bounded *Amélie play- a sonata* from the unbounded *Amélie play- the piano*: No proper part of any sonata playing is again a playing of the sonata (only of a part of it), while most eventualities of playing the piano (except the extreme cases of minimal playings, i.e., single keystrokes) have proper parts that are piano playings, too.

[30]This stand on punctuality allows for a definition of interval-based predicates that is considerably simpler than the one in Egg (1994, 1995).

Finally, telicity is defined as the explicit introduction of a change of state. E.g., the predicate *the train leave- the station* is telic because it refers to a change in the location of the train: Before this change, it is inside the station, after this change, it is outside the station. During the change it is neither inside nor outside the station.

This example shows that telic predicates refer to a constellation of three adjacent eventualities, a *preparatory phase* of the change, the eventuality at which the change takes place, and the *aftermath* of the change. These eventualities differ in that there is an unbounded (mostly stative) proposition P that holds for the aftermath, but does not hold for the preparatory phase. In the train example, this predicate would be the proposition that the train is outside the station. The example also suggests that during the eventuality of the change itself P is *undefined*.[31] (120) depicts this constellation:

(120)

$P(e')$ is false	$P(e)$ is undefined	$P(e'')$ is true
e'	e	e''

The distinction between telic and atelic yet bounded predicates is motivated by the fact that only the former are compatible with the perfect and allow the aftermath modification for durative adverbials (see section 1.1). This distinction is the main innovation of the classification of Egg (1994, 1995). It bridges the gap between approaches like Moens and Steedman's (1988), which emphasises the difference between telic and atelic predicates, and classifications like Krifka's (1992), where the boundedness distinction plays a prominent role.

The relations between the aspectual properties and the aspectual classes are summarised in diagram (121). It shows that all telic predicates are bounded and that all bounded predicates are interval-based:

(121)

	stative predicate	process predicate	intergr. predicate	change predicate
interval-based	−	+	+	+
bounded	−	−	+	+
telic	−	−	−	+

Now the three aspectual properties are defined, starting with **IB**:

(122) $\forall P.\mathbf{IB}(P) \leftrightarrow \exists e.P(e) \wedge \exists e'.e' \sqsubset e \wedge \neg P(e')$

In the extension of interval-based predicates P (like *dance*, *sing a song*, or *die*) there are eventualities with proper parts for which P does not hold.

Bounded predicates (e.g., *sing a song* or *build a house*) are defined in (123) (Krifka, 1992, 32):

[31] The distinction between false and undefined predicates is incorporated in *three-valued logics*, see, e.g., Blau (1978) or Pinkal (1991).

(123) $\forall P.\mathbf{BD}(P) \leftrightarrow \forall e \forall e'.P(e) \wedge e' \sqsubset e \rightarrow \neg P(e')$

Bounded predicates that hold for an eventuality e hold for no proper part of e. Hence, they also do not hold for eventualities of which e is a part.

Finally, the notion of telicity is defined in (124):

(124) $\forall P.\mathbf{TEL}(P) \leftrightarrow \exists P' \forall e.P(e) \rightarrow \text{BECOME}(P')(e)$

According to (124), a predicate P (e.g., *vanish* or *destroy Rome*) is telic iff all the eventualities it applies to can be described as a change of state for a certain predicate P'. The change is defined in terms of the operator BECOME, which characterises all telic predicates.

The definition of BECOME tries to capture the same intuitions as that of Dowty (1979), but assumes truth value gaps. It falls back on the schema (120) above: BECOME(P) holds for an eventuality e if P is false for an eventuality e' that immediately precedes e, undefined for e itself, but true for an e'' that immediately follows e. In addition, e must be *minimal* with respect to this constellation, i.e., it may have no proper part e''' that is surrounded by two eventualities for which P is false and true, respectively.

These definitions of the aspectually relevant properties **IB**, **BD**, and **TEL** entail the set-theoretic relations between them: Telic predicates are bounded, and bounded predicates are interval-based.

Telic predicates are bounded due to the definition of BECOME. Consider an arbitrary e from the extension of a telic predicate P. Then e is in the extension of BECOME(P'), for a certain P'. I.e., e is surrounded by two other eventualities e_1 and e_2 such that P' is false and true for them, respectively, and e is minimal with respect to this constellation. But this means that there is *no proper part* of e that is surrounded by two eventualities such that P' is false and true for them. Consequently, no proper part of e is in the extension of P, i.e., P is bounded.

One can also show that all bounded predicates must be interval-based: Let us assume a predicate P that is bounded yet not interval-based. Since it is not interval-based, every proper part e' of an eventuality e in the extension of P is in the extension of P, too. But by the boundedness of P, every such e' is not in the extension of P. I.e., the initial assumption is contradictory.

Aspectual properties were defined as *properties of propositions*. Thus, the aspectual classification applies to sentence radicals but not full sentences. This definition begs the question of how to classify predicates whose semantics is not of the propositional type (e.g., VPs). To determine the aspectual class of these predicates, their semantic representations are turned into propositions by existentially binding all but the last of their respective arguments.

E.g., this procedure returns the proposition $\lambda e \exists x \exists y.\mathbf{eat}'(x,y)(e)$ for *eat*. This proposition can then be the argument of properties of propositions like

IB. It emerges as interval-based but not bounded: If someone eats something at *e*, the same proposition may hold for some, but not all, proper parts of *e*. Thus, *eat* emerges as a process predicate.

The example shows that this procedure assigns an aspectual class even to predicates like *eat* where there are not-yet-filled slots for arguments that would influence the aspectual classification of the predicate projection of which they are a part. E.g., *Al eat- an apple* is telic, while *Al eat- apples* is a process (see in particular Krifka 1992 and Verkuyl 1993). However, since *eat* by itself introduces no boundaries whatsoever, I believe that it is justified to classify it as a process predicate.

To sum up this subsection, the aspectual classification underlying the presentation of the reinterpretation data is based on three properties of predicates and distinguishes four classes, viz., stative, process, intergressive and change predicates. Stative predicates are distinguished from the other groups by not being interval-based. Intergressive and change predicates are bounded whereas stative and process predicates are not, and change predicates are telic while the other groups of predicates are not. These relations between classes and properties of predicates are reflected in the implementation of the aspectual classification in terms of *sorts of eventualities* in section 2.2.4.

I conclude the presentation of the aspectual classification as assumed in this book with some comments on the relation between my classification and the nucleus structure of Moens and Steedman and on the distinction between 'punctual' and 'non-punctual' predicates, which I do not include in my aspectual classification.

1.6.3 My classification and the nucleus structure

Since I adopt the intuition of Moens and Steedman that the uninterrupted flow of eventualities is conceptually split up into nuclei, it is advisable to spell out the way in which this intuition is integrated into my approach. I assume that the main eventuality of every kind of predicate already introduces a nucleus (for bounded predicates) or may become part of one by reinterpretation.

For *stative* and *process predicates*, this means that the eventualities they denote may be integrated into nuclei if reinterpretation assigns to them a specific role in a larger nucleus structure. E.g., in *be in the pub at eight o'clock* (in the reading 'arrive there at eight'), the state of being in the pub emerges as the consequent state of a change of state from not being in the pub to being there. (Recall that nuclei break down into a preparatory phase, a culminative event, and a consequent state.) This also means that I deviate from Moens and Steedman in that I do not assume that process predicates invariably denote preparatory phases.

Predicates like *cough* (Moens and Steedman's point class) are also related to the nucleus structure in my approach: These predicates refer only to culminative events themselves, but reinterpretation may associate them with preparatory phases and consequent states.

For the culmination class of Moens and Steedman, my analysis is the same as theirs: These predicates refer to culminative events. But I assume (like Pulman) that these predicates also introduce information on preparatory phases and consequent states of these culminative events.

The main difference between my approach and Moens and Steedman's shows up for their culminated process class, e.g., for *build a house*: The involved culminative events in my analysis comprise *both* Moens and Steedman's preparatory phase and culminative event. Thus, the preparatory phase in my sense precedes that found in Moens and Steedman's analyses.

(125)
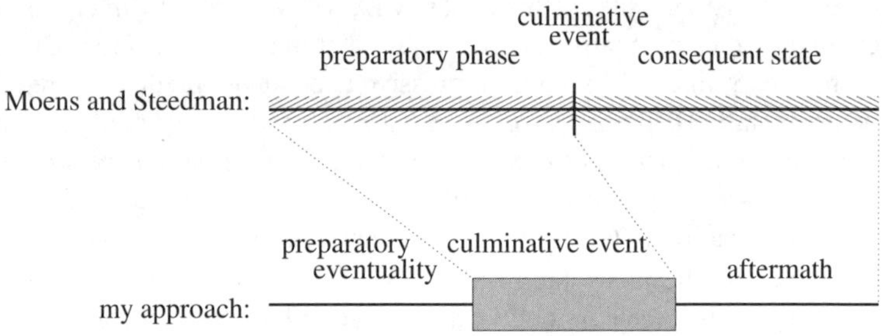

E.g., for *build a house* I regard the construction phase as part of the culminative event, thus, a preparatory phase of a building of a house precedes this construction. Moens and Steedman, in contrast, regard the construction as the preparatory phase. The *consequent state* in the nucleus structure of Moens and Steedman is the same as the one I assume; it is introduced explicitly in the semantics of telic predicates. To differentiate their analysis from mine, I will refer to the preparatory phase as *preparatory eventuality* and the consequent state as *aftermath* or *poststate*.

This comparison shows that for all predicates that introduce a change of state, the tripartite structure (120) is directly related to my view of the nucleus structure: The predicate *P* with respect to which the change of state takes place is false for the preparatory eventuality, undefined for the event itself, and true for the aftermath.

1.6.4 Phenomena of 'punctuality'

Semanticists strongly disagree over the question of whether *punctuality* (the property of referring to temporal entities that are extremely short or have no inner structure) is a main feature of aspectual classification. Punctuality features prominently in aspectual classifications like the ones of Vendler (1967) and Moens and Steedman (1988). Here it distinguishes accomplishment from achievement predicates (Vendler) and processes/culminated processes from points/culminations (Moens and Steedman). The former groups are non-punctual, e.g., *build a house*, the latter, punctual, e.g., *arrive*. In contrast, other researchers deny punctuality feature status, e.g., Parsons (1990) and Verkuyl (1993). I side with the latter group and do not integrate punctuality into my classification.

Data like (126) are cited as evidence for this feature:

(126) a The mountaineer climbed to the top in five hours
b # The mountaineer reached the top in five hours

While the time frame adverbial (TFA) *in five hours* specifies the (maximal) duration of the climbing in (126a), it does not pertain to the reaching of the top in (126b) but to another eventuality at the end of which the reaching of the top is situated (a preparatory phase in Moens and Steedman's terminology).

If *reach the top* is classified as a (punctual) achievement/culmination and *climb to the top*, as a (non-punctual) accomplishment/culminated process, the contrast between (126a) and (126b) can be modelled in terms of a non-punctual selection restriction of TFAs. This restriction is violated in (126b), which triggers reinterpretation.

I agree that expressions like (126b) are reinterpretation candidates, but do not regard these data as an argument for an aspectual feature of punctuality. This is motivated by the fact that the incompatibility of 'punctual' predicates like *cough* with TFA is not a hard and fast rule. Appropriately chosen TFA, as in (127), are compatible with 'punctual' predicates without reinterpretation (Pulman, 1997):

(127) Max coughed in .2 seconds

The seeming incompatibility of 'punctual' predicates and TFA thus boils down to the fact that one rarely uses TFA that refer to extremely short durations. Considerations of this kind suggest a different analysis for data like (126b):

They are attributed to another regularity in natural language, the so-called 'Duration Principle' (semantic construction may only combine expressions that do not introduce conflicting information on the duration of an eventuality), which closely interacts with aspectual semantics but must be distinguished from it. Chapter 5 provides a detailed argumentation of this point, so I just hint at the explanation here.

The need to reinterpret (126b) follows from the fact that eventualities in the extension of *the mountaineer reach- the top* have the typical duration of an *instant*. But, if a predicate is modified by a TFA, its main eventuality argument must have the duration that is specified in the semantics of the TFA. However, a duration of five hours and a duration of an instant are not compatible, which calls for reinterpretation. For (126a), the typical durations of eventualities in the extension of the modified expression *the mountaineer climb- to the top* are compatible with the five-hour duration introduced in the TFA, hence there is no need for reinterpretation.

These remarks conclude my account of the underlying aspectual classification which I assume for this book.

1.7 Conclusion

The review of previous literature on reinterpretation can be summarised as follows. There are detailed proposals for the integration of type coercion into semantic construction. These proposals include strategies for restricting the range of possible type coercions. I will build on these proposals in my own approach.

In contrast, the phenomenon of landing site coercion does not show up in the previous literature on reinterpretation. When phenomena which I presented under the heading of landing site coercion are treated in the literature, they are regarded as non-reinterpretation cases or as cases of type coercion. Hence, it is not possible to fall back on previously established analyses in my discussion of landing site coercion.

The discussion of previous approaches also identified a number of challenges in the analysis of reinterpretation phenomena that any analysis of reinterpretation must be able to handle. These challenges will be addressed in the subsequent analyses of type and landing site coercion.

- The analysis is expressive enough for an adequate coverage of reinterpretation data. It captures the two patterns of reinterpretation, type coercion and landing site coercion in a unified formalism.
- It provides a well-formed semantic representation for reinterpretation candidates and at the same time models any impending conflicts between the semantic contributions of its constituents.
- It distinguishes linguistic and extralinguistic contributions to the meaning of a reinterpretation candidate.
- It describes how these extralinguistic contributions are used to monotonically specify an underspecified result of semantic construction.
- It captures the cooccurrence of reinterpretation and issues of quantifier scope.
- The issue of delimiting the reinterpretation potential of an expression is crucial for such an analysis to avoid overgeneration.

2

Representing and Deriving Meaning

This chapter will outline the semantic representations of the meanings of reinterpretation candidates and their derivation. After a general introduction to formalisms for *underspecified* representations, one such formalism is presented in detail, viz., the Constraint Language for Lambda Structures (CLLS), in which the analyses of reinterpretation phenomena in this book are cast. CLLS was designed for the representation of all sorts of semantically underspecified expressions. CLLS is used to formulate the semantics of reinterpretation candidates (and other expressions) in terms of *constraints* over tree structures that correspond to λ-terms. Then a grammar fragment is sketched for the derivation of the proposed semantic representations of reinterpretation candidates. It is based on a simple phrase-structure grammar and an appropriate syntax-semantics interface.

2.1 Underspecification formalisms

This section introduces underspecification formalisms, which were designed for the representation of semantically underspecified expressions, i.e., expressions whose meaning can be only partially determined by semantic construction.

Consider the simple quantifier scope ambiguity (128), where either quantifier may outscope the other:

(128) Every woman loves a man

There are two readings for example (128), which I will gloss as '$\forall\exists$' and '$\exists\forall$'. An assertion of (128) is understood as $\forall\exists \vee \exists\forall$, a denial of (128), as $\neg\forall\exists \vee \neg\exists\forall$.

These two interpretations could not be captured if one simply determined the meaning of the ambiguous (128) as the disjunction of its possible disambiguations: In that case, one would falsely obtain $\neg(\forall\exists \vee \exists\forall)$ as the interpretation of the denial of (128).[32]

However, if we regard the meaning of the ambiguous expression as the set of its fully specified readings, and assume that understanding such an expression proceeds by forming the disjunction of this set, these interpretations follow directly. For (128), the meaning is thus $\{\forall\exists, \exists\forall\}$. The assertion of (128) is understood as the disjunction of its readings $\{\forall\exists, \exists\forall\}$; its denial, as the disjunction of its readings $\{\neg\forall\exists, \neg\exists\forall\}$, which yields the desired interpretations (van Eijck and Pinkal, 1996).

While this strategy would suffice for simple examples like (128), it would run into problems for more complex ambiguous expressions: Generating and enumerating all possible readings of these expressions may become a very involved task, which is neither efficient nor cognitively adequate. Thus, to characterize the set of possible readings for ambiguous expressions without enumerating the readings, a number of formalisms have been proposed that provide a compact description of the range of these readings in an *underspecified* representation. Examples for such formalisms are Quasi-Logical Form (QLF, Alshawi 1992), Underspecified Discourse Representation Theory (UDRT, Reyle 1993), Hole Semantics (Bos, 1996), Ambiguous Predicate Logic (Jaspars and van Eijck, 1996), Glue Language Semantics (Dalrymple et al., 1997), Minimal Recursion Semantics (MRS, Copestake et al. to appear), Underspecified Semantic Description Language (USDL, Pinkal 1996), the language of Context Unification (CU, Niehren et al. 1997), or Constraint Language for Lambda Structures (CLLS, Egg et al., Egg et al. 1998, 2001).

These formalisms augment semantic representations with metavariables and subordination relations between fragments of these representations. E.g., the semantics of (128) can be described in such a formalism. The description introduces the two quantifiers and the fact that they both subordinate (have scope over) the verb semantics, and that the arguments of the verb are variables that are bound by the quantifiers. The scope relation between the two quantifiers is left open. Ambiguity resolution can then be modelled as augmenting such descriptions, in (128), by information on the quantifier scope. This augmentation chooses one of the two feasible scope relations between the quantifiers. See section 2.2 below for the formal account of the semantics of (128).

I follow Pinkal (1996) and Niehren et al. (1997) here and regard these descriptions as *constraints* in a metalanguage (here, CLLS) that describe expressions in an object language (here, the typed λ-calculus). Since λ-terms

[32]This shows that the meaning of an ambiguous expression cannot be identified with its weakest reading, either, if there is one (for (128), $\forall\exists$). What is more, this strategy would not even generalize to all instances of quantifier scope ambiguity, since in some cases the readings do not stand in an entailment relation, e.g., in May's (1985) example *no one loves no one* with its two readings 'everyone is a lover' and 'everyone is loved'.

can be regarded as *tree structures*, descriptions of these λ-terms then emerge as *constraints on tree structures*.

Underspecified representations of ambiguous expressions are advantageous both from a semantic and a computational point of view. From the semantic perspective, there is a need for a representation of sentences with quantifier scope ambiguities. I.e., the goal is to express exactly and only the semantic contribution of such a sentence. E.g., the semantic representation of (128) may not rashly determine the scope between the two quantifiers.

From a computational point of view, formalisms for underspecified representations have the advantage of allowing one to choose freely the degree of disambiguation for an ambiguous expression. This means that disambiguation in a natural language processing system can be tailored to the specific needs of those components of the system that further process semantic representations.

E.g., the scope relations of the quantifiers in (128) or (129) are irrelevant for a machine translation system that translates (128) into German or (129) into English, since both are ambiguous in the same way. I.e., even if one could disambiguate the sentence that is to be translated, this disambiguation would be lost again in its translation; therefore, there is no need to invest the disambiguation effort. (NOM and ACC stand for nominative and accusative case, respectively.)

(129)	Einen	Mann	liebt	jede	Frau
	a	man.ACC	loves	every	woman.NOM

'Every woman loves a man'

Underspecification formalisms have mainly been used for the description of quantifier scope ambiguities. Recently, they have been extended to other phenomena as well, e.g., the interaction of ellipsis with phenomena like scope and anaphora. An example of the latter is the ambiguity of (130), where it is undecided whether Nigel walked Max's dog or his own dog. See, e.g., Sag (1976), Dalrymple et al. (1991), Gardent and Kohlhase (1996), Egg et al. (1998), and Egg et al. (2001) for detailed analyses of these and similar examples.

(130) Max walked his dog, and Nigel did, too

Reinterpretation is another field that lends itself to an account in terms of underspecification formalisms. In this book I will apply this kind of formalism to reinterpretation phenomena as well. This is motivated by the observation that reinterpretation candidates are semantically underspecified and that reinterpretation involves the integration of additional information into partial semantic representations.

Using an underspecification formalism for an account of reinterpretation has the additional advantage that one gets for free an analysis of scope ambiguity (after all, these phenomena are still the most prominent instances of ambiguity that are covered in such formalisms). Such an analysis is necessary since a comprehensive account of reinterpretation must be able to handle reinterpretation candidates that also exhibit quantifier scope.

After these remarks on underspecification formalisms, the next section presents the representation language that is used in this book for the underspecified account of reinterpretation.

2.2 CLLS

The goal of this section is to introduce the language CLLS. The presentation of CLLS closely follows Egg et al. (2001) but introduces the formalism only as far as it is needed for the purpose of this paper. In particular, the treatment of parallelism in CLLS is omitted. For full information on the treatment of parallelism, the reader is referred to Egg et al. (1998), and Egg et al. (2001). After an informal presentation of the basic ideas and goals behind the language CLLS in subsection 2.2.1, CLLS is formally defined in the subsections 2.2.2 and 2.2.3. Two more subsections are devoted to the issue of modelling type-theoretic and sortal information within CLLS and to a simplified representation of CLLS expressions.

2.2.1 The basic ideas and goals of CLLS

The language CLLS was designed to describe ambiguities of natural language in an underspecified fashion. It is a language of conjunctions of atomic constraints on *lambda structures* (or, *λ-structures*). λ-structures represent λ-terms by tree-like graphs. Nodes in λ-structures correspond to occurrences of subterms in the λ-term. E.g., the λ-structure (132) represents the formula (131) for one of the readings of (128).[33]

(131) $(\mathbf{every}'(\mathbf{woman}'))(\lambda x.(\mathbf{a}'(\mathbf{man}'))(\lambda y.\mathbf{love}'(x,y)))$

[33] Representations are simplified up to section 2.3 in that these structures cannot yet deal with reinterpretation issues. Furthermore, the semantics of determiners in λ-structures and constraints on λ-structures is represented by simple labelled nodes like the node 11 in (132). This node corresponds to the constant **every**′ in the λ-term (131). However, this is just shorthand for $\lambda P \lambda Q \forall x.P(x) \rightarrow Q(x)$. In principle, one could also describe the expanded λ-term by a λ-structure, but this would be extremely unwieldy because every variable binder (λP, λQ, and $\forall x$) as well as the operator $\rightarrow$ would be represented by a node of its own.

(132)

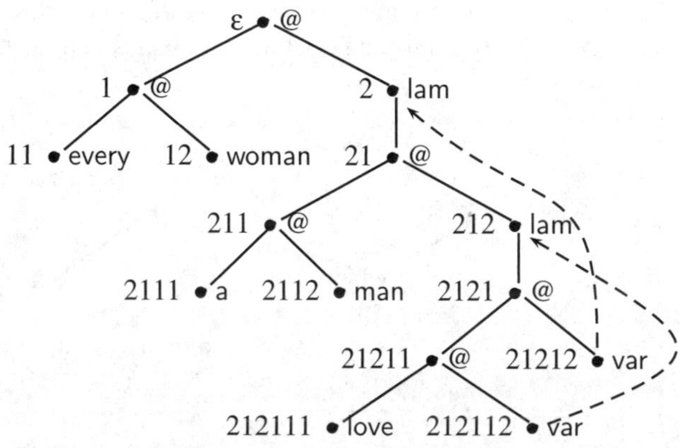

In λ-structures, nodes labelled by '@' stand for functional application, nodes labelled by lam, for a λ-abstraction, and nodes labelled by var, for a bound variable. Variable binding is represented by a dashed arrow from the variable node to the node for the binder. The arrow depicts a relation λ between var and lam nodes. In the example above, the λ-abstraction over the variable y in (131) is represented by the arrow from node 212112 to node 212. Modelling binding does not use explicit variable names, hence, α-equivalent closed λ-terms are represented by the same λ-structure. This explication of binding is crucial for underspecified descriptions of λ-structures, as in such descriptions variable names do not always suffice to model binding adequately.

This roundabout way of representing of λ-terms in terms of λ-structures is an extremely handy tool for semantic underspecification: Descriptions of λ-structures are just descriptions of trees, in this way, underspecified reference to λ-terms is possible.

These descriptions are cast in a logical language, to facilitate reading, they are often visualized by graphs. Note the difference between graphs for descriptions of λ-structures and graphs for λ-structures. The latter introduce *nodes*, the former, *node variables* (node variables are named X_i, where i is an appropriate subscript, usually, a natural number).

The descriptions introduce additional relations between nodes in order to talk about λ-structures in an underspecified way. In particular, descriptions comprise *dominance relations*. (A node ν_1 dominates ν_2 in a λ-structure if ν_1 must be above ν_2 in the λ-structure.) Dominance relations are represented graphically by dotted lines.

Reconsider, e.g., (128) and its two readings. As noted above, what both readings have in common is that they have the same quantifiers, both of them have scope over the verb, and the arguments of the verb are variables that are bound by the quantifiers. This common ground is captured in the description (133), where both X_1 and X_2 dominate X_3, while it remains open whether X_1 dominates X_2 or vice versa.

(133)

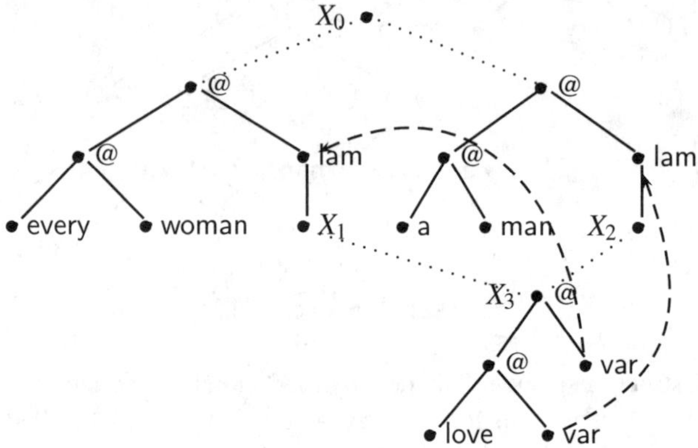

This description is satisfied by all λ-structures into which (133) can be embedded. In particular, it may be embedded into (132) and into the analogous λ-structure for the other reading of (128), which shows that (133) comprises the readings of the ambiguous (128) in an underspecified way. In this way, one can describe ambiguous expressions in CLLS in terms of partial descriptions of λ-structures.

However, (133) does not only license solutions corresponding to readings of (128); it can also be satisfied by λ-structures containing material not yet mentioned in the description. One could rule out these solutions by a general *constructiveness* restriction on these descriptions: Each node in a λ-structure that is described must be denoted by a variable in the description. While such a restriction would be appropriate for an account of scope ambiguity, it would be too strict for the proposed underspecified account of reinterpretation, which crucially involves the integration of additional material into semantic representations.[34]

But as soon as constructiveness is abandoned in an underspecification formalism, the *capturing problem* arises: How can we ensure proper and invariant binding of variables in an underspecified representation? The simple example (134) illustrates this problem in an analysis that is just as in CLLS, except that binding is modelled by variable names instead of directly relating the node variables for variable and its binder. This analysis is given in (135a), the actual CLLS analysis, in (135b):

(134) Every woman smiles

[34]It would also bar an underspecified analysis of ellipses, see Egg et al. (2001).

(135) a

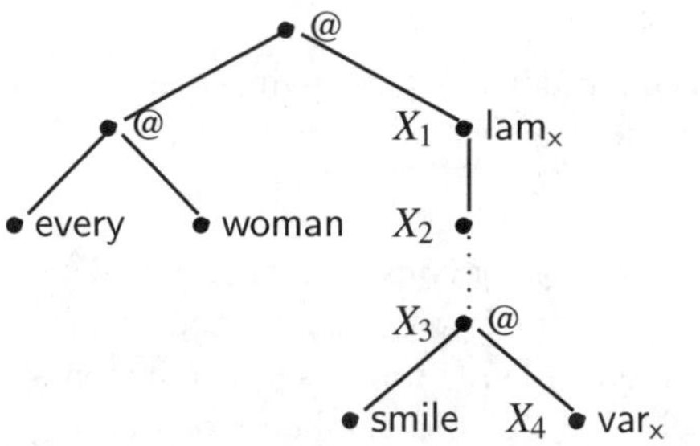

b

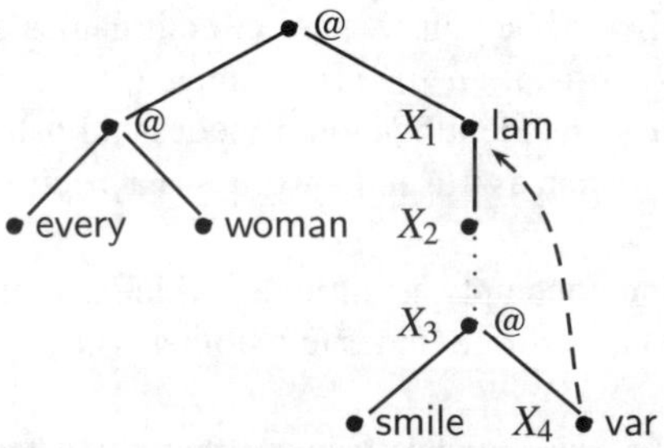

In (135a), the binding relation is expressed by the common subscript x of the labels of X_1 and X_4. Intuitively, this constraint is intended as a description of only those λ-structures in which this variable binding is preserved. However, (135a) comprises a gap in between X_2 and X_3.[35] Thus, (135a) can also be embedded into λ-structures where there is another node labelled by lam_x between the nodes that correspond to X_2 and X_3. In these structures, the binding relation as introduced by the common subscript x of X_1 and X_4 would be broken, since the variable would then be bound by this new, lower binder.

But as soon as variable binding is modelled in terms of λ as in (135b), such binding relations cannot be broken in the same way: The explicit relation between X_4 and X_1 cannot be abolished by any new material between the nodes that correspond to X_2 and X_3. In addition, due to the functional character of λ, it cannot relate a node that represents a bound variable to more than one lam node. Thus, the exclusive binding relation between X_1 and X_4 must be preserved in any λ-structure in which (135b) can be embedded. This solution of the capturing problem is one of the major innovations of CLLS and the main motivation for rendering λ-terms by λ-structures.

Next, λ-structures are assigned a formal representation as tree structures that are extended by additional relations (e.g., λ).

[35]This gap is introduced into the constraint for every NP by the syntax-semantics interface in order to anticipate potential scope ambiguities, see section 2.3.

2.2.2 Lambda structures

λ-structures are introduced formally, first, by giving a definition of tree structures, then, by extending tree structures to λ-structures.

Tree structures

Let Σ be a set of *function symbols* or *constructors*, f, g, a. They have a fixed *arity* as indicated by a superscript k; $k \in \boldsymbol{N}_0$. A (finite constructor) tree is a ground term (without variables) built from a set of function symbols. E.g., from the function symbols f^1, g^2, a^0 one can build the tree $f(g(a,a))$. *Paths* are words over $\boldsymbol{N}$. Tree nodes are identified with the path from the root to the node, the root is identified with the empty word ε. Path names are given as lowercase Greek letters like $\pi, \pi_1, \pi_2, \mu, \mu_1$. See example (132) for a tree (and λ-)structure which illustrates this identification of nodes and paths. Concatenation of words π and μ is written as $\pi\mu$, and a word π is a *prefix* of μ iff there is a word π_1 such that $\mu = \pi\pi_1$.

A *tree domain* Δ is a finite nonempty set of nodes which is prefixed-closed (i.e., $\pi\mu \in \Delta$ implies $\pi \in \Delta$) and closed under left siblings (i.e., if $\pi i \in \Delta$ then $\pi j \in \Delta$ for all $1 \leq j < i$).

A *tree structure* is a first-order model structure that characterizes a tree. Tree structures over Σ consist of a tree domain $\Delta \subseteq \boldsymbol{N}^*$ and a labelling relation $:f \subseteq \Delta^{n+1}$ for each n-ary function symbol $f \in \Sigma$, such that for all nodes $\pi \in \Delta$ and the maximal $n \in \boldsymbol{N}$ with $\pi n \in \Delta$, there is a unique symbol $f^n \in \Sigma$ such that $\pi{:}f(\pi 1, \ldots, \pi n)$. Thus, the number of children of a node is specified by the arity of its label. Two nodes may be labelled by the same constant without being equal.

The domain of a tree structure contains all nodes of the tree it characterizes, and its relations specify labelling and childhood within that tree. E.g., the domain of the tree structure for $f(g(a,a))$ is $\{\varepsilon, 1, 11, 12\}$. Its relations are $\varepsilon{:}f(1)$ (i.e., the root ε is labelled with f and has a single child 1), $1{:}g(11,12)$, $11{:}a$, and $12{:}a$.

Lambda structures and their extensions

The step to λ-structures then consists in extending tree structures with relations like the one for λ-binding. Σ contains the constructors var^0, lam^1, and ana^0, which are employed for the modelling of λ-binding and anaphora in the graphs. Then a *λ-structure* over Σ is a tree structure over Σ with tree domain Δ with the additional binary relations λ and ante on Δ such that $\lambda \subseteq \Delta \times \Delta$ is a partial function that maps every node $\pi \in \Delta$ with label var to a prefix of π which is labelled with lam and ante $\subseteq \Delta \times \Delta$, a partial function that maps every node $\pi \in \Delta$ with label ana to another node.

Finally, λ-structures are conservatively extended by two more relations between nodes. These relations, *dominance* and *disjointness*, are defined from the relations as specified in the definition of λ-structure.

Let Λ be a λ-structure and π, μ two of its nodes. Then π *dominates* μ ($\pi \triangleleft^* \mu$) if it lies above it, i.e., if π is a prefix of μ. The dominance relation is a partial order on the domain of Λ, i.e., reflexive, transitive, and antisymmetric.

Disjointness between two nodes means that neither one dominates the other, i.e., they lie on different branches of the λ-structure. Following Koller et al. (2000b), disjointness is defined in terms of a *branching point*: Two nodes π_1 and π_2 are disjoint ($\pi_1 \perp \pi_2$) iff there are paths π'_1 and π'_2 and different positive integers i, k such that $\pi_1 = \pi_0 i \pi'_1$ and $\pi_2 = \pi_0 k \pi'_2$, for some node π_0. The node π_0 is the branching point, the lowest node that dominates both the disjoint π_1 and π_2.

2.2.3 Syntax and semantics of CLLS

Now that λ-structures and their relations are defined, we can specify the constraint language for them. I assume an infinite set of *node variables*, ranged over by $X, Y, \ldots$, and choose relation symbols for all relations defined so far. To keep the presentation simple, the same symbols are used as for the relations themselves. The constraint language over λ-structures (CLLS) then has the following abstract syntax:

$$\begin{array}{llll} \varphi ::= & X{:}f^n(X_1,\ldots,X_n) & & (f^n \in \Sigma) \\ | & X \triangleleft^* Y & | & X \perp Y \\ | & \lambda(X) = Y & | & \mathsf{ante}(X) = Y \\ | & X \neq Y & | & \varphi \wedge \varphi' \end{array}$$

For the representation of semantically underspecified expressions, only *normal* constraints are used. A constraint φ is normal iff for any two distinct occurrences of labelling constraints $X{:}f(\ldots)$ and $Y{:}g(\ldots)$, φ comprises $X \neq Y$ – even if $f = g$.[36]

The semantics of CLLS is defined in the usual Tarski style. A constraint φ of CLLS can be evaluated to a truth value if a λ-structure Λ and a variable assignment α into the domain of Λ are given. A solution of φ is a pair (Λ, α) which satisfies φ.

Before turning to the introduction of types in CLLS, I present some ancillary definitions for notions recurrent in the analyses of reinterpretation phenomena in the following chapters.

For the notion of *fragments*, the definition of (Koller et al., 2000b, 15) is adopted. First, *connectedness* in a CLLS constraint φ is defined. Connected-

[36]This definition of normality, which is sufficient for my purpose of modelling reinterpretation, is augmented in Koller et al. (2000a). But since my syntax-semantics interface only produces constraints that comply to the additional conditions on normality in this paper, I need not go into them here.

ness in φ is the smallest binary equivalence relation over the set of variables of φ which contains all pairs (X_1, X_2) such that $X_1{:}f(\ldots X_2 \ldots)$ is a conjunct of φ.

Then a fragment of φ is a *maximal* subset of variables of φ that are pairwise connected in φ.[37] A fragment variable X is a *leaf* of the fragment if the fragment comprises no variable Y such that there is a labelling constraint $X{:}f(\ldots Y \ldots)$ in φ. Leaves are partitioned into *labelled leaves* and *holes*. For the latter, φ comprises no labelling constraint. As Koller et al. (2000b) show, such fragments have a tree-like structure, which in particular means that each fragment has a *root*, i.e., a unique node variable that dominates all variables of the fragment.

On the basis of these definitions, an intuitive notion of a *gap* in a constraint can be formalized: A constraint φ comprises a gap between two node variables X and Y iff X is a hole of a fragment and Y, the root of another fragment, and the relation $X \lhd^* Y$ holds.

2.2.4 Types in CLLS

In this subsection it is shown how type-theoretic and sortal properties of λ-terms are modelled in the corresponding λ-structures and in constraints on λ-structures. Type theory is an important tool in semantic construction, hence, modelling such properties in λ-structures is crucial, in particular, to rule out λ-structures that do not correspond to λ-terms. In addition, reference to such properties of λ-structures is a necessary prerequisite for my goal of describing the semantics of reinterpretation candidates in CLLS, since reinterpretation is characteristically triggered by the intention of avoiding impending type-theoretic or sortal conflicts between constituents of an expression.

Integrating types in CLLS

Type-theoretic information in CLLS constraints once again takes the form of constraints. The lexicon introduces type-theoretic constraints, which are then propagated throughout CLLS constraints. This propagation is based on the types associated with the labels '@' and 'lam', which model functional application and λ-abstraction in λ-structures.

The implementation of type-theoretic information for λ-structures and constraints on λ-structures follows Koller (1998): There is a typing system with *τ-types* for the types of nodes and *κ-types* that describe for each constructor f how the τ-type of a node that is labelled by $f(v_1, \ldots v_n)$ is related to the τ-types of the nodes of $v_1, \ldots v_n$.

κ-types of constructors f are of the form $(\tau_1, \ldots, \tau_n) \rightsquigarrow \tau$, where the

[37] As opposed to Koller et al. (2000b), the definition of a fragment includes a maximality condition. I am only interested in maximal fragments, which are used for the modelling of scopally ambiguous subconstituents in semantic representations.

$\tau_1,\ldots,\tau_n$ are the τ-types of the arguments of f. The τ-types are elements from a set T that is defined in the familiar way: (i) e and t are types, (ii) if τ_1 and τ_2 are types, then so is $\langle\tau_1,\tau_2\rangle$, (iii) nothing else is a type. This definition does not yet include sorts; it will be adapted later on in order to comprise sorts as well.

As examples for κ-types, consider those of the application (@) and of the lam constructor. The first constructor has the polymorphic κ-type $(\langle\tau_1,\tau_2\rangle,\tau_1) \rightsquigarrow \tau_2$. That is, the τ-type τ_2 of a node labelled by @ can only be determined with reference to the τ-types of the two arguments of @. This κ-type models the type-theoretic effect of functional application: the combination of an expression of type $\langle\tau_1,\tau_2\rangle$ with an expression of type τ_1 returns an expression of type τ_2.

The lam constructor has the polymorphic κ-type $(\tau_2) \rightsquigarrow \langle\tau_1,\tau_2\rangle$, where there are nodes ν_1,ν_2, and ν_3 such that $\nu_3{:}\mathsf{lam}(\nu_2)$ and $\lambda(\nu_1) = \nu_3$, and ν_1 is of type τ_1. Thus the τ-type of lam nodes depends on two factors: (i) the τ-type τ_1 of the var node or nodes that are mapped onto the lam node by the function λ, and (ii) the τ-type τ_2 of the sole argument of lam. Conversely, if the τ-type of a lam node is known as $\langle\tau_1,\tau_2\rangle$, the τ-type of all var nodes that are mapped onto this node by λ is τ_1.

For non-logical constructors like language and speak, the κ-types have an empty argument list, e.g., `nil` $\rightsquigarrow \langle e,t\rangle$ for language. This fixes the τ-type of the nodes labelled by them, e.g., $\langle e,t\rangle$ for nodes labelled by language. The constructor var may be of any κ-type with an empty argument list.

The interaction of τ-types and κ-types is illustrated by deriving the type of (136). The τ-type of ν_3 emerges as $\langle e,t\rangle$ (see the last paragraph). Thus, the κ-type of the application constructor returns t as the τ-type of ν_2 and e, as the τ-type of ν_4. Finally, the τ-type of ν_1 emerges as $\langle e,t\rangle$, because $\nu_1{:}\mathsf{lam}(\nu_2)$, $\lambda(\nu_4) = \nu_1$, and ν_4 is of type e.

(136)

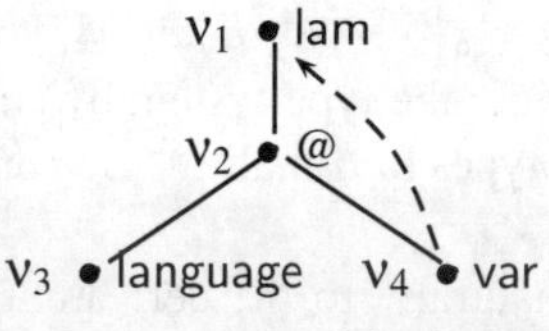

Since the κ-types of logical constructors model the type-theoretic effect of the corresponding operations within λ-terms, and non-logical constructors introduce the type of their corresponding λ-term in their κ-type, the τ-type of the root of a complex λ-structure equals the type of the λ-term to which the λ-structure corresponds. Thus, type-theoretic information restricts the class of possible λ-structures to those that are linguistically relevant in that they correspond to λ-terms. In constraints on λ-structures, κ-types of logical constructors are crucial in propagating type-theoretic and sortal information throughout the constraint. Constraints are well-typed if they have a solution.

Integrating sorts in CLLS

I extend this typing mechanism to introduce *sortal* information into λ-structures and constraints on λ-structures. This sort hierarchy reflects a hierarchy of conceptual categories (see Dölling 1995 for a discussion).

First, I assume a set of linguistic sorts S. There is a commutative and idempotent *join operation* '$\sqcup_S$' on S, which always maps two elements of S onto another element of S. For any two sorts s_1, s_2 there is a common most specific supersort $s_1 \sqcup_S s_2$ in S, i.e., $\langle S, \sqcup_S \rangle$ is a join semilattice. It has a 1-element, the most general sort' $\top$'. From the join operator, a (reflexive, transitive, and antisymmetric) relation '$\sqsubseteq_S$' can be defined in the usual way. $\sqsubseteq_S$ is called the *subsort relation*:

(137) $\forall s_1 \forall s_2 . s_1 \sqsubseteq_S s_2 \leftrightarrow (s_1 \sqcup_S s_2) = s_2$

The set S has no 0-element, since the meet operation on sorts '$\sqcap_S$' is not always defined. This models the fact that sorts may be incompatible. In the following, I will also assume a set of sort variables, which are indicated by lowercase Greek letters.

On the basis of this sort hierarchy one can define a hierarchy of a set of subtypes E of the type e with a function $f : S \rightarrow E$. To highlight the correspondence between sorts and types, subtypes e' of e are written with a subscript SORT, if f maps SORT onto e'. In particular, $f(\top) = e$, i.e., the subtype of e that corresponds to the 1-element of S is e itself. Hence, $e \equiv e_\top$. An example for a proper subtype of e is the type for eventualities, e_{EV}, whose subscript is the sort EV(entuality). As usual, this type is abbreviated as 's'.

There is a join operation '$\sqcup_E$' ($\sqcup_E : E \times E \rightarrow E$) and an ordering relation '$\sqsubseteq_E$' (called the *subtype relation*) on E. $\langle E, \sqcup_E \rangle$ is a join semilattice, too. The structure $\langle E, \sqcup_E, \sqsubseteq_E, e \rangle$ is induced on E by applying the function f to S, since $f : S \rightarrow E$ is an *isomorphism* between $\langle S, \sqcup_S, \sqsubseteq_S, \top \rangle$ and $\langle E, \sqcup_E, \sqsubseteq_E, e \rangle$.

This set E of subtypes of e is integrated into the type system by changing the first clause of the definition of the set of types to 'for all $e \in E$, e and t are types'.

This introduction of sorts carries over naturally to the derivation of the types of complex λ-structures in terms of τ- and κ-types. The derivation is based on constraints in the lexicon that model sortal restrictions of expressions like nouns or verbs. These restrictions are then propagated throughout CLLS constraints by the application and λ-abstraction node variables in the constraints. Their types involve the coindexation of type variables. For types that comprise subtypes of e this coindexation means that the sorts involved in these subtypes must be identical. E.g., if the types $\langle e_\alpha, t \rangle$ and $\langle e_\beta, t \rangle$ are coindexed, it follows that $\alpha = \beta$. Well-sorted constraints are those that have a solution.

Consider a simple example for a type coercion that is triggered by a sortal conflict:

(138) # Every bottle froze

The CLLS constraint for (138) is (139). Crucially, it must bring out the conflict between the two incompatible sorts THING and SUBST(ance) as introduced by the noun (semantically, a property of things) and the verb (semantically, a property of substances). The semantic contribution of the verb (the node variable X_9) is set off from the rest of the constraint by a dominance relation. Now the sortal restriction that is introduced in the node variable X_4 (the semantic contribution of the noun) must be propagated down to X_8, to model the fact that (139) has no constructive solution, i.e., that the gap between X_8 and X_9 may not be closed. (In contrast, the gap between X_6 and X_7 may be closed.)

(139)

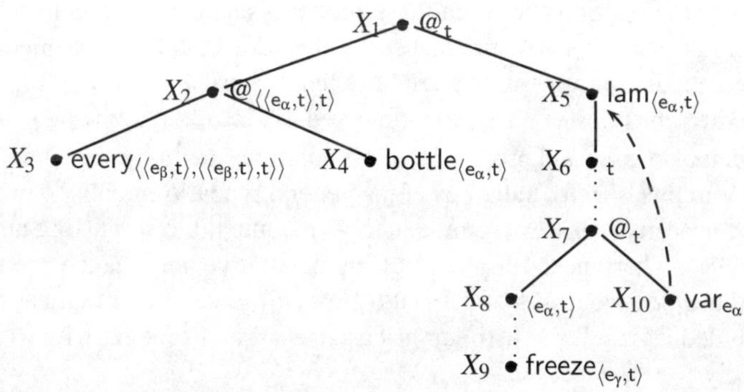

The lexicon introduces the κ-types $\mathtt{nil} \rightsquigarrow \langle e_\alpha, t\rangle$ and $\mathtt{nil} \rightsquigarrow \langle e_\gamma, t\rangle$ for bottle and freeze, respectively. It also provides the constraints $\alpha \sqsubseteq_S$ THING and $\gamma \sqsubseteq_S$ SUBST. In addition, every and all other labels that refer to determiners exhibit in their κ-type a coindexation of sorts. This type is $\mathtt{nil} \rightsquigarrow \langle\langle e_\beta, t\rangle, \langle\langle e_\beta, t\rangle, t\rangle\rangle$. This type models the fact that it makes only sense to interpret quantifiers in terms of different set-theoretic relations between properties of entities if these properties are sortally compatible (otherwise, the relation would always be one of non-intersection). The τ-type t of X_7 is introduced in semantic construction (see section 2.3.2).

The κ-type of X_2 enforces equating the sorts α and β. Because of the coindexation of the sorts in the τ-type of X_3, the τ-type of X_2 is determined as $\langle\langle e_\alpha, t\rangle, t\rangle$. This returns the τ-type $\langle e_\alpha, t\rangle$ for X_5. Due to the κ-type of lam, X_{10} has the τ-type e_α: The first part of the τ-type of X_5 is equal to the τ-type of every node variable that is mapped onto X_5 by the function λ. Since the τ-type of X_7 is t, X_8 carries the τ-type $\langle e_\alpha, t\rangle$, too. I.e., the type of X_4 is propagated down to X_8.

Thus, $X_8 \neq X_9$, due to the constraints on the sorts α and γ: $X_8 = X_9$ would ensue $\alpha = \gamma$, but no sort is a subsort of both THING and SUBST. Thus, (139) has no constructive solution, i.e., additional material must intervene between X_8 and X_9. This intervention is characteristic for reinterpretation.

This kind of type propagation reappears throughout the book to model type-theoretic incompatibilities that give rise to reinterpretation. To facilitate reading of CLLS constraints, however, I will abbreviate '$\langle \ldots e_\alpha \ldots \rangle$, where $\alpha \sqsubseteq_S$ SORT' as '$\langle \ldots e_{\text{SORT}} \ldots \rangle$'.[38]

The implementation of the aspectual classification

In the proposed analysis of reinterpretation, aspectual classes (and restrictions) are implemented as *sorts* of eventualities. In the same way, properties of predicates like telicity are modelled, which allows for a straightforward account of the relations between these properties and aspectual classes. E.g., *telicity* and *atelicity* are distinguished by the sorts $\pm$TEL. Consequently, the main eventuality argument of a telic predicate carries the sort +TEL, for instance, the semantics of *die* is then rendered as $\lambda x \lambda e_{+\text{TEL}}.\mathbf{die}'(x)(e)$.

Aspectual classes and properties of eventualities are integrated into a small type hierarchy (140) for subtypes of the general type EV(entuality). In this hierarchy, aspectual classes are modelled as incompatible sorts (Egg and Herweg, 1994). The types -IB and +TEL model stative and change predicates, while the types PROCESS and INTER(gressive) emerge as the meet of -BD (unboundedness) with +IB (interval-basedness), and of +BD with -TEL, respectively.

The more abstract types in the hierarchy can be used for the modelling of aspectual selection restrictions. E.g., the feature +IB may be used to express the selection restriction of the progressive operators for nonstative arguments (see section 3.2.1 for details).

[38] Chapter 5 is an exception here: In this chapter, the sorts get somewhat more complicated, hence, the presentation of the analysis becomes more readable if they are not included directly into the constraint graphs by means of this convention.

(140)

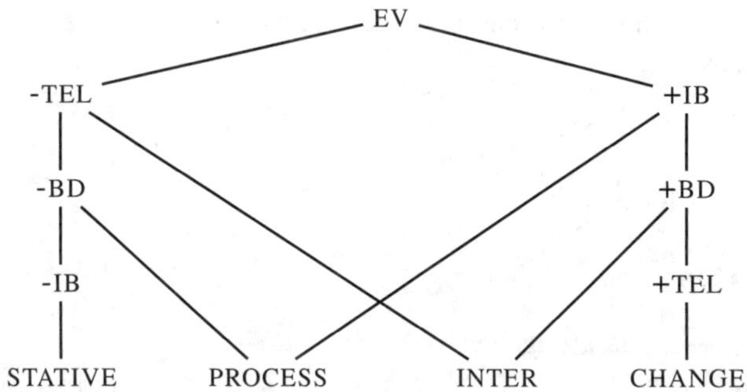

This implementation in terms of sorts does not necessarily carry fundamental ontological commitments. I.e., aspectual classes are not *ontologically relevant* distinctions (even though some aspectual boundaries might coincide with such distinctions) but mere linguistically induced *perspectives* on eventualities in the world. (This strategy seems also to be adopted in Pulman 1997.)

Dowty (1979) proposes another strategy of modelling aspect. He deducts the aspectual class of a predicate from its decomposition structure, hence, he needs no sortal distinction of eventualities. E.g., he characterizes all his achievement predicates in terms of a decomposition of the type BECOME(P), for a suitable proposition P. This strategy is very attractive for the description of verbs in isolation and can easily be adapted to aspectual classifications that differ from Vendler's (1967), which is adopted by Dowty (e.g., that of Egg 1995).

However, as soon as one tries to determine the aspectual class for the semantic representations of complex predicates, e.g., *eat an apple* or *Max dance- into the hall for two hours*, deducing their aspectual class from their decomposition structure gets very difficult because these structures tend to become very large. Hence, for a computational treatment of aspect it seems much more efficient to provide aspectual information explicitly. This applies in particular to the purpose of diagnosing potential aspectual mismatches that give rise to reinterpretation.

2.2.5 A shorthand notation for constraints on λ-structures

For the purposes of this book, constraints on λ-structures in their full beauty are often very complex. Therefore I will in many cases use a shorthand notation for CLLS constraints. These shorthand notations are related to constraints on λ-structures in the following way:

Fragments of constraints are given a two-dimensional notation in terms of (one alphabetic variant of) the corresponding λ-terms. I.e., var node variables are rendered as variables, and their lam node variables, by a binder for this specific variable. Sort information is encoded by sorted variables. E.g., (141) is rendered as (142):

(141)

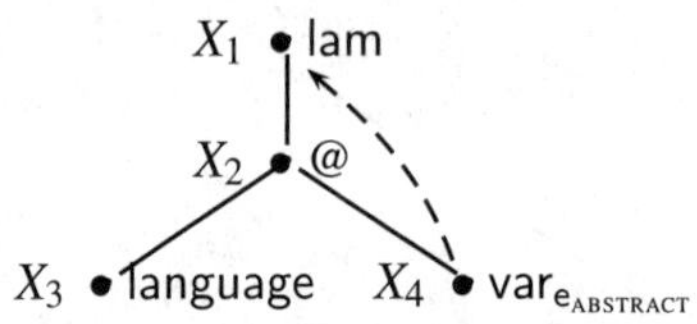

(142) $\lambda x_{\text{ABSTRACT}}.\textbf{language}'(x)$

This is the simplest case that applies only to fragments all of whose leaves are labelled, i.e., fragments without holes. When a fragment comprises a hole, it is indicated by '$\Box$' (called 'box' if the distinction to the hole to which it corresponds is relevant, otherwise, called 'hole', too.)

Consider for instance the fragment (143), which appears in λ-structures for expressions that comprise the NP *every language*. Its hole X_6 is represented as a box in the shorthand notation (144):

(143)

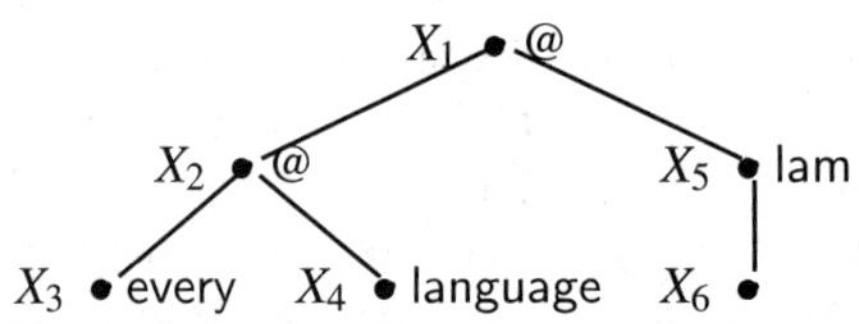

(144) $\forall x.\textbf{language}'(x) \rightarrow \Box$

One obtains (144) from (143) by replacing variables labelled by constants like every and language with the corresponding λ-terms, then working bottom-up by replacing application node variables by functional application of the λ-term for their left child to the λ-term for their right child. This yields $\lambda P \forall x.\textbf{language}'(x) \rightarrow P(x)$ for X_2. Since X_6 is replaced by a box, and lam node variables are replaced by λ-abstracting over the λ-term for their child, X_5 is replaced by (an arbitrary alphabetical variant of) $\lambda y.\Box$.[39] Applying the λ-term for X_2 to the one for X_5 returns (144) as the λ-term for X_1.

Finally, *dominance relations* are represented in the standard fashion (as dotted lines). In the shorthand notation, these dotted lines are drawn between boxes and whole fragments.

In order to become accustomed to this shorthand notation, consider (146), the representation for (145). It abbreviates (147) [= (133)]:

(145) [= (128)] Every woman loves a man

[39] λ-binding in (143) is vacuous, since X_5 is not linked to a var node variable. For lam node variables that are linked to var node variables, the corresponding λ-binder binds the variable (of the λ-calculus) that replaced the var node variables.

(146)

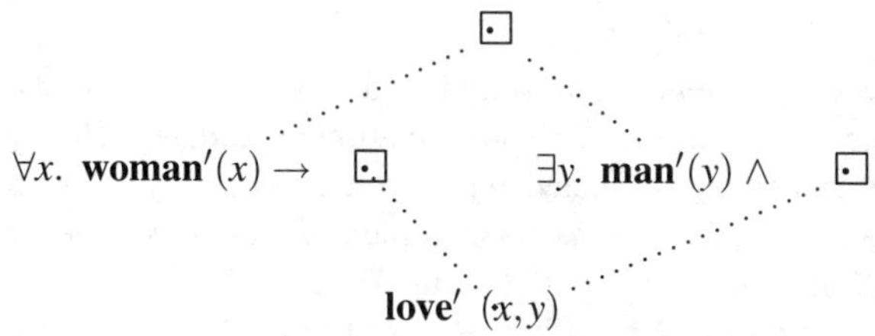

(147)

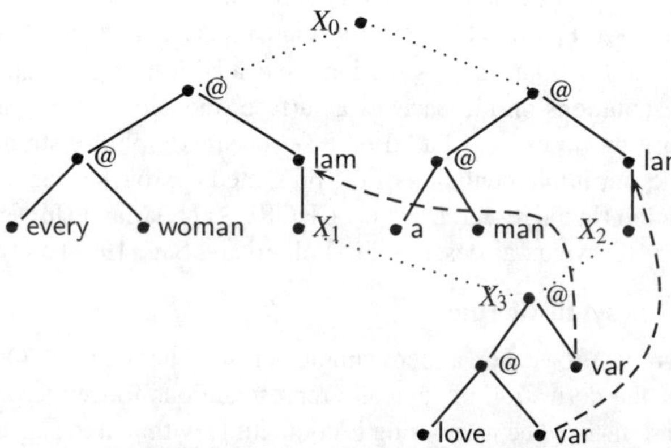

One aspect of CLLS is not represented directly in the shorthand notation: λ-bindings cannot be undone, even if binders and bound variables lie in different fragments. In the shorthand notation, such bindings are indicated in the names of the binders and the variables. E.g., the fact that the var node variable of the bottom fragment is bound by the lam node variable of the top fragment in (148a) is indicated in the abbreviated notation (148b) in that this var node variable is rendered by the variable name x, and the lam node variable, by λx:

(148) (a)

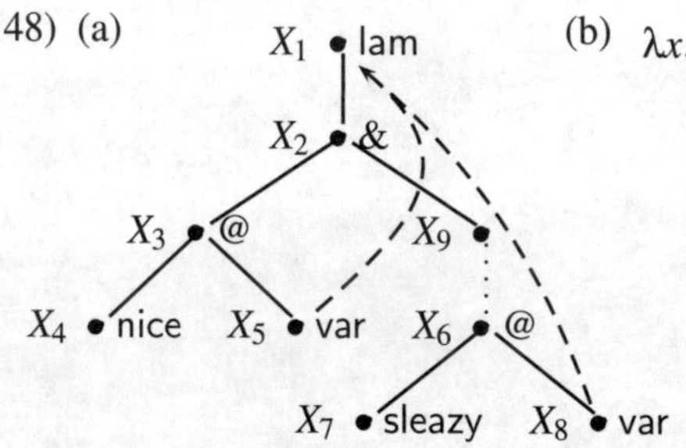

(b)

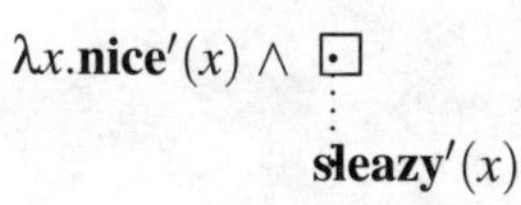

Finally, if a hole can only be identified with a fragment of a specific type, this is indicated by subscripting this type to the hole. E.g., the fact that the hole in (148b) must be identified with a fragment of type t could be expressed by writing '$\square_t$'.

2.3 The grammar fragment

This section introduces the grammar fragment for the construction of the proposed semantic representations of reinterpretation candidates. The syntactic phrase structure rules are associated with syntax-semantics interface rules that build semantic representations for complex expressions. The fragment is based on and fully compatible with that in Egg et al. (2001), except for interface rules that introduce R-positions. Rules of grammar and interface that are included in this latter fragment but are not needed for the purposes of the present book (in particular, those for relative clauses) are omitted.

The flexible semantic construction advocated in this book derives semantic representations on the basis of a surface-oriented syntactic analysis. For expository purposes, it is based on a set of simple phrase structure rules in this book; our implementation of the presented approach to flexible semantic construction (in the research project CHORUS at Saarland University) is built on the HPSG syntax as described in Pollard and Sag (1994) and Sag (1997).

2.3.1 The syntactic rules

The fragment is based on a set of simple phrase structure rules. Only rules relevant for the derivation of semantic representations for reinterpretation candidates are listed. The numbering is compatible with that in Egg et al. (2001), whence the gaps in the numbering.

(a1) `S` $\rightarrow$ `NP VP`
(a2) `VP` $\rightarrow$ `IV`
(a3) `VP` $\rightarrow$ `TV NP`
(a5) `VP` $\rightarrow$ `SV S`
(a8) `NP` $\rightarrow$ `Det` $\bar{\texttt{N}}$
(a9) $\bar{\texttt{N}}$ $\rightarrow$ `N`
(a14) `VP` $\rightarrow$ `CV VP`
(a16) `VP` $\rightarrow$ `Aux VP`
(a17) $\bar{\texttt{N}}$ $\rightarrow$ `AP N`
(a18) `AP` $\rightarrow$ `Adj`
(a19) `S` $\rightarrow$ `S Conj S`
(a20) `S` $\rightarrow$ `S Adv`
(a21) $\bar{\texttt{N}}$ $\rightarrow$ `N PP`
(a22) `PP`$\rightarrow$ `P NP`
(a13) $\alpha \rightarrow W$ if $(W, \alpha) \in Lex$

Most labels for syntactic categories are self-explanatory, except perhaps for the following: `Conj` refers to the category of subordinating conjunctions like *until* and *before*. Besides transitive and intransitive verbs (`TV` and `IV`, respectively), there is a category CV of control verbs like *begin* and a category SV for verbs with sentential complements like *believe*. Auxiliaries like *have* and *be* are of the category Aux.

The lexicon comprises a relation *Lex*, which relates words *W* and lexical categories $\alpha \in \{\texttt{Det}, \texttt{N}, \texttt{IV}, \texttt{TV}, \texttt{RV}, \texttt{Aux}, \dots\}$. Terminal productions **(a13)** expand lexical categories to words of this category.

The grammar is simplified in that sentence mood and tense are neglected. I.e., the category S corresponds to sentence radicals and not to full sentences. Also the construction of complex adverbials like durative and time frame adverbials and phenomena like agreement are omitted.

2.3.2 The syntax-semantics interface

The topic of this subsection is the derivation of the semantic representations as advocated in this book from the syntactic phrase-structure rules listed in the previous subsection. The presentation breaks down into four parts. First, the kind of interface I have in mind is introduced with a simple example, then I talk about special node variables ('scopenode' and 'topnode') that are crucial for semantic construction. Next, the syntax-semantics interface rules are presented, and, finally, a more involved example illustrates how the interface can be used to construct dominance diamonds as in (147) to represent scopally ambiguous expressions in an underspecified way.

The basic structure of the interface

The lexicon associates each atomic syntactic constituent with a CLLS constraint that models its semantic contribution. The task of semantic construction is to combine (or 'glue together') these smaller constraints (plus constraints associated with specific syntactic rules) into larger constraints for the semantics of syntactically complex constituents.

Since as much of the constraint construction as possible is factored out into the interface rules, entries in the semantic lexicon are extremely simple: Most of them introduce just one single labelling constraint.[40]

The syntax-semantics interface (SSI) specifies for each syntactic rule how the constraint for the emerging syntactic constituent is composed from the constraints of its immediate syntactic constituents (called 'IC constraints'). The IC constraints are conjoined with the constraint for the syntactic rule and, more importantly, specific node variables from the IC constraints are *equated* with node variables from the constraint for the syntactic rule. In terms of the glue metaphor, these variables are the 'gluing points' where one can stick constraints together.

---

[40]This holds for single-morpheme lexemes; the semantics of morphologically complex lexemes like *typist* is modelled by more involved constraints, see section 4.1.1.

The semantic representation for a constituent (modelled as the value of a feature like CONT) therefore indicates which node variables of its constraint form such gluing points. Interface rules refer to these gluing points, and, in addition, specify new gluing points for the emerging syntactic constituents. This strategy is the same as in the MRS interface (Copestake et al., to appear).[41] I assume two such gluing points for each constituent C, X^s_C (its *scopenode*) and X^r_C (its *topnode*).

But before elaborating the linguistic background of these node variables, I will first sketch how this interface is encoded in a typed feature structure formalism. In this way, the interface can be integrated into an HPSG grammar; versions of this interface were coupled to an HPSG parser in the research project CHORUS at Saarland University.

Here semantic information takes the form of a feature structure of type *cont*, whose features are TOPNODE, SCOPENODE, and CONSTRAINT. The first two features make available the local scopenode and topnode for semantic construction, their values are of a type *node_var*. The third feature for the constraint associated with a constituent is list-valued. The elements of the list are atomic constraints (labelling constraints, dominance constraints, λ-binding constraints, or anaphoric constraints). Consequently, conjoining constraints is implemented as appending such constraint lists.

These atomic constraints are of type *at_constr*; this type has four subtypes for each kind of atomic constraint. They can be implemented as atoms that have no internal structure in the grammar and are to be interpreted by an external module of semantic evaluation. Alternatively, they can be encoded as AVMs themselves, as e.g. in Richter and Sailer (2003). (149) illustrates an AVM for $\boxed{1} \lhd^* \boxed{2}$ (*at_dom_constr* is the type for dominance constraints):

(149)
$$\textit{at\_dom\_constr}\left[\begin{array}{ll}\text{ARG1} & \boxed{1}\\ \text{ARG2} & \boxed{2}\end{array}\right]$$

For ease of exposition, I will adopt the first option in the following. Consider, e.g., the CONT value for *Max smile-*:

(150)
$$\textit{cont}\left[\begin{array}{ll}\text{SCOPENODE} & \boxed{1}\\ \text{TOPNODE} & \boxed{2}\\ \text{CONSTRAINT} & \left\langle\begin{array}{l}\boxed{1} \lhd^* \boxed{4}, \boxed{1} \lhd^* \boxed{5}, \boxed{2}{:}\,@(\boxed{3},\boxed{4}), \boxed{3} \lhd^* \boxed{5},\\ \boxed{5}{:}\mathsf{smile}, \boxed{4}{:}\mathsf{max}\end{array}\right\rangle\end{array}\right]$$

[41] Note, however, that dominance relations are not separated into a specific feature in a CLLS-based interface, as opposed to MRS, where there is a list-valued feature H-CONS whose elements are dominance relations.

The constraint in (150) is depicted in its two-dimensional guise in (151). $X_1 \lhd^* X_2$ follows from $X_1 \lhd^* X_4$, $X_1 \lhd^* X_5$, $X_3 \lhd^* X_5$, and $X_2 : @(X_3, X_4)$:

(151)

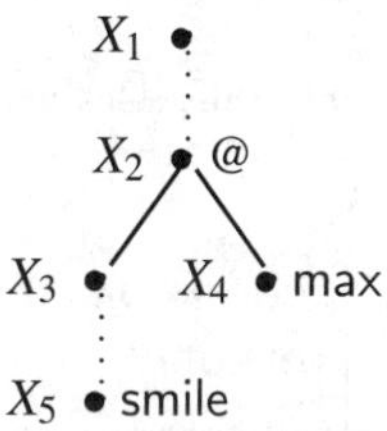

For the linguistic motivation of this semantic representation, see the next chapter (in particular, for the question of why there is a gap between X_3 and X_5). Here I will only show in detail how this constraint is derived from the CONT values of *Max* and *smile* in (152) on the basis of the simple syntactic structure (153):

(152) (a) $\begin{bmatrix} \text{SCOPENODE} & \boxed{1} \\ \text{TOPNODE} & \boxed{2} \\ \text{CONSTRAINT} & \left\langle \boxed{2}\text{:max}, \boxed{1} \lhd^* \boxed{2} \right\rangle \end{bmatrix}_{cont}$

(b) $\begin{bmatrix} \text{SCOPENODE} & \boxed{1} \\ \text{TOPNODE} & \boxed{2} \\ \text{CONSTRAINT} & \left\langle \boxed{2}\text{:smile}, \boxed{1} \lhd^* \boxed{2} \right\rangle \end{bmatrix}_{cont}$

(153)

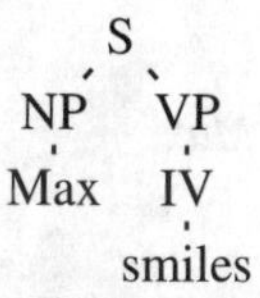

Two interface rules are needed to derive the constraint for the VP and the sentence, respectively. The first rule covers the VP case:

(154) $[_{\text{VP}}\ \texttt{IV}]$ $\overset{(b2)}{\Rightarrow}$

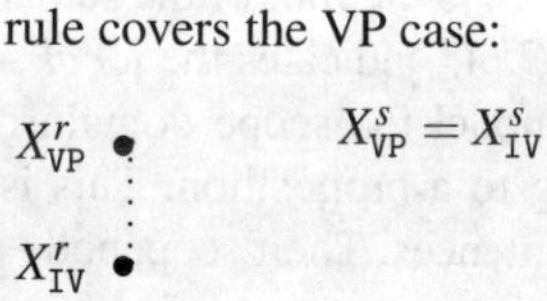

In prose: When a VP consists of an intransitive verb only, it inherits the scopenode from the verb, its topnode dominates the topnode of the verb. Since interface rules are encoded in the form of typed feature structures too, (154) is only shorthand for (155). However, to enhance readability, I will stick to the shorthand version in this book.

(155)
$$\begin{bmatrix} \text{SYNSEM}|\text{LOCAL} & \begin{bmatrix} \text{CAT} & \text{VP} \\ \text{CONT} & \begin{bmatrix} \text{SCOPENODE} & \boxed{1} \\ \text{TOPNODE} & \boxed{2} \\ \text{CONSTRAINT} & \text{APPEND}(\boxed{3}, \langle \boxed{2} \lhd^* \boxed{4} \rangle) \end{bmatrix} \end{bmatrix} \\ \text{DTRS} & \begin{bmatrix} \text{HEAD-DTR}|\text{SYNSEM}|\text{LOCAL} & \begin{bmatrix} \text{CAT} & \text{IV} \\ \text{CONT} & \begin{bmatrix} \text{SCOPENODE} & \boxed{1} \\ \text{TOPNODE} & \boxed{4} \\ \text{CONSTRAINT} & \boxed{3} \end{bmatrix} \end{bmatrix} \\ \text{COMP}|\text{DTRS} & \langle\rangle \end{bmatrix} \end{bmatrix}$$

This gives the following CONT value for the VP:

(156)
$$\begin{bmatrix} \text{SCOPENODE} & \boxed{1} \\ \text{TOPNODE} & \boxed{2} \\ \text{CONSTRAINT} & \left\langle \boxed{1} \lhd^* \boxed{4}, \boxed{2} \lhd^* \boxed{4}, \boxed{4}\text{:smile} \right\rangle \end{bmatrix}_{cont}$$

The second rule then derives the semantics of the sentence as a whole. It equates the scopenodes of NP, VP, and S and glues together the constraints of VP and NP by saying that their respective topnodes are immediate children of a new application node variable, which then becomes the topnode of the sentence:

(157) $[_{\text{S}}\ \texttt{NP VP}]$ $\overset{\text{(b1)}}{\Rightarrow}$

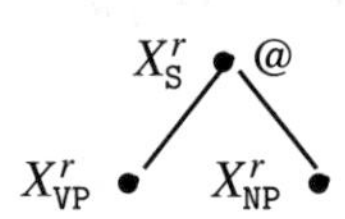

$X^s_{\text{S}} = X^s_{\text{NP}} = X^s_{\text{VP}}$

(157) derives (150) from (156) and the CONT value for *Max*.

Scopenode and topnode

I will now comment on the linguistic motivation behind the notions of scopenode and topnode. X^r_C is the *root* of the semantic contribution of the syntactic constituent below C. X^s_C indicates the *local scope domain* of C. Since scopenodes eventually model the scope domain of sentences, they are given the type corresponding to a proposition. This is relevant for scope islands like embedded finite sentences: Their scopenode indicates the maximal scope domain of a quantifier in such a scope island (excepting those that are introduced by an indefinite article).

This is brought about (i) by equating the scopenodes of a sentence and the NPs it contains, consider, e.g., (157), where this is done for the subject NP, and (ii) by a general lexical rule that for each lexical item L (except the indefinite article), its scopenode dominates its topnode: $X^s_L \lhd^* X^r_L$. This shows up, e.g., in the lexical entries in (152).

For instance, in the semantic representation of (158), given as (159) below, there are two scopenodes, X^s_M for the matrix sentence M, and X^s_E for the embedded sentence E. X^s_E dominates the quantifier of *every man* but not that for *a woman*:

(158) Max believes every woman loves a man

There are two topnodes too, one for each sentence. For either sentence, its topnode dominates that part of the constraint that models the *verbal nucleus*. This term refers to that part of a predicate that is made up by the verb relation or property plus its arguments, except the main eventuality argument (in a Davidsonian semantics). For the embedded sentence, the verbal nucleus consists of the verb semantics plus the variables bound by the quantifiers of *every woman* and *a man*. The verbal nucleus of the matrix clause consists of the verb semantics plus its two arguments, the constant **max**′ and the semantics of the embedded sentence. Verbal nuclei are of type $\langle s,t \rangle$ in a Davidsonian semantics, of type t, if eventualies are not arguments in verb meanings.[42]

In (159), the topnode X^r_M of the matrix sentence dominates the scopenode X^s_E, which means that *believe* has scope over the embedded sentence. (This was brought about by the interface rule **(b5)**, see below for details.) The resulting constraint models the three readings for (158): *Every woman* is in the scope of *believe*, and *a man* may take scope above, between, or below them.

(159)

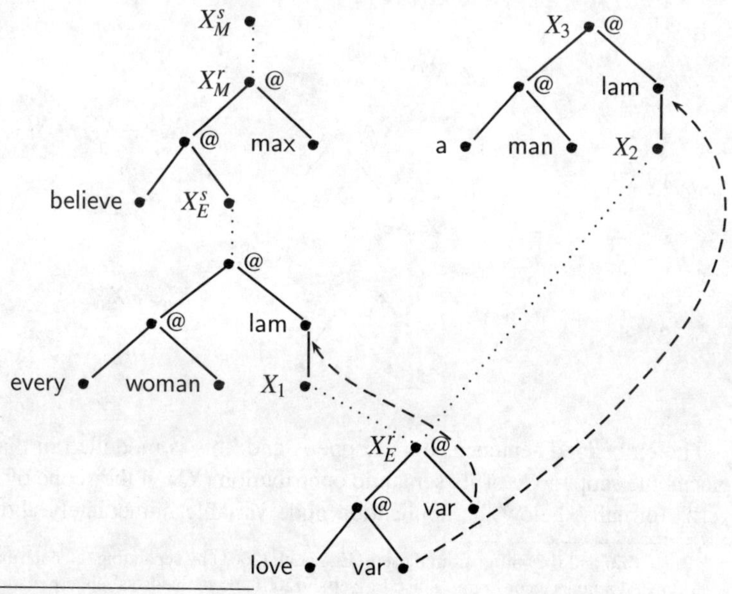

[42]This use of the term 'nucleus' is unrelated to its use by Moens and Steedman.

This constraint has three constructive solutions, in one *a man* has narrowest scope. Here, X_2 and X^r_E are mapped onto the same node, and so are X_1 and X_3. If we omit eventuality variables for simplicity, this solution corresponds to the λ-term(160):

(160) $\mathbf{believe'}(\mathbf{max'}, {}^\wedge\forall x.\mathbf{woman'}(x) \rightarrow \exists y.\mathbf{man'}(y) \wedge \mathbf{love'}(x,y))$

Here **believe′** is interpreted in the usual way as a relation between individuals *x* and properties of possible worlds *p*: The relation holds iff *p* holds for every belief world of *x* (i.e., every possible world compatible with *x*'s state of mind). Thus, (160) is true iff it holds in every belief world of Max that for every woman there is a man whom she loves.

The rules

Next, I list the interface rules that are relevant for the derivation of my semantic representations. Where necessary, numbers distinguish different constituents of the same category.[43]

$[_{\mathrm{S}}\ \mathtt{NP\ VP}]$ $\overset{(b1)}{\Rightarrow}$

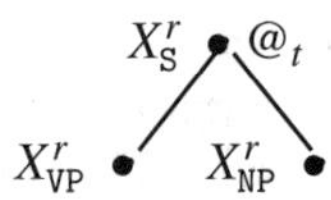

$X^s_S = X^s_{NP} = X^s_{VP}$

The type for X_1 is introduced in this interface rule.

$[_{\mathrm{VP}}\ \mathtt{IV}]$ $\overset{(b2)}{\Rightarrow}$

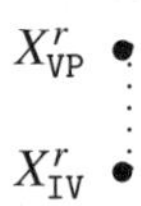

$X^s_{VP} = X^s_{IV}$

$[_{\mathrm{VP}}\ \mathtt{TV\ NP}]$ $\overset{(b3)}{\Rightarrow}$

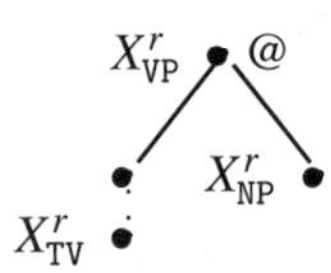

$X^s_{VP} = X^s_{TV} = X^s_{NP}$

$[_{\mathrm{VP}}\ \mathtt{SV\ S}]$ $\overset{(b5)}{\Rightarrow}$

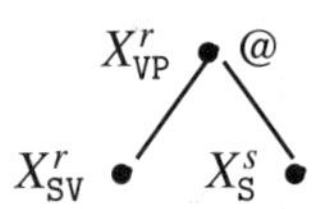

$X^s_{VP} = X^s_{SV}$

The embedded sentence S is a scope island, this is modelled in that **(b5)** places the scopenode of its semantic contribution (X^s_S) in the scope of the SV verb (formally, below the application node variable immediately above the

[43] Rules **(b2)** and **(b3)** differ from those in Egg et al. (2001) by separating the contribution of a verb by a dominance constraint. Since Egg et al. (2001) do not address reinterpretation, their interface rules use no such dominance constraints.

root $X^r_{\mathtt{SV}}$ for the semantics of this verb). Thus, quantifiers (except those introduced by an indefinite article) that arise in S are outscoped by SV. Constraint (159) is formed by this rule.

$[_{\mathtt{NP}}\ \mathtt{Det}\ \bar{\mathtt{N}}] \overset{(b8)}{\Rightarrow}$

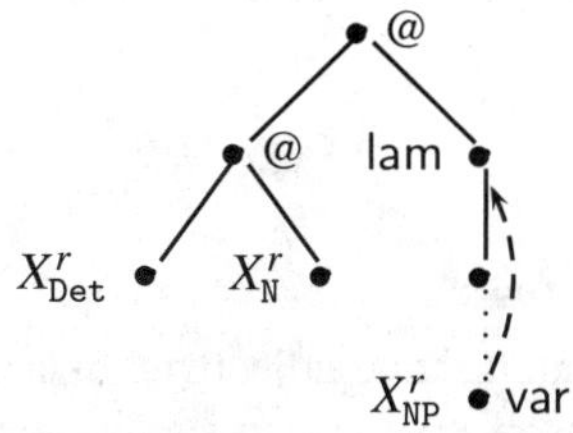

$X^s_{\mathtt{NP}} = X^s_{\mathtt{Det}}$

$[_{\bar{\mathtt{N}}}\ \mathtt{N}] \overset{(b9)}{\Rightarrow} X^r_{\bar{\mathtt{N}}}, X^r_{\mathtt{N}} \bullet \qquad X^s_{\bar{\mathtt{N}}} = X^s_{\mathtt{N}}$

$[_{\mathtt{VP1}}\ \mathtt{CV}\ \mathtt{VP2}] \overset{(b14)}{\Rightarrow}$

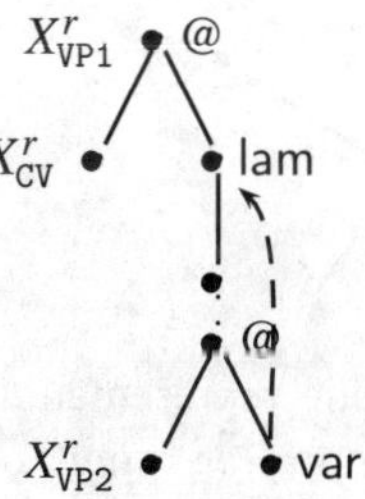

$X^s_{\mathtt{VP1}} = X^s_{\mathtt{CV}} = X^s_{\mathtt{VP2}}$

This rule is at the core of the proposed analyses of *begin*-sentences in section 3.1.1.

$[_{\mathtt{VP1}}\ \mathtt{Aux}\ \mathtt{VP2}] \overset{(b16)}{\Rightarrow}$

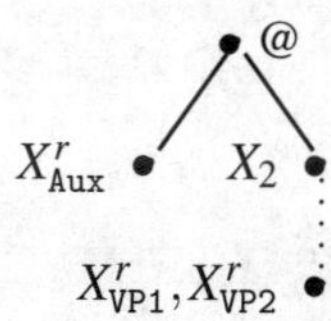

$X^s_{\mathtt{VP1}} = X^s_{\mathtt{Aux}} = X^s_{\mathtt{VP2}}$

Auxiliaries adjoin to VPs syntactically, but semantically, they map propositions on propositions. I.e., the type of $X^r_{\mathtt{Aux}}$ is $\langle\langle s,t\rangle,\langle s,t\rangle\rangle$, that of X_2, $\langle s,t\rangle$, and that of $X^r_{\mathtt{VP1}}$, $\langle e,\langle s,t\rangle\rangle$. This is handled in the interface rules in that the topnode $X^r_{\mathtt{VP1}}$ of the the emerging VP1 is the same as the topnode $X^r_{\mathtt{VP2}}$ of its immediate constituent VP2. Consequently, semantic construction by rule **(b1)** for a sentence S that consists of such a VP1 and its subject NP affects only the semantic contribution of the VP2 and ignores the contribution of the auxiliary: The topnodes of VP2 and subject are combined into a new application tree whose root is of type $\langle s,t\rangle$, thus fitting in with the semantic type of $X^r_{\mathtt{Aux}}$ and X_2.

$X^s_{\bar{\text{N}}} = X^s_{\text{AP}} = X^s_{\text{N}}$

$[_{\bar{\text{N}}}$ AP N$]$ $\overset{(b17)}{\Rightarrow}$

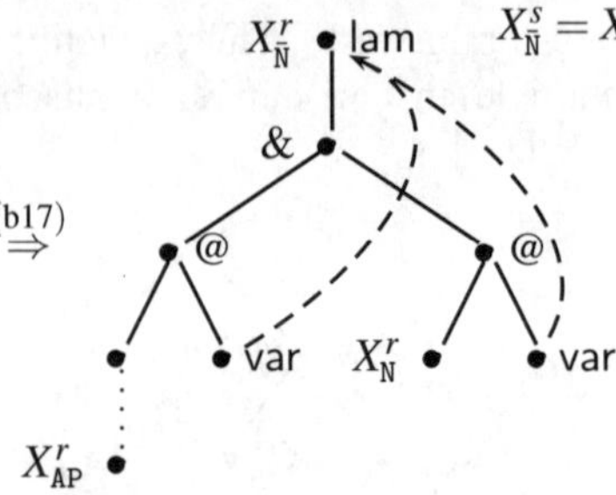

This rule handles intersective adjectives like *red-haired* or *fast*; the fragment excludes non-intersective adjectives like *former* or *alleged*.

$[_{\text{AP}}$ Adj$]$ $\overset{(b18)}{\Rightarrow}$ $X^r_{\text{AP}}, X^r_{\text{Adj}}$ • $X^s_{\text{AP}} = X^s_{\text{Adj}}$

Here I skip the level of Ā, which is not needed for my examples.

$X^s_{\text{S1}} = X^s_{\text{S2}} = X^s_{\text{Conj}}$

$[_{\text{S1}}$ S2 Conj S3$]$ $\overset{(b19)}{\Rightarrow}$

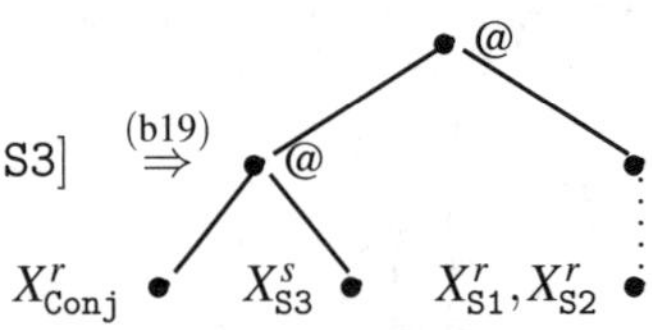

This rule forms the semantic representation for modification by clauses with a subordinating conjunction. It brings out the fact that these clauses (here, S 3) are scope islands. Section 3.2.5 shows that this interface rule also serves for the purposes of type coercion.

$X^s_{\text{S1}} = X^s_{\text{S2}} = X^s_{\text{Adv}}$

$[_{\text{S1}}$ S2 Adv$]$ $\overset{(b20)}{\Rightarrow}$

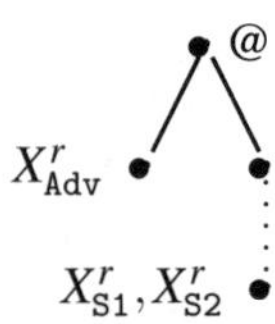

$X^s_{\bar{\text{N}}} = X^s_{\text{N}} = X^s_{\text{PP}}$

$[_{\bar{\text{N}}}$ N PP$]$ $\overset{(b21)}{\Rightarrow}$

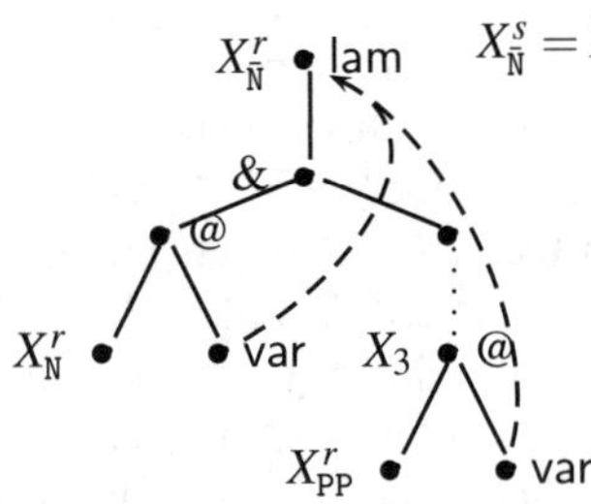

This rule is similar to **(b17)**. The gap above X_3 is the semantic position for NPs that are the object of the preposition and have narrow scope, e.g., in the reading of *every researcher of a company* that refers to everyone who is researcher in some company or other.

$[_{\text{PP}}\ \text{P NP}]$ $\overset{(b22)}{\Rightarrow}$

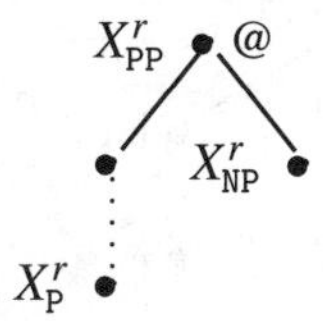

$X^s_{\text{PP}} = X^s_{\text{P}} = X^s_{\text{NP}}$

$[_\alpha\ W]$ $\overset{(b13)}{\Rightarrow}$ *Con*

Here *Con* is the CONT|CONSTRAINT value of the lexical entry W, whose syntactic category is α.

The syntax-semantics interface as it stands can deal with cases of type coercion, which are the topic of chapter 3. This shows up in particular in rules **(b2)**, **(b3)**, **(b15)**-**(b17)**, **(b19)**, **(b20)**, and **(b22)**, which introduce gaps into the constraints which they build. All these gaps are important for type coercion in that they mark the positions at which reinterpretation operators can be inserted.

For the description of landing site coercion phenomena, some small changes in the interface are inevitable. They affect only rules **(b17)**, **(b20)**, and **(b21)** and need to be motivated in some greater detail, and within the background of landing site coercion in general. Therefore these changes are postponed till chapter 4, the versions of these three rules in this chapter suffice for the treatment of type coercion.

An extended example

Finally, the fragment is illustrated by an extended example. The fragment directly forms underspecified representations of scope ambiguities ('dominance diamonds'), which will be demonstrated by the derivation of the semantics of (161), a variant of (133).[44] (Another detailed example is presented in section 3.1.1 where a step-by-step derivation of the semantic representation assumed for *begin*-sentences is given.)

(161) Every woman loves many men

First, the NP fragments are built from the constraints of the nouns and the determiners by rules **(b9)** and **(b8)**. For *every woman*, this returns the following constraint:

[44] This variant avoids the additional complexity that is introduced by the fact that the existential quantifier is not scopally restricted.

(162)

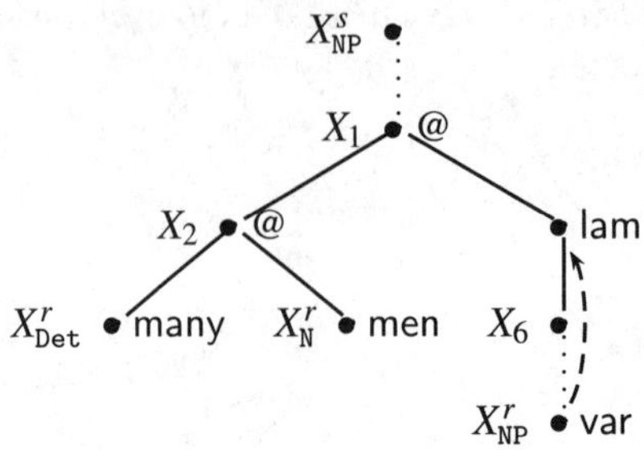

The topnode of the NP semantics X^r_{NP} is a fragment of its own. As a lexical item, the (non-indefinite) determiner carries the additional constraint $X^s_{Det} \lhd^* X^r_{Det}$, i.e., its scopenode dominates its topnode. Since $X^s_{NP} = X^s_{Det}$, the topnode of the NP X^s_{NP} must dominate X^r_{Det}. This dominance still includes identity, but the type of X^s_{NP} (of a proposition) does not match that of X^r_{Det} (of an intersection of properties). Thus, X^s_{NP} must dominate X_2. But since the type of X_2 is one of a functor from properties to propositions, X^s_{NP} must dominate X_1. The derivation of the semantics of *every woman* works analogously.

The major part of the semantics of the NP is expressed in the fragment below X_1; this fragment comprises the semantic contributions of the determiner and its N̄ argument. The scoping possibilities of the NP are represented in CLLS constraints by relating the root of this fragment to X^s node variables in the constraint. In the following, I will refer to such fragments as *N-fragments*.

The rule **(b3)** identifies the scopenodes of VP, verb, and NP, and combines the topnodes of verb and NP semantics into a new application tree (with a gap immediately above the verb topnode), whose root is the topnode of the VP:[45]

(163)

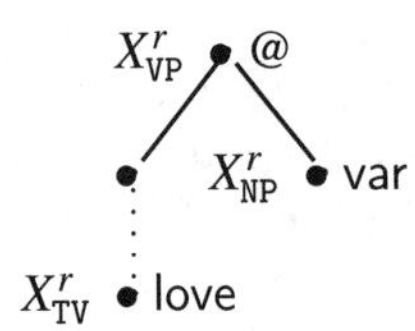

In this rule, the N-fragment of the NP *many men* (as seen in (162)) is not addressed at all, but we know that the daughter X_6 of the lam node variable in this N-fragment dominates X^r_{NP}. Accordingly, X_6 dominates X^r_{VP} in (163) ($X_6 \neq X^r_{NP}$, because the type of X_6 is t, that of X^r_{NP}, e), so that in the whole constraint for *love many men*, the N-fragment of the NP is positioned between X^s_{VP} (=X^s_{NP}) and X^r_{VP}:

[45]This gap is crucial for my analyses of type coercion in the case of sortal mismatches between a verb and its nominal arguments, see section 3.1.2.

(164)

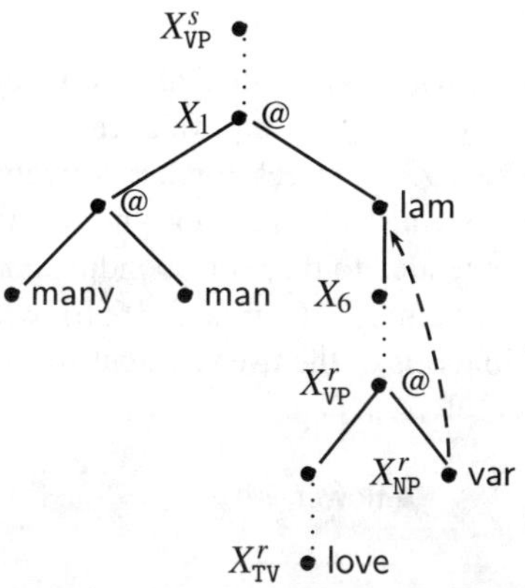

Finally, the sentence radical semantics is constructed from (164) and the constraint for *every woman* by rule **(b1)**. The semantic effect of this rule is pretty much the same as that of rule **(b3)**: Scopenodes of NP and VP are identified, their topnodes are combined in an application tree whose root becomes the new topnode. The N-fragment of the NP ends up between X^s_S (=X^s_{NP}) and X^r_S. This directly introduces the quantifier scope underspecification into the semantic representation of (161): We only know that the two N-fragments dominate the topnode of the sentence and are dominated by its scopenode, but it is not known which fragment dominates the other one.

(165)

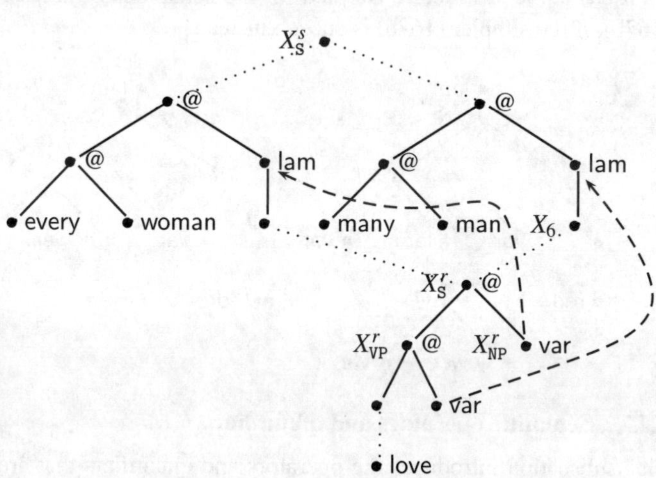

2.4 Further preliminaries

The sole goal of this section is the introduction of several formal preliminaries, which are presupposed in the following chapters.

2.4.1 The design of λ-structures

The design of λ-structures is somewhat flexible in that λ-structures may model different yet η-*equivalent* λ-terms. This equivalence on the level of λ-terms means that whenever two λ-structures model different yet η-equivalent λ-terms, the simpler one is chosen, which does not explicate the λ-abstraction. This strategy is then extended to the corresponding constraints on λ-structures. E.g., among the λ-structures (166a) and (166b), which correspond to the semantics of *flower* in terms of the η-equivalent $\lambda x.\mathbf{flower}'(x)$ and $\mathbf{flower}'$, respectively, (166b) is preferred:

(166) (a) (b)

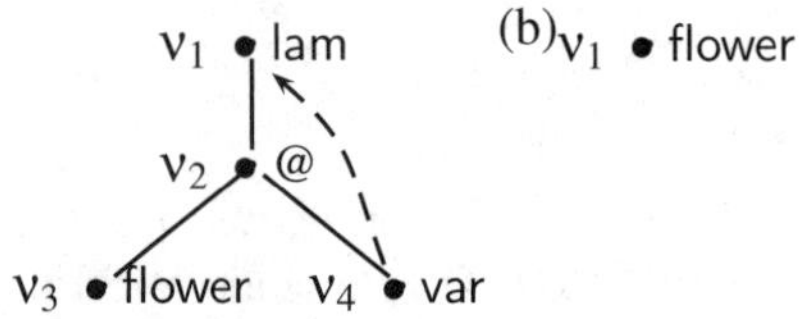

This strategy is also motivated by the fact that β-reduction on constraints on λ-structures is an extremely involved task (Bodirsky et al., 2001). That is, parsimony on explicating λ-abstraction in CLLS constraints keeps the constraints for the semantic representations of complex expressions as simple (and readable) as possible.

E.g., semantic construction returns the constraint (167a) for *red flower*, if (166a) is the λ-structure adopted for the semantics of *flower*; the simpler (167b), if the simpler (167b) is chosen instead.

(167) (a) (b)

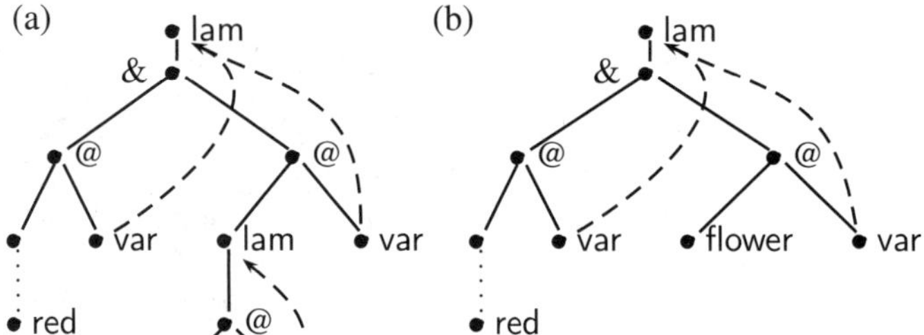

2.4.2 Semantic operators and quantifiers

This subsection introduces the operators and quantifiers that are used in semantic representations in the subsequent chapters.

The operator PROG

The semantics of the progressive is the operator PROG as defined in (168), which maps interval-based onto stative predicates:

(168) $\forall e \forall e' \forall P.\text{PROG}(P)(e) \leftrightarrow \exists e'.P(e') \wedge \tau(e) \sqsubset \tau(e')$

In prose: The progressive of a predicate P holds for an eventuality e iff there is another eventuality e' such that P holds for e' and the spatiotemporal extensions of e and e' stand in the (proper) part-of relation. ('τ' maps eventualities onto their spatiotemporal extension.)

(168) glosses over the so-called 'imperfective paradox' since it assumes the existence of a complete eventuality for which P holds even for the progressive of bounded predicates. But the paradox is that for bounded predicates (in contrast to unbounded ones) the existence of a complete eventuality e in the extension of P does not follow directly from the existence of a part e' of such an eventuality. Well-known examples highlight this fact: They assert the progressive of a bounded predicate P and at the same time deny the existence of a complete eventuality in the extension of P. E.g., in (169) the existence of a whole street-crossing of Max is ruled out by the *when*-clause:

(169) Max was crossing the street when he was hit by a truck

But if the progressive of *Max cross- the street* does not entail the existence of an eventuality of Max crossing the street, this raises the question of what status to assign to the eventuality for which the predicate holds. Answers to this question have been given in terms of inertia worlds (Dowty, 1979), continuation branches of events (Landman, 1992), defeasible entailments (Asher, 1992), and perspectives on events as part of ideal courses of events (Bonomi, 1997), to cite just a few analyses. Since the exact nature of the progressive is outside the scope of this book, I will not venture beyond the simple analysis (168).

The operator MAX

The maximality operator MAX resembles Herweg's (1991b) 'S-phase':

(170) $\forall e \forall P.\text{MAX}(P)(e) \leftrightarrow \exists e'.\tau(e) = \tau(e') \wedge P(e') \wedge \forall e''.e' \sqsubset e'' \rightarrow \neg P(e'')$

In prose: MAX(P) holds for an eventuality e iff P holds for an e' that spatiotemporally coincides with e, but for no e'' of which e' is a proper part. This definition ensures that MAX always returns a bounded predicate. It maps unbounded predicates onto intergressive predicates, for bounded predicates, it is the identity mapping. The type of MAX that accounts for these aspectual properties is $\langle\langle s_\alpha, t\rangle, \langle s_{f(\alpha)}, t\rangle\rangle$, where the function f is defined in (171).

(171) $f(\alpha) = \begin{cases} \alpha & \text{für} \quad \alpha \sqsubseteq_S +\text{BD} \\ \text{INTER} & \text{für} \quad \alpha \sqsubseteq_S -\text{BD} \end{cases}$

The operators PERF and the relation POST

The English perfect of a predicate P refers to *poststates* of eventualities in the extension of P. I assume a relation POST between eventualities and their poststates: $\text{POST}(e,e')$ iff e' is a state that follows and is adjacent to e. Change predicates lexically specify what their poststate looks like (as the argument of the operator BECOME that is specific for them). E.g., the poststate of coming home is one's being home.

Then the perfect operator PERF, which maps telic predicates P onto stative ones, is defined as follows: $\text{PERF}(P)(e')$ iff $\exists e.P(e) \wedge \text{POST}(e,e')$. I.e., PERF applied to a change predicate P entails $P'(e)$, where P' is the argument of BECOME in the decomposition of P and e, a poststate of an eventuality in the extension of P.[46]

The operator CAUSE

Next, *causation* is encoded in terms of the operator CAUSE. It relates two propositions P and Q: $\text{CAUSE}(P,Q)(e)$ iff $\exists e', e''.P(e'), Q(e'')$, e consists of e' and e', e' causes e'', and e'' may not start earlier than e'.[47] I.e., e' is a causing eventuality, e'', a caused eventuality. The relation of causing can be defined in terms of a counterfactual analysis (Dowty, 1979), which falls back on a relation of similarity between possible worlds: There is a world in which $P(e')$ and $Q(e'')$ hold, which is more similar to the real world than any world in which $P(e')$ and $\neg Q(e'')$ hold.

Causing and caused eventuality may, but need not, coincide temporally, consider, e.g., the painting of a picture (painting and the coming about of the picture coincide temporally) as opposed to causing the death of a person by putting poison in a wine bottle the day before.

The quantifier GEN

The semantics of agentive nouns like *typist* is modelled in terms of (one variant of) the generic quantifier GEN as discussed in Krifka et al. (1995): $\text{GEN}[x,e](R(x)(e), C(x)(e))$ iff $R(x)(e)$ usually entails $C(x)(e)$. The constant **usual**$'$ as used as an abbreviation in section 1.5.4 can be spelt out in terms of this quantification:

(172) $\mathbf{usual}' = \lambda P \lambda x.\text{GEN}[y,e](y\ \mathbf{in}'\ e \wedge y = x, P(y)(e))$

Thus, **usual**$'$ emerges as a relation between individuals x and properties P such that usually $P(y)(e)$ holds for eventualities in which a y that is identical

[46] In other languages, e.g., Thai, this entailment does not hold, because there is only a 'semi-perfect' operator that relates P with a poststate s of a *maximal part* of an eventuality in the extension of P. This includes, but is not restricted to, states that are the poststate of a complete eventuality in the extension of P (Koenig and Muansuwan, 2000).

[47] The last condition is formalised as the condition that all parts of e'' do not precede e': $\forall e.e \sqsubseteq e'' \rightarrow \neg e < e'$.

to x participates (**in**$'$ expresses this participation).

The operator PH

The core of the semantics of durative adverbs like *for two hours* is the 'P-quantity': $\lambda e.\text{PH}(P, \mathbf{Q})(e)$ holds for an eventuality e iff there is an e' in the extension of (the unbounded) P that spatiotemporally coincides with e, and a suitable measure function returns $\mathbf{Q}$ as the value of the length of e (see Egg 1995 for further discussion of the P-quantity).

The operator ITER

Iterativity is modelled in terms of the relation ITER. It maps properties of eventualities P onto the set of eventualities e such that e is equal to the convex closure (this is expressed by '$\bigcup$') of a set of eventualities E. The property P holds for the elements of E, but not for e:

(173) $\forall P \forall e.\text{ITER}(P)(e) \leftrightarrow \exists E. \bigcup E = e \wedge \neg P(e) \wedge \forall e'.e' \in E \rightarrow P(e')$

E must have more than one element, otherwise, P would hold trivially for the convex closure of E, which would be identical to its singleton element. E.g., an eventuality of Max playing the Moonshine Sonata does not count as an iteration of his playing the Moonshine Sonata.

If P is unbounded, (173) entails that the elements of E may not follow each other without interruption: Due to the cumulativity of P, this would otherwise mean that $\bigcup E$ is in the extension of P as well. E.g., even though one could (somewhat arbitrarily) split up a one-hour stay of Max in the pub into parts that last (say) five minutes each, this stay of Max does not count as an iteration of his staying in the pub. Consequently, every P-eventuality is *maximal*, which models the 'packaging' effect noted for the iterative operator.

The operator DUR

The operator DUR is similar to the operator PH in that it introduces a measure for the duration of an eventuality. As opposed to PH, however, it selects for bounded predicates only: $\lambda e.\text{DUR}(P, \mathbf{Q})(e)$ holds for an eventuality iff it is in the extension of P and the value of its temporal duration as measured by a suitable measure function is at least $\mathbf{Q}$.

The relation PREP

PREP introduces the relation between an eventuality and a preparatory eventuality for it. The property of being a preparatory eventuality of some other eventuality is bounded.

The quantifier MOST

The semantics of MOST is given in the usual fashion: $\text{MOST}(P, Q)$ holds iff $\frac{|P \cap Q|}{|P|} > \frac{1}{2}$, i.e., iff the cardinality of the intersection of P and Q divided by the cardinality of P is larger than $\frac{1}{2}$. In other words, the majority of the elements in P is also contained in Q.

The iota operator

'$\iota x.P(x)$' is of type e, it is defined as the only element in the extension of P. If the extension of P is not a singleton set, it is undefined. This operator is used for the semantic description of the definite article:

(174) $\lambda P \lambda Q.Q(\iota x.P(x))$

In prose: Properties P are mapped onto the set of properties Q that apply to the sole element in the extension of P.

This chapter laid out how semantic structures for reinterpretation candidates are represented and derived in the proposed approach. I presented underspecification formalisms in general, the representation language CLLS, and a grammar fragment which allows the derivation of the semantic representations I assume for reinterpretation candidates. In the next two chapters, CLLS and the grammar fragment are employed for the analysis of reinterpretation in natural language.

3

Type Coercion

The proposed analysis of reinterpretation phenomena accounts for reinterpretation by deliberately underspecifying the constraints on λ-structures for reinterpretation candidates. It exploits the possibility of representing semantically underspecified expressions in terms of partial descriptions for λ-structures. These descriptions are expressions of the representation language CLLS.

The account of reinterpretation is offered in two chapters. This chapter will present an analysis of type coercion, the next one will cover landing site coercion. Section 3.1 is devoted to type coercion in the nominal domain. I will then move on to aspectual cases of type coercion in section 3.2 and conclude with a brief summary of the proposed account in section 3.3.

Since the term *type coercion* has become established in the meantime, I will continue using it, even though it might suggest that such processes can merely adjust the type of an expression, similar to the processes proposed in Partee (1986). But in many cases of type coercion, there is a *sortal* shift, which changes not only the combinatory potential of an expression but also the way in which it relates to the commonsense ontology that underlies the semantic sorts.

To set the stage for the present chapter, I will recapitulate the intuitions on type coercion that emerged in chapter 1, employing the underspecification formalism introduced in chapter 2 to do so. Type coercion is recurrent in (but not restricted to) expressions with semantically mismatched constituents. For the semantics of these expressions, these mismatches show up in the fact that there is a functor-argument pair in which the argument does not fit in with the type-theoretic (including sortal) selection restrictions of the functor. This mismatch does not render the functor-argument structure ungrammatical, because an operator intervenes between functor and argument and mediates between their conflicting properties: It is applied to the argument, and the functor is applied to the result of this application (which then meets the selection restriction of the functor). Extralinguistic conceptual knowledge must provide this operator.

Type coercion is implemented in that for specific syntactic constituent structures, the syntax-semantics interface introduces R-positions into the corresponding semantic representations. Formally, the semantic contributions of potentially mismatched constituents are put into different fragments of the representation, which buffers any potential incompatibilities between them. The gaps between these fragments are positions where the information contributed by conceptual knowledge can be inserted to integrate it with the linguistic information.

Once the syntax-semantic interface has determined R-positions for type coercion in semantic representations for reinterpretation candidates, they are used for the integration of additional material into the semantic representation. This is depicted schematically in (175). Semantic construction yields (175a), a structure in which functor and argument are separated in fragments C_1 and C_2. The dominance relation between X_2 and X_3 determines the position where additional material (in the form of a fragment Op for a type coercion operator) must be integrated (175b). Then this material is added to the semantic representation (175c), and, finally, this new representation has a constructive solution, the λ-structure (175d):

(175)

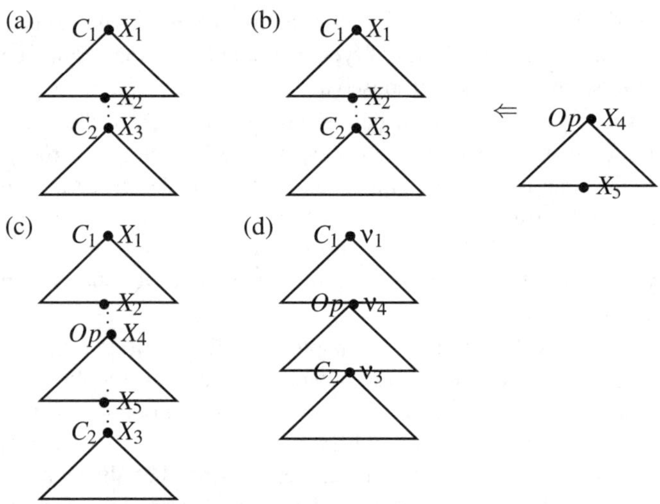

This account of type coercion addresses a number of issues that were identified in the review of competing approaches to type coercion.

- The analysis provides a well-formed semantic representation for reinterpretation candidates and at the same time, models any potential mismatches between their constituents.
- It distinguishes the linguistic and extralinguistic parts of the meaning of

reinterpretation candidates.

- It describes how the various knowledge sources interact during reinterpretation.
- It delimits the range of potential reinterpretations to avoid overgeneration.
- It can handle the cooccurrence of reinterpretation and quantifier scope.

The proposed approach to type coercion will now begin with an investigation of type coercion in the nominal domain.

3.1 Type coercion in the nominal domain

Reinterpretation cases that exhibit non-sortal type-theoretic mismatches are discussed in section 3.1.1, while reinterpretation candidates with sortal mismatches are the subject of section 3.1.2.

3.1.1 Type coercion for type-theoretic mismatches

As a paradigmatic example of type coercion for type-theoretic mismatches, consider sentences like (176a) [= (29a)] and (176b) [= (29b)], whose matrix verb is *begin*.

(176) a Max began to read a novel

b # Max began a novel

The goal is to assign both syntactic variants of the verb (control verb and transitive verb) the same semantic representation as a relation between an individual and a property, viz., the begin-relation that relates eventualities e, properties P (of type $\langle e, \langle s,t\rangle\rangle$), and individuals x iff e is an initial part of an eventuality in the extension of $\lambda e'.P(x)(e')$.

If the second syntactic argument of the verb is a VP, as in (176a), it provides the required property P in its semantics, hence, semantic composition can proceed straightforwardly. Thus, the proposed semantic representation of *begin* accounts directly for the R-free[48] variant of *begin* whose second argument is a VP. If the second argument of *begin* is an NP, reinterpretation is called for to mediate between the conflicting types of verb and NP. It will be shown that the semantics of *begin* provides a suitable input for reinterpretation in this case.

From the viewpoint of syntax, *begin* is underspecified in that its second subcategorised argument is either an NP or a VP. Depending on the instantiation of this argument as NP or VP, different rules of the syntax-semantics interface (**(b3)** and **(b14)**, respectively) apply to build the semantic representation of the constituent that consists of *begin* and its second argument.

[48]This term refers to expressions that need not undergo reinterpretation.

The analysis of *begin*-sentences commences with R-free cases as (176a), then reinterpretation candidates as (176b) are expounded in detail.

The case of *begin* as control verb

As noted in chapter 1, NPs in the VP complement of *begin* may, but need not, outscope the matrix verb, which introduces scope ambiguity. This scope ambiguity shows up if *every novel* replaces *a novel* in (176a):

(177) Max began to read every novel

The two readings of (177) [=(36a)] that exhibit wide and narrow scope of the universal quantifier, respectively, are the following:

(178)

a $\lambda e \forall x.\mathbf{novel}'(x) \rightarrow \mathbf{begin}'(\mathbf{max}', \lambda y \lambda e'.\mathbf{read}'(y,x)(e'))(e)$

b $\lambda e.\mathbf{begin}'(\mathbf{max}', \lambda y \lambda e' \forall x.\mathbf{novel}'(x) \rightarrow \mathbf{read}'(y,x)(e'))(e)$

These scoping possibilities must be captured in an appropriate semantic representation for (177). (178a) refers to eventualities e such that for every novel, Max started to read it at e (i.e., he read at least some pages in every novel). Elements of (178b) are eventualities e' that are an initial part of Max's reading every novel. As an extreme case, even an eventuality in which Max read only some pages in the first of the novels may be such an e', if it is part of an eventuality of Max's reading every novel.

The explicit reference to eventuality variables and their binders in the proposed account of *begin*-sentences necessitates a more complex semantic representation of determiners: Semantically, NPs are functions from expressions of type $\langle e, \langle s,t \rangle\rangle$ to expressions of type $\langle s,t \rangle$. Consequently, the semantics of determiners is of type $\langle\langle e,t \rangle, \langle\langle e, \langle s,t \rangle\rangle, \langle s,t \rangle\rangle\rangle$. E.g., the λ-term for *every* is $\lambda P \lambda Q \lambda e \forall x.P(x) \rightarrow Q(x)(e)$. Node variables that are labelled by every correspond to this λ-term.

I will now show the derivation of the CLLS representation of (177). The constraint for the semantics of *every novel* is (179). Its topnode X^r_{NP} is the var node variable at the bottom of the right branch, while its scopenode dominates the N-fragment of *every novel*. X^r_{NP} corresponds to the variable bound by the quantifier in the λ-term for (177). See section 2.3.2 (p.91) for the derivation of constraints for NPs.

(179)

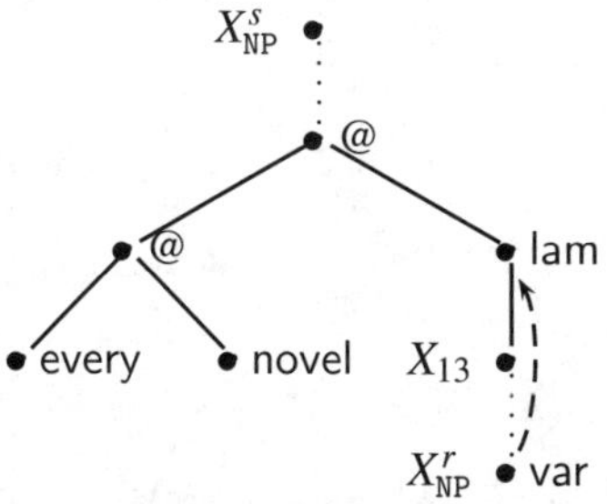

Next, rule **(b3)** builds the semantics of the VP *to read every novel*; the semantic contribution of the verb is a node variable labelled with read. Its topnode corresponds to the nucleus of the VP.

(180)

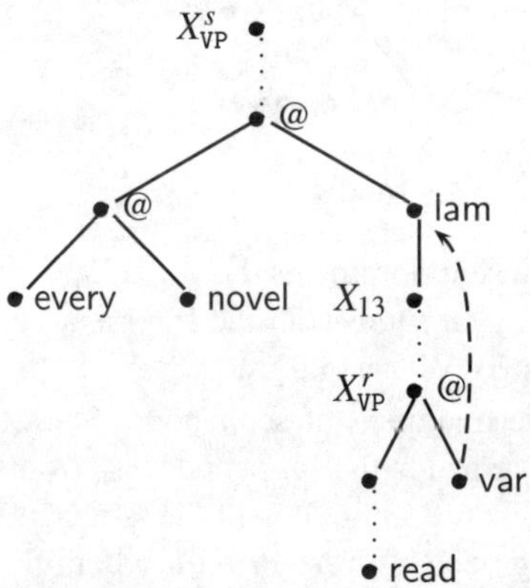

The semantics of the matrix clause VP (*begin- to read every novel*) is then derived by rule **(b14)** and the constraint of the verb, a node variable labelled with begin, which corresponds to the begin-relation. For convenience, rule **(b14)** is repeated as (181). The node variables X^r_{VP1}, X^r_{CV}, and X^r_{VP2} are the topnodes of the constraint for matrix clause VP, control verb, and VP argument, respectively.

(181) $[_{\mathrm{VP1}}$ CV VP2$]$ $\overset{\text{(b14)}}{\Rightarrow}$

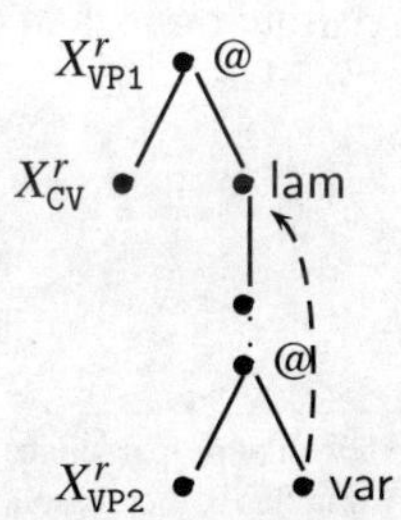

$X^s_{\mathrm{VP1}} = X^s_{\mathrm{CV}} = X^s_{\mathrm{VP2}}$

Note that this rule ignores any N-fragments in the semantic representation of the VP argument of *begin*. The resulting constraint for the matrix clause is given in (182).

(182)

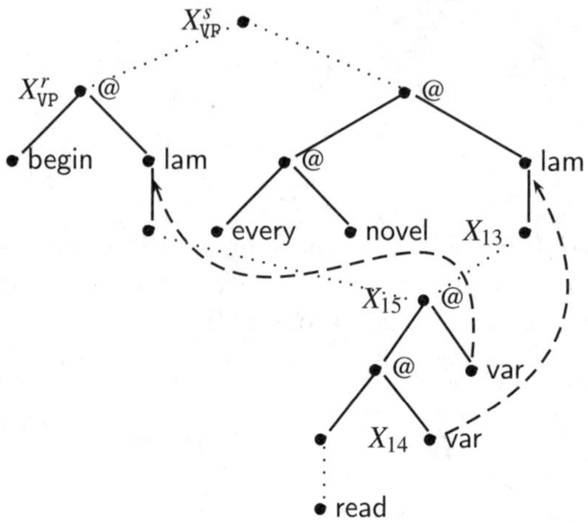

In (182), X_{13} dominates X_{15} because it dominates the var node variable X_{14} (the root of the constraint (179) for *every novel*) in the fragment below X_{15}. The root X^r_{VP} corresponds to the matrix VP semantics.

In this step of the derivation, the treatment of scopenodes is crucial. For control verbs like *begin*, rule **(b14)** equates the scopenode X^s_{VP} of the matrix VP with those of the verb and of its VP complement. This means that the fragment below X^r_{VP} and the N-fragment of *every novel* are both dominated by X^s_{VP} and dominate the node variable X_{15}, but are not related in any other way. Thus, (182) represents the scope ambiguity between *begin* and *every novel*.

The final step in the derivation merely consists of the integration of the constraint for the semantics of the subject NP by rule **(b1)**. The semantic contribution of the NP *Max* is just a node variable labelled by max.[49] The final result of semantic construction is then (183):

[49]This simplifies the representations of proper names for expository purposes: They are given a first-order representation (node variables that correspond to constants of type *e*). Nothing hinges on this simplification for the proposed treatment of type coercion. But for ellipsis reconstruction representing proper names as generalised quantifiers would be indispensable (see Egg et al. 1998 and Egg et al. 2001).

(183)

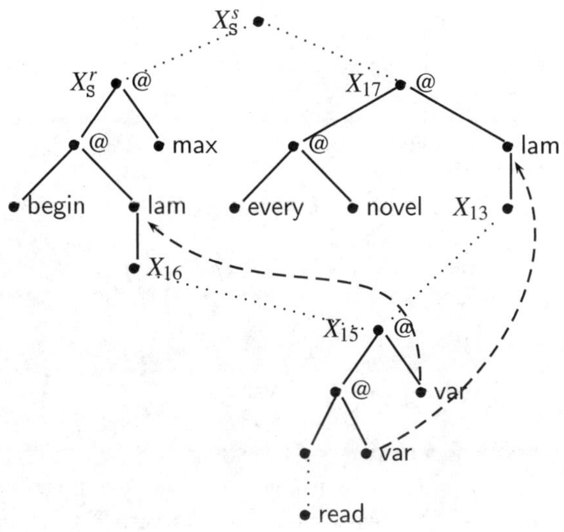

This completes the derivation of the semantics of the example (177). The constraint (183) exhibits the same kind of dominance diamond structure as that of (184) [= (161)].

(184) Every woman loves many men

For the case of *begin* as a control verb the constraint (183) brings out the fact that any kind of nominal quantifier within its VP argument can take scope over or below *begin*. Attributing the NP in the VP argument of *begin* scope over the matrix verb can then be modelled by conjoining (183) with the dominance relation $X_{13} \triangleleft^* X^r_S$. Narrow scope of this NP with respect to *begin* emerges by conjoining (183) with $X_{16} \triangleleft^* X_{17}$ (the root of the N-fragment of *every novel*).

The first option leads to the constructive solution (185), in this solution X_{13} and X^r_S refer to the same node, and so do X_{16} and X_{15}. This λ-structure corresponds to the λ-term (178a), which stands for the first of the two readings of (177). Giving *begin* scope over the NP leads to another constructive solution, where X_{16} and X_{17}, and X_{13} and X_{15} refer to the same node. This second solution corresponds to (178b).

(185)

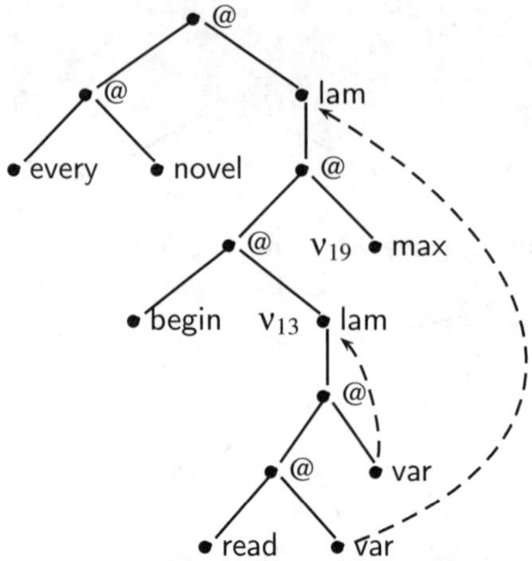

This analysis of *begin* as a control verb does not yet directly relate the semantic contributions of the two arguments of the verb. E.g., in the λ-structure (185), these contributions appear on different branches of the tree, as v_{19} and below v_{13}, respectively. This means that so far, the analysis does not address the requirement that the two arguments must match sortally, which shows up, e.g,. in (186).

(186) # London began to phone Max

(186) calls for reinterpretation since the NP *London* fails to meet the selection restriction of the verb *phone* for a subject NP that refers to persons. This will be modelled straightforwardly by an appropriate κ-type of the label begin in section 3.1.2.

To sum up, the analysis captures the meaning of the verb for R-free expressions like (177). It remains to be shown that it can be extended to reinterpretation candidates like (176b).

The case of *begin* as transitive verb

Now the proposed analysis will be applied to *begin*-sentences where the verb subcategorises for two NP arguments. Since both syntactic variants of *begin* are assigned the same semantic representation, viz. the begin-relation (see p.101), the semantics of the second NP argument of *begin* does not match the semantics of the verb. Hence, to obtain well-formed semantic representations of such sentences, type coercion is called for that mediates between the begin-relation and the semantic contribution of the NP.

In addition, sentences like (187) [= (36b)] are scopally unambiguous, since the quantifier always outscopes the verb *begin*:

(187) # Max began every novel

If we interpret (187) in the sense of 'Max began to read every novel', it lacks one of the two readings of its explicit counterpart (177), viz., (178b), where *begin* has scope over the quantifier. (187) and (177) share the reading (178a) with wide scope of the quantifier. Other control verbs exhibit this scoping pattern too, e.g., *fail*:

(188) a Max failed to pass every exam

b # Max failed every exam

While (188a) is ambiguous between a reading in which Max failed each and every exam (wide scope of the NP) and another, weaker one in which he did not pass every exam (but perhaps some of the exams; wide scope of *fail*), (188b) exhibits only the stronger reading of (188a).

Semantic construction for (187) crucially uses the interface rule **(b3)**, since *begin* is a transitive verb here. The resulting constraint is (189):

(189)

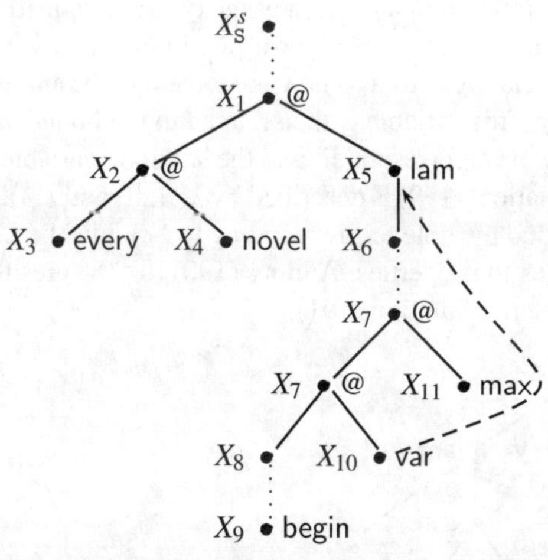

But this means that without any further assumptions, semantic construction for (187) returns a constraint where there is no scope ambiguity between *begin* and its object NP, as desired.

To derive one of the readings of (187), one has to derive a solution from its semantic representation (189). As it stands, (189) has no constructive solution, because the gap between X_8 and X_9 cannot be closed (as opposed to the one between X_6 and X_7, which are both of the type of a proposition): X_8 is of type $\langle e, \langle e, \langle s,t \rangle \rangle \rangle$ (the type of a transitive verb), while X_9 has the type of an operator from expressions of type $\langle e, \langle s,t \rangle \rangle$ to expressions of the same type.

Thus, this mismatch must be bridged by an appropriate reinterpretation operator, whose constraint is inserted into this gap. Well-typed solutions of (189) comprise additional material between X_8 and X_9, viz., a fragment whose root is of the type of a transitive verb, and which comprises a hole with the same type as X_9. This kind of fragment is depicted in (190). Here X_{12} can be labelled by any label rel $\in \Sigma$ that assigns the τ-type $\langle e, \langle e, \langle s,t \rangle\rangle\rangle$ to X_{12}, e.g., read. Boxed variables indicate where the operator constraint is connected to constraint (189):

(190)

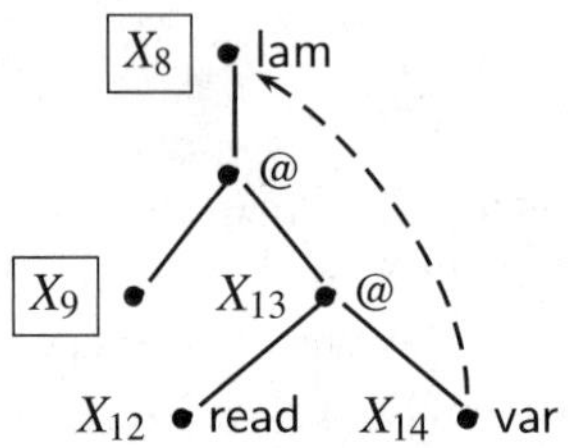

The idea behind (190) is that the part of the constraint below X_{13} stands for the property that is the second argument of the begin-relation (which comes in via X_9). This property is composed of a relation of the type of a transitive verb (corresponding to X_{12}) applied to a variable (corresponding to X_{14}). λ-binding this variable (in terms of relating it to X_8 via λ) becomes important after integrating (190) with (189): This variable is then related to the bound variable of the semantics of *every novel* (corresponding to the var node variable X_{10} in (189). In the shorthand notation, (190) is described by $\lambda z.\Box(\mathbf{read}'(z))$, where $\mathbf{read}'$ corresponds to X_{12} and the hole (corresponding to X_9) must be filled by an operator from properties to properties. Adding (190) to (189) results in a constraint with the constructive solution (191):

(191)

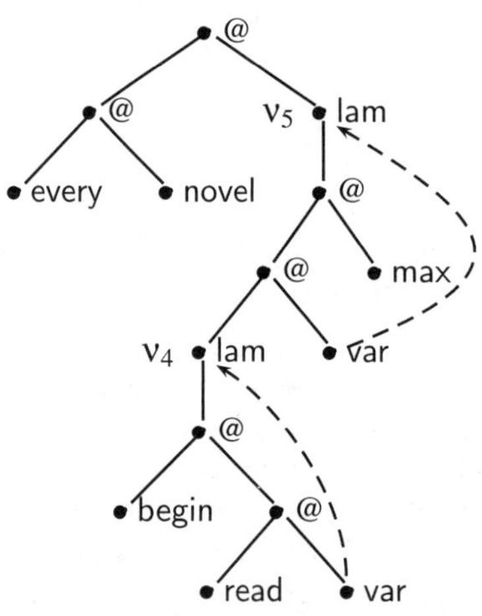

This solution corresponds to a λ-term that is equivalent to (178a); the λ-term to which the λ-structure (185) corresponds. To see this, consider first the λ-term corresponding to the tree below ν_4 in (191):

(192) $\lambda x \lambda u \lambda e.\mathbf{begin}'(u, \lambda y \lambda e'.\mathbf{read}'(y,x)(e'))(e)$

Applying this to a variable z and to the constant $\mathbf{max}'$, and subsequently abstracting over z returns (193) as the λ-term corresponding to the tree below v_5:

(193) $\lambda z \lambda e.\mathbf{begin}'(\mathbf{max}', \lambda y \lambda e'.\mathbf{read}'(y,z)(e'))(e)$

Finally, applying $\lambda P \lambda e \forall z.\mathbf{novel}'(z) \rightarrow P(z)(e)$ to (193) yields (194), which is α-equivalent to (178a):

(194) $\lambda e \forall z.\mathbf{novel}'(z) \rightarrow \mathbf{begin}'(\mathbf{max}', \lambda y \lambda e'.\mathbf{read}'(y,z)(e'))(e)$

I.e., the proposed analysis of *begin* handles both syntactic variants of *begin* and, what is more, brings out their semantic similarity. This similarity was outlined for the sentence pair (177) and (187), which both refer to the start of novel-related activities by Max.

It is now time to reconsider the problems noted for Pustejovsky's analysis of sentences like (187), which comprise the transitive variant of *begin*. The first problem is the scope of the object NP: Pustejovsky must assume scope of the verb over the NP, which clashes with intuitions on the meaning of such sentences. In his approach, this is the only way of expressing the fact that for the transitive *begin* the reinterpretation operator mediates between the conflicting types of verb and object NP

The proposed account addresses this problem in that it distinguishes two parts of the semantics of an NP, viz., the N-fragment and the node variable that corresponds to the bound (λ-calculus) variable (the root of the NP). Then reinterpretation operators can intervene between the semantic contributions of the verb and of its object NP without determining their scope relation: The constraint (189) showed that the two parts of the object NP semantics end up in different fragments, hence, integrating a coercion operator into the fragment that comprises the NP root does not affect the NP's N-fragment. The scope of this fragment with respect to the begin-relation falls out independently (and correctly) during semantic construction for (187).

The second class of problems stemmed from the question of where to draw the boundary between linguistic and conceptual knowledge. Assuming a semantic Qualia Structure and composition processes that access suitable qualia in order to derive operators that mediate between conflicting functor-argument pairs privileges certain readings for (187) (the 'reader' and the 'author' readings), in that they are the only ones that can be derived compositionally. But this does not fit in with the fact that appropriate contexts may make other readings available.

In the discussion of Pustejovsky's approach (section 1.3.5), I have argued that the source of these mediating operators is conceptual knowledge: The range of information that may be integrated here by far exceeds the material that could sensibly be integrated into the semantic lexicon. Therefore I represent the semantics of sentences like (187) in such a way that the derivation of full meanings from these representations must fall back on conceptual knowledge. I.e., they are semantically ambiguous, a full interpretation can only be obtained by integrating a piece of conceptual knowledge with the result of semantic construction. E.g., for (187), conceptual knowledge introduces some contextually appropriate novel-related activity.

In this way, Pustejovsky's intuitions can be explained differently: The prominence of the 'author' (agentive) and the 'reader' (telic) readings of (187) follow from the fact that generic conceptual knowledge (which is accessed during the derivation of these readings) is available regardless of context factors while context-specific conceptual knowledge is not. However, specific items of conceptual knowledge (like the fact that Max is a professor of literary studies) might be more salient than pieces of generic conceptual knowledge and hence trigger other interpretations of *begin*-sentences. In sum, my approach can handle the issues in the semantics of *begin* that were problematic for Pustejovsky's approach.

3.1.2 Type coercion for sortal mismatches

Many cases of type coercion in the nominal domain involve sortal incompatibilities, in particular, between verbs and their NP arguments. These cases are studied extensively by Dölling (1992, 1995, 1998). I refer to them as cases of *sortal type coercion*. The intuitions that underlie their analyses in this book were considerably influenced by Dölling's work. For ease of exposition, eventuality variables and their binders are ignored in this section (except where indicated).

Consider, e.g., sentence (195) [= (62)]. A λ-term for its literal reading would be ill-formed, since it would introduce conflicting sortal restrictions on a universally bound variable. As discussed in section 1.4.4, the subject NP restricts this variable to one sort (here, THING), while the verb restricts it to another, incompatible sort (here, SUBST[ance]).

(195) # All the bottles froze

The impending sortal conflict in (195) can be resolved in terms of a reinterpretation operator that mediates between the conflicting sorts by mapping the property of freezing onto the property of *containing* a substance that is freezing (a property of things). Consequently, the interpretation of (195) is that the content of every bottle froze.

This section offers an analysis of reinterpretation for cases of sortal type coercion that captures the insights of Dölling's work while at the same time focussing on the problem of how to delimit R-positions.

The analysis is introduced with simple cases of sortal mismatches between an intransitive verb and its NP argument. It is then generalised to sortal type coercion for verbs with more than one NP argument, sortal type coercion within NPs, control verbs, and so-called 'ham sandwich' cases, for which the reinterpretation strategy is different. Further subsections are devoted to type coercion for semantically well-formed expressions and to the anaphoric potential of NPs.

The analysis

Potential sortal conflicts between a verb and its NP arguments are anticipated in semantic representations in that verb and NP semantics are not combined directly. This buffers any such conflicts between them and leaves room for the integration of a reinterpretation operator to mediate between these conflicts.

Formally, there is an R-position between the verb semantics and the semantics of its argument(s). It is determined in the syntax-semantics interface in terms of dominance constraints between the semantic contributions of the verbs and the contributions of their arguments. I.e., the relevant rules (repeated for convenience in (196)) set off the semantic contribution of the verb in a fragment of its own.

Two of these rules build constraints for VPs; **(b2)** for VPs that consist of an intransitive verb only, **(b3)**, for VPs that break down into a transitive verb and its object NP. In either case, the constraint of the verb (whose root is $X^r_{\mathtt{IV}}/X^r_{\mathtt{TV}}$) is in a different fragment than the topnode $X^r_{\mathtt{VP}}$ of the VP. **(b3)** separates the constraint of a transitive verb from constraint of its object NP, whose topnode is $X^r_{\mathtt{NP}}$.

When **(b1)** constructs the semantics of a sentence, the constraints of NP and VP are in the same fragment, since their topnodes $X^r_{\mathtt{NP}}$ and $X^r_{\mathtt{VP}}$ are immediate daughters of the sentence topnode $X^r_{\mathtt{S}}$. But since the constraint of the verb is set off in a fragment of its own in the VP constraint, it is set off from the constraint of the subject NP as well.

(196) 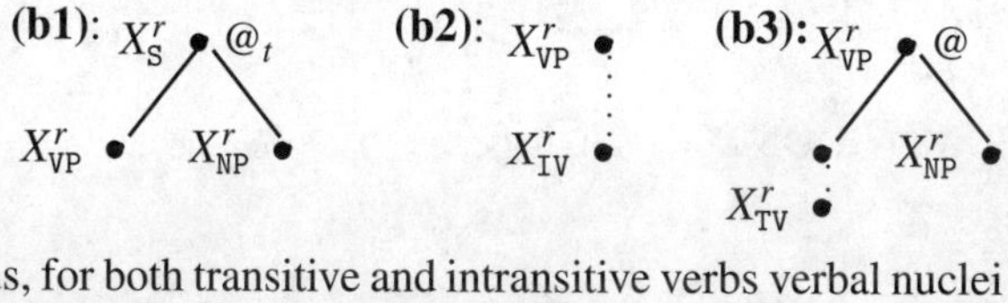

Thus, for both transitive and intransitive verbs verbal nuclei are represented by two fragments in a CLLS constraint, one for the semantic contribution of the verb, and one that comprises the topnodes of the constraints of its arguments. In this way, any sortal restrictions that the verb might impose on its arguments are buffered; the constraint is not ill-formed if the arguments fail to comply to these restrictions.

As an example of the effect of these rules, consider (197), the semantic representation of sentence (195). The verbal nucleus (with topnode X_7) is derived through **(b2)** and **(b1)**, the fragment X_9 models the semantic contribution of *freeze*. Here the incompatibility of the types $\langle e_{\text{THING}}, t \rangle$ and $\langle e_{\text{SUBST}}, t \rangle$ of X_8 and X_9 models the sortal mismatch between NP and VP, which rules out a constructive solution for (197).

(197)

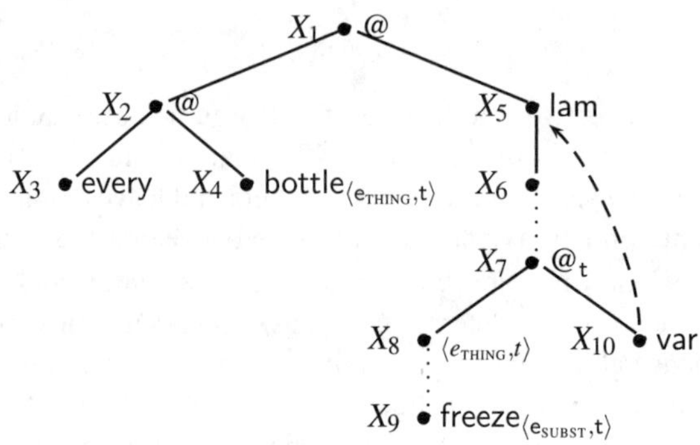

The lexical entries of noun and verb introduce sortal information in their κ-types, which determines the τ-types of X_4 and X_9 as $\langle e_{\text{THING}}, t \rangle$ and $\langle e_{\text{SUBST}}, t \rangle$, respectively. It was shown in (139) how the constructor types of the labels lam, @, and every propagate the type constraint for X_4 down to X_8, whose type emerges as $\langle e_{\text{THING}}, t \rangle$.[50]

Next I will show how the extralinguistic contribution to the meaning of (195) in its preferred reading (which is contributed by conceptual knowledge that bottles are containers for liquids) is integrated into the result of semantic construction.

This extralinguistic contribution is also expressed in the form of a constraint, which fills the gap between X_8 and X_9. Its heart is the container-content relation CONT. It is first rendered in the simplified representation, then in the full glory of CLLS:

(198) $\lambda x_{\text{THING}} \exists y_{\text{SUBST}}.\mathbf{CONT}(x,y) \wedge \Box(y)$

[50]The gap between X_6 and X_7 is introduced in the syntax-semantics interface for purposes of scope underspecification. In (195), it is irrelevant, since only the subject bears scope. X_{10} corresponds to the argument position of *freeze*. CLLS constraints show no unwanted interaction between gaps introduced to model quantifier scope ambiguity and those for the modelling of type coercion, see Koller et al. (2000b).

(199)

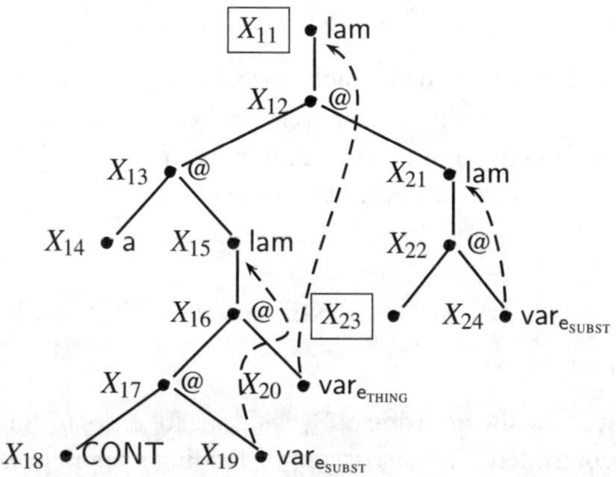

X_{18} carries the label for the two-place predicate **CONT** that relates containers and their contents. X_{11} and X_{23} are to be equated with the hole and the root of the R-position in (197). The names of such node variables in the constraint of a reinterpretation operator are boxed.

The constraint for the meaning of (195) after type coercion is (200), which conjoins the constraints (197) and (199) with the equations $X_8 = X_{11}$ and $X_{23} = X_9$. Its constructive solution corresponds to the λ-term (201) [= (63)], the desired representation for sentence (195).

(200)

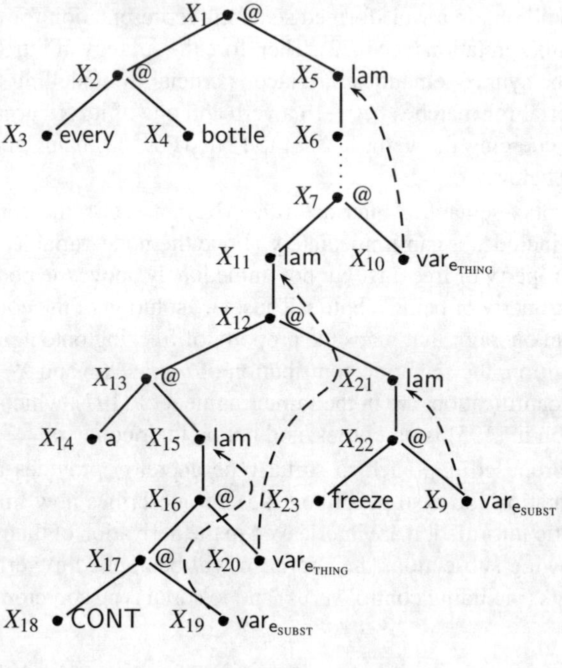

(201) $\forall x_{\text{THING}}.\textbf{bottle}'(x) \rightarrow \exists y_{\text{SUBST}}.\textbf{CONT}(x,y) \wedge \textbf{freeze}'(y)$

In prose: Every bottle has a content which froze.

In the simplified version, the type coercion process is depicted in (202), where the left hand side constraint is the simplified version of (197) (the irrelevant gap between X_6 and X_7 has been ignored).

(202)
$$
\begin{array}{lll}
\forall x_{\text{THING}}.\textbf{bottle}'(x) \rightarrow \boxdot\ (x) & & \\
\quad\quad\quad\quad\vdots & \Leftarrow & \lambda z_{\text{THING}} \exists y_{\text{SUBST}}.\textbf{CONT}(z,y) \wedge \boxdot\ (y) \\
\lambda y_{\text{SUBST}}.\textbf{freeze}'\ (y) & &
\end{array}
$$

In the proposed analysis, the insertion of R-positions for cases of sortal type coercion is strictly controlled. The discussion of Dölling's approach to reinterpretation in section 1.4.4 showed that the strategy of avoiding impending sortal conflicts between two constituents C_1 and C_2 of an expression by unrestricted insertion of R-positions in semantic representations would lead to overgeneration: This would allow the insertion of reinterpretation operators that adapt C_1 to C_2 or vice versa. But only one of the possibilities actually occurs.

E.g., in (195) the quantification in the reinterpreted meaning of (195) is on bottles, not on contents of bottles. But if one mediated between the conflicting sorts in (195) in terms of an operator that maps bottles onto their content, one would obtain a well-formed semantic representation for exactly this inadequate interpretation (see p.32). Therefore the strategy of introducing R-positions in the syntax-semantics interface is crucial to modelling the observation that sortal mismatches between a verb and one of its NP arguments are resolved by coercing the verb, but not the NP. (For the 'ham sandwich' cases, see p.120 below.)

Due to the syntax-semantics interface rules **(b2)** and **(b8)**, the constraint (197) for (195) includes a gap immediately above the node variable X_9 that introduces the property of freezing, but not immediately above the node variable X_4 for the property of being a bottle. Thus, any solution of the constraint must comprise an operator that maps the property of freezing onto a property of things. In addition, the semantic contribution of *bottle* (X_4) and X_3, which introduces the quantification, are in the same fragment of (197), which shows that quantification in (195) is on bottles, and not on their contents.

In sum, the proposed approach to sortal type coercion provides a well-formed representation for examples like (195) and describes how linguistic and extralinguistic information are interleaved in the derivation of their meaning. In the following subsections the approach will be applied to verbs with several arguments (including control verbs) and to sortal type coercion within NPs.

Sortal type coercion for verbs with several arguments

As noted in section 1.4.1, *each* argument of a verb may introduce a sort that is not compatible with the sortal restriction imposed on the argument by the verb, which gives rise to type coercion. The sentences (203)-(205) illustrate this phenomenon:

(203) # The capital phoned Max

(204) # Max phoned the capital

(205) # London phoned Brighton

If one assumes that only persons can be agents and recipients of phone calls (and that this is encoded in the semantics of *phone*), the sort LOC(ation) that is involved in the NPs *the capital*, *London*, and *Brighton* does not fit in with the verbal restrictions in either subject or object position, which calls for reinterpretation. Generally, if a verb has n arguments ($n \in \mathbf{N}_0$), there are $2^n - 1$ reinterpretation possibilities.

The proposed approach was introduced by cases of sortal type coercion that involve intransitive verbs. It will now be shown that it covers instances of sortal type coercion that affect verbs with several NP arguments as well.

For each of the sentences (203)-(205), the interface rules **(b1)** and **(b3)** build a constraint for its verbal nucleus that comprises two fragments, one for the verb semantics, and one for its arguments. The relevant part of this constraint is (206):

(206)

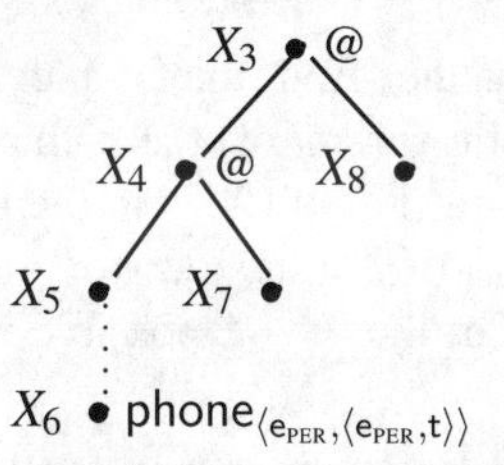

Isolating the semantic contribution of the verb in a constraint of its own suffices to represent the fact that type coercion can affect any number of nominal arguments of the verb, as illustrated in (203)-(205). E.g., in (206) the gap between X_5 and X_6 is sufficient to block the propagation of the sortal restrictions of the verb (expressed in the type of X_6, where PER is the sort for persons) to either of the node variables X_7 and X_8, which model the arguments of the relation of telephoning.

On the basis of (206), the reinterpretations that take place in (203)-(205) are described in (207)-(209). Recall that $\iota x.P(x)$ refers to the sole element in the extension of P:

(207) $\boxdot\ (\iota x_{\text{LOC}}.\mathbf{capital}'(x), \mathbf{max}')$

$$\Leftarrow \quad \lambda x \lambda z_{\text{LOC}} \exists y_{\text{PER}}.\mathbf{in}'(y,z) \wedge \boxdot\ (y,x)$$

$\mathbf{phone}'$

(208) $\boxdot\ (\mathbf{max}', \iota x_{\text{LOC}}.\mathbf{capital}'(x))$

$$\Leftarrow \quad \lambda x_{\text{LOC}} \lambda z \exists y_{\text{PER}}.\mathbf{in}'(y,x) \wedge \boxdot\ (z,y)$$

$\mathbf{phone}'$

$\boxdot\ (\mathbf{london}', \mathbf{brighton}')$

(209) $$\Leftarrow \lambda x_{\text{LOC}} \lambda z_{\text{LOC}} \exists y_{\text{PER}} \exists u_{\text{PER}}.\mathbf{in}'(y,x) \wedge \mathbf{in}'(u,z) \wedge \boxdot\ (u,y)$$

$\mathbf{phone}'$

The constraints on the left are the result of the semantic composition, the intervening constraint on the right models the extrasemantically derived type coercion operator. The constructive solutions of these constraints correspond to the λ-terms for the readings that someone in the capital called Max (210), that Max called someone in the capital (211), and that someone in London phoned someone in Brighton (212):

(210) $\exists y_{\text{PER}}.\mathbf{in}'(y, \iota x_{\text{LOC}}.\mathbf{capital}'(x)) \wedge \mathbf{phone}'(y, \mathbf{max}')$

(211) $\exists y_{\text{PER}}.\mathbf{in}'(y, \iota x_{\text{LOC}}.\mathbf{capital}'(x)) \wedge \mathbf{phone}'(\mathbf{max}', y)$

(212) $\exists y_{\text{PER}} \exists u_{\text{PER}}.\mathbf{in}'(y, \mathbf{brighton}') \wedge \mathbf{in}'(u, \mathbf{london}') \wedge \mathbf{phone}'(u,y)$

The more complex operators can be put together from the simpler operators. E.g., the operator in (209) is an (alphabetic variant of) the combination of the operators in (207) and (208), i.e., the insertion of (208) in the hole of (207). Hence, for n-ary predicates, one needs only n basic operators (one for each argument of the predicate), to derive all of the $2^n - 1$ possible reinterpretation operators.

Thus, the proposed analysis captures sortal type coercion for verbs with more than one NP argument as well.

Sortal type coercion within NPs

Consider next the case of sortal type coercion within NPs, which is instantiated by the sentence (213) [= (65)]:

(213) # Most red-haired teams fell ill

Recall that there seem to be two possible ways of mediating between the conflicting sortal restrictions of the constituents: Either the noun *team* is coerced into a property of persons, or the adjective *red-haired* and the verb *fall ill* are both coerced into a property of groups. But the quantification in (213) is on teams, not on their members. I.e., the latter option is chosen, although it involves two reinterpretations instead of one for the former option.

The strategy of introducing the type coercion potential of expressions in the syntax-semantics interface suffices to block the unwanted first reinterpretation option and to enforce the second option. The relevant interface rule **(b17)** for the modification of an N by an AP (which returns N̄) is repeated here in part as (214). It separates the semantic contribution of the AP (whose topnode is X^r_{AP}) in a fragment of its own:

(214)

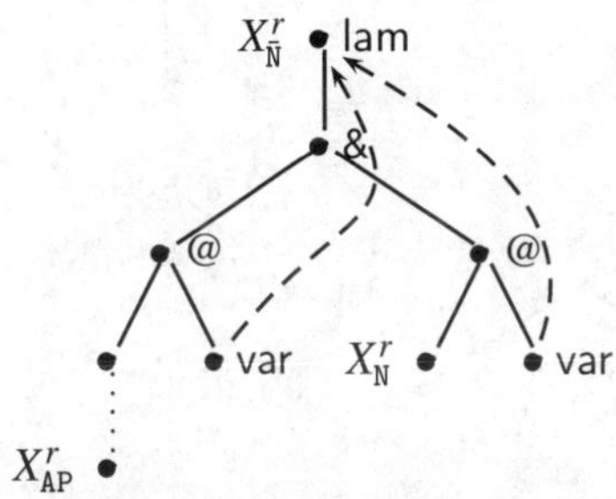

The semantic representations of *team*, *red-haired*, and *fall ill* are appropriately labelled node variables. The node variable for *team* has the type $\langle e_{\mathrm{GROUP}}, t\rangle$. The fact that both *red-haired* and *fall ill* introduce a property of persons is expressed in their type $\langle e_{\mathrm{PER}}, t\rangle$.

Rules **(b18)** and **(b17)** derive the following semantic representation of the N̄ constituent *red-haired team*:

(215)

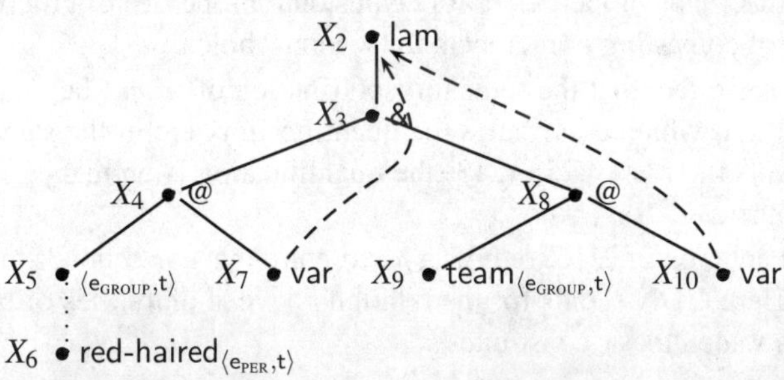

This constraint exhibits a gap between the node variables X_5 and X_6, but not above X_9, i.e., even at this early stage of semantic construction it is evident that any sortal conflict between the adjective and the noun would have to be resolved in terms of an operator that pertains to the adjective, and not to the noun.

Note that the fact that $\lambda(X_7) = \lambda(X_{10})$ in (215) has consequences for the type of the variable X_5. The types of X_7 and X_{10} must be identical, because they are mapped onto the same lam node variable by λ. Consequently, any sortal restrictions are propagated from X_5 to X_9 and vice versa, which entails the type $\langle e_{\text{GROUP}}, t\rangle$ for X_5.

The rest of the derivation of the semantic representation for (213) is straightforward, returning (216):

(216)

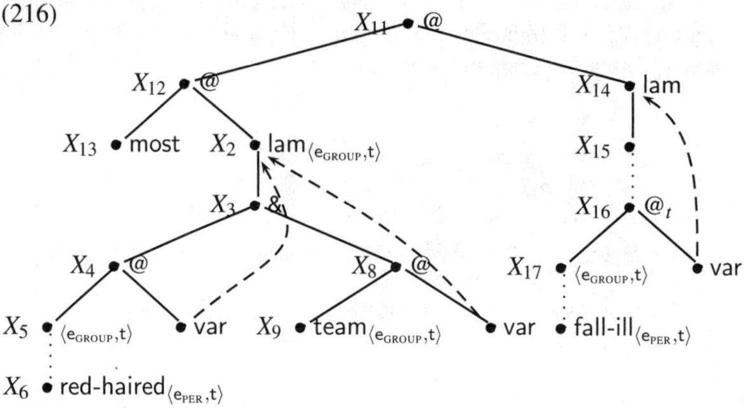

Since the type $\langle e_{\text{GROUP}}, t\rangle$ (for a property of groups) is propagated from the node variable X_9 to both X_5 and X_{17} (crucial for the latter propagation are the types of X_{13} and X_2, see p.77), the only chance of deriving a well-formed solution for (216) is to use both gaps in the constraint to insert additional material that mediates between the conflicting sorts. To this end, one can use an operator that maps properties P of persons onto properties of groups, viz., the property of consisting of members for whom P holds.

Once again the fact that the semantic contribution of *team* (the node variable X_9) and X_{13}, which contributes the quantification, are in the same fragment highlights the fact that in (213) the quantification is on teams, and not on their members.

This augmentation of (216) returns a λ-structure that corresponds to the λ-term (217). Here **CON** stands for the relation between pluralities of persons y and groups x such that y constitutes x.

(217) $$\text{MOST}(\lambda x_{\text{GROUP}}.\mathbf{team}'(x) \wedge \exists y_{\text{PER}}.\mathbf{CON}(y,x) \wedge \mathbf{red\text{-}haired}'(y), \\ \lambda x_{\text{GROUP}} \exists y_{\text{PER}}.\mathbf{CON}(y,x) \wedge \mathbf{fall\text{-}ill}'(y))$$

(217) expresses the meaning of (213) after type coercion, viz., that more than 50% of the teams whose members are red-haired are teams whose members fell ill.

Sortal type coercion for control verbs

The proposed analysis of sortal type coercion will next be applied to control verbs.[51] These verbs require that their subject NP complies with the selection restriction of the verb that is the head of the VP argument, otherwise type coercion is called for. This shows up, e.g., in the reinterpretation candidate (218) [= (186)], where *London* does not meet the selection restriction of *phone*:

(218) # London began to phone Max

In other words, sortal selection restrictions from the VP argument of the control verb percolate to its NP argument. This percolation can be captured by assigning an appropriate type to the semantics of control verbs, viz., $\langle\langle e_\alpha, \langle s,t\rangle\rangle, \langle e_\alpha, \langle s,t\rangle\rangle\rangle$. Due to this type, the sort of the NP argument of the begin-relation must be compatible with the sortal restriction of the VP-argument of the begin-relation. The semantic representation of (218) is then the constraint (219):

(219)

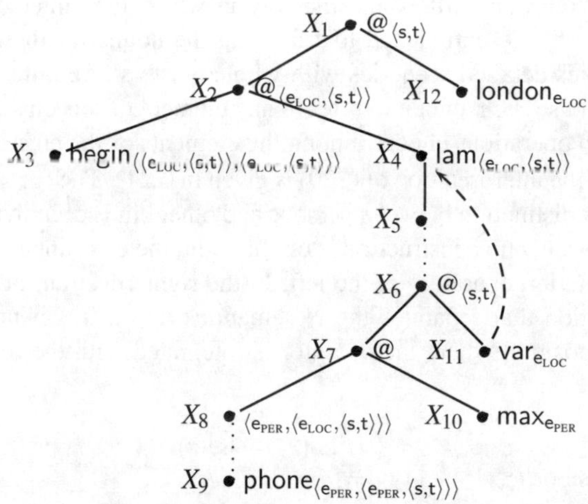

The types of the node variables X_3 and X_{12} enforce the typing of X_4 by $\langle e_{\text{LOC}}, \langle s,t\rangle\rangle$. This sortal information is propagated (via X_{11}) down to X_8, whose type is determined as $\langle e_{\text{PER}}, \langle e_{\text{LOC}}, \langle s,t\rangle\rangle\rangle$. But this type is incompatible with the type $\langle e_{\text{PER}}, \langle e_{\text{PER}}, \langle s,t\rangle\rangle\rangle$ of X_9, which bars an equation of the variables X_8 and X_9. I.e., (219) has no constructive solution, which models the fact that (218) is a reinterpretation candidate.

Reinterpretation for (218) can then proceed in the same fashion as for the example (203) above.

[51] The discussion of control verbs makes eventuality variables and their binders explicit to ensure compatibility with the analyses of *begin*-sentences in section 3.1.1. In this case, the interface rule **(b1)** assigns the type $\langle s,t\rangle$ to the root of the sentence.

Sortal type coercion for 'ham sandwich' cases

Finally, the proposed analysis of sortal type coercion is applied to the 'ham sandwich' cases. These cases showed that in specific contexts there are alternative patterns of type coercion. In particular, Nunberg-style examples like (220) show that – at least in some professional jargons – there are additional strategies of mediating a sortal mismatch between a verb and its subject NP. In (220), quantification is on customers, not on sandwiches, which calls for type coercion for the $\bar{\text{N}}$ in terms of an operator from properties of food onto properties of its consumers:

(220) # Every ham sandwich complained

This coercion potential of nouns seems to be restricted to nouns referring to entities highly relevant for the respective context (e.g., dishes for a restaurant context, and musical instruments for a music context). This suggests attributing this potential to the fact that in highly specialised contexts common knowledge of the relevant entities and the way in which they interact with other entities is so firmly entrenched that uttering the nouns for these relevant entities invokes detailed sceneries with whole clusters of entities. Consequently, one can use such a noun to refer to any element of this cluster, and let reinterpretation operations choose among the elements of the cluster.

The analysis of the interpretation of (220) is given in (221). The sorts $\pm$PER model the relevant distinction between persons and other kinds of individuals. Here the result of semantic construction is on the right, the extralinguistically derived reinterpretation operator, on the left. In the right constraint, there is a dominance relation that separates the $\bar{\text{N}}$ semantics into a fragment of its own. This is the position where the operator is integrated with the result of semantic construction:

(221)

$$\lambda z_{+\text{PER}} \exists y_{-\text{PER}}.\mathbf{consume}'(z,y) \wedge \boxdot\,(y) \Rightarrow \quad \forall x.\ \boxdot(x) \rightarrow \boxdot(x)$$

$$\lambda y_{-\text{PER}}.\mathbf{hamsandwich}'\,(y) \qquad \lambda y_{+\text{PER}}.\mathbf{complain}'(y)$$

(221) as a whole has a constructive solution that corresponds to the λ-term (222) for the proposition that every consumer of a ham sandwich complained:

(222) $\forall x_{+\text{PER}}.(\exists y_{-\text{PER}}.\mathbf{consume}'(x,y) \wedge \mathbf{hamsandwich}'(y))$
$\rightarrow \mathbf{complain}'(x)$

This analysis begs three questions: (a) How can one derive a constraint like the right hand side in (221), in particular, the R-position above the $\bar{\text{N}}$ semantics? (b) Is it acceptable to have two R-positions in this constraint (above the $\bar{\text{N}}$ and the VP semantics)? (c) Why is the correct R-position chosen in (221)?

The answer to the first of these question lies in my view of the lexicon in professional jargons where 'ham sandwich' cases abound. I assume a certain context-dependence of the lexicon, i.e., these jargons have special lexical entries for nouns that relate to highly relevant entities: These entries indicate that the nouns may undergo type coercion too.

Formally, this is modelled in terms of a constraint for these nouns that consists of two node variables that are related by a dominance relation. The upper node variable is the topnode of the noun's semantic contribution. E.g., in a restaurant context, *ham sandwich* would get the representation (223):

(223)
$$\begin{array}{ll} X^{r}_{\mathrm{N}} & \bullet\ \langle \mathsf{e,t} \rangle \\ & \vdots \\ X_1 & \bullet\ \mathsf{hamsandwich}_{\langle \mathsf{e}_{\text{-PER}},\mathsf{t}\rangle} \end{array}$$

If this representation is used for the derivation of (221), it introduces the additional R-position within the NP semantics. Then the interface rules need not be altered in any way to obtain (221).

Thus, ham sandwich cases show that, sometimes, the strategy of hard-wiring the determination of R-positions in the syntax-semantics interface must be complemented by additional lexical fine-tuning in order to cover all aspects of reinterpretation. In chapter 4, other cases are pointed out in which syntactic constituent structure by itself is not sufficient for the determination of R-positions.

The second question is answered in the affirmative: Neither R-position is dispensable, since the standard pattern of sortal type coercion is not ruled out in professional jargons. The standard and the special pattern may even coexist in a single sentence, e.g., in (224):[52]

(224) # Every ham sandwich is parked out back

The interpretation of (224) is that every consumer of a ham sandwich has a car that is parked out back. I.e., quantification is over persons, although neither the $\bar{\mathrm{N}}$ nor the VP semantics refer to persons, which is highlighted in its semantic representation (225):

(225)
$$\begin{array}{ccc} & \forall x.\ \boxdot\,(x) \rightarrow & \boxdot\,(x) \\ & \vdots & \vdots \\ \lambda y_{\text{-PER}}.\mathbf{hamsandwich}' & (y) & \lambda y_{\text{-PER}}.\mathbf{be\text{-}parked\text{-}out\text{-}back}'(y) \end{array}$$

Thus, to derive the desired interpretation of (224), one needs both R-positions in (225) to coerce both the $\bar{\mathrm{N}}$ and the VP semantics.

[52]This example was pointed out to me by Manfred Pinkal.

The answer to the third question (why the correct R-position is chosen in (221), to which one may add the question of why (224) is interpreted as a quantification over persons) requires a closer investigation of the factors that select between different feasible reinterpretation options, if the semantic representation of a reinterpretation candidate does not determine which option must be chosen. Examples like (220) and (224) corroborate Nunberg's (1993) assumption that such choices are driven by contextual relevance: If the hearer expects a reinterpretation candidate to be about persons, he chooses a reinterpretation that returns such a sentence, if there are various reinterpretation options. But still it is fair to say that further work is necessary to determine the full range of factors that influence these choices and to integrate them into a formal account of reinterpretation.

3.1.3 Type coercion for semantically well-formed expressions

This subsection is devoted to cases of type coercion that are not triggered by impending mismatches between constituents of an utterance. I will show that these cases are also covered by the proposed approach to reinterpretation.

Type coercion induced by anaphoric relations

The first kind of type coercion for semantically well-formed expressions is due to subsequent anaphoric reference to constituents of these expressions, as in (226), where the subject of the first sentence is the antecedent of the pronoun *he* in the second sentence:

(226) # The ham sandwich is nice. He smiles.

The constraint for the first sentence of (226) is (227). It has a constructive solution, since *be nice* introduces no sortal restriction for persons for its subject NP. In such solutions, X_6 and X_7 would denote the same node, which would equate the sorts -PER and α and thus spread X_7's sortal restriction all over the constraint, in particular, to X_{13} (whose type would then be $e_{\text{-PER}}$).

(227)

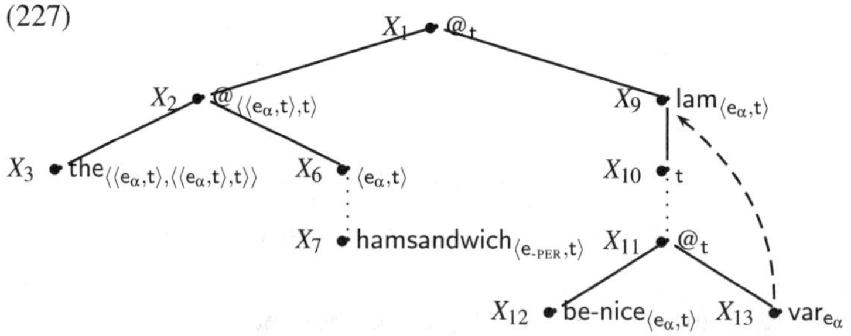

The λ-term corresponding to the constructive solution of (227) would be (228). It states that the unique ham sandwich is nice:

(228) $\textbf{be-nice}'(\iota x.\textbf{hamsandwich}'(x))$

But before such a constructive solution can be derived, the second sentence of the example must be processed. The resulting constraint for the example as a whole includes a top-level conjunction whose arguments are the constraints for the two sentences and an anaphoric link between *he* and *the sandwich*, which is modelled by the anaphoric relation ante between the ana node variable X_{17} of the pronoun and the topnode X_{13} of its antecedent NP (depicted by a dashed arrow). Not directly relevant sortal information is omitted to enhance readability:

(229)

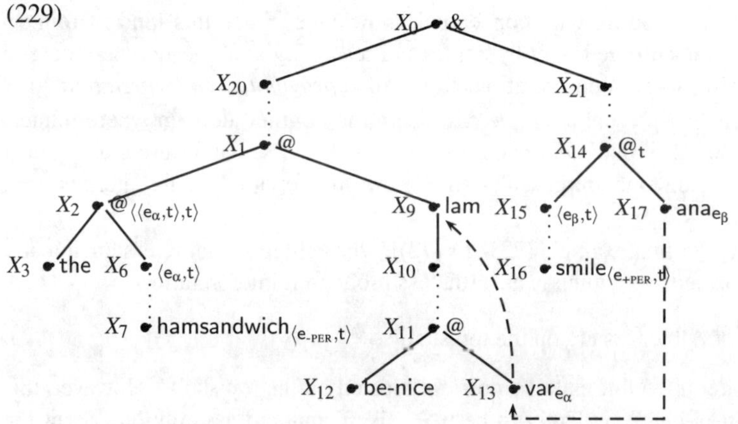

Sortal restrictions percolate along these anaphoric relations in that their arguments have the same type. Hence, constraint (229) for both sentences has no constructive solution: For the second sentence of (226), whose semantics is given in the fragments below X_{14}, a constructive solution would entail closing the gap between X_{15} and X_{16}, thus, $\beta = +\text{PER}$. Then the sortal restriction of X_{16} would carry over to X_{17}, and from there via the ante-link to X_{13}. But then, the type of X_{13} would be $e_{+\text{PER}}$, hence, $\alpha = +\text{PER}$. This would percolate to X_6, whose type then emerges as $\langle e_{+\text{PER}}, t\rangle$. But then the gap between X_6 and X_7 could no longer be closed due to conflicting sortal restrictions on X_6 and X_7.

Type coercion as outlined for (220) would insert material between X_6 and X_7 in the form of a fragment with a root of type $\langle e_{+\text{PER}}, t\rangle$ and a hole of type $\langle e_{-\text{PER}}, t\rangle$. This would yield a constructive solution for the resulting constraint for (226). It corresponds to the λ-term (230), which states that the contextually unique ham sandwich consumer is nice and smiles:

(230) $\textbf{be-nice}'(\iota x_{+\text{PER}} \exists y_{-\text{PER}}.\textbf{consume}'(x,y) \wedge \textbf{hamsandwich}'(y)) \wedge$
$\textbf{smile}'(\iota x_{+\text{PER}} \exists y_{-\text{PER}}.\textbf{consume}'(x,y) \wedge \textbf{hamsandwich}'(y))$

This is only a first sketch of the way in which CLLS can handle reinterpretation cases that are triggered by anaphoric relations across sentence boundaries. What has to be investigated further is the question of exactly *when* one can actually go from CLLS constraints to their solutions. While the above example has shown that one may not rashly go for a locally feasible constructive solution for a single sentence in a larger discourse, it seems unrealistic to assume that solutions are derived only after a discourse as a whole has been processed.

Pragmatic reinterpretation

This section focusses on reinterpretation cases without impending semantic mismatches, whose reinterpretation is motivated by the incompatibility of their literal reading with conceptual knowledge. Since this kind of reinterpretation is enforced only by contextual reasoning and not by type-theoretic (including sortal) considerations, it is called *pragmatic reinterpretation.*

I will first present a simple case from the nominal domain where reinterpretation takes place but cannot be explained on semantic grounds. Then I will move on to the representations for the problematic Nixon sentences from section 1.4.2.[53]

Consider first example (231) [= (72)], whose literal reading is semantically well-formed, but which is nevertheless prone to reinterpretation:

(231) # All tenors are on the top shelf

Its literal reading is ‘all tenors are located on the top shelf’. However, this reading is highly unlikely to be true, given standard assumptions about the weight that shelves can bear.

But as argued in the introduction (0.1.2), hearers are extremely reluctant to impute defective utterances to speakers, no matter whether the defect would result from semantic mismatches or from an incompatibility of the utterance with conceptual knowledge. They assume that speakers observe pragmatic rules (in particular, Grice’s *cooperative principle*). To uphold this assumption, hearers take recourse to reinterpretation to make up for impending conflicts between utterances like (231) and conceptual knowledge.

Type coercion in (231) follows the pattern described for the ‘ham sandwich’ cases of sortally triggered type coercions: It is technical jargon that is used in specific contexts (e.g., in a CD store). Thus, the lexicon is different in that the semantic representations of nouns for entities that are highly relevant in these contexts specify that the nouns may be reinterpreted. Formally, the constraint for *tenor* comprises two node variables that are related by a dominance relation:

[53] Further instances of pragmatic reinterpretation are discussed in section 3.2.4 (for the aspectual domain) and section 4.1.2 (for landing site coercion).

(232) $X_1 \bullet \langle \mathsf{e,t} \rangle$

$X_2 \bullet \mathsf{tenor}_{\langle \mathsf{e}_{\text{PER}},\mathsf{t} \rangle}$

The constraint for (231) thus emerges as the right hand side of (233):

(233)

$$\forall x. \boxdot\,(x) \rightarrow \boxdot\,(x)$$

$$\lambda z \exists y.\mathbf{recording\text{-}of}'(z,y) \wedge \boxdot\,(y) \;\Rightarrow$$

$$\lambda y_{\text{PER}}.\mathbf{tenor}'\,(y) \qquad \lambda y_{\text{THING}}.\mathbf{on\text{-}top\text{-}shelf}'(y)$$

This constraint has a solution (since THING subsumes PER[son]), but in order to derive a solution that is compatible with conceptual knowledge, reinterpretation introduces an operator that maps the property of being a tenor onto the property of being a recording of a tenor. The operator is depicted on the left hand side of (233).

In the constraint that results from conjoining both sides of (233), universal quantification is over recordings, not over tenors. This fits in with intuitions on the interpretation of (231). (233) as a whole has a constructive solution, which corresponds to (234). This λ-term denotes the proposition that every recording of a tenor is on the top shelf:

(234) $\forall x.\exists y(\mathbf{recording\text{-}of}'(x,y) \wedge \mathbf{tenor}'(y)) \rightarrow \mathbf{on\text{-}top\text{-}shelf}(x)$

The second instance of pragmatic reinterpretation discussed in this subsection are the Nixon sentences like (235) from section 1.4.2:

(235) [=(54)] (#) Nixon saw himself

The suggested analysis associates anaphora with *two* identity relations. Anaphors introduce the property of being identical to some entity y that that is identical to the referent of the antecedent. This property is the restriction in an existential quantification, but may be coerced (as indicated by the underline in the semantic representation (236)):

(236) [=(56)] $\exists y.(\underline{\lambda z.z = \mathbf{nixon}'})(y) \wedge \exists x.(\underline{\lambda z.z = y})(x) \wedge \mathbf{see}'(y,x)$

In prose: Some individual y identical to Nixon saw some individual x identical to y, in short, Nixon saw Nixon.

The semantic representation of (235) is the following constraint:

(237)

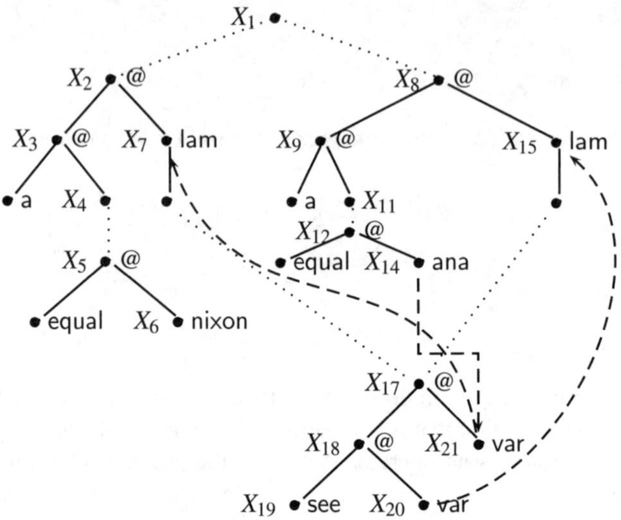

The label equal introduces the relation of identity '=' (its type is the polymorphic $\langle\alpha,\langle\alpha,t\rangle\rangle$, for any type α). X_{14} is ante-linked to X_{21}, the root of the constraint of its antecedent *Nixon*. The constructive solution of (237) corresponds directly to (236), here X_{14} is interpreted in the same way as X_{21} (viz., as the bound variable y of the λ-calculus). However, in an appropriate context either of the identity relations (below X_5 and X_{12}) could be coerced by inserting the constraint for an appropriate reinterpretation operator between X_4 and X_5 and X_{11} and X_{12}, respectively, as discussed in section 1.4.2.

To conclude the presentation of the proposed approach to type coercion in the nominal domain, I will use it to model the influence of type coercion on the anaphoric potential of NPs.

3.1.4 Type coercion and the anaphoric potential of NPs

Section 1.4.5 discussed Fauconnier's (1985) distinction between 'open' and 'closed' coercion operators (which he calls 'connectors'). I argued that this distinction does not fit the data in that some reinterpretation operators are neither open nor closed operators: They do not affect the anaphoric potential of NPs, even if they are part of an expression where type coercion takes place. The relevant examples showed that the original referent of *the wine* is still accessible after coercion, while the newly introduced referent for the *container* of the wine is not:

(238) # The wine was labelled. It had a spicy, slightly confected finish

(239) *The wine was labelled. It was mouth-blown

This influence on the anaphoric potential can be attributed to the notion of R-position: Coercing an NP affects its anaphoric potential, coercing a verb does not change the anaphoric potential of any NP. The explanation rests on two pillars: First, reinterpretation operators cannot by themselves introduce additional anaphorically accessible referents. Second, the anaphoric potential of an NP is jointly determined by its determiner and the interpretation of the $\bar{N}$ sister of the determiner. If this interpretation changes due to reinterpretation of the $\bar{N}$ constituent, the anaphoric potential of the whole NP changes accordingly. But if reinterpretation affects a verb, no new accessible referents are introduced, and the interpretation of any NPs' $\bar{N}$ constituents remains the same – and so does the anaphoric potential of these NPs.

Therefore anaphoric reference to the definite NP is impossible in sentences like (240). Reinterpretation inside the NP changes the meaning of its $\bar{N}$ constituent to the property of being a omelet eater. Thus, the NP introduces an accessible discourse referent for the omelet eater, there is no longer an accessible referent for the omelet available:

(240) * The mushroom omelet left without paying. It was inedible

In contrast, reinterpretation of a verb leaves the anaphoric potential of all NPs unchanged and does not introduce new referents to which one could refer anaphorically. This accounts for (238) and (239).

This leaves us with seeming counterexamples where *both* the original and the newly introduced referent seem to be accessible:

(241) # Most French authors are in room 116. They are bound in leather.

(242) # Most French authors are in room 116. They are great artists.

But here my explanation is that in this case different R-positions are at stake. I will show this with the quantification test introduced in section 1.4.4 to detect R-positions. Consider first a scenario in which (241) is uttered and the majority of *books* by French authors, though not the books of the majority of French authors, are in room 116. This is possible, which shows that one option is the coercion of *French authors*, which returns the interpretation 'most books by French authors'.

In contrast, (242) is compatible with a scenario where the books of the majority of the French authors, but not necessarily the majority of books by French authors, are in room 116. I.e., *be in room 116* is coerced to yield the interpretation 'be the author of books in room 116'.

But then the influence of type coercion on the anaphoric potential can be explained: VP-coercion does not affect the anaphoric potential of NPs, NP-coercion changes it for the relevant NP. If either option is possible, there is a choice between NP- and VP-coercion.

This concludes the presentation of my approach to type coercion in the nominal domain. Its goal was to capture a wide range of phenomena within a general framework and at the same time to include the results and intuitions of previous work.

3.2 Type coercion in the aspectual domain

Type coercion is triggered in the aspectual domain by the fact that expressions like durative adverbials or temporal conjunctions exert aspectual selection restrictions on the predicates which they modify or for which they subcategorise. This section will focus on aspectual type coercion that involves the progressive, the perfect, and temporal conjunctions; the account of type coercion for durative adverbials and time frame adverbials is deferred until chapter 4, since it follows directly from the analysis of landing site coercion for these adverbials.

3.2.1 Type coercion for the progressive

Aspectual type coercion can be found in progressive predicates. Since the progressive maps interval-based or non-stative predicates onto stative ones, (243a) is in need of reinterpretation, as the argument of the progressive operator is a stative predicate. In contrast, (243b)-(243d), where the arguments of the progressive are a process, an intergressive, and a telic predicate, respectively, are directly interpretable. The reinterpretation strategy that is needed for cases like (243a) is type coercion, there are no cases of landing site coercion for the progressive.

(243) a # Charlotte was being silly

b Charlotte was singing

c Charlotte was playing a sonata

d Charlotte was building a house

The interpretation of (243a) is that Charlotte – although she is not a silly person in general – was *acting* silly. This interpretation is quite common for stative predicates in the progressive.

This aspectual characterisation of the progressive does not account for all reinterpretation cases involving the progressive, e.g., reinterpretation candidates like (244a) and (244b) are not covered. The explanation of such examples is deferred until chapter 5, where I will show that these cases follow from the non-aspectual *Duration Principle*.

(244) a # Nigel was winning the race

b # The light was flashing

In the grammar fragment, the semantic contribution of the progressive operator PROG (as defined in section 2.4.2) is modelled as a labelled node variable. Since PROG maps interval-based onto stative predicates, this variable carries the type $\langle\langle s_{+\text{IB}}, t\rangle, \langle s_{-\text{IB}}, t\rangle\rangle$.

The interface rule **(b16)** that constructs the semantics of a progressive VP1 from the semantic contributions of its immediate constituents, the progressive auxiliary and a VP2, is repeated in part as (245):

(245)

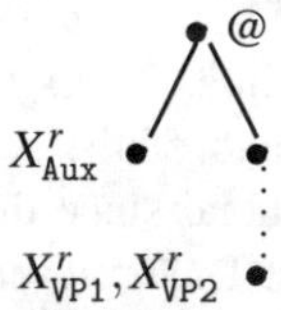

In (245), the semantic contributions of the progressive auxiliary and the VP are separated in different fragments of the constraint, which models the possibility of type coercion for functor-argument pairs where the progressive is the functor.

For (243b), semantic construction returns the constraint (246). Starting with (246), I ignore for the rest of this chapter R-positions in the constraints that are not relevant for aspectual reinterpretation.[54]

(246)

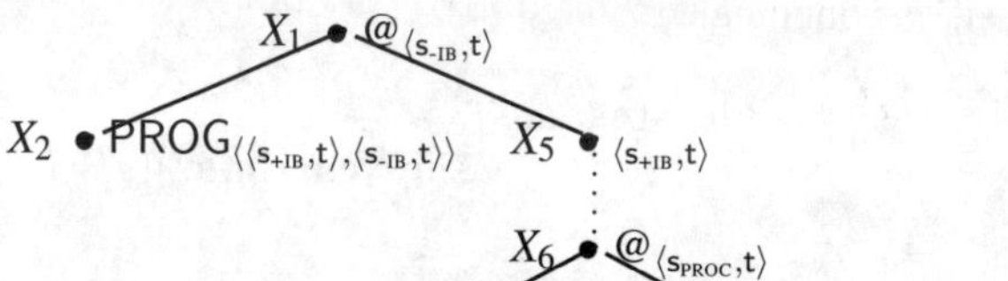

The type of the node variable X_2, $\langle\langle s_{+\text{IB}}, t\rangle, \langle s_{-\text{IB}}, t\rangle\rangle$, determines the types of the node variables X_1 and X_5. These types model the restriction of the argument to nonstative predicates (variable X_5) as well as the fact that the result of applying the progressive operator to a predicate returns a stative predicate (variable X_1).

(243b) is an R-free expression. Accordingly, its semantic representation (246) has a constructive solution. This solution corresponds to the λ-term (247) for the set of all eventualities that are part of an eventuality of Charlotte's singing:

[54] These R-positions are introduced for the purpose of modelling type coercion that is driven in particular by sortal mismatches between verbs and their arguments. E.g., in (246), there should be an R-position above the semantic contribution of the intransitive verb *sing* (the node variable labelled by sing). This R-position follows from the interface rule **(b2)** for VPs that consist of an intransitive verb only.

(247) $\lambda e_{\text{-IB}}.\text{PROG}(\lambda e'_{\text{PROC}}.\textbf{sing}'(\textbf{charlotte}')(e'))(e)$

In contrast, examples like (243a) must be reinterpreted. Following Herweg, I assume that their interpretation is due to type coercion in terms of a *maximality operator* MAX as defined in section 2.4.2. Thus, (243a) refers to maximal phases of Charlotte's silliness. But the introduction of maximal phases of silliness pragmatically (not semantically) ensues phases of non-silliness. This means that Charlotte is not a silly person in general. Otherwise, her silliness could not be restricted to certain phases.

Accordingly, for the semantic representation of cases like (243a), the gap between the semantic contributions of the progressive and of the sentence radical it applies to, which is introduced in (245), is crucial since the constraints for these examples have no constructive solutions. The representation of (243a) in the simplified CLLS notation is (248):[55]

(248) $\text{PROG}_{\langle\langle s_{\text{+IB}},t\rangle,\langle s_{\text{-IB}},t\rangle\rangle}(\;\boxdot_{\langle s_{\text{+IB}},t\rangle})$

$\qquad\qquad\vdots$

$\qquad\qquad\textbf{be-silly}'_{\langle e,\langle s_{\text{-IB}},t\rangle\rangle}(\textbf{charlotte}'_{e})$

Inserting MAX into (248) yields a structure whose minimal solution corresponds to a λ-term for the set of eventualities in which a maximal phase of Charlotte being silly is ongoing:

(249) $\lambda e_{\text{-IB}}.\text{PROG}(\lambda e'_{\text{INTER}}.\text{MAX}(\lambda e''_{-\text{IB}}.\textbf{be-silly}'(\textbf{charlotte}')(e''))(e'))(e)$

3.2.2 Type coercion for durative adverbials

Durative adverbials select for unbounded predicates and return intergressive ones. Hence, (250) need not be reinterpreted, while (251) must undergo reinterpretation (by preference, in terms of an iterative operator). However, type coercion is only one option for such aspectual mismatches, and the account of type coercion for these examples follows trivially from the (more involved) analysis of the landing site coercion that is also possible for some of these cases. Therefore the analysis of such examples is deferred until section 4.2.1.

(250) Charlotte sang for two hours

(251) # The light flashed for two hours

[55] Recall that annotating a hole with a type means that the hole is to be identified with a fragment of this type. The type INTER of the λ-abstracted variable e' in (249) is due to the fact that MAX maps unbounded predicates onto intergressive ones.

3.2.3 Type coercion for time frame adverbials

Like durative adverbials, time frame adverbials (TFA) such as *in 20 minutes* are involved in both type coercion and landing site coercion patterns. They select for bounded predicates and return a predicate whose aspectual class is that of the predicate they modify.

This means that there are literal readings for (252) and (253), but not for (254) and (255):

(252) Ariadne played the sonata in 20 minutes

(253) Max tore down the house in 20 minutes

(254) # Max ran in 20 minutes

(255) # Max was here in 20 minutes

Characteristically, an aspectual mismatch such as in the last two examples is resolved in terms of landing site coercion. (E.g., in (254), the adverbial may pertain to a *preparatory eventuality* of Max's running.) For some cases, including (254), but not (255), type coercion is also possible: In the type coercion reading of (254) there is a fixed distance which Max runs. Since once again the account of type coercion follows from the account of landing site coercion, the analysis of these cases is postponed until section 4.2.2.

3.2.4 Type coercion for the perfect

The perfect operator (as defined in section 2.4.2) maps predicates *P* onto the property of being an aftermath of an eventuality in the extension of *P*. The argument of the operator must specify this aftermath (formally, as the argument of an operator BECOME). Thus, the operator selects for telic predicates. This explains the literal understanding of sentences like (256). Here the argument of the perfect operator (the proposition that Max goes away) introduces the aftermath proposition that Max is away. Thus, (256) refers to an absence of Max at the moment of utterance that is the aftermath of his going away:

(256) Max has gone away

In contrast, atelic predicates involve no such aftermath proposition in their semantics. Since reference to an aftermath is crucial for the semantics of the perfect, this contrast is the reason for the selection restriction of the perfect for telic predicates.

If the perfect operator is applied to atelic predicates, context or conceptual knowledge must provide an aftermath proposition.

(257) # Max has had the measles

(258) ? I have sneezed

(259) ? Amélie has played a sonata

The preferred interpretation of (257) is that Max is now immune to the measles as a result of having had them once. For (258) and (259) it is more difficult to get an interpretation; one must assume that somehow sneezing or playing the sonata had some (contextually supplied) consequence that held at the time of utterance.

This observation agrees with Depratere's (1998) view of the present perfect. She notes that the present perfect invariably expresses the fact that some (one or several) states of affairs obtain at (and are relevant for) the moment of utterance t_0. However, for telic[56] present perfect expressions, a distinguished state of affairs holds at t_0, e.g., in (256), Max's absence, which is an non-cancellable entailment of the expression, whence the contradiction in (260):

(260) * Max has gone away and is present right now

Depending on the context, there may be other states of affairs whose holding at t_0 follows from (256). E.g., if speaker and hearer of this sentence had some private matter to discuss but could not do so as long as Max was present, (256) would entail that it is now possible for them to discuss this matter.

In contrast, for atelic predicates as in (258) there is no such distinguished state of affairs whose holding at t_0 invariably follows. Thus, (258) only makes sense in a context that associates sneezing with some consequence or other. E.g., in a context in which sneezing is heavily tabooed, (258) might entail that Max is now embarrassed and that the witnesses of his sneezing have a low opinion of him now. But this entailment is strongly context-dependent.

I.e., I agree with Depraetere that telic and atelic predicates behave differently in the perfect tense, due to the requirement of the perfect operator that for perfect forms of *every* kind of predicate *P* there must be *at least one* poststate that is associated with *P*. If *P* provides this poststate in its semantics (i.e., is telic), no reinterpretation is necessary, but, if *P* fails to provide it because it is atelic, reinterpretation is called for that introduces it, in other words, which maps an atelic predicate *P* onto a telic predicate.

Examples (257)-(259) suggest an analysis of the reinterpretation for the atelic argument of a perfect operator in the following way: The information of the atelic predicate *P* is retained, but regarded as part of a larger eventuality description, viz., as the *cause* part in the description of a *causation*. The *result* part of this causation description then provides an aftermath proposition, i.e., one which holds for the aftermath of the causation. Only extralinguistic

[56]Like Dowty's (1979) reconstruction of Vendler's classes, she identifies the notions of boundedness and telicity, see section 1.1 for discussion.

knowledge about what might be a result of *P*-eventualities can specify how to integrate the atelic *P* into the description of a causation.

The resulting description of a causation is a telic predicate that fits in with the selection restriction of the perfect operator. After reinterpretation, the perfect of the atelic predicate *P* thus is a stative predicate that denotes the property of being the aftermath of this causation.

As an example of this kind of reinterpretation, consider (257). Its interpretation draws on the conceptual knowledge that no one can catch the measles twice, as their first attack makes their victims develop antibodies, which prevent a second attack. Hence, there is a salient causal link from having the measles to becoming immune to them. This link licenses a reinterpretation for (257) in terms of a causation structure whose result is immunisation against the measles. The resulting causative change predicate (roughly 'becoming immune to the measles by having them') fulfills the selection restriction of the perfect. Thus, what is conveyed by (257) is not just that there was a time in the past when *Max have- the measles* held but that Max is in the aftermath of an eventuality of becoming immune to the measles by having them, i.e., that he is immune to them now.

Hence, it is felicitous to answer (257) to someone worrying about the possibility of Max getting the measles. In this context, the relevance of (257) does not lie in the information that Max had the measles sometime in the past. But the information that Max is immune to measles now is highly relevant, which makes the response felicitous.

This is different for examples like (258) and (259): In a normal context it is difficult to think of eventualities that are direct poststates of sonata playings or sneezings. Hence, the move from these predicates to complex causative structures where the predicates describe the cause is not straightforward. Differences in the acceptability of perfects of atelic predicates *P* are thus explained in terms of how easy it is to come up with a potential consequence for eventualities in the denotation of *P*.

But as soon as specific contexts introduce such a potential consequence, the acceptability of these examples rises immediately: For instance, if Amélie passed a round in a musicians' competition by playing a sonata, sentence (259) becomes quite acceptable and is interpreted as expressing the fact that Amélie is in the aftermath of passing a round and, hence, a competitor in the next round of the contest. Similarly, in a country where playing music is forbidden by law, (259) is acceptable as well, this time, however, it is interpreted as stating that Amélie has rendered herself liable to prosecution by playing the sonata.

Semantic construction for sentence radicals in the perfect once again uses the interface rule **(b16)** in (245). In the simplified CLLS representation, the semantics of (257) emerges as (261), where '**imm-measles**′' abbreviates the stative property of being immune to the measles. (CAUSE relates two predicates *P* and *Q* such that *P* characterises a causing, and *Q*, a caused eventuality, see section 2.4.2.)

(261) $\lambda e_{\text{-IB}}.\text{PERF}(\boxdot_{\langle s_{+\text{TEL}},t\rangle})(e)$

$$\Leftarrow \quad \lambda e'_{+\text{TEL}}.\text{CAUSE}(\Box, \text{BECOME}(\textbf{imm-measles}'(\textbf{max}')))(e')$$

$\lambda e''_{\text{-IB}}.\textbf{have-measles}'(\textbf{max}')(e'')$

Semantic construction yields the constraint on the left of (261). It has no constructive solution, due to the incompatibility between the two sorts +TEL and -IB. Adding the constraint on the right (the contribution of the reinterpretation process) returns a constraint with a well-formed constructive solution.

It corresponds to the λ-term (262), which denotes the set of aftermaths or poststates of Max's becoming immune to the measles as the result of his having had the measles. This entails that during the poststate, Max is immune to the measles (this property is expressed as the argument of BECOME).

(262) $\lambda e_{\text{-IB}}.\text{PERF}(\lambda e'_{+\text{TEL}}.\text{CAUSE}(\lambda e''_{\text{-IB}}.\textbf{have-measles}'(\textbf{max}')(e''), \lambda e''_{+\text{TEL}}.\text{BECOME}(\textbf{imm-measles}'(\textbf{max}'))(e''))(e'))(e)$

The perfect is also a domain where pragmatic reinterpretation is quite frequent. The first group of cases are illustrated by (263) (taken from Herweg 1990):

(263) (#) Trevor has fallen down

(263) is felicitous in a context where its literal reading is false, since the aftermath of Trevor's falling (i.e., his lying on the floor) no longer holds, but where some result of Trevor's fall (e.g., a wound on his forehead) is at issue. Rather than rejecting (263) because of the incompatibility of its literal reading with the context, the hearer assumes the speaker to be cooperative and takes to reinterpretation. This reinterpretation introduces a change of state that was caused by Trevor's falling, viz., his getting injured. Hence, (263) in the above context does not express that Trevor is lying on the ground (this would be wrong) but that he is in the aftermath of getting injured by falling.

The reinterpretation is depicted in (264). It once again embeds the original predicate into a complex causative expression as the predicate that indicates the *cause*. It returns a constraint whose constructive solution corresponds to (265). This λ-term denotes the set of aftermaths of Trevor's getting injured by falling, i.e., a set of eventualities in which Trevor is injured because of a fall.

(264) $\lambda e_{\text{-IB}}.\text{PERF}(\boxdot_{\langle s_{+\text{TEL}},t\rangle})(e)$

$$\Leftarrow \quad \lambda e'_{+\text{TEL}}.\text{CAUSE}(\Box, \lambda e''_{+\text{TEL}}.\textbf{injure-oneself}'(\textbf{trevor}')(e''))(e')$$

$$\lambda e''_{+\text{TEL}}.\ \textbf{fall-down}'(\textbf{trevor}')(e'')$$

(265) $\lambda e_{\text{-IB}}.\text{PERF}(\lambda e'_{+\text{TEL}}.\text{CAUSE}(\lambda e''_{+\text{TEL}}.\textbf{fall-down}'(\textbf{trevor}')(e''), \lambda e''_{+\text{TEL}}.\textbf{injure-oneself}'(\textbf{trevor}')(e''))(e'))(e)$

Other instances of pragmatic reinterpretation for the perfect are cases of the so-called 'experiental perfect', like, e.g., in (266). The experiental perfect of an expression P is true in case there is at least one P-eventuality in the past. For (266), P is the property of climbing the Matterhorn:

(266) (#) Reto has climbed the Matterhorn

The reinterpretation operator that is called for here maps predicates P (of all aspectual classes) onto the telic predicate that introduces a change of state from there being no P-eventuality in the past to there being at least one such eventuality:

(267) $\lambda P \lambda e_{+\text{TEL}}.\text{BECOME}(\lambda e' \exists e''.P(e'') \wedge e'' < e')(e)$

This experiental reinterpretation is very often triggered by an incompatibility of the (semantically well-formed) literal reading of a telic predicate in the perfect with the context. E.g., if (266) is uttered in a context where Reto is introduced to someone at a cocktail party, the poststate of climbing the Matterhorn (being on top of the Matterhorn) obviously does not obtain, but reinterpreting (266) as an experiental perfect is a way out here: Stating that one is in the aftermath of a change of state from there being no previous eventuality of Reto's climbing the Matterhorn to there being at least one such eventuality, amounts to introducing Reto as someone who knows what it is like to climb the Matterhorn because he has done it at least once.[57]

Formally, (266) is interpreted by type coercion, the operator for the experiental perfect is inserted between the semantic contribution of the perfect and of the sentence radical *Reto climb- the Matterhorn*. The resulting constraint has a constructive solution that corresponds to the λ-term (268). This term eventually boils down to the property of succeeding an eventuality of Reto's climbing the Matterhorn:

(268) $\lambda e_{\text{-IB}}.\text{PERF}(\lambda e'_{+\text{TEL}}.\text{BECOME}(\lambda e'' \exists e_{+\text{TEL}}.\textbf{climb}'(\textbf{reto}', \textbf{matterhorn}')(e) \wedge e < e'')(e'))(e)$

[57] Depratere (1998) and Moens and Steedman (1988) discuss similar cases of the experiental perfect. Sometimes it reconciles conflicting aspectual properties of the perfect and its argument, as, e.g., in the perfect of the stative (i) [= (19)]:

(i) # Have you ever loved a woman?

This subsection explained the data in the field of type coercion for the perfect that centred on the distinction between telic predicates, which specify the aftermath of the members of their extensions, and atelic predicates, which do not.

3.2.5 Type coercion for temporal conjunctions

Type coercion is also frequent for temporal conjunctions. They have been investigated in particular for German in the work of Herweg (1990, 1991b). His analyses are also cast in a Davidsonian framework and emphasise the aspectual selection restrictions of these conjunctions. Type coercion for temporal conjunctions is illustrated with *until*. This conjunction is particularly interesting since it exerts aspectual selection restrictions on both its subordinate clause and the main clause that is modified by the *until*-clause.

The semantics of *until* is first introduced with a simple example that does not involve reinterpretation:

(269) Max was nervous until Ariadne arrived

(269) expresses the fact that Max's being nervous was terminated by Ariadne's arrival. This is reflected in the semantic representation of *until* in (270):

(270) $\lambda P \lambda Q \lambda e_{\text{-BD}} \exists e'_{\text{+BD}}.P(e') \wedge Q(e) \wedge e \supset\!\subset e'$

It maps a bounded predicate P and an unbounded predicate Q onto the set of eventualities in the extension of Q that *abut* onto an eventuality in the extension of P ('$\supset\!\subset$' expresses this relation). Two eventualities e and e' abut iff e precedes e' and is adjacent to it.[58]

The aspectual selection restrictions of *until* may give rise to type coercion, which is illustrated in the following sentences:

(271) a # Max checked his watch until Ariadne arrived

b # Max was nervous until Ariadne was here

c # Max checked his watch until Ariadne was here

In (271a), an iterative reinterpretation of the main clause predicate returns the preferred interpretation that Max checked his watch *repeatedly*. The subordinate clause is the target of reinterpretation in (271b): By an ingressive interpretation of the predicate *Ariadne be- here* one obtains a bounded predicate that is compatible with *until*. The resulting reading is that Ariadne's *arrival* terminated Max's nervousness. Finally, (271c) comprises both these reinterpretations.

[58]This representation of *until* neglects the question of whether the conjunction involves some proximality requirement. This would mean that the eventuality described in the semantics of the main clause must be placed within a preparatory eventuality of the eventuality as described in the semantics of the subordinate clause (see Herweg 1991b for a discussion of this requirement).

In the CLLS representation, the semantics of *until* is given as a labelled node variable that corresponds to the λ-term (270). Its type is $\langle\langle s_{+\text{BD}},t\rangle, \langle\langle s_{-\text{BD}} \sqcap_S \alpha,t\rangle,\langle s_\alpha,t\rangle\rangle\rangle$, i.e., the subordinate clause must be bounded, the main clause, unbounded. In addition, the whole construction (consisting of *until* and the two clauses) inherits the aspectual class of the main clause.

The semantic representation for sentence (271) is built by the syntax-semantics interface rule **(b19)**. Here S1 is the resulting complex sentence, S2, its main and S3, its subordinate clause:

(272)

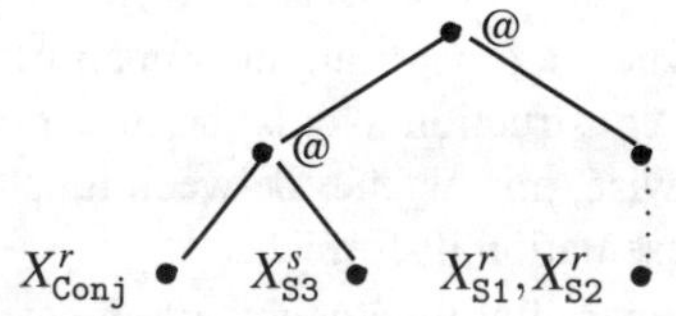

Note that this rule accesses the scopenode of the subordinate clause (X^s_{S3}). I.e., this clause is a scope island, non-indefinite quantifiers that are introduced by NPs in this clause cannot achieve wide scope over the conjunction. E.g., (273) is unambiguous, it cannot mean that for everyone, Max waited until he arrived:

(273) Max waited until everybody arrived

(b19) yields the semantic representation (274) for (271c). Here the semantic contribution of *check one's watch* is abbreviated by a labelled node variable (X_{15}) that corresponds to a property **CW**.

(274)

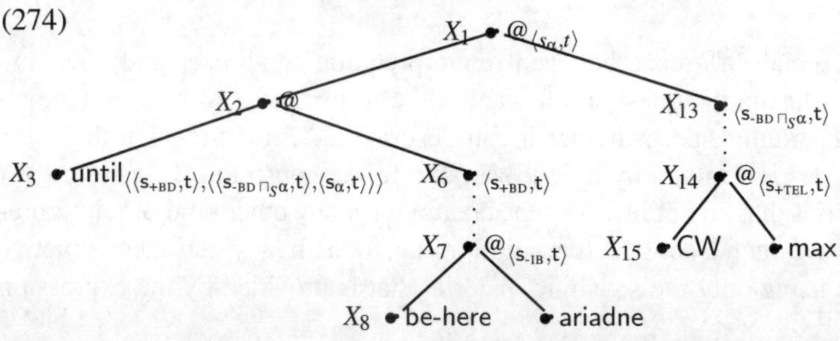

In this constraint, the semantic contributions of both clauses are not in the same fragment as the semantics of *until*. I.e., type coercion may – and in the case of (271c) must – affect either clause. (274) has no constructive solution since both the gap between X_6 and X_7 and the gap between X_{13} and X_{14} cannot simply be closed due to the types of the node variables involved. The types of X_6 and X_{13} are determined by the type of X_3 that is contributed by the conjunction.

3.3 Conclusion

At the end of this chapter, I will briefly summarise the proposed treatment of type coercion. Type coercion – as well as other kinds of reinterpretation – is a process in which the full meaning of a reinterpretation candidate is derived by enriching a well-formed but not yet fully determined (hence underspecified) result of semantic construction with material from extralinguistic sources. Since type coercion cases are semantically underspecified, they are described in terms of an *underspecification formalism*.

Formally, type coercion is modelled in the following way. At 'R-positions' (i.e., positions in semantic structures where a functor-argument pair might be affected by reinterpretation) semantic construction avoids the direct combination of functor and argument. Otherwise, mismatches between functor and argument could render the whole representation ill-formed.

Instead, the potentially conflicting material of functor and argument is separated in different fragments that are related only in terms of a connecting dominance relation. The resulting semantic representations are therefore constraints that consist of several fragments. From a different point of view, such a connecting dominance relation opens up a gap within a constraint on λ-structures.

Due to this gap between the fragments of functor and argument, any incompatibilities of type or sort between the two do not introduce contradictions into the resulting constraints. Semantic construction can therefore steer clear of conflicts of type or sort for reinterpretation candidates: It returns a non-contradictory constraint on λ-structures (i.e., a constraint that has a solution) for cases of reinterpretation as well as for cases that can be interpreted directly.

The crucial difference between reinterpretation candidates and other expressions lies in the question of whether the respective constraint has a *constructive* solution, i.e., whether it can describe a λ-structure such that each of its nodes is denoted by a node variable in the constraint. Constraints for expressions that do not involve type coercion (or any other kind of reinterpretation) have such a constructive solution. I.e., one already gets a constructive solution using only the semantic material that is provided by the expression itself.

But even for these cases it is important to introduce gaps at R-positions, since some cases of reinterpretation are enforced not by semantic mismatches between constituents of an expression but in order to make a (well-formed) expression fit in with conceptual knowledge or due to subsequent anaphoric references to entities introduced in the expression.

Except for these cases, constraints for expressions that need type coercion have no constructive solution. To turn them into constraints with such a constructive solution, additional information – in the form of further constraints – is needed. This information complements that provided by semantic construction. But, nevertheless, such constraints are not ill-formed structures that have to be 'repaired' in some way, but constraints that exhibit a specific kind of underspecification, i.e., have no constructive solution.

The gaps that are inserted at R-positions determine where this additional material is inserted to fully specify the meaning of the respective type coercion case. This material is to be contributed by extralinguistic sources. Thus, semantic construction strictly restricts itself to the semantic parts of such a meaning, which leaves enough space for extralinguistically derived material.

In this way, one can describe how reinterpretation operators that have been derived from extralinguistic knowledge sources are integrated into a semantic representation. As a consequence of this kind of modelling type coercion, constraints on tree structures do not express a partial order on a set of semantic components or 'building blocks' (the output of semantic construction). This distinguishes CLLS dominance relations from the subordination relations that hold between the parts of the semantic representation, e.g., in UDRT (Reyle, 1993).

Since the result of semantic construction leaves room for the integration of additional information, the integration of this information can be formalised as a monotonic process, which need not undo results of semantic construction. This monotonic addition of information models the resolution of the semantic underspecification introduced by reinterpretation. The specification may be only partial, which makes possible a treatment of reinterpretation in which various stages of resolution can be expressed.

The analysis of type coercion which was proposed in this chapter also took into account the cooccurrence of reinterpretation and quantifier scope. For type coercion in the case of *begin*-sentences, it correctly identified the scope relations between matrix verb and object NP; for cases where sortally triggered type coercion cooccurs with quantifier scope ambiguity, the analyses did not predict any unwanted readings.

To prevent overgeneration for the proposed analysis of type coercion, an exact determination of R-positions is indispensable. To this end, I adopted the basic strategy of associating specific syntactic constituent structures (e.g., AP-$\bar{\text{N}}$ structures) with R-positions. For each of these structures there may be a semantic mismatch between the constituents, the corresponding interface rule hence introduces a gap between their semantic contributions.

However, this strategy, while doing part of the job, does not yet cover all the data. Therefore, it was augmented by lexical means, i.e., the lexical entry for an expression may specify a certain reinterpretation potential for the expression. This augmentation allows the extension of my analysis to the 'ham sandwich' cases as well.

4

Landing Site Coercion

This chapter presents an analysis of the phenomenon of *landing site coercion* as introduced in the preceding sections. First the basic issues for an analysis of landing site coercion (LSC) are recapitulated. Section 4.1 is then devoted to LSC in the nominal domain. Here the groundwork of the analysis will be laid by investigating closely related phenomena within the realm of compositional semantics. Aspectual cases of landing site coercion will be treated in section 4.2.

The last section of this chapter broadens the perspective of the proposed treatment. The analysis of landing site coercion as expounded in this chapter is applied to a number of related issues, most prominent among them the representation of the so-called 'repetitive'/'restitutive' ambiguity of *again*-sentences. This shows on the one hand that landing site coercion is no isolated fringe phenomenon but closely related to other phenomena of natural language semantics. On the other hand, only if an analysis of LSC is extendable to related issues is it more than an ad hoc solution but provides deeper insights into the principles and mechanisms of semantic composition.

As in the preceding chapter, I will begin with a brief recapitulation of the phenomenon of landing site coercion as sketched in the introduction (0.1.5). This recapitulation will clothe the phenomenon in the underspecification formalism CLLS.

Landing site coercion is characteristically triggered by a mismatch between a functor and its argument in a functor-argument structure. To avoid this mismatch, the argument is augmented. This introduces a new part of the argument which fits the selection restriction of the functor and to which the functor may be applied alternatively (hence this additional part is often referred to as an alternative 'landing site' for the functor). Thus, an adequate analysis of LSC in the framework of underspecification should provide a semantic representation that does not fix in advance the position of a functor in a functor-argument structure. The functor may have scope over the argument as a whole or over only part of it.

The abstract schema for LSC as presented in the introduction can now be cast in the framework of CLLS: First, semantic construction returns a structure in which a functor and its argument (whose respective fragments are F and A) are both dominated by a common node variable X_0, but their scope is not determined (275a). The gap between X_0 and A is the position into which the reinterpretation operator is to be inserted (275b). This operator conjoins the argument with additional information that is given in two fragments Op_1 and Op_2 (separated by the gap between X_7 and X_8). It is inserted immediately above A, i.e., $X_5 = X_2$ (275c), finally, the hole in the functor fragment dominates the root of Op_2, which returns a dominance diamond similar to the ones encountered in the treatment of quantifier scope ambiguities (275d):

(275)

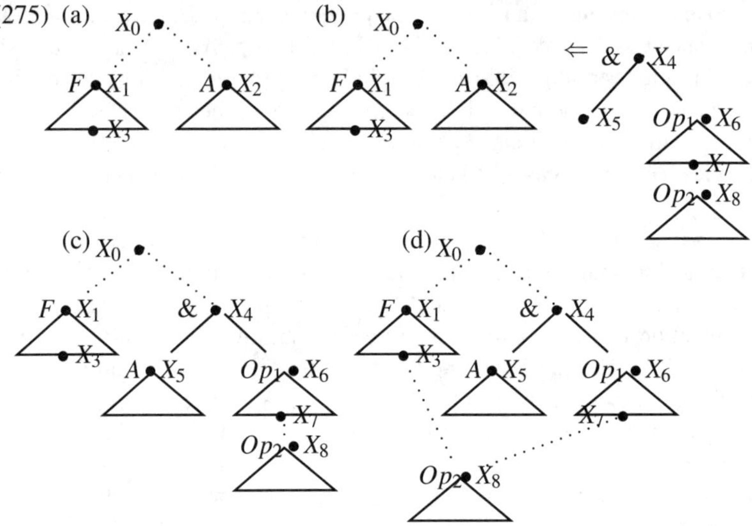

The issues noted for a satisfactory analysis of reinterpretation in the discussion of previous work on reinterpretation in chapter 1 apply to an account of LSC as well:

- the analysis provides well-formed representations for reinterpreted expressions
- it distinguishes linguistic and non-linguistic parts of the meaning of a reinterpretation candidate
- it describes the interaction of linguistic and non-linguistic knowledge in determining the full meaning of a reinterpretation candidate
- to avoid overgeneration, it delimits the range of reinterpretation possibilities it licenses

The last issue is particularly relevant for an analysis of landing site coercion. This can be illustrated with the LSC pattern of *aftermath modification*: To mediate the mismatch between the selection restriction of a durative adverbial (for an unbounded predicate) and the predicate it modifies, the notion of an aftermath is introduced into the semantics of the modified predicate (in the form of a stative predicate). The modifier can then pertain to this predicate. (276) [= (9)] (in the interpretation that Amélie left and her subsequent absence lasted for two hours) exemplifies aftermath modification:

(276) # Amélie left for two hours

(276) shows that LSC arises in modification structures, among them constituents that consist of a modifying adverbial and a modified sentence radical. This suggests that it is straightforward to determine – and to delimit – R-positions for LSC in the syntax-semantics interface by restricting them to modification structures. However, comparing (276) to the following examples shows that this strategy does not suffice on its own:

(277) a # Amélie played the sonata for two hours

b Amélie left yesterday

(277a) and (277b) have the same constituent structure as (276), in addition, they share the adverbial phrase and the modified sentence radical, respectively, with (276). Still, aftermath modification is not possible for either of them.

The case of the German durative adverbials as noted in section 1.5.1 illustrates the issue of delimiting the LSC potential of an expression more drastically. These adverbials come in two variants with the same meaning, either as a temporal NP in the accusative case, or as such an NP plus the adverbial *lang* 'long'. Examples are *einen Tag (lang)*, 'for one day' or *zwei Stunden (lang)*, 'for two hours'.

But only the variants without *lang* participate in LSC. E.g., only the first of the German translations of (276) in (278) can be interpreted in the sense of a two hours' absence of Amélie. In contrast, (278b) cannot undergo aftermath modification. Since a reinterpretation in terms of an iterative type coercion is highly unlikely, it is rated as ungrammatical.

(278) a # Amélie ging zwei Stunden weg
Amélie went two hours away
'Amélie went away for two hours'

b * Amélie ging zwei Stunden lang weg
Amélie went two hours long away
'For two hours, Amélie went away'

In sum, overgeneration is a serious problem for analyses of LSC. Even if one adopts the strategy of coupling LSC potential with specific syntactic constituent structures, this is only a first approximation that calls for further, more fine-grained (perhaps even lexeme-specific) techniques to block the prediction of unattested LSC interpretations.

4.1 Landing site coercion in the nominal domain

In this section, the formal analysis of landing site coercion is introduced with an investigation of the phenomenon of LSC in the nominal domain. After a recapitulation of the relevant LSC phenomena, the account of LSC starts with an analysis of the modification of agentive nouns (as in *fast typist*). This looks like a deviation – after all, modifying agentive nouns is not an instance of LSC in itself – but there are good reasons for the detour: Developing an analysis of this phenomenon will prove extremely useful for the proposed account of LSC, because of the similarity between this kind of modification and LSC. This strategy also focusses on the similarities between agentive modification and LSC without glossing over their distinctions.

Consider (279), a simple case of nominal landing site coercion. It has an in principle unlimited number of readings. While the reading that comes to mind immediately is 'road whose purpose is an activity that proceeds fast', i.e., road along which one can move fast, it was noted in section 1.5.3 that specific contexts (e.g., street cleaning, or post offices) may trigger other readings like 'road that can be cleaned fast' or 'road such that it does not take long to distribute the post in it'.

(279) # fast road

As an instance of landing site coercion, this expression has the following properties:

First, the landing site of the functor (the semantics of *fast*) is *variable*: It need not pertain to the argument (the semantics of *road*) as a whole but can be applied only to a suitable part of it. This part of the argument, however, is not determined lexically, it has been introduced by a coercion process. If the functor is applied to this part only, it may become embedded in the scope of a scope-bearer within the argument.

This variability can give rise to structural ambiguity: Since this embedded position of the functor within the argument is only an option, the functor might as well apply to the argument as a whole, in which case it would outscope the scope-bearer in the argument.

However, this potential ambiguity might be blocked by the properties of the involved functors and arguments. E.g., in the preferred reading of *fast road*, the functor may in principle appear within and without the scope of a (partial) functor PUR that maps entities onto their purpose (formalised as properties of eventualities). But the types of functor and argument immediately resolve this potential ambiguity because they bar an application of the functor to the argument as a whole.

Hence, in all readings of *fast road* the functor pertains to a part of the argument only. E.g., in the reading 'road whose purpose is an activity that proceeds fast' the only thing that is considered to be fast is the *activity* for which the road is used. This part of the argument is provided by an operator that augments the argument with information on a purpose. The core of this operator is the functor PUR. Another operator that might be used for the interpretation of *fast road* introduces the notion of a *task* that is associated with an entity in a given context (e.g., for the post office scenario).

Second, the representation that models this variability of the landing site for the functor is not wholly provided by semantic construction, but falls back upon *knowledge from extralinguistic sources* like conceptual knowledge. In particular, the additional landing site for the functor within the argument is not inherent in the argument, it is derived by a reinterpretation process that augments the argument.

This is the reason why the number of readings of (279) is not fixed. Its meaning is not fully specified by semantic construction, the part of the argument that provides a further landing site for the functor must be derived with the help of extralinguistic knowledge. These parts of the argument in (279) refer to certain aspects of roads.

But the semantics of *road* does not make explicit all these aspects of roads, like, e.g., the fact that roads may be associated with specific tasks. Even if one might argue that the purpose of a road should be part of the definition of *road*, the possibility of pertaining *fast* in (279) to a purpose of the road is just one of very many possibilities. This speaks against including reference to a purpose in the semantics of nouns like *road* and justifies analysing (279) as a case of reinterpretation.

Thus, the argument as provided by lexical semantics does not suffice, it must be augmented. For the reading 'road whose purpose is an eventuality that proceeds fast', the augmentation can be described as as intersection of the semantics of *road*, glossed here by '$\lambda x.\mathbf{road}'(x)$', with $\lambda x \exists P.\mathrm{PUR}(x,P)$, the property of having a purpose (purposes are characterised by a property of eventualities). The augmented argument is given in (280) (in prose, the set of roads with some purpose).

(280) $\lambda x.\mathbf{road}'(x) \wedge \exists P.\mathrm{PUR}(x,\underline{P})$

But to yield the desired reading for the semantics of *fast road* ('road whose purpose is fast'), the functor must apply only to the underlined part of the augmented argument (280), viz., the existentially quantified variable P that is the second argument of PUR:

(281) $\lambda x.\mathbf{road}'(x) \wedge \exists P.\text{PUR}(x, \lambda e.\mathbf{fast}'(e) \wedge P(e))$

The representation (281) specifies the result of LSC for the relevant reading of (279). The derivation of the representations for such LSC cases is the topic of the following subsections.

4.1.1 Modification of agentive nouns

I will now discuss the modification of agentive nouns (*agentive modification* for short). Due to the similarity of this kind of modification to landing site coercion, its description provides a good introduction to ideas and techniques that will be reused in the LSC account. Recall that in modification structures, the semantics of the modifier is a functor and the semantics of the modified element, the argument.

As an example of agentive modification, consider (282):

(282) fast typist

The meaning of agentive nouns is composed of the meanings of verb stem and of affix. Thus, if one paraphrases *typist* (roughly) as 'person who usually types', this meaning is composed in the following way:

(283) *typist*: $\underbrace{\text{'person who usually'}}_{\text{contribution of the affix}} \ \ldots \ \underbrace{\text{'types'}}_{\text{contribution of the stem}}$

Now the challenge of such examples lies in the observation that the modifier may pertain to the noun as a whole or to the verb stem only. The first case is trivial, it gives the reading 'fast person who usually types', but the second case is not. Here the reading is 'person who usually types fast'.

The meaning of agentive nouns is modelled with the generic operator GEN (see section 2.4.2). The semantic representation for *typist* is (284a), the set of individuals y such that when y participates in an eventuality e, e is usually a typing of y. This takes into account the fact that these nouns are not only used to refer to professions.

(284) a $\lambda x.\text{GEN}[y,e](y \ \mathbf{in} \ e \wedge y = x, \underline{\mathbf{type}'(y)(e)})$
b $\lambda P \lambda x.\mathbf{fast}'(x) \wedge P(x)$
c $\lambda x.\mathbf{fast}'(x) \wedge \text{GEN}[y,e](y \ \mathbf{in} \ e \wedge y = x, \mathbf{type}'(y)(e))$
d $\lambda x.\text{GEN}[y,e](y \ \mathbf{in} \ e \wedge y = x, \mathbf{fast}'(e) \wedge \mathbf{type}'(y)(e))$

The meaning of *fast* is given in (284b) (it maps properties of individuals P onto the intersection of P with the property of being fast), then the trivial reading of *fast typist* is (284c), the set of fast individuals who usually type. The interesting reading is modelled in (284d), here the modifier pertains to the underlined part of its argument (284a) only. The gloss is 'set of individuals who usually type fast'.

The reading in which the modifier pertains to the argument as a whole is less preferred than the other, hence, must be motivated by context. E.g., in the context of a race where some of the participants happen to be typists, (282) may be used to refer to someone who is a typist and who is running fast. Other examples show that the preference for the reading where only part of the agentive noun is modified varies in strength. Consider for instance *beautiful dancer*, where the preference of the reading 'someone who usually dances beautifully' over the reading 'someone who is beautiful and usually dances' is less pronounced.

This analysis is similar to that presented by Larson (1998) in that it attributes the ambiguity of agentive modification to the semantics of agentive nouns and to different attachment sites for the adjective. See section 1.5.4 for a discussion of Larson's proposal.

Agentive modification and LSC are *similar* in that they share the same kind of potential structural ambiguity: Agentive modification may cause a functor (the semantics of a modifier of an agentive noun) to pertain either to its argument (the semantics of this noun) as a whole or to only a suitable part of it. Thus, the functor may appear inside or outside the scope of an operator in the argument. For *fast typist*, this means that the functor may apply to the verb stem semantics or to the semantics of the noun as a whole. In the first case, it is inside the scope of the quantifier GEN, in the second case, it is not. This is the same pattern as expounded for *fast road* and its interpretation (281), where the functor could in principle appear inside or outside the scope of the operator PUR (if the second option were not directly ruled out by sortal incompatibility).

As will be shown in this section, this similarity is modelled in that in both agentive modification and LSC the eventual semantic representation takes the form of a *dominance diamond* as in the semantic representation of examples with scope underspecification, e.g., (146).

Schematically, the two diamonds are depicted in (285). For agentive modification (285a), the argument (the semantics of *typist*) contributes two fragments: The bottom fragment F_3 in this diamond is the verb stem semantics, it is in the scope of the functor fragment F_1 (the semantics of *fast*). The rest of the argument F_2 (the affix semantics, which comprises in particular the scope-bearing operator) and the functor are scopally underspecified; both dominate the embedded fragment F_3.

(285)

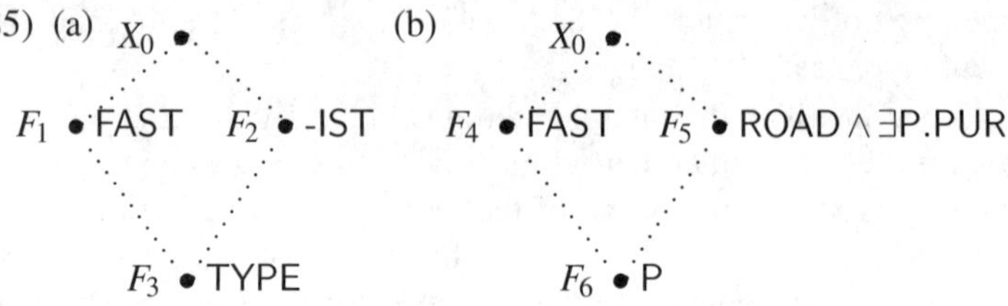

In the (b) diamond for LSC, fragment F_5 is the augmented semantic contribution of *road*, which includes the information that the road has a purpose P. The existentially quantified variable P constitutes the bottom fragment F_6, scope between the functor F_4 and F_5 is open.

So much for the similarity between agentive modification and LSC; the former *differs* from the latter in that the proper part of the argument to which the functor may alternatively apply is fixed right from the start: In the case of agentive nouns, this part is the semantic contribution of the verb stem that makes up the noun together with the nominalisation affix. This means that semantic composition already determines the range of possible readings, no recourse to extrasemantic knowledge is necessary. Therefore agentive modification is a phenomenon of compositional semantics.

This is different for LSC, even though the functor may pertain to only part of the argument in LSC cases, too: The part of the argument that provides an additional landing site for the functor is not fixed semantically. Its derivation crucially depends on extralinguistic knowledge, thus, the range of readings is not delimited by semantic construction.

I will now propose an account of agentive modification that brings out its similarities and differences to LSC. The difficult task for semantic construction is to obtain the underspecified semantic representations for the structural ambiguity that characterises agentive modification. If no coercion takes place here, this representation must be put together compositionally: The semantic representations of functor and argument and the interface rule that combines them are to be specified in such a way that the resulting constraint has two potential (constructive) solutions, one for each reading, e.g., for *fast typist*, the required solutions are the λ-structures that correspond to the λ-terms (284c) and (284d).

For the argument (here, the semantics of an agentive noun) this means that its constraint comprises two nonempty parts C_2 and C_3 that are connected by a dominance relation between two of its node variables X_4 and X_5. This dominance relation opens up a gap which makes C_3 an additional landing site for the semantics of specific modifiers like *fast*. The argument schema is given in (286).

(286)

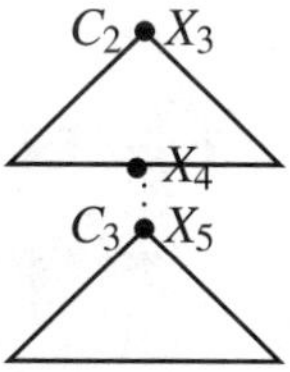

In a linguistic sign for such an agentive noun, the root X_3 of the constraint for its semantics is the value of the attribute CONT|TOPNODE (see section 2.3.2). I.e., the syntax-semantics interface rules can refer to it. In a similar fashion, the root X_5 of the embedded fragment C_3 should be accessible to the interface rules. To this end, a new attribute CONT|INTNODE (for 'internal node') is introduced into the CONT feature of a linguistic sign. Its value is the root of the dominated fragment X_5. If the semantics of a lexeme (e.g., *walk*) has no such twopartite structure, the value of CONT|INTNODE is not specified.

In constituent structures where an adjective modifies a noun, or an adverbial modifies a sentence radical, the interface rule may now address both the CONT|TOPNODE and the CONT|INTNODE value of the modified expression. In this way, it can relate the modifier fragment and the two fragments of the modified expression independently. In particular, it can give the modifier fragment scope over the embedded fragment of the modified expression but leave open the scope of the modifier fragment and the main fragment of the modified expression.

Semantic construction for these modification structures thus yields a dominance diamond like (287). Here fragment C_1 comprises the functor, X_5 is the CONT|INTNODE and X_3, the CONT|TOPNODE value of the argument. (287) is underspecified, as C_1 may be above or below C_2:

(287)

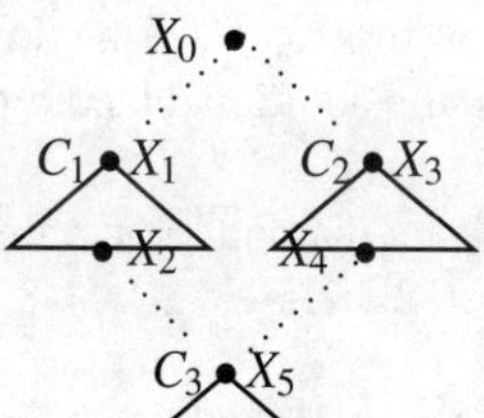

The two constructive solutions of this diamond can be derived just as in the case of scope ambiguities, they are (288a) and (288b):

(288) (a) 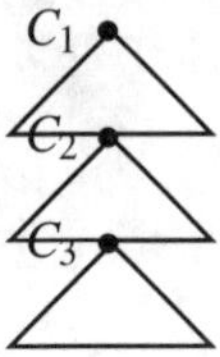

(b) 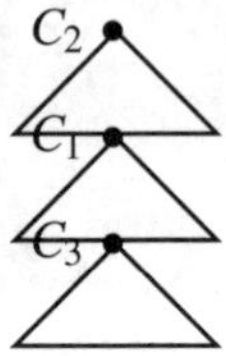

These two structures correspond to the two possibilities for the functor-argument combination in *fast typist*: The functor (modelled as part of C_1) may apply to the argument as a whole (C_2 and C_3), or to only a part of the argument (C_3). That is, the constraints of functor and argument together with the interface rule that combines them are sufficient for a compositional derivation of the ambiguity in the modification of agentive nouns.

This schema is now fleshed out with an account of the derivation of the semantics of *fast typist*. The constraint for the adjective is a node variable of type $\langle e,t\rangle$ with label fast, the one for the noun is (289):

(289) 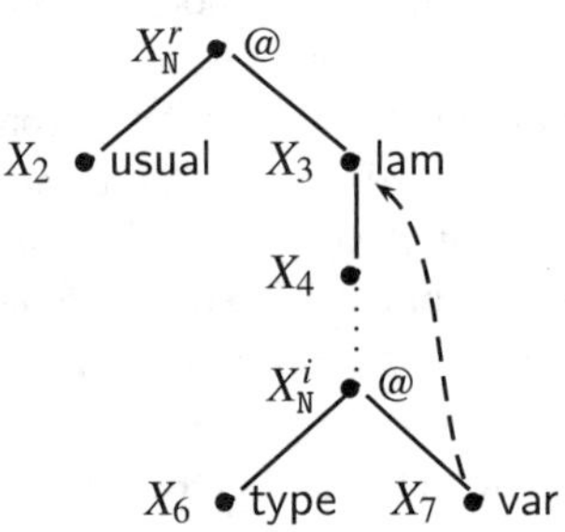

Here X_2 corresponds to the constant **usual**$'$ as defined in section 2.4.2. It abbreviates the generic quantification on eventualities:

(290) $\textbf{usual}' = \lambda P \lambda x.\text{GEN}[y,e](y\ \textbf{in}'\ e \wedge y = x, P(y)(e))$

The constructive solution of this constraint corresponds to (284a).[59] (289) says that the values of CONT|TOPNODE and CONT|INTNODE in the linguistic sign for *typist* are X_N^r and X_N^i, respectively. Thus, the additional landing site is the fragment below X_N^i.

The interface rule that constructs the dominance diamond structure (287) is a revised version of the rule **(b17)** from section 2.3.2:

[59]If different λ-structures (or constraints for them) correspond to η-equivalent λ-terms, the simplest one is chosen (see section 2.4.1). Thus, the λ-abstraction for the first argument of **usual**$'$ is not explicated in (289). (167) contrasts alternative constraints on λ-structures of different complexity for η-equivalent λ-terms.

(291) $[_{\bar{\mathrm{N}}}\ \mathrm{AP}\ \mathrm{N}]$ $\overset{(b17)}{\Rightarrow}$

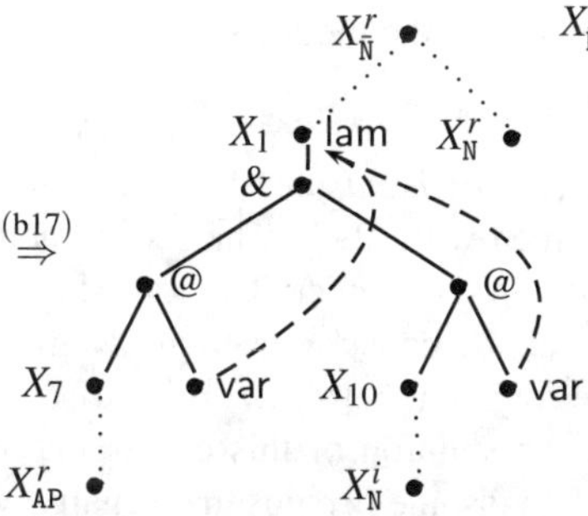

$X^s_{\bar{\mathrm{N}}} = X^s_{\mathrm{AP}} = X^s_{\mathrm{N}}$

This rule gives the fragment below X_1 scope over the embedded fragment of the argument (the one below X^i_{N}). The functor becomes a part of this fragment by identifying X_7 and X^r_{AP} (if there is no sortal mismatch between the node variables to bar this). The rule does not specify the scope between the fragment below X_1 and the main fragment of the argument (with root X^r_{N}). It presupposes that $X^r_{\mathrm{N}} \lhd^* X^i_{\mathrm{N}}$, which is fulfilled, e.g., in (289), the constraint for *typist*.

For *fast typist*, semantic construction results in the dominance diamond (292). The two constructive solutions of (292) correspond to the λ-terms for the two readings of *fast typist* (284c) and (284d).

(292)

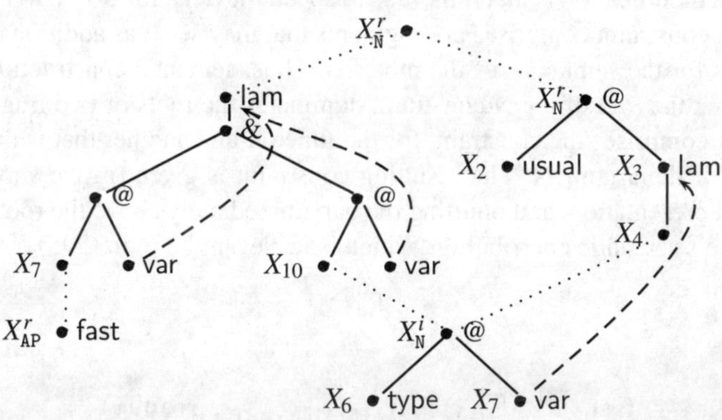

This strategy of anticipating the ambiguity of agentive modification in the syntax-semantics interface is complemented by the possibility of blocking the ambiguity lexically. This is needed for expressions like *handsome typist*, which do not exhibit the ambiguity of *fast typist*. This blocking is effected by an additional constraint in the semantics of adjectives like *handsome*: Its CONT|TOPNODE value (which is inherited to the AP as X^r_{AP}) is disjoint to a node variable X_b that dominates both the CONT|TOPNODE and

CONT|INTNODE values of the modified noun:[60]

(293) $X_b \lhd^* X^r_{\mathrm{N}} \wedge X_b \lhd^* X^i_{\mathrm{N}} \wedge X_b \perp X^r_{\mathrm{AP}}$

Thus, the semantics of *handsome typist* is (292) (with handsome as the label of X^r_{AP}) conjoined with (293). The second conjunct rules out the ambiguity inherent in the first conjunct: The lowest X_b that fulfills the conjoined constraints is X^r_{N}, i.e., the constraints entail $X^r_{\mathrm{AP}} \perp X^r_{\mathrm{N}}$. Thus, the left fragment must dominate the fragment below X^r_{N}, otherwise, X^r_{N} would dominate X^r_{AP}.[61] The sole constructive solution of this constraint corresponds to the λ-term (294) for the set of handsome persons that usually type. Thus, overgeneration is avoided for cases like *handsome typist.*

(294) $\lambda x.\mathbf{handsome}'(x) \wedge \mathrm{GEN}[y,e](y \;\mathbf{in}\; e \wedge y = x, \mathbf{type}'(y)(e))$

This concludes the account of the modification of agentive nouns. It has prepared the ground for the analysis of landing site coercion, which will be expounded in the next subsection.

4.1.2 The formal representation of landing site coercion

The representation of LSC is expounded for *fast road.* It resembles cases like *fast typist* in that the constraint for the functor (the adjective semantics) is related to that of the argument (the noun semantics) via the value of the CONT|INTNODE of the noun. The difference between the case of *fast road* and agentive modification is that *road* fails to specify a value for CONT|INTNODE, since its constraint comprises no fragments that may serve as additional landing sites for the semantics of the modifier. Thus, semantic construction only states that the root of the N̄ constraint dominates the roots of two fragments, one that comprises the constraint for the functor, and another that is the constraint for the argument. The resulting constraint is given (in the simplified CLLS representation, and omitting the gap immediately above the root of the adjective's semantic contribution, which is irrelevant here) in (295).

(295)

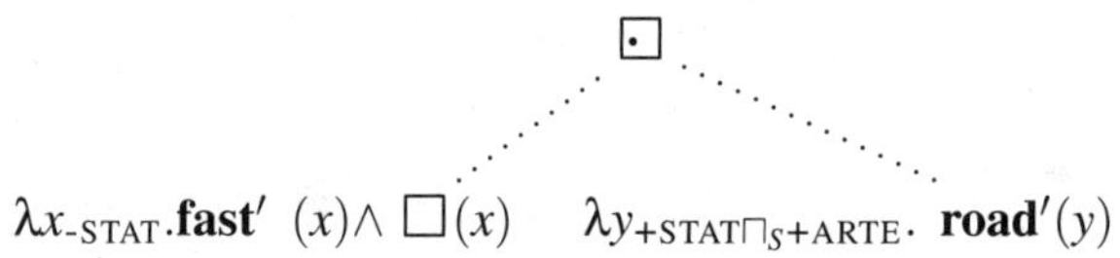

[60] This strategy presupposes that the values of X^r_{N} and X^i_{N} of the modified noun (its topnode and the root of its embedded fragment) are available for the adjective, e.g., via a syntactic feature like the MOD feature of HPSG (Pollard and Sag, 1994).

[61] The constraint cannot be expressed more directly as $X_{10} \lhd^* X^r_{\mathrm{N}}$: Since X_{10} is introduced by the interface rule (**b17′**), it cannot be referred to in the semantics of the adjective. The complexity of (293) is motivated by the fact that it will also be employed to characterise those adjectives that block LSC. For the case of *handsome typist* and the like, '$X^r_{\mathrm{AP}} \perp X^r_{\mathrm{N}}$' as a special case of (293) would have been sufficient.

(295) is well-formed but has no constructive solution, due to a sortal conflict between functor and argument. The functor selects for properties of entities with (im-)proper parts that may undergo some change (characteristically, a change of location), but the argument is a property of entities that have no such parts (see the discussion on p.47). This incompatibility is modelled by the sorts $\pm$STAT[ionary]. For eventualities, the distinction coincides with $\pm$IB: +IB is the meet of the sorts EV[entuality] and -STAT, hence, a subsort of -STAT. Analogously, +STAT $\sqcap_S$ EV = -IB. In prose: stationary eventualities are stative, non-stationary ones, interval-based. (The sorts that model the aspectual classes were introduced in section 2.2.3, see in particular (140).) The sort +ARTE stands for 'artefact'.

The constraint (295) can be augmented in terms of an LSC that bridges the sortal conflict. One can insert an operator directly above the argument that introduces an additional landing site for the functor. For (295), one of the possible augmentations is given in (296), it introduces the notion of purpose (in the form of a property of eventualities P). This property is not yet determined aspectually. The operator (296) is restricted to artefacts, as indicated by the sort on the λ-abstracted variable. The root of the dominated fragment in this operator fills in the missing value of CONT|INTNODE for the modified expression.

(296) $\lambda x_{+\text{ARTE}}.\Box(x) \wedge \exists P.\text{PUR}(x, \boxdot)$

$$P$$

After closing the gap above P, this constraint corresponds to a λ-term that denotes a set of artefacts with some property Q that have a purpose P. The reason for this underdetermination is that a hole in a λ-structure corresponds to all expressions in the λ-calculus that have the type specified by the hole (in (296), this type is $\langle e_{+\text{ARTE}}, t \rangle$).

Combining the two constraints (295) and (296) in such a way that the argument fills in the first hole of (296) yields the constraint (297):

(297)

$$\boxdot$$

$$\lambda x_{-\text{STAT}}.\ \textbf{fast}'(x) \wedge \boxdot(x) \quad \lambda x_{+\text{STAT}\sqcap_S+\text{ARTE}}.\textbf{road}'(x) \wedge \ \exists P.\text{PUR}(x, \boxdot)$$

$$P$$

Here the structural ambiguity is directly resolved; due to the sortal incompatibility between -STAT and +STAT$\sqcap_S$+ARTE the functor cannot dominate the argument as a whole. The sole constructive solution of (297) corresponds to the λ-term (298) for the set of roads whose purpose is an eventuality that proceeds fast. The type of the argument of **fast**′ is +IB, since P is a property of eventualities and -STAT$\sqcap_S$ EV = +IB.

(298) $\lambda x_{+\text{STAT}\sqcap_S+\text{ARTE}}.\mathbf{road}'(x) \wedge \exists P.\text{PUR}(x, \lambda e_{+\text{IB}}.\mathbf{fast}'(e) \wedge P(e))$

This analysis deliberately leaves open the exact nature of the purpose of the road (while Pustejovsky assumes that this purpose is invariably to drive on the road). It takes into account that roads may serve a different purpose in different contexts. Once again the reinterpretation operation is monotonic in that it *augments* an underspecified semantic representation as provided by semantic construction. Like the pattern of type coercion, it does not undo results of semantic composition.

However, lexemes like *red* block LSC, e.g., in (299):

(299) red car

Semantic construction returns (300) as the constraint for the semantics of (299). While this constraint has a constructive solution (with $X^r_{\text{N}} = X_{10}$), it does not by itself block LSC.

(300)

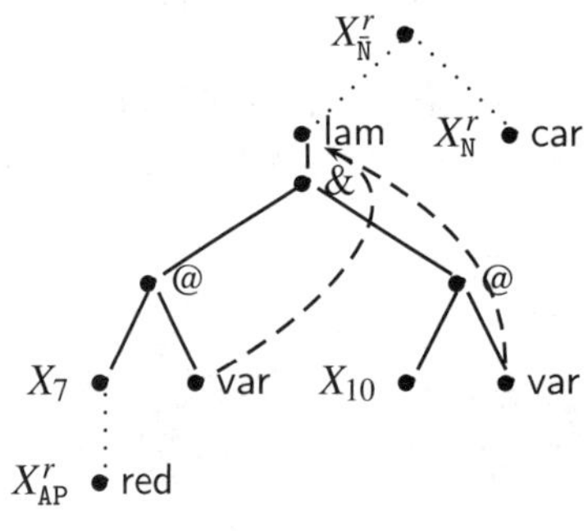

Thus, if the argument in (300) is augmented by a reinterpretation operator like (296), a dominance diamond as in (297) arises. For simplicity, the quantification over P is ignored in (301).

(301)

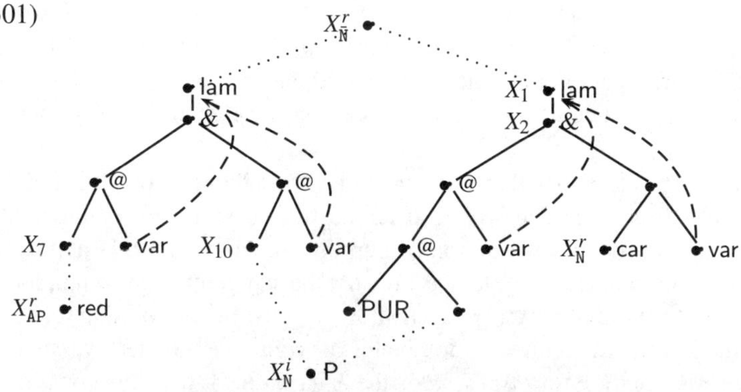

To block unwanted LSC for *red car* in structures like (301), the strategy against unwanted ambiguity for agentive modification (for *handsome typist* and the like) is reused. This provides a direct and efficient handle on the issue of control. I assume that *red* belongs to the adjectives that introduce the constraint (302) [= (293)] to block LSC.

(302) $X_b \lhd^* X^r_{\bar{\mathrm{N}}} \wedge X_b \lhd^* X^i_{\bar{\mathrm{N}}} \wedge X_b \perp X^r_{\mathrm{AP}}$

Because of (302) the additional landing site $X^i_{\bar{\mathrm{N}}}$ of the argument in (301) as introduced by (296) is not available for the constraint that comprises the functor, i.e., the left fragment dominates the right one in solutions of (301): Any X_b that dominates both $X^r_{\bar{\mathrm{N}}}$ and $X^i_{\bar{\mathrm{N}}}$ dominates X_2, and X^r_{AP} can thus only be disjoint from such an X_b if $X_{10} \lhd^* X_b$ and hence $X_{10} \lhd^* X_1$. The constraint (302) deliberately leaves open whether $X^r_{\bar{\mathrm{N}}}$ and $X^i_{\bar{\mathrm{N}}}$ are disjoint (as they are after LSC) or not (as in the case of agentive modification). Note that $X^r_{\mathrm{AP}} \perp X^r_{\bar{\mathrm{N}}}$ would have been too weak a constraint to bar the unwanted solution in (301).

But LSC must also be barred for cases in which the argument – and not the functor – disallows it. This case is exemplified by (303):

(303) fast comet

(b17′) returns for (303) the semantic representation (304) (in the simplified CLLS notation), in analogy to the case of *fast road* above.

(304)

Since this kind of constraint was shown to be the input for LSC, there is the danger of applying LSC for *fast comet* as well. It is the task of appropriately modelled lexical entries of nouns like *comet* to indicate that they disallow the kind of LSC that makes reference to the purpose of an entity as it was employed for *fast road*. Formally, this is effected by subsuming the sort of the λ-abstracted variable in the representation of *comet* under -ARTE. This states that comets are not artefacts. The additional subsumption under -STAT models the fact that comets are nonstationary objects that do undergo changes of location.

This typing determines that *fast comet* disallows the kind of LSC that was possible for *fast road*: The typing of the abstracted variable in the operator (296), which introduces the notion of purpose, specifies that it is applicable for expressions that refer to artefacts only. At the same time, the compatibility of the sorts -STAT and $\text{-STAT}\sqcap_S\text{-ARTE}$ allows a constructive solution for (304) where the left fragment directly dominates the right one. I.e., the eventual semantic representation for *fast comet* is the λ-term (305), which is not derived by LSC like (297).

(305) $\lambda x_{\text{-STAT}\sqcap_S\text{-ARTE}}.\mathbf{fast}'(x) \wedge \mathbf{comet}'(x)$

Finally, LSC in the nominal domain also comprises cases of pragmatic coercion where reinterpretation takes place but cannot be explained on semantic grounds. The following example, whose literal reading is semantically well-formed, may nevertheless undergo reinterpretation:

(306) (#) fast car

Its literal reading is 'car that is moving fast'. However, in many contexts, no cars are moving fast, and the expression is attributed to cars that are not moving fast, which is incompatible with its literal reading.

Landing site coercion for (306) is the same as the one for *fast road* (297). The only difference to the case of *fast road* is that the reinterpretation is not triggered by impending sortal mismatches. The reinterpretation yields the reading 'car whose purpose is fast driving'.

So far, the examples presented have involved only modified expressions whose semantic representation is simple in that it consists of one single fragment only. But modified expressions might have a semantic representation that consist of several fragments that are *not* available as additional landing sites for the semantics of a modifier.

Schematically, the constellation is depicted in a constraint like (292), except that the embedded fragment A_2 of the argument constraint is not an additional landing site, hence, its root does not appear as the value of a CONT|INTNODE feature and is not dominated by the fragment F that comprises the constraint for the functor. The resulting structure is (307), where X_6 stands for the CONT|INTNODE value of the argument:

(307)

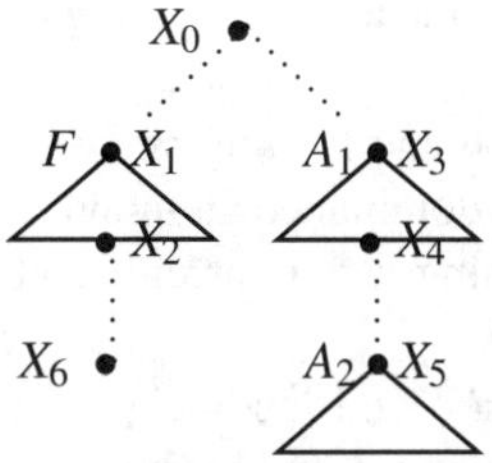

As it stands, (307) cannot rule out the possibility of inserting F below A_1 and above A_2, even if A_2 is not a landing site for a functor. The result of semantic construction for (308) (the constraint for the noun semantics is (223)) instantiates this schema, here, $X^r_{\bar{N}}$ corresponds to X_0, A_1 consists of X^r_N only ($X^r_N = X_3 = X_4$), and A_2 is made up exclusively of X_{11} ($X_5 = X_{11}$):

(308) # fast ham sandwich

(309)

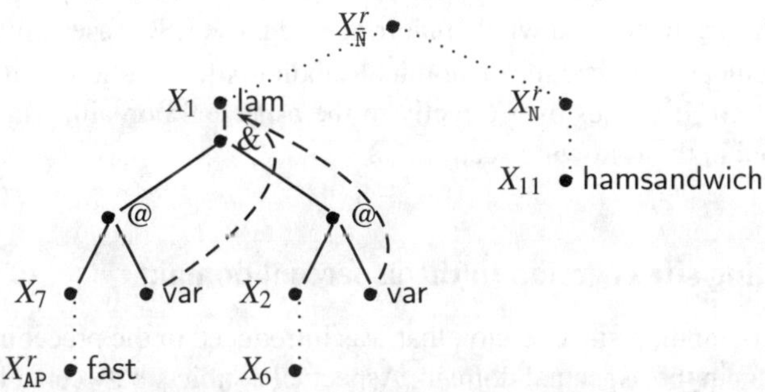

The gap between X^r_N and X_{11} can only be used for the purposes of type coercion (see section 3.1.2). To prevent the fragment below X_1 from being inserted in this gap, one must add an explicit statement that the hole in the embedding fragment (X_4 or X^r_N, respectively) does not properly dominate the CONT|INTNODE value (X_6). This calls for an extension of the underspecification formalism; see Koller and Niehren (2000) for further motivation of such an extension.

Note that this statement is compatible with LSC for (308) in analogy to (297), the resulting interpretation would be 'ham sandwich which is to be eaten fast' (i.e., whose purpose is fast). Here X^r_N and X_6 would be disjoint. The statement is also compatible with a type coercion interpretation of (308) as in (221), which inserts additional material between X^r_N and X_{11}, but combines the constraints of AP and N directly as for (303). Here the interpretation would be 'fast-moving ham sandwich consumer'; X_6 would be identical to X^r_N.

To sum up, attributing LSC to lexical semantics in the way proposed in this section reuses the largest part of the analysis that was introduced for agentive modification. This brings out the similarities and differences between LSC and agentive modification and provides a direct means for avoiding overgeneration for reinterpretation analyses.

The similarity between agentive modification and landing site coercion is modelled in that both phenomena give rise to a dominance diamond structure that directly models the variability in positioning a functor either above or within its argument.

The difference between agentive modification and landing site coercion is captured in that, first, the characteristic structural ambiguity is regarded as the *result of semantic construction* for agentive modification cases, while for LSC cases it is attributed to the *result of a further augmentation* of the constraint provided by semantic construction. This models the fact that cases of agentive modification have a fixed set of readings whereas LSC cases have an in principle unlimited number of readings. Second, the potential ambiguity as represented by the dominance diamond is resolved immediately in most LSC cases, since it was the very fact that the functor may not be directly applied to the argument as a whole that triggered these LSC cases initially.

This concludes the account of nominal landing site coercion in the proposed approach. It carries over directly to the aspectual domain, which will be expounded in the following section 4.2.

4.2 Landing site coercion in the aspectual domain

The pattern of landing site coercion that was introduced in the preceding section reappears in the aspectual domain. Aspectual conflicts between a functor and its argument can be resolved not only by type coercion but also by pertaining the functor to only a suitable part of the argument, i.e., by landing site coercion. These aspectual instances of LSC are the topic of this section.

The conceptual foundation and restriction of the pattern of LSC uses the tripartite event structure ('nucleus') in the form presented in section 1.6.3. I.e., eventualities can have preparatory eventualities and aftermaths or poststates associated with them. LSC operators must refer to one of these, which prevents unwanted proliferation of LSC readings. As in the nominal domain, extrasemantic knowledge about specific types of eventualities and their potential preparatory eventualities and aftermaths is needed to derive the appropriate LSC operators.

The pattern of aspectual landing site coercion reappears in other linguistic phenomena. Hence, an appropriate description of aspectual LSC will be of use for additional, seemingly unrelated issues like the repetitive and the restitutive interpretation of *again*-sentences and the modification of indefinite pronouns as in *everyone in this room*. These other issues are discussed in section 4.3.

4.2.1 Landing site coercion for durative adverbials

The prime instance of landing site coercion in the aspectual domain is to be found in the modification of predicates by durative adverbials (DA) like *for two hours*. Recall that these adverbials impose an aspectual selection restriction of unboundedness on predicates they modify. The aspectual class of the resulting predicate is intergressive, since the DA has a bounding effect but does not introduce a change of state.

Hence, (310) [= (250)] need not be reinterpreted, since *Charlotte sing-* is an unbounded predicate. In contrast, the durative adverbials in (311) [= (251)] and (312) modify bounded predicates, which calls for reinterpretation. (311) undergoes type coercion: The resulting reading is iterative; it talks about a whole *series* of flashings. For (312), both landing site coercion (LSC) and type coercion are available.

(310) Charlotte sang for two hours

(311) # The light flashed for two hours

(312) # Amélie went to Oxford for two years

Let us ignore the type coercion interpretations of examples like (311) or (312) for a while (until p.166). Then the intuition regarding the meaning of examples like (312) is this: The DA does not pertain to the argument as a whole (it does not measure the length of Amélie's going to Oxford) but only to that part of the argument that specifies the *aftermath* of her trip to Oxford, viz., her stay there.

My claim that this aftermath modification of (312) is an instance of landing site coercion is based on observations like the following. First, (the sentence radical of) (312) as a whole is a telic predicate like *Amélie go- to Oxford*. This is illustrated by the fact that this reading of (312) specifies an aftermath in the same way as *Amélie go- to Oxford*, which shows up in the perfect version of (312):

(313) # Amélie has gone to Oxford for two years

(313) denotes the set of all eventualities that last for two years and are the aftermath of Amélie's going to Oxford. I.e., this sentence entails that at the moment of utterance, Amélie is staying in Oxford.

This shows that the aftermath modification of (312) cannot be derived by applying the semantics of the durative adverbial to its argument (the semantics of *Amélie go- to Oxford*) as a whole. In that case, the resulting predicate would have to be intergressive, i.e., it would not specify an aftermath in its semantics.

Second, the intuition is that the aftermath modification of (312) returns a property of eventualities that need not have a length of two years themselves, analogously to the intuition about *fast road*, whose semantics was a property of things that are not themselves fast. This is illustrated by sentences like (314):

(314) # Amélie moved to Oxford for two years in two days

The time frame adverbial *in two days* limits the duration of Amélie's move itself to a maximum of two days, hence, the temporal information of the durative adverbial cannot likewise pertain to the move but must make reference to another eventuality.

The semantics of DA assumed in the proposed analysis is given in the λ-term (315):

(315) $\lambda P \lambda e_{\mathrm{INTER}}.\mathrm{PH}(\lambda e'_{\mathrm{-BD}}.P(e'), \mathbf{2yrs'})(e)$

The core of (315) is the notion of 'P-quantity' as defined in section 2.4.2. $\mathrm{PH}(P, \mathbf{2yrs'})(e)$ holds iff there is an e' such that $P(e')$ and e and e' coincide spatiotemporally, and an appropriate measure function determines the temporal duration of e as two years. Then (315) can be glossed as a function that maps unbounded properties of eventualities P onto the (intergressive) property of being such a P-quantity (the property of having a length of two years and spatiotemporally coinciding with an eventuality in the extension of P).[62]

In CLLS the semantics of *for two years*, which corresponds to (315), looks like (316) (recall that the simpler CLLS constraint is preferred out of two constraints that correspond to different yet η-equivalent λ-terms, see section 2.4.1). The aspectual impact of the DA is modelled in the type of its topnode $X^r_{\mathtt{Adv}}$:

(316)

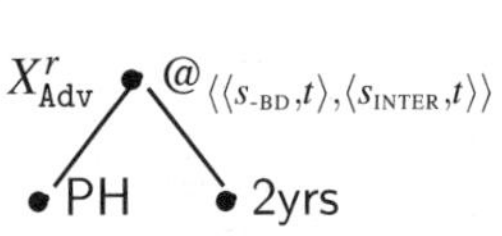

The next building block of my analysis is a syntax-semantics interface rule that relates the semantics of a DA and of the sentence radical it modifies. The strategy of introducing LSC potential in the syntax-semantics interface, which was used in the proposed analysis of LSC in the nominal domain, will

[62]The complexity of this representation emerges invariably as soon as one assumes a sortal distinction (in terms of incompatible sorts) somewhere between stative predicates and bounded predicates. For instance, Krifka (1989) and Dölling (1998) distinguish stative predicates as properties of *states* from intergressive predicates as properties of *events*. Galton (1984) and Herweg (1991b) model unbounded predicates as properties of *times* and bounded predicates, as properties of *events*.

For all such approaches, modifying a stative predicate by a DA involves mapping from a property of entities of one sort onto properties of entities of another sort that is incompatible with the first sort. This calls for an analysis of DA as a non-intersective modifier (see, e.g., the analyses of Herweg 1991b and de Swart 1998).

once again be employed for aspectual LSC. To this end, I adopt a new version **(b20′)** of the interface rule **(b20)**:

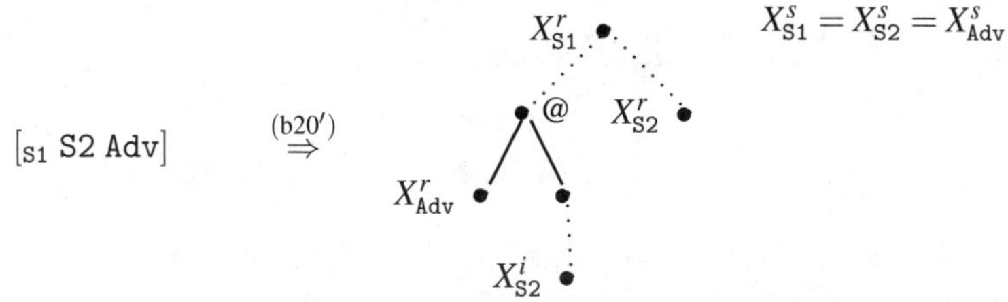

Like rule **(b17′)**, this rule relates the semantics of the functor to the CONT|INTNODE value of the argument (here, $X^i_{\mathtt{S2}}$). $X^r_{\mathtt{S1}}$, the root of the constraint for the constituent as a whole, dominates the roots of the fragments of both subconstituents.

Semantic construction for LSC examples in the aspectual domain follows the pattern described for nominal LSC. The argument fails to specify the value of CONT|INTNODE, hence, semantic construction cannot directly relate functor and argument, it only specifies that the root of the new constraint dominates them both.

For example (312), the resulting constraint is (317). Here the semantics of the modified expression is considerably simplified (to a node variable labelled by gtO) to enhance readability:

(317)

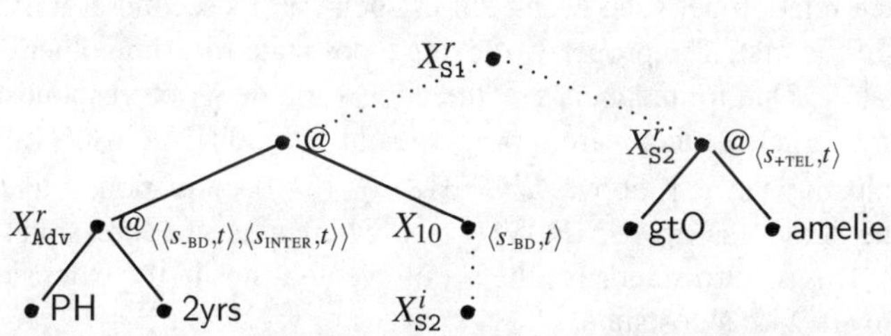

This structure has no constructive solution, where $X_{10} = X^r_{\mathtt{S2}}$, due to the conflicting aspectual requirements of functor and argument: The type of $X^r_{\mathtt{Adv}}$ determines the type of X_{10} as $\langle s_{\text{-BD}}, t\rangle$, which is incompatible with the type of $X^r_{\mathtt{S2}}$.

Landing site coercion can be used to obtain a solution of the constraint. It augments the argument in (317) with an additional landing site for the functor. The LSC operator for (317) is (318) in the abbreviated, and (319) in the full CLLS notation:

(318) $\lambda e_{+\text{TEL}}.\square(e) \wedge \exists e'.\ \boxdot\ (e')$

$\lambda e''_{\text{-IB}}.\ \text{POST}(e,e'')$

(319)

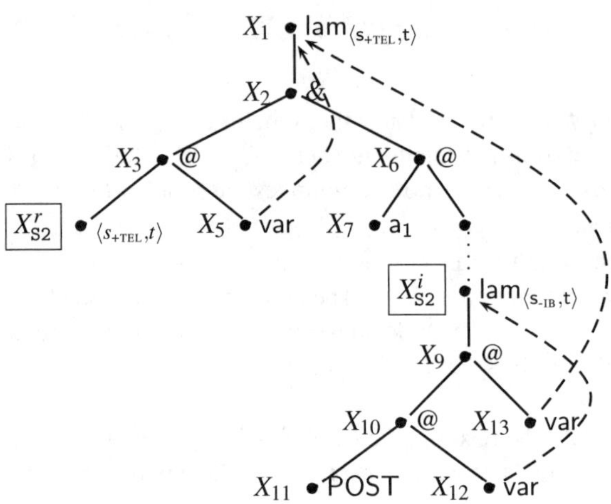

The operator introduces the notion of aftermath: X_{11} corresponds to POST, a two-place relation between eventualities such that its second argument is a poststate of the first. The property of being a poststate for some other eventuality is stative. Due to its label 'a_1', the node variable X_7 corresponds to the λ-term $\lambda P \exists x.P(x)$, a functor from properties of individuals to truth values.

After closing the gap above X^i_{S2}, (318) or (319) corresponds to any λ-term of the kind $\lambda e.\varphi(e) \wedge \exists e'.\text{POST}(e,e')$, where φ is an expression of type $\langle s_{+\text{TEL}}, t\rangle$. This λ-term stands for the set of eventualities in the extension of a telic predicate with a poststate.

This operator is only applicable to arguments that refer to eventualities which are conceptually linked to a poststate. This is only the case for telic predicates, which give information on this poststate in their semantics. This restriction is modelled by the sort $\langle s_{+\text{TEL}}, t\rangle$ for X_1 in (319) (it is propagated down to X^r_{S2}).

The boxed node variables indicate how (319) is integrated with (317): They are the variables that are to be identified with the topnode and the intnode (i.e., the CONT|TOPNODE and the CONT|INTNODE value) of the argument in (317), which returns (320):

(320)

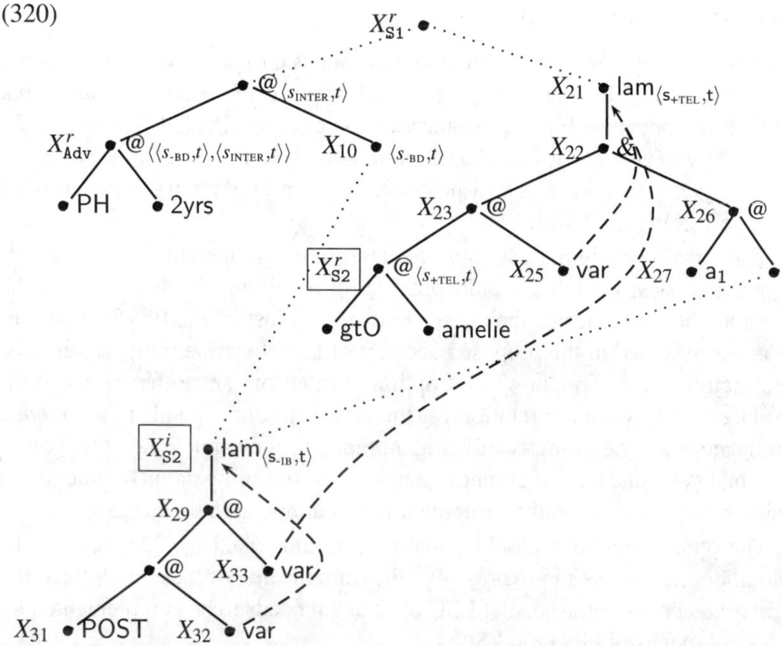

The abbreviated representation of (320) is (321):

(321)

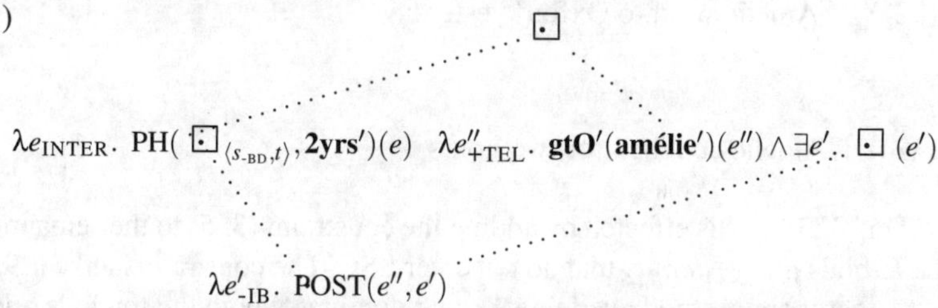

There is no ambiguity in this structure due to the aspectual selection restrictions: In the only constructive solution of (320)/(321), the left fragment immediately dominates the bottom fragment, with the right fragment dominating everything else. This solution corresponds to the λ-term (322), which denotes the set of events of Amélie's going to Oxford whose poststate lasted two years:

(322) $\lambda e''_{+TEL}.\mathbf{gtO}'(\mathbf{amélie}')(e'') \wedge$
$$\exists e'_{INTER}.PH(\lambda e_{-IB}.POST(e'', e), \mathbf{2yrs}')(e')$$

Hence, the conclusion is that the proposed account of LSC allows the derivation of the semantics of the aftermath modification of (312).

The issue of overgeneration

At this point, the analysis sketched for (312) begs the question of how to avoid overgeneration. There are two potential cases of overgeneration for aspectual LSC. First, one must block a reinterpretation of cases like (312) in terms of a *preparatory eventuality*, i.e., an interpretation where the time frame adverbial *for two years* pertains not to a poststate but to a preparatory eventuality of Amélie's going to Oxford.

This case is problematic because a reinterpretation operator that introduces a preparatory eventuality would provide an additional landing site for the functor (the semantics of the durative adverbial) just like (319). Such an operator is assumed in the proposed account of LSC for time frame adverbials, see section 4.2.2. This unwanted option is ruled out since the fragment introduced by this reinterpretation for the argument corresponds to a *bounded* predicate (viz., the property of being a preparatory eventuality of some other eventuality), hence, is no potential landing site for an operator fragment that can directly dominate only a fragment for an unbounded predicate.

The other potentially troublesome case is illustrated in (323) and (324): Modifiers as well as the expressions they modify may block LSC, thus, the proposed account of aspectual LSC once again needs to be complemented by a lexical means of blocking LSC:

(323) Amélie went to Oxford yesterday

(324) # Amélie coughed for two hours

For (323), this is effected by adding the constraint (325) to the semantics of adverbials like *yesterday* that do not enter LSC. The constraint is like (293): It says that there is a node variable X_b that dominates both the topnode and the scopenode of the modified `S2` and is disjoint to the modifying `Adv`'s topnode:

(325) $X_b \lhd^* X^r_{\mathtt{S2}} \wedge X_b \lhd^* X^i_{\mathtt{S2}} \wedge X_b \bot X^r_{\mathtt{Adv}}$

The semantics of *yesterday* is a labelled node variable that corresponds to the λ-term $\lambda P \lambda e.P(e) \wedge \mathbf{time}'(e) \sqsubseteq \mathbf{yesterday}'$, i.e., it intersects properties of eventualities with the property of having a temporal extension that is part of yesterday.

Due to (325), the adverbial *yesterday* always pertains to its modified VP as a whole, even if the VP were augmented by an LSC as in (320). In this case, the constraint would look like this:

(326)

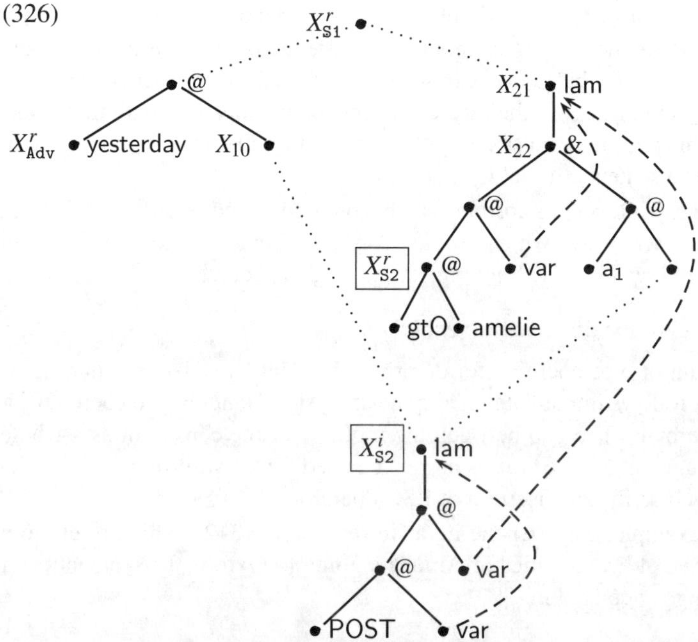

The blocking of LSC works in analogy to the case of (299): Any X_b can only dominate both X^r_{S2} and X^i_{S2} and still be disjoint to X^r_{Adv} in a solution of (326), if $X_{10} \lhd^* X_b$, and, since $X_b \lhd^* X_{22}$, $X_{10} \lhd^* X_{21}$.

For (324), blocking of LSC works through the type of the involved argument: The operator (319) only applies to telic arguments, but the semantics of *Amélie cough-* is an intergressive predicate. Thus, the verb lexically determines that its projections disallow LSC as in (321).

In sum, the difference in interpretation between (312) on the one hand and (323) and (324) on the other hand can be captured by the strategy of associating specific constituent structures, among them adverbial modification of sentence radicals, with LSC potential, and complementing this strategy with lexeme-specific blocking mechanisms that prevent overgeneration of LSC.

Yet another twist to the issue of controlling aspectual LSC follows from Hitzeman's (1993, 1997) analysis of temporal adverbials. She assigns durative adverbials in sentence-initial position the additional information that the temporal entity measured by the DA starts at the moment of utterance. Consequently, LSC for sentences with a sentence-initial DA in the future tense should be ruled out, e.g., (327):

(327) * For two hours, Amélie will go to the pub

LSC as in the case of (312) would impose conflicting requirements on the interpretation of (327): In a simple temporal semantics, the future tense indicates that Amélie's going cannot start before the moment of utterance and hence extends into the future. Consequently, the aftermath (her being in the pub) starts somewhere in the future. But this is incompatible with the condition that this aftermath must start at the moment of utterance, since its length is given by a sentence-initial DA.

Most of my informants corroborate this prediction and refuse an LSC reading for such sentences, which provides additional evidence for the proposed analysis of cases like (312) in terms of landing site coercion.

Type coercion for durative adverbials

The account of type coercion for durative adverbials was deferred until now, because it follows immediately from the analysis of landing site coercion for these adverbials: The gap between the root X^r_{S1} of the constraint as a whole and the fragment for the argument may be used for the insertion of TC operators as well as for the insertion of LSC operators.

As an example, consider the iterative reading of (312), which refers to a whole series of eventualities of Amélie's going to Oxford. The semantics of this reading is depicted in (328):

(328)

$$\boxdot \qquad \Leftarrow \lambda e_{\text{PROC}}.\text{ITER}(\square)(e)$$

$$\lambda e_{\text{INTER}}.\text{PH}(\square_{\langle s\text{-BD},t\rangle}, \mathbf{2yrs}')(e) \qquad \lambda e_{+\text{TEL}}.\mathbf{gtO}'\cdot(\mathbf{amélie}')(e)$$

The left hand side constraint in (328) is (317), the result of semantic construction for (312). The right hand side constraint is the iterative operator that mediates between the conflicting aspectual properties of functor and argument. It accepts arguments of any aspectual class and returns a process predicate. The core of the iteration operator is the relation ITER as defined in section 2.4.2.

Augmenting (317) as in (328) returns a constraint with a constructive solution that corresponds to the λ-term (329):

(329) $\lambda e_{\text{INTER}}.\text{PH}(\lambda e'_{\text{PROC}}.\text{ITER}($
$$\lambda e_{+\text{TEL}}.\mathbf{gtO}'(\mathbf{amélie}')(e))(e'), \mathbf{2yrs}')(e)$$

This λ-term stands for the set of eventualities of two years' length that are spatiotemporally coextensive to an iteration of eventualities of Amélie's going to Oxford.

After this account of LSC and TC for durative adverbials, the next section is devoted to LSC for time frame adverbials.

4.2.2 Landing site coercion for time frame adverbials

The second group of potential candidates for landing site coercion in the aspectual domain are cases of modification by time frame adverbials like *(with)in five minutes*. I will first analyse reinterpretations that involve time frame adverbials (TFA) whose head is *within* as instances of LSC. Since the discussion of reinterpretation for TFA usually centres around TFA whose head is *in*, the choice of *within*-TFA will then be explained by showing that *in*-TFA do not suggest themselves as prime examples of reinterpretation phenomena, as their semantics is more involved than is often assumed.

Time frame adverbials whose head is *within*

Analysing specific interpretations of expressions that comprise *within*-TFA in terms of LSC is motivated by expressions like (330)-(332):

(330) # I will be in my office within three hours

(331) # Max ran within five minutes

(332) (#) Max built a house within five months

(330) means that the speaker's presence in his office starts some time within the next three hours (but has not started yet), (331) has a reading that the running started after five minutes. I.e., the TFAs do not measure the length of the eventuality argument of the sentence radicals they modify but specify how long it takes *until* the presence/the running starts. (332) can (but need not) be interpreted in a similar fashion, which results in an ambiguity: The building may have lasted (up to) five months, or may have started after (up to) five months.

These readings, where the TFA indicates how long it takes until an eventuality sets in, are called 'pre-readings'. They can be explained in terms of an aspectual selection restriction of *within*-time frame adverbials: They modify only bounded predicates, hence, the modification of the unbounded *I be- in my office* and *Max run-* by such a TFA calls for reinterpretation. One possibility here is a landing site coercion that introduces the notion of a *preparatory eventuality*. The modifier may then pertain not to its argument as a whole but only to the newly introduced part of the argument that specifies the preparatory eventuality. This explanation provides a formalisation of the intuitions of Moens and Steedman. As (332) shows, this reinterpretation is optional if a bounded predicate is modified by a TFA.

The semantics for TFA like *within five minutes* is the following:

(333) $\lambda P \lambda e_{\alpha}.\mathrm{DUR}(\lambda e'_{+\mathrm{BD}\sqcap_S \alpha}.P(e'), \mathbf{5min}')(e)$

Recall that $\lambda e.\mathrm{DUR}(P, \mathbf{5min}')(e)$ is the set of eventualities in the extension of P with a duration of (at least) five minutes. The sorts indicate that the operator is only applicable to bounded predicates; the aspectual class of the argument is propagated to the result of the application of the operator.

In CLLS, the semantics of *within five minutes* is given by the following constraint, which corresponds to (333). The aspectual selection restriction shows up in its type:

(334)

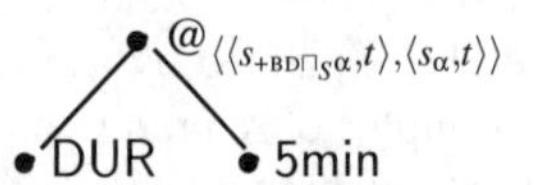

As in the case of durative adverbials, rule **(b20′)** builds the constraint for a constituent that consists of a *within*-TFA and the expression it modifies. This rule introduces LSC potential in that it relates the semantics of the functor to the CONT|INTNODE of the argument. E.g., the result of semantic construction for (331) is (335):

(335)

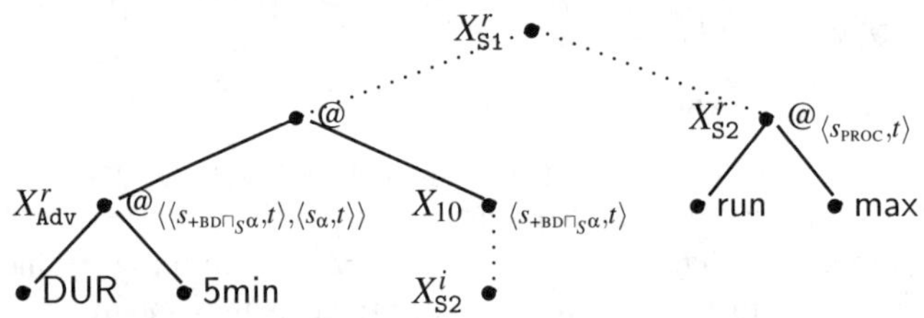

This constraint has the same structure as (317) above. It also has no constructive solution, since the types of functor and argument bar equating X_{10} and $X^r_{\mathtt{S2}}$.

The LSC operator that is needed for these TFA cases is given in the constraint (336a), its abbreviated version, by (336b). Since the derivation of these pre-readings by means of LSC works in close analogy to the derivation of aftermath readings for durative adverbials, the analyses are only presented in the abbreviated CLLS version after (336a):

(336) (a)

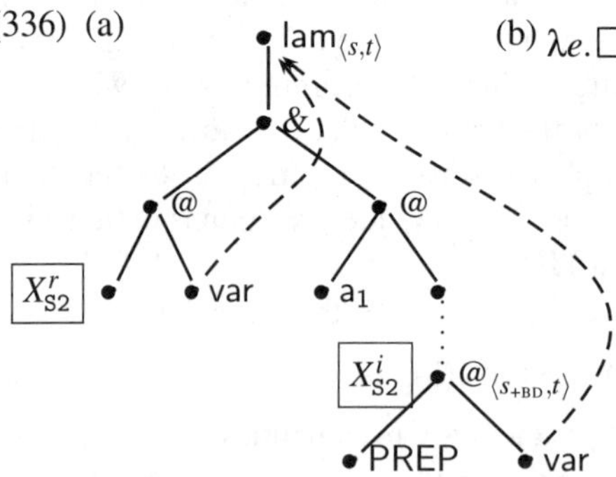

(b) $\lambda e.\Box(e) \wedge \exists e''.\ \boxdot\ (e'')$

$\lambda e'_{+\mathrm{BD}}.\ \mathrm{PREP}(e',e)$

PREP is a two-place relation between eventualities such that its first argument is a preparatory eventuality of the second argument. Being a preparatory eventuality of some eventuality is a bounded predicate. The node variables to be equated with the topnode and the intnode of the argument in constraint (335) are boxed. No aspectual restrictions are encoded on X^{r}_{S2}, (336) can apply to predicates of all aspectual classes. This models the fact that LSC is an option for cases where a *within*-TFA models a bounded predicate too, as shown by (332).

(336) introduces an additional landing site, viz., the fragment for the property of being a preparatory eventuality. The root of this fragment is the value of CONT|INTNODE of the argument to which (336) applies.

Integrating (336) with the result of semantic construction for (331) gives rise to (337), a dominance diamond like (321).

(337)

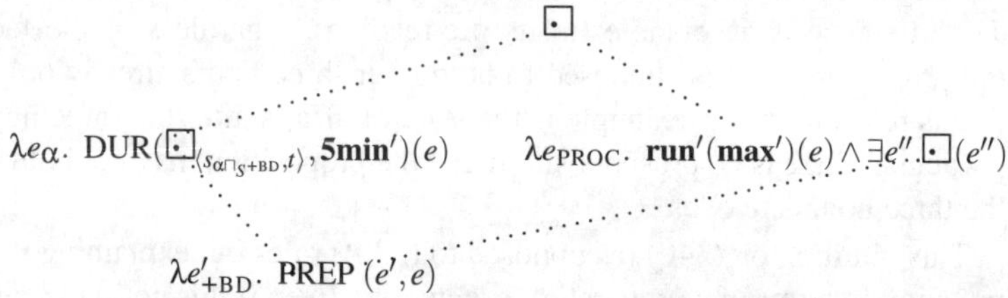

Its sole constructive solution corresponds to the λ-term (338), which stands for the set of runnings of Max that have a preparatory eventuality whose length is five minutes:

(338) $\lambda e_{\text{PROC}}.\mathbf{run'}(\mathbf{max'})(e) \wedge \exists e'_{+\text{BD}}.\text{DUR}(\lambda e''_{+\text{BD}}.\text{PREP}(e'',e),\mathbf{5min'})(e')$

Modelling the pre-readings for examples like (330)-(332) in terms of LSC has the additional advantage that the analysis carries over directly to examples like (339).

(339) ? Algernon spilled his coffee within five minutes

Moens and Steedman adduce this kind of example to show that pre-readings are subject to conceptual licensing, which suggests an analysis in terms of reinterpretation. This shows up in (339) in that it is inacceptable – except in humorous contexts –, since a pre-reading is barred conceptually: There is no preparatory eventuality that is conceptually linked to spilling one's coffee.

Examples like (339) would be problematic for approaches to *within*-TFA that either assume a semantics for *within* that is so underspecified that it also captures pre-readings or attributes them to a second reading of *within*. Such strategies were proposed for *in*-TFA, e.g., in Dowty (1979) and Pulman (1997), respectively. Extending these approaches as they stand to *within*-TFA would risk predicting that examples like (339) are acceptable. Thus, additional blocking mechanisms would have to be integrated in these approaches to derive the nonacceptability of these examples.

Time frame adverbials whose head is *in*

After analysing pre-readings for expressions with *within*-TFA, I will now outline why I do not focus on pre-readings for expressions with *in*-TFA. The point is that the case of *in*-TFAs is less clear than the one of *within*-TFA, it needs a more thorough discussion, which would go beyond the scope of this book. The crucial difference between the two kinds of TFA shows up in the analogue of (330):

(340) # I will be in my office in three hours

Imagine that a clerk who is already sitting in his office utters this sentence. The utterance is acceptable (in its pre-reading), regardless of the fact that the proposition that is supposed to hold after three hours already holds. All that is relevant in this example is the state of affairs after the three hours. In particular, there is no presupposition that the proposition may not hold before the three hours are over.

This intuition on (340) (as opposed to (330)) rules out explaining its interpretation in terms of a preparatory eventuality. Even if this notion leaves a lot of leeway for specification, the preparatory eventuality must be over once the main eventuality sets in - unless this notion is weakened beyond sense. Therefore an analysis of (340) in terms of a three hours' preparatory eventuality is too strong, since it falsely rules out the described scenario.

While this suggests an approach to the semantics of *in*-TFA that captures their pre-readings either by a vague semantics or a second reading for *in*, these strategies would run into problems for cases like (341), which do behave like their counterparts with *within*-TFA:

(341) ? Algernon spilled his coffee in five minutes

Regarding pre-readings of *in*-TFA as an option that is introduced in the lexicon cannot directly explain why (341) is not acceptable in normal contexts. Thus, either approach cannot account for the whole range of pre-readings for *in*-TFA, hence, further investigation on the semantics of *in*-TFA is called for to explain these data.

Type coercion for time frame adverbials

It remains to present an account of the type coercion examples that involve time frame adverbials. Recall that type coercion may arise if TFAs modify process predicates as in (342), but not if they modify stative predicates as in (343):

(342) # Max ran within 20 minutes

(343) # Max was here within 20 minutes

In one reading of (342), one can assume that Max always runs a fixed distance, which licenses the insertion of the operator MAX between the semantics of the adverbial and the semantics of *Max run-*. Since there is a homomorphism between an eventuality of (directed) movement and the path traversed during this eventuality, the introduction of boundaries for the path ensues also boundaries for the eventuality itself (see Krifka 1995 for a detailed description of such homomorphisms). There is no type coercion for (343), since conceptual reasoning cannot derive boundaries for the eventuality of Max's being here in the same way.

De Swart (1998) provides a similar example, where TC is licensed by conceptual knowledge that programs (at least ideally) terminate, which suggests a reinterpretation in terms of the maximality operator:

(344) # The program ran in four minutes

The analysis of the TC reading of (342) is (345). The left side represents the semantic part of the interpretation of (342), and the right side, the reinterpretation operator, which is to be inserted between the top hole and the semantic contribution of the predicate.

In the left constraint, two fragments are dominated by a common hole but are not otherwise related. The reason for this is that the interface rule connects the constraints of the adverbial and modified predicate via the latter's CONT|INTNODE value, but the predicate fails to provide this value. The constraint for the reinterpretation operator involves the function f as defined in section 2.4.2. It maps the sort PROC (for process predicates) onto INTER (for intergressive predicates), which fulfills the aspectual selection restriction of the time frame adverbial:

(345)

$$\boxdot \qquad \Leftarrow \lambda e''_{f(\beta)}.\mathrm{MAX}(\square_{\langle s_\beta,t\rangle})(e'')$$

$$\lambda e_\alpha.\mathrm{DUR}(\boxdot_{\langle s_{\alpha\sqcap_S+\mathrm{BD}},t\rangle},\mathbf{20min'})(e) \qquad \lambda e'_{\mathrm{PROC}}.\mathbf{run'}\,(\mathbf{max'})(e')$$

(345) as a whole has a constructive solution, which is derived by identifying the fragment for the durative adverbial with the top hole and closing all remaining gaps. The resulting λ-term (346) stands for the set of maximal runnings of Max with a duration of up to 20 minutes.

(346) $\lambda e_{\mathrm{INTER}}.\mathrm{DUR}(\lambda e''_{\mathrm{INTER}}.\mathrm{MAX}(\lambda e'_{\mathrm{PROC}}.\mathbf{run'}(\mathbf{max'})(e'))(e''),\mathbf{20min'})(e)$

4.2.3 Landing site coercion for *quickly*

One more case of aspectual landing site coercion can be found in expressions that comprise the adverbial *quickly*. It selects for nonstative predicates, which is illustrated by the fact that there is no literal reading for sentences like the following:

(347) # Ariadne will be in her office quickly

Sentence (347) means that a preparatory eventuality of Ariadne's presence in her office is passing or will pass quickly. The presence itself cannot be characterised as quick. (347) presupposes that Ariadne is not in her office at the moment of utterance.

For nonstative predicates, reinterpretation is optional, e.g., in (348):

(348) (#) Ariadne went to her office quickly

Apart from the literal reading that Ariadne moved fast, there also is the reading – in analogy to (347) – that some preparatory eventuality of Ariadne's going elapsed quickly.

The counterpart of (339) is once again odd:

(349) ? Ariadne spilled her coffee quickly

These data suggest an analysis in terms of reinterpretation where the adverbial pertains to a preparatory eventuality of an eventuality in the extension of the modified predicate. Formally, the analysis of these examples follows the pattern as spelt out in detail for *within*-TFA.

This concludes the exposition of the phenomenon of landing site coercion and its proposed representation. The following section is devoted to extensions of the LSC analysis to related linguistic phenomena.

4.3 Further applications

From the viewpoint of semantic composition, the problematic issue of landing site coercion and agentive modification was the question of how to model *optional* insertion of the semantics of a syntactic constituent C_1 within the semantic representation of another syntactic constituent C_2, in particular, within the semantic representation of a syntactic atom (i.e., a word). Recall, e.g., agentive modification as in *beautiful dancer*, where there is the option that the adjective pertains semantically only to the verb stem *dance* and is in the scope of the nominal affix.

This optionality is essentially due to the fact that C_1 is no argument of C_2, but something that may optionally be combined with C_2, e.g., a modifier. The standard way of inserting material arbitrarily deep into the semantics of a constituent, viz., λ-abstraction and subsequent β-reduction, is barred here, because the insertion is only optional (hence not anticipated in the semantics of C_2 by an appropriate λ-abstraction).

Landing site coercion and agentive modification are just two instances of this problem, where a non-argument C_1 applies semantically to only part of another constituent C_2. I will show that the techniques for the treatment of landing site coercion and agentive modification generalise to other instances of this problem. The focus will be on the repetitive/restitutive ambiguity of sentences that comprise *wieder* (the German counterpart of *again*), which probably is the most prominent case here. Another case presented in this section is modification of 'indefinite' pronouns like *someone* (e.g., in *someone who knows English*).

4.3.1 Ambiguity in *wieder*-sentences

Ambiguity arises from the interaction of *wieder* 'again' with telic verbs. This ambiguity can be modelled in terms of semantic structures that do not yet determine whether the adverbial pertains to the whole semantics or only to a part of the semantics of the verb it modifies. The compositional derivation of the latter case is a long-standing problem of semantic theory. I will now apply my approach to this issue.

(350) is a simple example for the relevant ambiguity. It has two readings which differ only in their presuppositions. In the 'repetitive' reading, Max must have opened all the windows before, the 'restitutive' reading only presupposes that all the windows were open before:

(350) daß Max alle Fenster wieder aufmachte
that Max all windows again opened
'that Max opened all windows again'

The interpretation of such sentences is influenced by the position of the adverbial. This effect is highlighted in the following minimal pair of examples (based on similar examples presented by Tibor Kiss):

(351) a (*) daß Max einen Kuchen wieder aß
that Max a cake again ate
'that Max ate a cake again'
b daß Max wieder einen Kuchen aß

Any interpretation (be it repetitive or restitutive) of (351a) has a ruminant flavour, in which Max either eats the same cake twice or restores the cake's location (in his stomach). With respect to syntax and semantics, the sentence is fine; the inacceptability is only due to conceptual knowledge, whence the brackets around the asterisk.

Switching the object NP and *wieder* yields a sentence with far less unappetising readings, which do not enforce one single cake to be involved in the repetitions. (351b) has the preferred (repetitive) reading that Max ate a cake and had previously eaten another cake.

Therefore it is not implausible to expect the interpretation of (350) to change as soon as the object NP and *again* are switched:

(352) daß Max wieder alle Fenster aufmachte

The general view on such sentence pairs is that switching the object NP and *again* as in (352) rules out the restitutive reading. But I claim that the influence of word order on the semantics of (350) and (352) is more subtle than is usually assumed. The analysis of these sentences which will be presented in this section refines the general view and offers an explanation for it.

In the following, I will focus on cases like (350) and (352), where the presupposition of the restitutive reading is related to the aftermath proposition as introduced in the semantics of these predicates. E.g., for *Max open- the window* this proposition is *the window be- open.*[63] Before presenting my own account of the data, I will first discuss previous approaches to the subject.

Previous approaches

The first main current of approaches follows the intuition of Generative Semantics (McCawley, 1971, Lakoff, 1971) and models the repetitive/restitutive ambiguity by (syntactic or semantic) scope variation of a semantically invariable *wieder* (Dowty, 1979, von Stechow, 1996). The second current claims that the adverbial is ambiguous but its scope is fixed (Blutner and Jäger, 2003, Kamp and Roßdeutscher, 1994).

The first group of approaches decompose the semantics of telic verbs using operators like CAUSE and BECOME (see section 2.4.2). E.g., Dowty represents *open* as (353). In this decomposition (adapted here), $P(x)$ introduces the cause of the causation, some activity of the subject of *open*; **open**′ stands for the stative property of being open:

(353) $\lambda y \lambda x \exists P.P(x)\text{CAUSE BECOME}(\mathbf{open}'(y))$

The semantics of *wieder* itself is simple. Omitting details not relevant for the present discussion (see Egg 1995), it is the identity mapping for properties P of eventualities and introduces the presupposition that there is a preceding eventuality in the extension of P:

(354) $\lambda P.P$, on the presupposition that $\exists e'.e' < e \wedge P(e')$

The predicate over which *wieder* has scope determines the property that must hold of the presupposed eventuality introduced by the adverbial. Modification by *wieder* has no other semantic effect. I.e., the scope ambiguity of

[63] This does not exhaust the number of challenging issues for a semantics of *wieder*-sentences, for other cases see in particular Fabricius-Hansen (1983).

wieder merely determines different presuppositions.

The repetitive/restitutive ambiguity can then be be attributed to two different scope positions of *wieder*, above the whole verb for the repetitive reading, and below BECOME, for the restitutive reading. The presupposition of the restitutive reading is a part of the presupposition of the repetitive reading; the latter entails the former. E.g., the presupposition of the repetitive reading of *Max open- the window again* is that Max opened the window before, which entails the presupposition of its restitutive reading that the window was previously open (otherwise, Max could not have opened it before).

This strategy can describe the semantics of *wieder*-sentences straightforwardly, but faces the problem of how to insert the meaning of *wieder* in the semantics of the verb. To this end, Dowty proposes a meaning postulate that claims equivalence between repetitive and restitutive readings of *wieder*-sentences. The postulate is given in an adapted form as (355), where the repetitive reading appears on the left side of the equivalence relation, and the restitutive reading, on the right side:

(355) $\forall p \forall q.\Box[\mathbf{again}'(p \text{ CAUSE BECOME}(q)) \leftrightarrow p \text{ CAUSE BECOME}(\mathbf{again}'(q))]$

But this meaning postulate is problematic in that it allows one to infer the repetitive reading from the (weaker) restitutive reading. This problematic inference turns out to be responsible for the unwanted side effects noted in Zimmermann (1993) for this postulate.

Von Stechow (1996, 2003) rephrases these intuitions of Generative Semantics by a *syntactic* decomposition of complex verbs like *open* in the framework of Generative Grammar. The relevant part of the syntactic structure of (350) and (352) (without *wieder*) is depicted in (356).

(356)

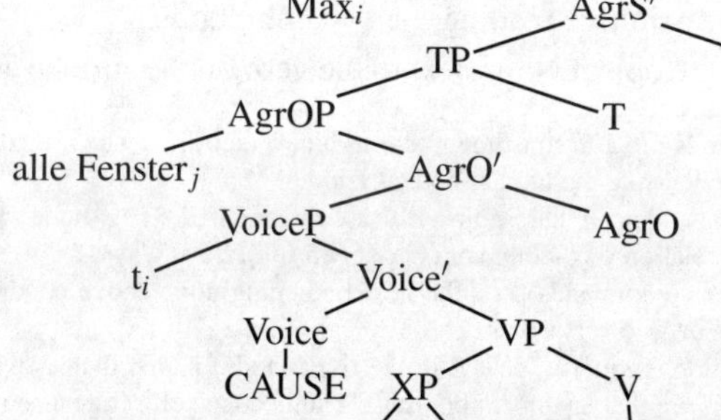

In this syntax tree the verb is introduced not in a single leaf node but in the VoiceP as a whole. The adjective *offen*, 'open', denotes the property (being open) that holds for the second argument of the verb in the aftermath of *auf-machen*-eventualities. The crucial assumption of this analysis is that there are different *adjunction positions*[64] for an adverbial like *wieder* in such a syntactic structure, within and without the subtree that corresponds to the complex verb. If the syntactic position of the adverbial determines its semantic scope,[65] this makes possible a syntactic reconstruction of the different scope positions of the adverbial: *Wieder* may be adjoined to the XP, which gives it narrow scope with respect to BECOME. The relevant fragment of the syntax tree would in that case be (357):

(357)

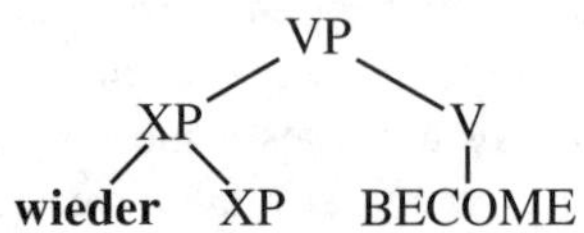

Alternatively, *wieder* may be adjoined to VoiceP or a higher phrase, which means that the whole verb is in its scope.[66]

This analysis not only aims at reconstructing the repetitive/restitutive ambiguity, its second goal is to account for the semantic effect of word order variation in *wieder*-sentences. It predicts different interpretations for (350) and (352). These differences follow from the assumption that in order to receive case, NPs move from their positions within VoiceP (as indicated by the traces t_i and t_j) into the specifier position of their respective agreement phrase (AgrS and AgrO) on the surface structure.

Consequently, the deep structure position of *wieder* (and hence its scope relation to CAUSE and BECOME) cannot be uniquely reconstructed when it appears next to the verb on the surface as in (350). The movement of the object NP results in the surface order 'object NP before adverbial' if the adverbial is adjoined to XP or to VoiceP. (Word order can be directly read off the tree of the syntactic surface structure.) But since these syntactic positions give rise to different scope positions for *wieder*, (350) may have either the repetitive or the restitutive reading, i.e., is ambiguous.

In contrast, if the object NP is next to the verb on the surface as in (352), the

---

[64] Adjunction of an XP to a Y constituent returns a new (sub)tree, whose daughters are the XP and the Y, respectively, while the mother node is another Y.

[65] Formally: A constituent *A* has scope over a constituent *B* iff its node α *c-commands* β, the node of *B*. The relation of c-command is defined in various ways, for (356) the following definition suffices: α c-commands β iff the next branching node above α dominates β, and β does not dominate α or vice versa.

[66] In (356), inflection (formerly located in the INFL node) is distributed over several nodes. 'AgrSP' and 'AgrOP' are the agreement phrases for subject and object, respectively. 'TP' stands for tense phrase. Finally, the VoiceP is the place where the syntactic material that determines the voice is located. In German, the Voice node is in particular the position of the passive auxiliaries *werden* and *bekommen*. See von Stechow (1996) for further explanations of the syntactic framework.

adverbial must be adjoined to AgrOP or higher. Otherwise, it could not appear to the left of the object NP in the syntactic surface structure. Semantically this means that it outscopes CAUSE and BECOME, i.e., only the repetitive reading should be possible.

But Blutner and Jäger (2003) point out a restitutive reading for (352), which runs counter to the predictions of the approach. This reading can be glossed as 'all windows had been open before *simultaneously*, and Max restituted this state of affairs'. I.e., CAUSE has widest, *wieder*, intermediate, and the quantifier, narrowest scope.[67]

Considering the problems of these scope ambiguity approaches to the semantics of *wieder*-sentences, Blutner and Jäger (2003) argue against the appropriateness of these approaches in general. They attribute ambiguity and invariant scope position to *wieder*. In their analysis (358), the material to the right of the oblique expresses the presupposition:

(358) $\lambda P \lambda e.P(e)/\exists e'.e' < e \wedge f(P)(e')$

In prose: Semantically, *wieder* is the identity mapping for properties of eventualities P and presupposes a preceding eventuality in the extension of $f(P)$. f is an open parameter, which can be instantiated as either identity mapping or a function RES. RES maps (telic) properties of eventualities P onto the stative aftermath proposition involved in P. E.g., RES applied to the semantics of *Max open- the window* returns the property of eventualities e that the window is open at e.

The crucial point of this analysis is that the ambiguity of the function f mimicks the effects of a scope ambiguity of *wieder* without having to assign different scope positions to *wieder*. The two different instantiations of f determine two different presuppositions, one that comprises the complete semantics of the verb, and another that comprises only those parts of the semantics of the verb that are in the scope of BECOME. But as noted above, the sole effect of assigning different scope positions to *wieder* was the determination of these two presuppositions.

This predicts two readings each for (350) and (352), which are summarised by (359) and (360), respectively. These two representations are different because the scope of *wieder* and the object NP determines whether the universal quantifier appears in the presupposition or not:

(359) $\lambda e \forall x.\mathbf{window}(x) \rightarrow \mathbf{open}'(\mathbf{m},x)(e)/$
$$\exists e'.e' < e \wedge f(\lambda e''.\mathbf{open}'(\mathbf{m},x)(e''))(e')$$

[67]Previous analyses of causative operators in the literature define causation either as a relation between two propositions (as, e.g., in Dowty 1979) and a relation between an individual and a proposition (as, e.g., in von Stechow 1996). In this book, the former type of analysis is assumed, which is crucial for the proposed analysis of type coercion for the perfect in section 3.2.4.

(360) $\lambda e \forall x.\mathbf{window}(x) \rightarrow \mathbf{open}'(\mathbf{m},x)(e)/$
$\exists e'.e' < e \wedge f(\lambda e''.\forall x.\mathbf{window}(x) \rightarrow \mathbf{open}'(\mathbf{m},x)(e''))(e')$

According to (359), (350) has a repetitive reading (f is identity), which carries the presupposition that Max has opened every window before. If f is RES, one arrives at a restitutive reading for (350) with a presupposition for every window that it was open before.

If f is identity, (360) yields a repetitive reading for (352), which presupposes a previous eventuality of Max's opening every window. This reading is similar to the first reading derived from (359) but differs from this reading in that it does not require that the set of windows are identical for either opening eventuality (see p.181f. for further discussion). In (360), f can also be instantiated as RES. In the formal framework of Blutner and Jäger (2000), (362) can be derived from (361), i.e., the presupposition would be that the windows were open simultaneously before:

(361) $\text{RES}(\lambda e' \forall x.\mathbf{window}(x) \rightarrow \mathbf{open}'(\mathbf{m},x)(e'))$

(362) $\lambda e' \forall x.\mathbf{window}(x) \rightarrow \mathbf{open}'(x)(e')$

This is the appropriate presupposition for the restitutive reading for (352) that Blutner and Jäger pointed out. However, (360) does not describe the assertion of this reading correctly, since it gives the universal quantifier scope over CAUSE and BECOME in every reading of (352). The representation does not decompose the semantics of the verb, which prevents the quantifier from taking scope over only part of the verb semantics.

But the assertion in the restitutive reading of (352) is only that Max brought about a state of every window being open. This does not entail that he manipulated each and every window (compare the discussion of the simpler (365) below). Formally, this means that in an appropriate representation of this reading, the universal quantifier must be outscoped by CAUSE and BECOME.

Finally, some comments are in order on Blutner and Jäger's (2003) argument against an account of the repetitive/restitutive ambiguity in terms of a scope ambiguity for *wieder*, because the proposed analysis of *wieder*-sentences assumes scope ambiguity for *wieder*. The argument focusses on sentences like (363):

(363) daß sich wieder Delawaren in New Jersey ansiedelten
that REFL again Delawares in NJ settle
'that Delawares settled in New Jersey again'

The presupposition of the restitutive reading of (363) is already fulfilled if *some* Delawares had once lived in New Jersey before the settling event, not necessarily those Delawares whose settling down in New Jersey is asserted in (363). I.e., the scope of *wieder* includes the existential quantifier of the semantics of *Delawaren*. In addition, *wieder* has scope between BECOME and the aftermath proposition in the decomposition of *sich ansiedeln* 'settle (intrans.)', since the relevant reading is restitutive. If one furthermore assumes that *sich ansiedeln* involves the notion of causation (roughly, the resulting semantics would be 'causing a change of one's own residence'), a contradiction arises: The existential quantifier of *Delawaren* must outscope CAUSE (to bind the variable for the agent of the cause in the verb decomposition), CAUSE outscopes *again* (by transitivity; CAUSE always outscopes BECOME, and BECOME has scope over *again*), and *again* outscopes the existential quantifier. (Note that CAUSE and BECOME invariably occur in the same fragment, i.e., *wieder* cannot intervene scopally between them.)

This scope puzzle presupposes an analysis of *sich ansiedeln* as a causative verb, and of *sich* as true reflexive. However, to my mind, *sich* in the case of *sich ansiedeln* is just a grammatical marker, which can be described along the lines of Grimshaw's (1982) 'intrinsic clitics' in Romance. Such markers are introduced by a lexical rule, they are in complementary distribution with NP objects but are not themselves objects. Semantically, they have a *decausativising* effect. I.e., if they are combined with a verb whose semantic decomposition structure is (roughly) $P(x)$ CAUSE(BECOME($Q(y)$)), where x and y are linked to the subject and the object NP, respectively, the decomposition structure for the meaning of the result of the combination is merely BECOME($Q(y)$). Since in this second, smaller decomposition only y must be linked to a syntactic argument of the verb, it is linked to the subject NP, thus, the result of the combination is intransitive. See also Wunderlich (1997) for an analysis of this phenomenon in German.

But without causativity for *sich ansiedeln*, the scope puzzle disappears. The semantics of *sich ansiedeln* comprises only the operator BECOME. But since BECOME has no individual argument, the existential quantifier may slip under BECOME and *wieder* without leaving any variables unbound. Then (363), too, may be explained in terms of a structural ambiguity: *Wieder* may take wide or narrow scope with respect to BECOME.

Compare (363) to (364), where *sich ansiedeln* is replaced by the truly causative verb *kaufen*, 'buy'. This example no longer exhibits the reading that could give rise to the scope puzzle of Blutner and Jäger. At the end of this subsection a semantic representation of the two sentences will be given that highlights the difference between them.

(364) daß wieder Delawaren in New Jersey Land kauften
that again Delawares in NJ land bought
'that Delawares bought land in New Jersey again'

In sum, the discussion of previous approaches to the repetitive/restitutive ambiguity shows that the derivation of the semantic representations that represent the possibilities of scope interaction between *wieder*, complex verbs, and quantifiers is still a problematic issue.

The analysis

Now the repetitive/restitutive ambiguity for sentences like (350) and (352) will be derived. First, the range of its readings is specified for each of these sentences. It is helpful to start with the simpler variant of these two sentences that contains no *wieder*:

(365) daß Max alle Fenster aufmachte

In (365), the scope between CAUSE and the universal quantifier is open. Apart from the preferred reading ('for every window: Max opened it') there is the reading 'Max brought it about that all windows were open'. This reading is much less preferred than the other, hence shows up only in special contexts, in particular if the first reading is explicitly denied:

(366) Erst war nur die Hälfte aller Fenster auf, aber dann machte Max alle Fenster auf
'First only half of the windows were open, but then Max opened all windows'

Consequently, an underspecified semantic representation of (365) should leave open the scope of quantifier and CAUSE and be compatible with exactly two meanings, one for each of the two scoping possibilities. (367) is the CLLS representation of (365).[68]

(367)

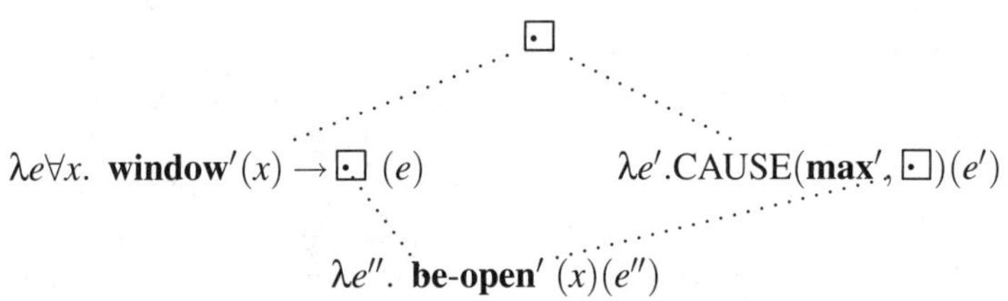

(367) has two constructive solutions, which correspond to λ-terms for the two readings of (365):

(368) $\lambda e \forall x.\mathbf{window}'(x) \rightarrow \text{CAUSE}(\mathbf{max}', \lambda e''.\mathbf{be\text{-}open}'(x)(e''))(e)$

(369) $\lambda e'.\text{CAUSE}(\mathbf{max}', \lambda e \forall x.\mathbf{window}'(x) \rightarrow \mathbf{be\text{-}open}'(x)(e))(e')$

This result paves the way for the derivation of the repetitive/restitutive ambiguities in (350) and (352). The intuitions on (352) are that it has only three

[68] Since CAUSE and BECOME invariably occur in the same fragment, BECOME is omitted in the following representations for expository reasons. In addition, CAUSE is simplified to a relation between an individual (the agent of the cause), a proposition (which characterises the caused eventuality), and an eventuality.

readings, although there are three scope bearers (**again**′, ∀, and CAUSE):

(a)Max opened every window; there was a preceding event of Max's opening every window
(**again**′ < ∀ < CAUSE; 'repetitive')

(b)Max brought it about that all windows were open simultaneously; he had done so before
(**again**′ < CAUSE < ∀; 'repetitive'; see the discussion on (365))

(c)all windows had been open before simultaneously, and Max restituted this state of affairs
(CAUSE < **again**′ < ∀; 'restitutive'; the reading pointed out by Blutner and Jäger (2003))

In each of these readings **again**′ outscopes the universal quantifier. This leaves exactly three scoping possibilities for CAUSE.

Similar considerations regarding the readings of (350) reveal that it has three readings too:

(d)for every window: Max opened it, and he had done so before
(∀ < **again**′ < CAUSE; 'repetitive')

(e)for every window: Max opened it, and the window had been open before
(∀ < CAUSE < **again**′; 'restitutive')

(f)Max brought it about that all windows were open; every window had been open before
(CAUSE < ∀ < **again**′; 'restitutive'; see once again the discussion on (365) above)

The common ground of these three readings is scope of the universal quantifier over **again**′.

This suggests an influence of word order on semantic scope: A scope-bearing adverbial to the left of an NP outscopes this NP. I.e., although word order influences the semantics of *wieder*-sentences, the order of object NP and *wieder* influences only the scope of these two constituents themselves. It does not determine the scope of the adverbial and CAUSE, which allows repetitive and restitutive readings for both word orders.

The differences and similarities of the readings can be attributed to scope relations between two of the three scope bearers in these sentences. There are three such pairs of scope bearers, each of which has a semantic effect of its own.

- The scope relation between **again**′ and CAUSE determines the traditional dichotomy between repetitive (**again**′ < CAUSE) and restitutive readings (CAUSE < **again**′).

- CAUSE and ∀ determine whether *every* member of the extension of the quantifier restriction is affected by an eventuality as specified in the quantifier scope (∀ < CAUSE) or not (CAUSE < ∀). This distinction was introduced in the discussion of the readings of (365).
- The scope of ∀ and **again′** determines *identity criteria* of the entities involved in the NP semantics. E.g., the readings (a) and (d) differ in that Max closes the same set of windows twice in (d), in (a), the set of windows may change. Since the scope between ∀ and **again′** is fixed by word order, this criterion distinguishes (350) and (352).

If one encodes these three alternatives as binary features ±REP(etitive), ±EVE(ry), and ±ID(entity), the readings (a)-(f) instantiate the six possible combinations of these features. (Only +REP,-EVE,+ID and -REP,+EVE,-ID would express contradictory scope relations.)

The intuitions about the readings and the relations between them can now be read off these features immediately. E.g., the similarity between the readings (a) and (d) (which was noted in the discussion on Blutner and Jäger's proposal) follows from the fact that they share the features +EVE and +REP. I.e., both readings are repetitive and there is an opening eventuality for every window. The difference between them rests in the feature ID: The set of windows may change between the two openings in (a), which is -ID, but not in (d), which is +ID.

The semantic representations in CLLS for (350) and (352) are (370) and (371), respectively. Each constraint has three constructive solutions, depending on the position of CAUSE, while the scope of ∀ and **again′** is fixed:

(370)

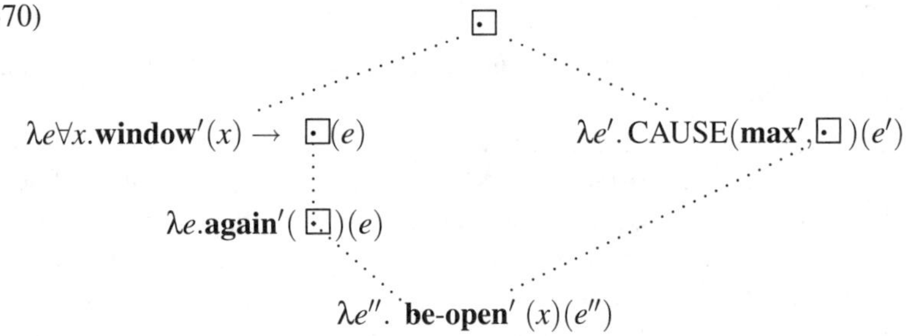

(371)

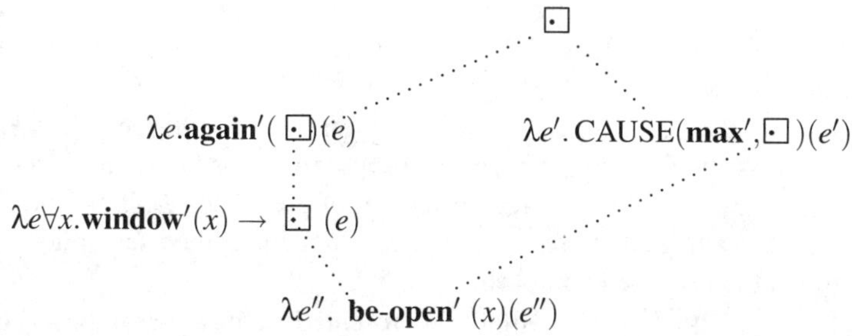

At this point, the task of semantic construction is over. The representations (370) and (371) comprise the repetitive/restitutive ambiguities of the sentences (350) and (352) but incorporate the restrictions imposed on these sentences by the order of the object NP and *wieder*.

The derivation of the preferred readings of (350) and (352) can then be modelled in an optimality theory (OT) framework that takes these underspecified representations as input. In this book, the OT processing of these representations can only be sketched (see Kager 1999, Prince and Smolensky 2004 for OT in general and Blutner and Jäger 2003 or Egg 1999 for OT analyses of *wieder*-sentences). The idea is that a preferred reading is selected with the help of *OT constraints*, which are ranked and may be violated. The reading with the fewest violations of OT constraints wins (several violations of lower-rank constraints are less severe than violating a constraint of higher rank). Two OT constraints are relevant for this task:

(372) Do not insert arguments into their heads semantically

(373) Minimise presuppositions

Constraint (372) accounts for the strong preference against the reading of (365) that is enforced in (366). The second constraint expresses preference for restitutive readings, formally, by giving CAUSE scope over **again**$'$. (372) is ranked higher than (373).

Among the readings (a)-(c) for (352), only the repetitive (a) complies to the strong (372). This explains the general view on sentences like (352). For them, the repetitive interpretation is strongly preferred, because an attempt to comply to the pro-restitutive constraint (373) would enforce violation of (372): Due to the scope of **again**$'$ over $\forall$, scoping **again**$'$ below CAUSE would give CAUSE scope over $\forall$, too.

From the readings (d)-(f) for (350), only (f) violates the strong constraint (372). This explains why both the repetitive (d) and the restitutive (e) are prominent interpretations of (350), with a slight preference for (e) over (d), because (e) violates neither constraint. Reading (d) can be enforced by a marked intonation which shifts the sentence accent from the verb to the adverbial (Fabricius-Hansen, 1983).

In sum, the general view on the interpretation of sentence pairs like (350) and (352) follows from the approach proposed in this book: It emerges as the result of an optimality-theoretic selection of preferred readings from a set of available readings that are captured by an underspecified semantic representation in the proposed approach.

I conclude this section with the representations of the examples (363) and (364). Their representations are (374) and (375), respectively. For expository reasons, the aftermath propositions of both *sich ansiedeln* and *kaufen* are extremely simplified:

(374)

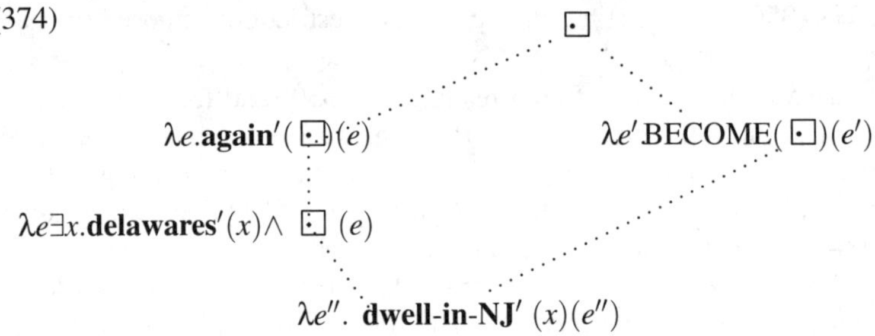

(375)

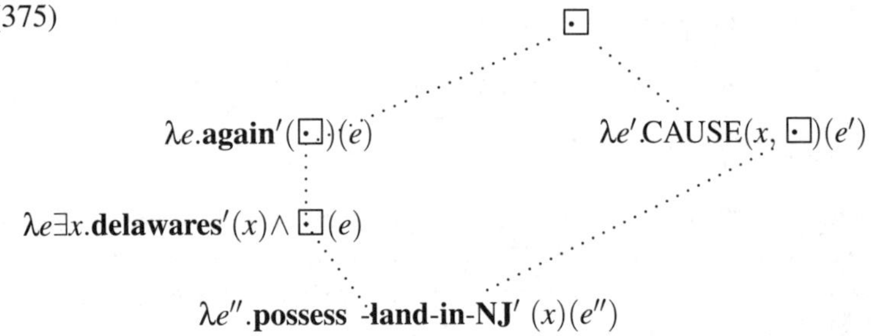

The critical reading of (363) has widest scope for BECOME, narrowest scope for the existential quantifier, with *wieder* taking intermediate scope. One of the constructive solutions of (374) corresponds to a λ-term for this reading:

(376) $\lambda e'.\mathrm{BECOME}(\lambda e.\mathbf{again}'($
$$\lambda e''\exists x.\mathbf{delawares}'(x) \wedge \mathbf{dwell\text{-}in\text{-}NJ}'(x)(e''))(e))(e')$$

(376) denotes the set of changes from there being no Delawares dwelling in New Jersey to there being some Delawares dwelling there. (376) presupposes

a previous dwelling of some (perhaps different) Delawares in New Jersey.

A reading that would be analogous to (376) is not available as a solution of (375), since the quantifier fragment must always outscope the fragment that comprises CAUSE in order to prevent unbounded variables. I.e., the scope ambiguity of (375) is only apparent while it is real in (374), where the quantifier fragment need not bind a variable in the fragment on the right side. The sole constructive solution of (375) corresponds to the λ-term (377) for a *repetitive* interpretation that some Delawares bought land in New Jersey (formally, brought it about that they possess land there), with the presupposition that there was a preceding buying of land in New Jersey by some Delawares:

(377) $\lambda e.\mathbf{again}'(\lambda e'\exists x.\mathbf{delawares}'(x)\wedge$
$\mathrm{CAUSE}(x, \lambda e''\mathbf{possess\text{-}land\text{-}in\text{-}NJ}'(x)(e''))(e'))(e)$

The difference in scope ambiguity potential between sentences (363) and (364) is highlighted in the proposed analysis. The lack of ambiguity of (375) means that the scope puzzle of Blutner and Jäger does not arise for the truly causative (364).

4.3.2 Other potential applications

Apart from the repetitive/restitutive ambiguity, there are other cases where the proposed analysis of landing site coercion looks promising as the solution to problems of semantic composition. In order not to stray too much further from the topic of this book, only one of these cases is sketched here, viz., modification of indefinite pronouns like *someone* or *everything*, whose syntactic category is NP.

Intuitively, these nouns are cases of 'incorporation' of a noun by a determiner (this is suggested by their morphology, especially in the case of *something*). The fact that it is possible to modify these NPs with typical noun modifiers (adjective phrases, preposition phrases, and relative clauses), as well as the semantic spellout of this kind of modification substantiates this intuition. Consider the following examples:

(378) Something new appeared

(379) Everyone in this room is dancing

The semantics of the involved NPs is the set of properties that a new thing has and the set of properties of every person in this room. I.e., the modifier semantics seems to have been applied to the semantics of the 'incorporated' noun first. The result of this application would then be the argument of the semantics of the determiner that is the other part of the NP.

However, expressing this intuition syntactically requires tampering with the syntax of these NPs.[69] In the proposed approach, these intuitions are rephrased in a semantic way: I assume a fragment in the semantics of the NP for the 'incorporated' noun that is an additional landing site for the semantics of a modifier (its root X^i_{NP} is the CONT|INTNODE value in the lexical entry for *something*). Then the constraints for both modifier and NP semantics are put together by an interface rule that relates the CONT|INTNODE value of the adjective with X^i_{NP}. I.e., this rule is basically **(b17′)**; the account of agentive modification is generalised to these cases.

The semantic representation of *something new* is then a dominance diamond with the embedded fragment as its bottom element; the semantics of the modifier and the rest of the NP semantics show up in the two fragments whose scope is not yet specified. The diamond expresses the fact that the modifier may outscope its argument as a whole or only the 'incorporated' noun.

(380)

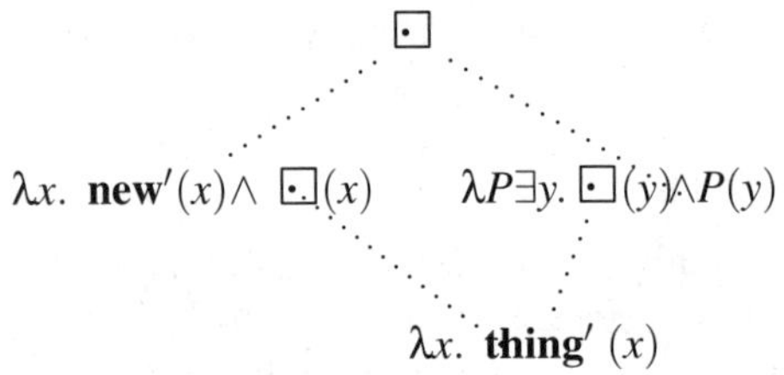

This potential ambiguity is immediately resolved: The left fragment that comprises the modifier semantics has a hole for a fragment of type $\langle e,t \rangle$, the right fragment is of type $\langle\langle e,t \rangle,t \rangle$ and has a hole for a fragment of type $\langle e,t \rangle$, too, and the dominated fragment is of type $\langle e,t \rangle$. I.e., in the only constructive solution of this constraint the right fragment has widest scope, the solution corresponds to $\lambda P \exists y.\mathbf{new}'(y) \wedge \mathbf{thing}'(y) \wedge P(y)$, as desired.

In sum, the analysis proposed for landing site coercion and agentive modification is not an ad hoc measure but is also applicable to other cases of semantic construction where there is *optional* insertion of the semantics of a non-argument constituent into the semantic representation of another constituent. In particular, it can be carried over directly to the analysis of the long-standing semantic problem of the repetitive/restitutive ambiguity of *wieder*-sentences, where it fits in with rather subtle distinctions between the readings of such sentences.

[69] In analogy to a potential syntactic approach to agentive modification in section 1.5.4, a syntactic structure of *something new* which directly models these intuitions would have to be [some-[thing new]], see, e.g., Abney (1987).

4.4 Conclusion

In this chapter the proposed approach to reinterpretation, which was developed in chapter 3 on type coercion data, was applied to phenomena of landing site coercion. Casting the analyses in the representation formalism CLLS provided the necessary expressivity to cover these phenomena as well.

The basic strategy of modelling landing site coercion is the same as in the account of type coercion presented. The result of semantic construction for LSC cases is not yet fully determined and must be enriched with material from extralinguistic sources to obtain a fully specified meaning. Formally, the constraints for the semantic representation of LSC cases are well-formed but have no constructive solution. In these constraints, once again the semantic contributions of constituents of expressions that might mismatch semantically are separated into different fragments of the constraint for the expression.

Landing site coercion differs from type coercion in that it gives rise to functor-argument structures where the functor (typically, the semantic contribution of a modifier) does not necessarily dominate its argument (as contributed by the respective modified expression) as a whole. Instead, the argument may be augmented in such a way that it comprises an additional *landing site* (in the form of an additional fragment) to which the functor may be applied alternatively.

Consequently, the formal spellout of R-positions for LSC is more involved than the one for type coercion: The functor is related to the argument in terms of the *intnode* of the argument. The intnode is the root of the fragment for the additional landing site. But since the argument as it stands has no such fragment, it must be augmented by a reinterpretation operator that comprises such a fragment and hence provides an intnode for the argument.

The resulting structure is familiar, it is the 'diamond structure' that is characteristic for underspecified representations of quantifier scope ambiguities. I.e., the proposed account of LSC falls back on already established structures. The fragment of the argument for the additional landing site is the bottom element of this diamond structure, it is dominated by the other two elements, viz., a fragment that comprises the functor, and a second fragment comprising the original (uncoerced) argument.

R-positions for LSC are determined in the syntax-semantics interface again, i.e., the potential of an expression to undergo LSC is associated with specific constituent structures, in particular, modification structures. It is a question for further research whether every modification structure may give rise to LSC. In that case, one could go beyond syntax-semantics interface rules like (**b17′**) and (**b20′**) and encode the way in which they combine the constraints of modifier and modified expression as the semantic part of the head-adjunct schema of an HPSG grammar. (In a similar fashion, it seems worthwhile to investigate the question of whether the property of introducing R-positions for type coercion is related to the head-complement schema.)

This basic strategy of determining R-positions for LSC is complemented by additional fine-tuning that avoids attributing reinterpretation potential to expressions that are not reinterpretation candidates. In particular, this allows a distinction between adjectives or adverbials that may undergo LSC and those that may not. Examples for the latter group are *red* or *yesterday*; they carry additional constraints in their semantics that block LSC.

In addition, careful design of reinterpretation operators also contributes to the exact determination of the LSC potential of linguistic expressions. E.g., the aspectual selection restriction of the aftermath operator (319) as opposed to the preparatory eventuality operator (336a) makes it possible to model the fact that aftermath modification is only available for telic predicates, while modification of preparatory eventualities as the result of reinterpretation occurs for predicates of all aspectual classes. For aspectual LSC, it is furthermore assumed that the only available reinterpretation operators refer to the *nucleus structure* of eventualities.

The phenomenon of LSC was shown to be similar to several problematic cases for semantic construction that do not involve reinterpretation. The common ground between LSC and these cases is that they are all semantically functor-argument structures where a functor may pertain to part of its argument only. The difference between LSC and these compositional cases is that for the latter the additional landing site for the functor is already present in the argument, it need not be introduced by reinterpretation.

In particular, agentive modification as in the case of *fast typist* belongs to these cases, since it involves readings in which the adjective pertains only to the verb stem of the agentive noun. Other such cases were the repetitive/restitutive ambiguity of sentences with *again* and the modification of NP expressions like *something* or *everyone*.

The presented approach to LSC generalises to these problematic cases for semantic construction in that these cases can be characterised by the same structures as expressions that undergo LSC. At the same time, the approach brings out the differences between LSC and these cases as well. This shows that the approach of LSC captures a more general regularity of natural language.

In sum, the proposed approach to reinterpretation is expressive enough to cover both type coercion and landing site coercion with their whole range of data. This concludes the account of the two patterns of reinterpretation. The next chapter will explore a piece of extralinguistic knowledge that frequently interacts with reinterpretation, viz. the duration information that is associated with predicates and expressions that modify or subcategorise for predicates.

5

The Duration Principle

The preceding chapters of this book showed how the syntax and semantics of reinterpretation candidates contribute to their meaning. It was emphasised that extralinguistic knowledge (like the fact that beverages usually have containers and that the typical duration of a sonata is shorter than a day) is required for the full determination of the meaning of a reinterpretation candidate, but up to now the book has focussed on the linguistic side of reinterpretation.

To complement the account of the linguistic aspects of reinterpretation, this chapter will now venture beyond the boundaries of syntax and semantics and explore at least one piece of conceptual knowledge that plays an important role in reinterpretation, viz., the *typical duration* of eventualities that is associated with, but not part of, the semantics of predicates. This duration information is of additional interest for the topic of this book since it not only triggers its own reinterpretations, it also constrains cases of aspectually triggered reinterpretation.

Duration information is investigated to back up the claim made in the introduction that reinterpretation is not restricted to m-expressions (expressions with semantically conflicting constituents). Incompatibility of a semantically well-formed expression with conceptual knowledge gives rise to reinterpretation, too. One instance of this general observation is the *Duration Principle*, according to which information on the duration of an eventuality that is introduced by various linguistic expressions must be compatible:

Semantic construction may only combine expressions if they do not introduce conflicting information on the duration of an eventuality.

Constraints on such a duration may be exact as in the TFA *in five hours*, or nonspecific, as in the progressive, which merely introduces a duration that is longer than an instant (since its semantics talks about proper parts of an eventuality). Predicates constrain the *typical duration* of their main eventuality arguments. E.g., the typical duration of eventualities in the relation denoted by *play a sonata* ranges from minutes to hours. I will often refer to this by saying that a predicate is 'associated' with a certain duration. As indicated by the term 'typical,' predicates attribute to their main eventuality arguments a default duration, which can be overridden by special contexts.

As an illustration of the duration principle at work, consider the following examples:

(381) # Max played soccer on the beach for three months

(382) # Ariadne will play the Moonlight Sonata in twenty seconds

(381) is a case of type coercion in that its meaning involves an *iterative* notion, i.e., Max played soccer on the beach repeatedly for three months. However, from an aspectual point of view, nothing motivates this reinterpretation: Durative adverbials select for unbounded arguments and *Max play- soccer on the beach* is a process predicate. My claim is that this reinterpretation is due to an attempt to avoid an impending violation of the duration principle.

In a literal reading, the sentence would refer to an eventuality that lasts (at least) three months due to the semantics of the adverbial, and whose duration extends from some minutes to some hours due to the typical duration associated with *Max play- soccer on the beach*. These mismatched duration constraints would violate the DP, which triggers iterative reinterpretation. Since the iterative of an expression is associated with a longer duration that the expression itself, this reinterpretation makes *Max play- soccer on the beach* and the adverbial compatible in terms of the DP: An iteration of soccer playings may well last months, which reconciles (381) with the DP.

Example (382) is another semantically well-formed reinterpretation candidate. It instantiates landing site coercion where a functor does not apply to its argument as a whole: The time frame adverbial measures a preparatory eventuality associated with Ariadne's recital rather than the length of the recital itself. But there is no need for aspectual reinterpretation here, since the time frame adverbial (which selects for bounded arguments) modifies an intergressive predicate in (382). The sole reason for the reinterpretation is an incompatibility of duration constraints. The literal reading of the sentence would refer to an eventuality that lasts (at most) 20 seconds and whose typical duration extends over (at least) several minutes.

This impending DP violation is avoided by a landing site coercion that provides an additional landing site in the argument which refers to a preparatory eventuality of the recital. The functor is then applied to that part of the argument only, which is licensed by the DP: The typical duration of such a preparatory eventuality is quite nonspecific and thus compatible with the duration introduced by the TFA.

The reinterpretations in (381) and (382) rely heavily on the assumption that things are normal. This shows that the association of predicates with duration constraints is *context-dependent*. Thus, in a context where someone possesses extraordinary stamina (and perhaps tries to set a new world record) or can play the piano extremely quickly, these two sentences may be acceptable in their literal meaning. But as we know that such talents are rare enough to assume their absence in human beings, we take recourse to reinterpretation and neglect – as I will do in the following – these exceptional contexts.

The need to reinterpret such sentences vanishes as soon as the adverbials are replaced by others that introduce durations compatible with those associated with the respective predicates, as in (383) and (384):

(383) Max played soccer on the beach for the whole evening

(384) Ariadne will play the Moonlight Sonata in 50 minutes

Investigating and formalizing the Duration Principle is an exploration of the interaction of linguistic and extralinguistic information within reinterpretation processes: The DP is not part of aspectual semantics itself but functions as a constraint on the range of feasible reinterpretations within the realm of aspect. The reason for this is that aspectual reinterpretations often change the typical duration involved in the affected predicates. Factoring out the effects of this principle and the effects of aspectual reinterpretation deepens our understanding of reinterpretation data.

Since the DP may also trigger its own reinterpretations, its investigation illustrates my claim that not all instances of reinterpretation are triggered by impending semantic mismatches between the constituents of an expression. In addition, the DP offers an alternative account of data that are usually attributed to an aspectual feature of 'punctuality'. This feature figures prominently in some other aspectual classifications, but the straightforward explanation of the crucial data in DP terms (as well as some additional problems that ensue from giving punctuality aspectual status) justifies its omission in my aspectual classification. The Duration Principle can also be used to model semelfactive predicates (the 'once-only' predicates of Galton 1984).

The chapter is structured as follows. Section 5.1 offers a formalization of the Duration Principle. It applies to the semantic representations (in the form of CLLS constraints) that were introduced in the preceding sections. Duration information is represented by elements of an additional sort hierarchy below the sort EV(entuality). When such information blocks the derivation of a constructive solution for a constraint, it triggers reinterpretation.

Next, the DP will be established as an independent regularity of natural language by showing that it is applicable to a wide range of data (section 5.2). In section 5.3 I will expound how the DP interacts with reinterpretation in that it constrains the range of feasible reinterpretations. This interplay of reinterpretation and the Duration Principle explains seemingly unruly behaviour of aspectual reinterpretations. Section 5.4 concludes with an excursus on data that seem to motivate an aspectual feature of 'punctuality'.

5.1 Formalization of the Duration Principle

This section first presents the modelling of duration constraints, which is the foundation of the proposed account of the Duration Principle. In a second step, it is shown how these constraints are integrated into the semantic representations used in this book.

5.1.1 Modelling duration constraints

Duration constraints often are not overly exact, e.g., they may express information like the fact that playing a sonata does not take days. To model this property, constraints on temporal duration are encoded in terms of *temporal granularities*:[70] I assume a set S of *absolute* temporal granularities, e.g., seconds, minutes, or days ($\langle S, < \rangle$ is a strict partial order). Duration constraints are modelled by convex sets of such granularities. E.g., associating *to play a sonata* with $\{min, hour\}$ describes the fact that the typical duration of the playing of a sonata ranges from some minutes to some hours, the extremely short duration of a cough is modelled by associating $\{\frac{sec}{10}\}$ (i.e., the granularity of tenths of seconds) with *cough*.

There is also a set of *relative* temporal granularities, modelled by the set $N_0 \cup \{\infty\}$. The notion of a minimal eventuality or *instant* is modelled by its element 0.

The relation between these two sets is not fixed right from the start but varies with the context, which models the fact that only context can tell what counts as an instant. Formally, the two sets are related by a function $f : S \mapsto N_0$. f has two parts: A constant function f_1 that maps elements of S below a certain $s_0 \in S$ onto 0 and a bijective structure-preserving function f_2 (whose domain are all $s \in S$ with $s_0 \leq s$) such that $f_2(s_0) = 0$ and for all s_1, s_2 in the domain of f_2, $s_1 < s_2$ entails $f_2(s_1) < f_2(s_2)$. f is context dependent in that s_0 is not yet fixed. In a normal context, $s_0 = \frac{sec}{10}$. Thus, slow motion contexts are those in which $s_0 < \frac{sec}{10}$, quick-motion contexts, those in which $s_0 > \frac{sec}{10}$.

The three possibilities are illustrated in the following diagrams, which depict the function f in the normal context (385), a slow-motion (386), and a quick-motion context (387):

[70] This notion of temporal granularities was introduced in Worm (1994).

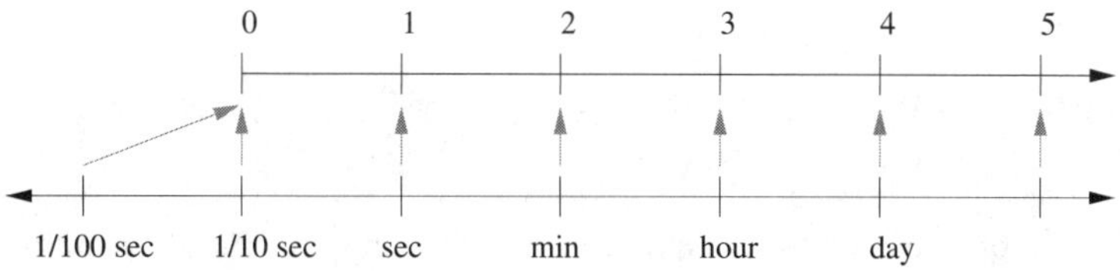

(385)

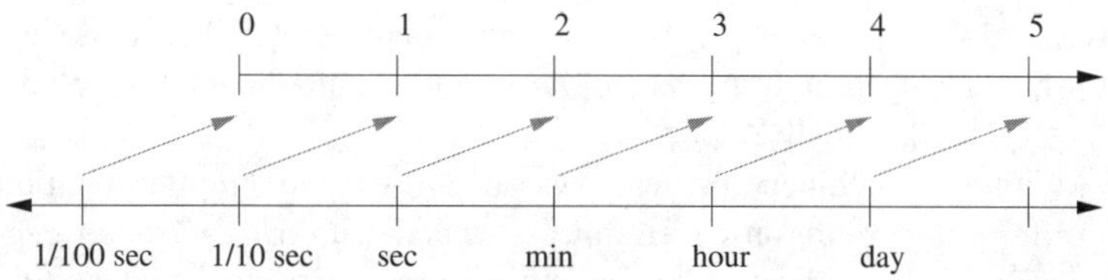

(386)

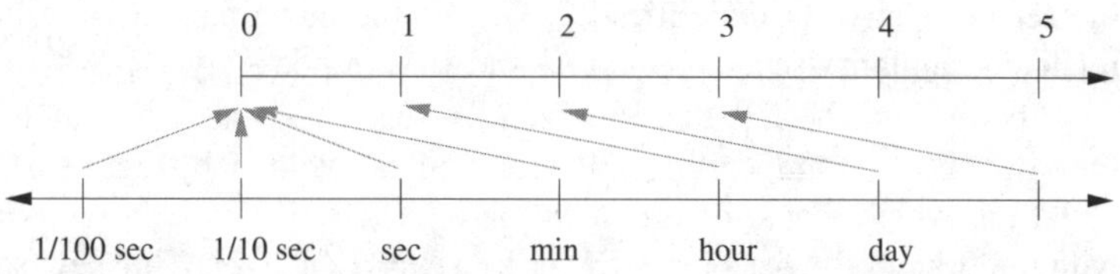

(387)

Thus, each predicate is associated both with its set S_1 of absolute granularities, and with a set of relative granularities, $\{y|\exists x.x \in S_1 \wedge y = f(x)\}$ (i.e., the range of $f \restriction S_1$).

This context-dependent mapping makes possible a reformulation of the definition of a property of 'punctuality' that is relative to contexts: Punctual predicates are associated with the relative granularity set $\{0\}$. E.g., the predicate *cough* is associated with this set in a normal context.

Compatibility with respect to the DP can then be modelled as a nonempty intersection of the involved granularity sets. E.g., an argument fulfills the DP restriction of its function if its granularity set overlaps with the granularity set that represents the durative selection restriction of the function.

For examples like (381), where there is DP-triggered type coercion, one must first model durative selection restrictions of operators like the iterative or the progressive. They are expressed in terms of *relative* granularities, e.g., the argument of the progressive is restricted to predicates with a relative granularity set whose largest member is larger than 0.

Furthermore, the influence of operators like the iterative or the progressive on the typical durations of their arguments P is to be represented: Eventualities in the extension of the progressive (the iterative) of P may have a shorter (longer) duration than those in the extension of P itself. This influence is modelled by functions that map the (relative) granularity set of P onto the granularity set of the progressive/iterative of P. The function for the progressive is (388a), for the iterative, it is (388b), where 'SM' is a function that maps a set on its smallest member:

(388) a $\lambda X.\{x|x < \mathrm{SM}(X)\} \cup X$

b $\lambda X.\{x|x > \mathrm{SM}(X)\}$

The progressive changes the constraint on temporal duration in that it augments the set of granularities S associated with its argument. It adds the granularities that are smaller than the smallest member of S. The iterative, in contrast, maps the granularity set S of its argument onto the set of all granularities larger than the smallest member of S.

With this machinery, one can describe DP-triggered reinterpretations, e.g., in (381). The duration constraint associated with *Max play- soccer on the beach* is given by the set $\{min, hour\}$. Assuming a normal context, this yields the set of relative granularities $\{2,3\}$. For the adverbial, the absolute and relative granularity sets are $\{month\}$ and $\{6\}$, respectively.

To comply to the DP, these granularity sets would have to match, which they do not. The impending DP violation is avoided by iterative reinterpretation, which maps the argument onto an iterative expression associated with the granularity set $\{x|x > \mathrm{SM}(\{2,3\})\} = \{x|x > 2\}$. This new set has a nonempty intersection with $\{6\}$, i.e., after reinterpretation, the durative adverbial and *Max play- soccer on the beach* are compatible with respect to the DP.

5.1.2 Integrating duration constraints and CLLS constraints

The proposed analysis of the Duration Principle is based on the account of reinterpretation that was given for reinterpretation candidates that are m-expressions. To derive well-formed semantic representations for them, gaps were introduced into their representations in terms of dominance constraints so that the semantic contributions of the mismatched constituents appear in different fragments of the constraint. Consider, e.g., (389), the CLLS representation of (381), where the semantic contributions of functor and argument are both dominated by the root of the constraint (‘**PSOB**′’ abbreviates the property of playing soccer on the beach):

(389)

$$\boxdot$$

$$\lambda e.\mathrm{PH}(\boxdot, \mathbf{3months}')(e) \qquad \lambda e'.\ \mathbf{PSOB}'(\mathbf{max}')(e')$$

These gaps also allow for the integration of the material provided by the DP-triggered iterative reinterpretation into the constraint. For these examples, it is thus advantageous to assign reinterpretation potential even to semantically well-formed expressions (as opposed to de Swart 1998).

These constraints are now augmented with duration information. Then the solution of a constraint depends not only on the type-theoretic and sortal properties of its node variables, it also depends on the duration information associated with the node variables. Formally, gaps in CLLS constraints may only be closed if the duration information of the involved node variables is compatible. Otherwise, these gaps are used for the insertion of additional information into the constraints. This predicts that DP-triggered reinterpretations affect the same positions in CLLS constraints as semantically triggered reinterpretation.

To integrate the DP into the proposed account of reinterpretation, duration information is modelled in terms of a set D of subsorts of EV. The elements of D correspond to the set N_C of convex subsets of $N_0 \cup \{\infty\}$ (excluding the empty set). This correspondence takes the form of a *homomorphism* from $\langle N_C, \cup, \subseteq, N_0 \cup \{\infty\}\rangle$ into $\langle D, \sqcup_S, \sqsubseteq_S, \text{EV}\rangle$.[71] Thus, two duration sorts have a common subsort if the corresponding granularity sets have a nonempty intersection.

Duration sorts carry mnemonic names: The sort that corresponds to the granularity set $\{a,b,c\}$ is written (in boldface) as **a_b_c**. Sorts that correspond to a granularity set $\{x|x \geq n\}$ for $n \in N_0$ are rendered as '**≥n**'. E.g., the duration sort for the playing of a sonata (minutes or hours) is in a normal context rendered as '**2_3**'. (Due to the correspondence of granularity sets and duration sorts, it is not possible to list these sorts exhaustively.)

The notion of compatibility in terms of the DP thus emerges as compatibility of the involved subsorts of D. Associating predicates with duration constraints is formalized as assigning the main eventuality argument of a predicate a specific element of the set D.

However, the subsorts of D differ from the other sorts that are assumed in this book: Conceptual knowledge associates them with predicates, hence, they do not show up in their lexical entries. Thus, the formalization of duration information in terms of sorts does not give it the status of linguistic knowledge.

Modelling duration information in terms of sorts is all it takes to integrate the DP into the proposed account of reinterpretation: In its sortal guise, duration information can exert its constraining power just like any other sortal information. Whenever a constructive solution of a constraint is to be derived, the closure of a gap in the constraint may cause constraints on the duration of an eventuality to become unified. But if these restrictions are incompatible, the closure of the gap is blocked. Hence, the only way to derive a solution for the constraint in question is to augment the constraint by additional material,

[71] This means that there is a function $f : N_C \mapsto D$ which is structure-preserving in that $f(N_0 \cup \{\infty\}) = \text{EV}$ and for all $n_1, n_2 \in N_C$ it holds that $f(n_1 \cup n_2) = f(n_1) \sqcup_S f(n_2)$ and that $n_1 \subseteq n_2 \rightarrow f(n_1) \sqsubseteq_S f(n_2)$. The operator $\cup$ is only defined for elements of N_C whose union is likewise convex.

i.e., by reinterpretation.

Consider, e.g., the constraint (389) in its non-abbreviated form.

(390)

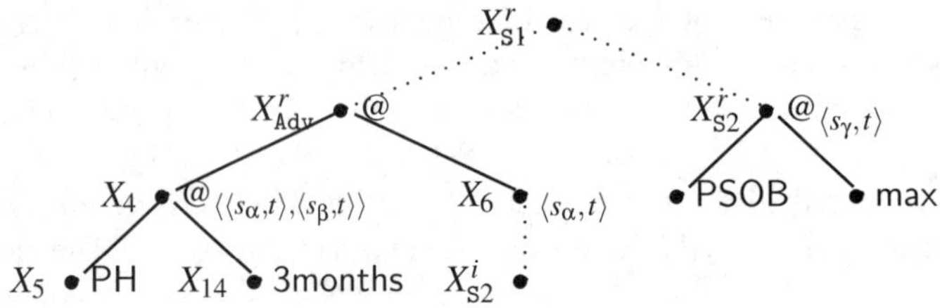

The aspectual constraints on the sorts α, β, and γ are $\alpha \sqsubseteq_S -\text{BD}$, $\beta \sqsubseteq_S$ INTER, and $\gamma \sqsubseteq_S$ PROC. In a normal context, the durational constraints are $\alpha \sqsubseteq_S \mathbf{6}$ (the argument of the durative adverbial must be compatible with a duration of months), $\beta \sqsubseteq_S \mathbf{6}$ (the result of the modification has a duration of months, too), and $\gamma \sqsubseteq_S \mathbf{2\_3}$ (playing soccer on the beach has a typical duration of minutes or hours).

This means that (390) has no constructive solution, since in such a solution X_6 and X^r_{S2}, and hence the incompatible sorts α and γ, would have to be identified. Thus, additional information must be inserted into the gap above X^r_{S2} to mediate between α and γ.

This augmentation involves an iterative operator as illustrated in (391). Here the result of semantic construction is on the left, the extralinguistically derived operator, on the right. The constructive solution of (391) corresponds to (392), the proposition that Max played soccer on the beach repeatedly for three months. Here the conflicting sorts α and γ are buffered by the iterative operator. The durative constraints on α from the durative adverb and *Max play- soccer on the beach* (after coercion) are the compatible $\alpha \sqsubseteq \mathbf{6}$ and $\alpha \sqsubseteq \mathbf{\geq 3}$. The latter constraint emerges through the application of the function (388b) to the granularity set associated with the modified sentence radical *Max play- soccer on the beach.*

(391)

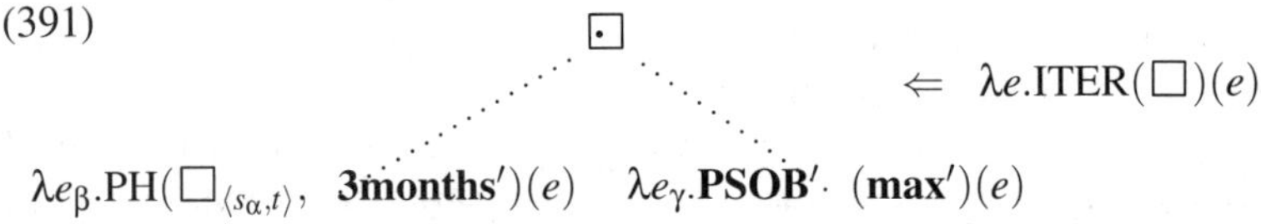

(392) $\lambda e_\beta.\text{PH}(\lambda e'_\alpha.\text{ITER}(\lambda e_\gamma.\mathbf{PSOB'}(\mathbf{max'})(e))(e'), \mathbf{3months'})(e)$

(382) is an example in which the Duration Principle enforces landing site coercion. Semantic construction returns a constraint for (382) that has no constructive solution due to the DP. Here $\alpha \sqsubseteq_S +\text{BD}$, $\beta \sqsubseteq_S$ INTER, and (in a normal context) $\alpha \sqsubseteq_S \mathbf{1}$ and $\beta \sqsubseteq_S \mathbf{2\_3}$.

(393)

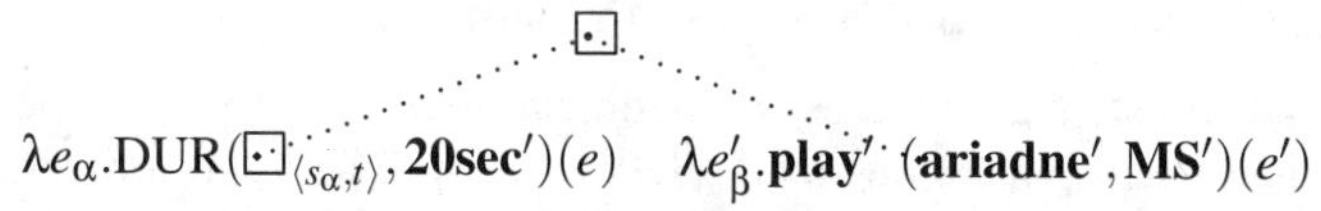

The landing site coercion for (382) augments the semantics of the argument in order to provide an additional landing site for the functor. This augmentation introduces a preparatory eventuality for Ariadne's playing the sonata as shown in section 4.2 for cases of aspectually triggered reinterpretations.

The operator that is inserted directly above the right dominance daughter in (393) is (394) [= (336)], which introduces the notion of a preparatory eventuality, with $\gamma \sqsubseteq +\text{BD}$. The associated duration constraint is quite nonspecific, as a first approximation, the duration may range from seconds to months, i.e. $\gamma \sqsubseteq \mathbf{1\_2\_3\_4\_5\_6}$:

(394)

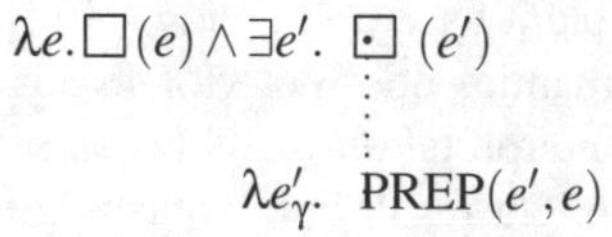

The result of this augmentation is the structure (395). This structure has only one constructive solution, in which the left dominance daughter immediately dominates the embedded fragment of the right dominance daughter. In this solution, $\alpha = \gamma$ (hence, $\alpha \sqsubseteq \mathbf{1}$); the incompatible sorts α and β pertain to different eventuality arguments. The solution corresponds to the λ-term (396), which denotes the set of Ariadne's playings of the Moonlight Sonata that have a preparatory eventuality of 20 seconds' length.

(395)

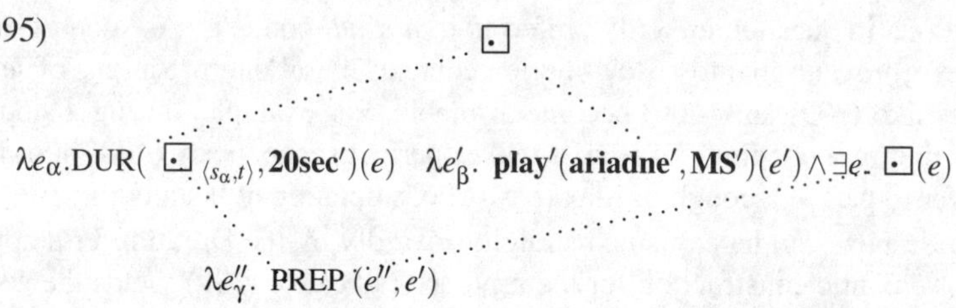

(396) $\lambda e'_\beta.\textbf{play}'(\textbf{ariadne}', \textbf{MS}')(e') \wedge$

$$\exists e_\alpha.\text{DUR}(\lambda e''_\alpha.\text{PREP}(e'', e'), \textbf{20sec}')(e)$$

In this section a Duration Principle was introduced: Semantic construction may only combine expressions if this does not bring about conflicting constraints on the duration of eventualities. Impending violations of this principle trigger reinterpretations, which alter the typical duration associated with the modified predicate so that the Duration Principle is met. The non-aspectual nature of the examples given in this section shows that the Duration Principle is not an aspectual phenomenon.

5.2 Applications of the Duration Principle

The DP was illustrated with cases of modification by durative and time frame adverbials. Other applications of the DP show up for the progressive, time point PPs like *at six o' clock sharp*, and adverbs like *suddenly*.

5.2.1 The progressive

The progressive operator requires an interval-based argument, which accounts for the contrast between (397) and (398) in that only the former is acceptable in a literal reading:

(397) Max was building a house

(398) # Max was being silly

But this selection restriction cannot explain why (399) and (400) [= (38)] undergo type coercion, although their semantics does not violate this selection restriction. (399) has a (preferred) interpretation that Max is *about* to reach the top (i.e., some eventuality that might result in the reaching but not the reaching itself is in progress), and (400) is (preferably) understood as referring to a whole *series* of coughs.

(399) (#) Max was reaching the top

(400) (#) Max was coughing

Worse still, there is yet another twist to these two sentences, which is indicated by the brackets around the hash signs in (399) and (400). The reinterpretations in question are only preferred in *normal* contexts. As soon as one moves from a normal to a slow-motion context, literal interpretations of sentences like (399) and (400) become available. For example, during a slomo recording of a coughing of Max it makes perfect sense to say (400) in order to refer to part of a cough of Max (e.g., Max's opening of his mouth).

These facts can be explained straightforwardly by the Duration Principle. First, semantic construction for the sentence radical of (399) yields the constraint on the left in (401):

(401)

$$\lambda e.\mathrm{PROG}(\boxdot_{\langle s_\delta,t\rangle})(e) \qquad \Leftarrow \qquad \lambda e''.\mathrm{ITER}(\Box)(e'')$$

$$\lambda e'_\varepsilon.\mathbf{cough}'(\mathbf{max}'),(e')$$

The durative selection restriction of the progressive operator is modelled by constraining the sort δ of the main eventuality argument of the first argument of PROG to a subsort of the sort $\geq\mathbf{1}$. In prose, the argument of the progressive operator must be 'non-punctual' (as defined in the preceding section) in a given context.

The context-dependence of this reformulation of 'punctuality' is crucial here. While the typical duration associated with the eventualities in the extension of *Max cough-* and *Max reach- the top* is the same throughout (the set $\{\frac{sec}{10}\}$), the result of applying the function f from absolute to relative temporal granularities to $\frac{sec}{10}$ may differ. In a normal context, this result is 0. I.e., the sort ε of the main eventuality argument of *Max cough-* is subsumed by $\mathbf{0}$. This makes ε incompatible with δ, which bars a constructive solution for the left side of (401).

Thus, (400) must undergo type coercion in order to derive a constructive solution for the left side of (401). An iterative reinterpretation suggests itself here, since the iterative of a predicate is associated with a longer duration than the predicate itself. This reinterpretation is depicted by (401) as a whole; on the right is the operator that buffers the conflicting sorts δ and ε. Both the progressive and *Max cough-* after type coercion impose onto δ the constraint $\delta \sqsubseteq \mathbf{\geq 1}$. The constructive solution of (401) corresponds to the λ-term (402), which denotes the proposition that a repetition of coughs by Max is ongoing:

(402) $\lambda e.\mathrm{PROG}(\lambda e''_{\delta}.\mathrm{ITER}(\lambda e'_{\varepsilon}.\mathbf{cough}'(\mathbf{max}')(e'))(e''))(e)$

But this reinterpretation was only necessitated by the fact that f maps $\frac{sec}{10}$ onto 0 in a normal context. As soon as one moves on to a slomo context – where $f(\frac{sec}{10}) > 0$ – one obtains the constraint that ε is a subtype of an element d of D (the set of sorts that model duration constraints) such that d and $\mathbf{\geq 1}$ have a common subtype. Then the DP no longer blocks a constructive solution for the right hand side constraint in (401), because δ and ε can be equated.

The analysis of (399) is as follows. The result of semantic construction for (399), which calls for reinterpretation in a normal context, is analogous to the one presented on the left hand side in (401). The constant '**RTT**′' stands for the property of reaching the top ($\delta \sqsubseteq \mathbf{\geq 1}, \varepsilon \sqsubseteq \mathbf{0}$):

(403) $\lambda e.\mathrm{PROG}(\boxdot_{\langle s_\delta, t\rangle})(e)$

$\vdots$

$\lambda e'_{\varepsilon}.\mathbf{RTT}'\ (\mathbf{max}'), (e')$

The reinterpretation for (399) that mediates between the incompatible duration information of PROG and its argument is a case of type coercion in which the operator (404) maps properties of eventualities P onto the property of being a preparatory eventuality of a P-eventuality:[72]

(404) $\lambda e_{\alpha} \exists e'_{\beta}.\Box(e') \wedge \mathrm{PREP}(e, e')$

[72]This operator does not address a problem with the status of the involved P-eventuality that is closely related to the imperfective paradox (see section 2.4.2): The existence of a preparatory eventuality for a P-eventuality does not in itself guarantee the existence of the P-eventuality.

The constraints $\alpha \sqsubseteq$ +BD and $\beta \sqsubseteq$ +TEL apply. The duration associated with the preparatory eventuality in (404) is modelled by $\{min, hour, day, week\}$ (because the culminative event is a climbing). Thus, in a normal context, $\alpha \sqsubseteq$ **2_3_4_5**. $\beta \sqsubseteq$ +TEL restricts the reinterpretation to telic predicates and thus blocks potential overgeneration in that no such reinterpretation is available, e.g., for progressives of stative predicates (405):

(405) * Amélie was being there

Inserting (404) between functor and argument in the semantics of (399) leads to a constraint whose constructive solution corresponds to (406), the set of eventualities that spatiotemporally coincide with a proper part of an eventuality in the extension of a predicate. This predicate expresses the property of being a preparatory eventuality of an eventuality of Max reaching the top. (406) models the fact that (399) does not entail Max's reaching the top, since the progressive has widest scope. The conflicting sorts δ (= α) and ε (= β) are again buffered:

(406) $\lambda e.\mathrm{PROG}(\lambda e''_{\delta}\exists e'_{\varepsilon}.\mathbf{RTT}'(\mathbf{max}')(e') \wedge \mathrm{PREP}(e'', e'))(e)$

In sum, the interpretation of examples like (399) and (400), in which the progressive applies to 'punctual' predicates, can be modelled in terms of the DP. The intuitions about these examples are encoded directly: They are acceptable in a slow-motion context but not in a normal context.

5.2.2 Time point PPs

The next area of application for the Duration Principle is time point PPs like *at six o'clock sharp* or *at that moment*. At a first glance, time point PPs seem to be compatible with stative predicates (like (407); although, surprisingly, ingressive reinterpretation is optional here, which is expressed by putting the hash sign in brackets) and some intergressive (409) and change predicates (412):

(407) (#) Nigel was in the pub at noon sharp

(408) # Nigel ran at noon sharp

(409) Nigel coughed at noon sharp

(410) # Nigel played the sonata at noon sharp

(411) # Nigel went to the pub at noon sharp

(412) Nigel vanished at noon sharp

Process predicates (408) as well as certain intergressive (410) and change predicates (411) must undergo an ingressive reinterpretation in order to be compatible with time point PPs.

Once again the Duration Principle can account for the data: Time point PPs select for predicates that are associated with an *instantaneous* duration. For the interval-based predicates in (408)-(412), the contrasts in acceptability between (408), (410), and (411) vs. (409) and (412), respectively, follow immediately, the predicates *Nigel cough-* and *Nigel vanish-*, are associated with such a duration in a normal context, but *Nigel run-*, *Nigel play- the sonata* and *Nigel go- to the pub* are not.

Formally: Predicates that are modified by time point PPs must have the type $\langle s_\alpha, t\rangle$, where $\alpha \sqsubseteq \mathbf{0}$. In addition, the typical duration associated with an ingressive is modelled by the singleton set $\{\frac{sec}{10}\}$, i.e., an instant in a normal context.

The granularity sets associated with *Nigel run-*, *Nigel play- the sonata*, and *Nigel go- to the pub* comprise only absolute granularities that are larger than $\frac{sec}{10}$. I.e., all these granularities are mapped onto relative granularities that are greater than zero in a normal context. Only an ingressive reinterpretation returns an expression that is compatible with time point PPs in DP terms. The predicates *Nigel cough-* and *Nigel vanish-*, in contrast, are associated with absolute granularity sets that comprise $\frac{sec}{10}$, i.e., in a normal context their modification by time point PPs does not violate the DP.

Finally, a stative predicate like *Nigel be- in the pub* is associated with the granularity set $\{\frac{sec}{10}, sec, min, hour\}$. The intuition behind this association is that the typical duration associated with the property of being in a pub may be very short or extend up to some hours. This duration information ties in with the fact that stative predicates are divisive (they hold for every part of eventualities in their extension). Hence, in a normal context, *Max be- in the pub* is compatible with a time point PP *both* in its literal reading and in an ingressive reinterpretation.

However, this regularity seems to have exceptions, which shows up, e.g., in that stative predicates like *Max be- a smoker* are not compatible with time point PPs:

(413) # Max was a smoker at six

The difference between (407) and (413) could be attributed to the intuition that the involved predicates should be associated with different typical durations, even though both are stative: The typical duration of habits far exceeds the typical duration of a stay in the pub. Formally, the property of being a smoker would be associated with the granularity set $\{month, year\}$ (i.e., habits typically last months or years). Hence, in a normal context, no literal reading is available for (413).[73]

The proposed analysis predicts context-depencency for the compatibility of predicates with time point PPs. This is illustrated by (414):

(414) (#) At that moment, the Neanderthal Man died out

In a normal context, *die out* is not compatible with time point PPs; its typical duration is modelled by a set of absolute granularities whose smallest member is larger than $\frac{sec}{10}$. But in a historical 'time-lapse' perspective that condenses whole thousands of years into single moments, examples like (414) are acceptable, which fits in with my analysis.

5.2.3 *Suddenly*

Adverbials like *suddenly* present another case that lends itself to an explanation in terms of the DP. These adverbials are similar to time point PPs in that they are compatible with some, but not all, intergressive and change predicates. (As opposed to time point PPs, these adverbials carry an aspectual selection restriction for a bounded argument.)

(415) Suddenly, Nigel coughed

(416) # Suddenly, Nigel played the sonata

(417) # Suddenly, Nigel went to the pub

(418) Suddenly, Nigel vanished

For (416) and (417) ingressive reinterpretation is called for. The explanation of these data in DP terms is the same as that of time point PP data: *Suddenly* selects for arguments that are associated with an instantaneous duration, i.e., carry the type $\langle s_\alpha, t\rangle$, where $\alpha \sqsubseteq \mathbf{0}$. The granularity sets for *Nigel cough-* and *Nigel vanish-*, but not for *Nigel play- the sonata* and *Nigel go- to the pub*, comprise $\frac{sec}{10}$. The contrasts in acceptability of the above examples follow directly.

This predicts that acceptability judgements for sentences with *suddenly* may vary with the context, which is borne out by examples like the following, which are acceptable in a historical 'time-lapse' context:

(419) (#) Suddenly, the Neanderthal Man died out

[73]The difference between (407) and (413) might also be attributed to the distinction between stage and individual level predicates (Kratzer, 1995): *Be in the pub* is an SLP, *be a smoker*, an IP. (The intuitive correlation between the two explanations would be that IPs are associated with longer durations than SLP.)

5.2.4 Semelfactive eventualities

The subsection on further applications of the DP concludes with *semelfactivity*. Predicates like *Max win- his first race* and *Max be- born* are semelfactive or 'once-only' (Galton, 1984). The extension of such predicates is a singleton set. E.g., as winning one's first race presupposes never having won a race before, no repetition of this eventuality is possible. Or, to put it a different way, once Max has won his first race, the resulting poststate (that he has won at least one race) cannot be undone. This entails that the *preparatory eventuality* and the *aftermath* of the winning of one's first race extend infinitely (on one side each). Semelfactivity partitions the group of change predicates. It shows up in the incompatibility of once-only predicates with frequency adverbials:

(420) * Max won his first race five times

One might describe semelfactivity by the property **NR**. For an eventuality in the extension of a semelfactive predicate P there is no preceding, succeeding, or properly overlapping P-eventuality:

(421) $\forall P.\mathbf{NR}(P) \leftrightarrow$
$$\forall e.P(e) \rightarrow \neg\exists e'.P(e') \wedge (e' < e \vee e < e' \vee (e \circ e' \wedge e \neq e'))$$

If P occurs as the argument of the operator ITER, a contradiction arises: The semantics of ITER expresses the fact that there are at least two P-eventualities. But to derive this contradiction, one would have to encode the property **NR** directly in the semantics of predicates.

The Duration Principle allows this encoding of the property of semelfactivity. The core idea centres on the fact that change predicates P restrict the vicinity of P-eventualites e: A specific proposition P' is false for the preparatory eventuality of e, but true for the aftermath of e. Formally, P' shows up in the semantic decomposition of P as the argument of the change-of-state operator BECOME. If P is semelfactive, the typical duration of the preparatory eventuality and aftermath of P-eventualities is *infinite*. This is expressed by associating P' (and its negation) with the granularity set $\{aeon\}$, which is mapped to ∞ by the function f in every context.

Then the incompatibility between semelfactive predicates and the iterative operator follows directly: Iterating a semelfactive predicate P would yield a constellation with at least two P-eventualities e_1 and e_2. The aftermath of the first eventuality e_1 and the preparatory eventuality of the second eventuality e_2 must overlap for two reasons. First, e_1 and e_2 are not adjacent: e_1 is a change of state, whose aftermath must be undone by an intervening change of state before another change of state of the same kind as e_1 can occur. Second, the aftermath of the first eventuality is of infinite duration, hence, does not end before the prephase of e_2 begins. The resulting constellation is depicted in (422):

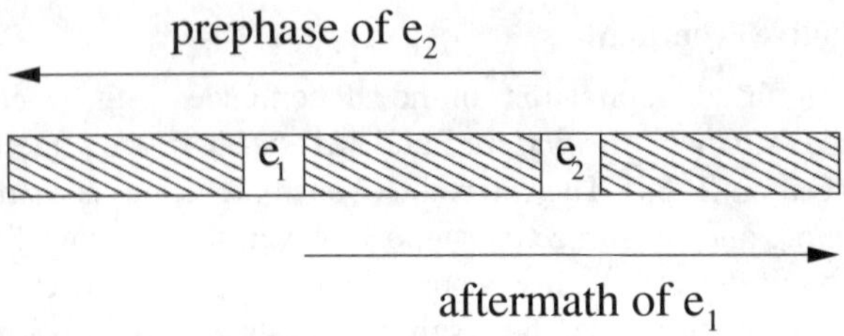

(422)

Here P' is both false and true for the intersection of the preparatory eventuality of e_2 with the aftermath of e_1, which is a contradiction.

This section has presented a number of applications of the DP in order to establish this principle as a pervasive (and non-aspectual) regularity of natural language.

5.3 Interaction of aspectual reinterpretation and DP

This section is devoted to the interaction between aspectual reinterpretation and the Duration Principle. The DP is an additional licensing condition for this kind of reinterpretation. I.e., one must take into account that reinterpretations may change the typical duration associated with the predicates they affect, this holds in particular for reinterpretations that use operators like the progressive or the iterative operator.

This interaction explains for quite a number of aspectual reinterpretation candidates why their range of possible reinterpretations is restricted: From the viewpoint of aspectual semantics, one could mediate between the mismatched constituents in different ways, but some of these possibilities would return semantic representations that violate the Duration Principle.

The prime example of the influence of the DP in the realm of aspect is the choice between different feasible reinterpretations in cases where the selection restriction of a durative adverbial (unbounded) is not met. E.g., from an aspectual point of view, the necessary type coercion in (423) and (424) could introduce either an iterative or a progressive operator between functor and argument.[74] Both operators mediate between the conflicting aspectual properties of functor and argument by mapping the bounded argument onto an unbounded expression:

(423) # Max played the 'Flying Dutchman' on his stereo for 10 minutes

(424) # Max played the 'Flying Dutchman' on his stereo for 5 months

However, this potential ambiguity does not show up in (423) and (424): In

[74] *Max play- the 'Flying Dutchman' on his stereo* is an intergressive predicate (playing an opera on one's stereo involves no aftermath), hence, reinterpreting the sentence by aftermath modification (see section 4.2.1) is ruled out.

the first sentence, progressive reinterpretation is the only option, in the second, the iterative reinterpretation. The reason for this is that both operators affect the duration associated with the predicates that undergo coercion: As spelt out in (388b), an iterative operator lengthens the typical duration associated with its argument. In contrast, the typical duration associated with the progressive of a predicate *P* can be shorter than that of *P* itself (388a).

Considering the typical duration of Wagner operas (some hours), the Duration Principle selects the interpretation of sentences (423) and (424). In order to make the typical duration of playing such an opera compatible with the duration of ten minutes, the progressive reinterpretation must be chosen. Likewise, only the iterative operator can make the duration associated with the modified predicate compatible with the duration of five months.

This interplay of aspectual selection restrictions and Duration Principle also accounts for the freedom of reinterpretation for sentence (425):

(425) # Amélie went to Oxford for one year

Since both an iteration of eventualities in the extension of *Amélie go- to Oxford* and the aftermath of such an eventuality may last one year, only the context (Amélie as a scholar or as a commuter) can determine the relevant reinterpretation of the modified predicate.

Another example of this interplay of the DP with aspectual reinterpretation is (426):

(426) # Max went to the 'Fox and Hounds' for five years

As the progressive does not lengthen the typical duration associated with its argument, a progressive reinterpretation of the modified predicate in (426) would fall prey to the Duration Principle, since the duration associated with the progressive of *Max go- to the 'Fox and Hounds'* is as incompatible with a duration of five years as that associated with the predicate itself. Similarly, the typical duration of aftermaths of pub-goings is definitely shorter than five years (no one stays in the pub for that long), thus, the durative adverbial cannot pertain to such an aftermath. Hence, the only feasible interpretation left is one in which a whole series of pub-goings is at stake: Iterative reinterpretations lengthen the typical duration associated with the involved predicates, which makes (426) compatible with the Duration Principle.

Such cases of the DP constraining the range of aspectually feasible reinterpretations may also affect time frame adverbials. Consider, e.g., the contrast between (427) and (428):

(427) # Ariadne will run in 30 minutes

(428) # Ariadne will run in three weeks

While (427) is ambiguous between a reading in which Ariadne ran a fixed distance in 30 minutes and one in which she started running after 30 minutes, (428) exhibits only the reading that she started running after three weeks.

In either sentence, the impending violation of the aspectual selection restriction (for a bounded argument) of the respective time frame adverbial can in principle be avoided either by a type coercion that introduces boundaries for the running eventuality (in terms of the operator MAX) or by a landing site coercion that augments the (unbounded) modified predicate *Ariadne run-* with information on a suitable preparatory eventuality, which provides a (bounded) landing site for the adverbial (see section 4.2.2 for details). These reinterpretations yield the two ways of understanding (427). However, the DP constrains these possibilities in that the duration introduced by the adverbial must match the one associated with the predicate to which the adverbial is eventually applied. This blocks the type coercion possibility for (428), since the typical duration associated with *Ariadne run-* after type coercion (in the range from minutes to hours; the operator MAX does not change the duration associated with its argument) is not compatible with a duration in the range of entire weeks.

Finally, for semelfactive predicates the Duration Principle interacts with aspectual reinterpretation as well. Consider, e.g., sentence (429):

(429) * Max won his first race for five years

This sentence exhibits the by now familiar aspectual incompatibility between a durative adverbial and its bounded argument. While such examples are usually reinterpreted in order to get a well-formed interpretation, this is impossible for (429): All reinterpretation options that are imaginable from an aspectual point of view are blocked by the Duration Principle.

First, assuming an iterative operator between functor and argument to mediate between their aspectual differences is ruled out by the conflict between an iterative operator and the semelfactivity of the argument (see section 5.2.4). Second, avoiding the aspectual clash between the durative adverbial and the bounded predicate by a progressive operator is ruled out by the DP: It blocks the applicability of the progressive operator to *Max win- his first race*, as the latter is 'punctual' in a normal context. Finally, a third reinterpretation option where the durative adverbial pertains to the aftermath of the winning is ruled out directly by a mismatch between the durations that would be assigned to this aftermath by the predicate (infinite) and by the adverbial (some years).

Accounting for such restrictions on reinterpretations of semelfactive predicates by the Duration Principle has the additional advantage of correctly predicting that semelfactivity is not a hard and fast property of predicates, but one that can be overwritten by context. This shows up for cases of aftermath modification by durative adverbials:

(430) * Smith & Co. built the bridge for ten weeks

(431) # The sappers built a bridge across the Danube for ten weeks

(432) * Max died for two days

(433) # My terminal died for two days

(434) # The whale swallowed Jonah for three days

The first two examples illustrate the fact that even for creation predicates there is a certain leeway in attributing typical durations to their aftermaths. While for these predicates the typical duration associated with their aftermaths is infinite, which is shown by the inacceptability of (430) (the example is Hitzeman's), conceptual knowledge like the fact that sappers are more likely to construct non-permanent (pontoon) bridges can license an LSC reading for (431), i.e., a reading that the bridge was in existence for ten weeks.

I attribute these different interpretations to conceptual knowledge about bridges and their builders that may overwrite default duration information associated with *build*. In contrast, Hitzeman (1993) distinguishes change predicates that allow aftermath modification and those that do not in terms of different aspectual classes (change predicates with and without an explicit aftermath.) However, this would introduce massive ambiguity into the lexicon, since the group of change predicates that allow aftermath modification, but only in very specific contexts, is quite large: Hitzeman would have to assume two readings for each member of this group, which can be avoided in my approach.

E.g., this group of change predicates also comprises predicates of destruction and consumption. Usually, *die* and *swallow* give rise to semelfactive predicates, as illustrated by (432), but Pustejovsky's example (433) as well as (434) show that this is only a default.

This section showed how the Duration Principle and aspectual reinterpretation interact. The (non-aspectual) DP constrains feasible aspectual reinterpretations, which explains why finding good examples for tests for aspectual classes is often such a messy affair: One has to tailor one's sentences carefully to comply to the Duration Principle. Unless this principle is factored out, the acceptability and the interpretation of many sentences in the domain of aspect seem to be quite unpredictable. Sorting out DP effects in aspectual reinterpretation cases therefore contributes to a deeper understanding of aspectual reinterpretation.

5.4 Excursus: Duration Principle and 'punctuality'

The chapter on the Duration Principle concludes with an excursus on 'punctuality', which is a prominent feature in some aspectual classifications but is not included in the aspectual classification assumed in this book (see section 1.6). In this section I will justify the omission of punctuality from this aspectual classification. My claim is that once the Duration Principle has been established there is no need for an aspectual feature of punctuality, since phenomena that have often been attributed to punctuality turn out to be just special cases of the DP.

After some remarks on the definitions of an aspectual feature of punctuality in the literature, the arguments that are adduced for such a feature will be reviewed. I will show that these arguments can be given an alternative explanation in terms of the DP. Finally, I will adduce general problems that arise if one assumes an aspectual feature of punctuality.

5.4.1 Definitions of 'punctuality'

This subsection presents a number of definitions that have been given for an aspectual feature of punctuality and discusses the ways in which this feature is integrated in aspectual classifications.

Basically, there are two different viewpoints on punctuality. Punctuality is defined either as the property of denoting extremely short (perhaps even durationless) temporal entities (e.g., Vendler 1967 or Piñón 1997) or as the property of denoting entities that *lack inner structure* (e.g., Pianesi and Varzi 1994, Moens and Steedman 1988, or Steedman 1997). These two viewpoints are related in that extremely short temporal entities are bound to have no inner structure. The reverse implication, however, does not hold: Temporal entities without an inner structure need not be durationless.

From the perspective of the Duration Principle, the first viewpoint on punctuality only takes into account contexts where the flow of time is normal and ignores slow- and quick-motion contexts. The second viewpoint, in contrast, at least suggests some context-dependence of punctuality: The slower the flow of time is, the more fine-grained details of an eventuality may become recognisable and, hence, relevant for the classification of an eventuality as structured or unstructured.

There is also considerable disagreement over the question of how to integrate a feature of punctuality into an aspectual classification. I will illustrate this with the aspectual classifications of Vendler (1967), Moens and Steedman (1986, 1988), and Piñón (1997).

Vendler's classification neglects the distinction between intergressive and change predicates. Instead, bounded predicates are divided into punctual ones ('achievement' predicates, e.g., *die*) and nonpunctual ones ('accomplishment' predicates, e.g., *build a house*). Vendler cross-classifies punctuality with boundedness, where punctual predicates are defined as those that are applicable to points of time (1967, 106f.; see section 5.4.2 below). This yields the well-known four groups *stative predicates* (punctual and unbounded), *process predicates* (not punctual and unbounded), *accomplishment predicates* (not punctual and bounded), and *achievement predicates* (punctual and bounded).

But this classification is peculiar in that stative predicates are grouped together with predicates like *explode* or *die*. These predicates make rather strange bedfellows, which is often noted in the literature on Vendler's taxonomy, e.g., in Verkuyl (1989). If they behave in the same way, they do so for very different reasons. Take, e.g., the fact that members of both groups usually do not occur in the progressive. For 'achievement' predicates, this follows from the fact that they are associated with an instantaneous duration in a normal context, which is incompatible with the durative selection restriction of the progressive.

In contrast, progressive stative predicates *P* are problematic because their semantics would (in a literal reading) boil down to the semantics of *P* itself: The progressive returns a stative predicate that refers to parts of eventualities in the extension of *P*, which would be equivalent to *P* due to the divisivity of stative predicates. Such a progressive expression would be ruled out pragmatically: The request 'be succinct' of the conversation maxim of manner (Grice, 1975) enforces the choice of the less complex of two equally informative expressions.

Other approaches introduce punctuality as a feature that does not apply to stative predicates. This avoids postulating common aspectual properties for stative and 'achievement' predicates. E.g., Moens and Steedman cross-classify non-stative predicates with the features '±consequence' (having a poststate, i.e., telicity) and '±punctuality'. The resulting classes are 'process' $(-c,-p)$, 'point' $(-c,+p)$, 'accomplishment' $(+c,-p)$, and 'achievement' $(+c,+p)$. Examples are *run*, *cough*, *build a house*, and *win the race*, respectively.

This classification acknowledges the existence of bounded atelic predicates: The 'point' class is a subgroup of the intergressive predicates of my classification. But it is problematic in that it neglects the fundamental aspectual boundary of *boundedness*. Hence, there is no way of distinguishing between intergressive predicates like *Ariadne play- a sonata* and process predicates like *Ariadne run-*: Both are atelic and not punctual, hence, would have to be classified alike, in spite of their difference with respect to boundedness.

Piñón (1997) models accomplishments and achievements by assigning to them fundamentally different temporal entities, viz., *happenings* with duration vs. durationless *boundary happenings*. Achievements are initial or final boundaries of happenings. E.g., *Max reach- the top* would be modelled as the initial boundary of a happening of Max being at the top, *Max leave- the top*, as the final boundary of such a happening.

While Piñón uses this analysis only to subclassify the group of telic predicates, the distinction should carry over to the intergressive aspectual class as well, since the difference between, e.g., *Amélie play- a sonata* and *Amélie cough-* is the same as that between an accomplishment and an achievement predicate. However, such an extension seems to be no straightforward matter. If one tried to fit in intergressive predicates in Piñón's classification, one would have to assume that they denote boundaries of certain happenings. But, then, what are the happenings of which the boundary happenings in the extension of *Amélie cough-* are a part? In addition, it is difficult to assign an orientation to these boundary happenings: Are they the beginning or the end of another happening?

Finally, there is the question of whether one could use the definition of punctuality offered in this book to characterise an aspectual feature. (Punctuality was defined as the context-dependent property of having the relative temporal granularity set $\{0\}$.) The following two subsections will provide arguments against this option: First, the usual arguments in favour of such a feature can be rephrased in terms of the DP (section 5.4.2), second, there are severe problems for such a feature (section 5.4.3).

5.4.2 Arguments for 'punctuality'

After the presentation of various proposals for the way in which an aspectual feature of 'punctuality' can be defined and integrated into aspectual classifications, I will now turn to the arguments that are to be found in the literature for such a feature.

The progressive

(In-)compatibility of bounded predicates with the progressive is one of the prime arguments for a punctuality feature. The fact that progressives of some bounded predicates must undergo reinterpretation is attributed to punctuality of the predicates. E.g., (435) [= (38)] is (preferably) understood iteratively:

(435) (#) Max was coughing

This is attributed to a selection restriction of the progressive operator that requires not only interval-basedness but also non-punctuality of its argument.

However, I showed that this regularity depends on the context. As soon as one moves to a slow-motion context, sentences like (435) are acceptable in their literal reading. I.e., there is no way of classifying predicates once and for all with respect to punctuality, at best one can state preferences or classify them for normal contexts only. In contrast to my DP analysis of examples like (435), an analysis that tries to explain such data in terms of an aspectual feature of punctuality cannot capture this context-dependence.

Time frame adverbials

The second main argument for punctuality is the observation that bounded predicates behave differently if they are modified by TFA like *(with)in two hours*, which was noted, e.g., in Moens and Steedman (1986). For one group of predicates (those that are grouped as 'non-punctual'), TFA specify the maximal temporal duration for the eventualities in the extension of the modified predicate. This holds, e.g., for *Ariadne build- a house* in (436). In contrast, TFA specify for a second group of predicates (the 'punctual' ones) the duration of a temporal entity that extends from a contextually given starting point to the beginning of the eventualities denoted by the modified predicates. E.g., (437) is understood in this way:

(436) (#) Ariadne built a house in two months

(437) # Max vanished in two hours

This difference can also be illustrated by the observation that (437) is synonymous to the sentence (439), where the preposition *in* is replaced by *after*, while the analogous pair (436) and (438) need not be synonymous (Piñón, 1997), if (436) is understood literally:

(438) Ariadne built a house after two months

(439) Max vanished after two hours

These contrasts between the interpretations of (436) and (437) are then attributed to a selection restriction 'bounded and nonpunctual' of time frame adverbials (TFA).

However, only the choice of duration in the TFA brings about this contrast. As soon as the TFA introduces a very short temporal duration, which is more in harmony with intuitions about the usual length of eventualities in the extension of predicates like *vanish*, sentences in which a TFA modifies a 'punctual' predicate, like the Pulman-style (440), are interpreted in analogy to (436): Here it is the vanishing itself that lasts for .2 seconds. Conversely, modification of *non-punctual* predicates by time frame adverbials may give rise to the same special interpretation as encountered in (437). This happens in cases like (441), where the duration introduced by the adverbial is too short to match the typical duration associated with the modified predicate.

(440) Max vanished in .2 seconds

(441) # Ariadne built a house in five days

These findings tie in with the fact that the pattern of synonymy between these sentences and their variants with *after* instead of *in* is exactly the opposite of that encountered for (436) and (437): There must be synonymy between (441) and (443), but not between (440) and (442):

(442) Max vanished after .2 seconds

(443) Ariadne built a house after five days

I.e., giving TFA an aspectual selection restriction for non-punctual predicates is too coarse to predict whether cases of modification by time frame adverbs must undergo reinterpretation.

The Duration Principle offers a unified and straightforward explanation for all these data. The contrast between (436) and (437) follows from an impending DP violation in (437) that calls for reinterpretation. The typical duration of vanishings is incompatible with a length of two hours as introduced by the TFA. (436) exhibits no such incompatibility. What is more, the interpretation of the sentences (440) and (441) is also predicted by the DP: It licenses the literal interpretation for (440) (the typical duration of vanishings is compatible with a time span of tenth of seconds) but not for (441) (building houses is associated with a temporal granularity of months or years, but not of days).

Pulman (1997), following Dowty (1979), proposes another way of explaining the contrast in interpreting bounded expressions modified by TFA by a punctuality feature. He assumes a lexical ambiguity of TFA. In one reading, they modify non-punctual predicates and specify the maximal duration of the temporal entities (times or eventualities) in the extension of these predicates, in another reading, they apply to punctual predicates and specify the maximal duration of another temporal entity that abuts a temporal entity in the extension of the modified predicate.

But this kind of account would run into problems for (440) and (441) and also for the contrast between (444) and (445). Both sentences would exemplify the postulated second reading of the respective TFA (since *the mountaineer reach- the top* and *Algernon spill- his coffee* would both be regarded as punctual), but the inacceptability of (445) cannot be explained by this account:

(444) # The mountaineer will reach the top within five days

(445) * Algernon spills his coffee in five minutes

In contrast, I assume that (444) undergoes landing site coercion to avoid a DP violation. LSC introduces a predicate for a preparatory eventuality of reaching the top. The time frame adverbial then applies to this predicate. Conceptual knowledge about this kind of eventuality licenses this LSC, e.g., climbing to the top can be a preparatory eventuality of reaching the top. No such LSC is possible for (445), since there is no preparatory eventuality associated with the spilling of coffee (Moens and Steedman, 1986).

In sum, the selection restriction of time frame adverbials need not include 'non-punctuality'. The restriction 'bounded' suffices, as the DP interacts with aspectual selection restrictions and exerts all these restrictions that seemed to be due to a 'non-punctuality' restriction.

Time point PPs

The next argument for an aspectual feature of punctuality centres around time point PPs. The fact that predicates differ with respect to their compatibility with these PPs is often attributed to a punctual selection restriction.

Following Vendler (1967), a predicate is punctual if it may pertain to points of time. This is fulfilled for 'achievement' predicates, which pertain to points of time only (like *Nigel vanish-*), and for stative predicates, which, although they hold for extended periods of time, hold for any point of time within these periods (like *Nigel be- in the pub*). Process predicates and 'accomplishment' predicates have no points of time in their extension.

If one now assigned a punctual selection restriction to time point PPs (where punctuality is defined in the Vendler style), the contrasts in acceptability as presented in the examples (407)-(412) would follow directly (see section 5.2.2 for details), except that the optional reinterpretation of cases like (407), where a time point PP modifies a stative predicate, remains a mystery (this problem also arises for the classifications of Moens and Steedman and Piñón).

However, Vendler's notion of punctuality is problematic in that it extends to stative predicates as well. But as soon as one restricts the punctuality feature to nonstative predicates, as in the analyses of Moens and Steedman and Piñón, an account of the above data in terms of a punctuality feature fails to explain why (most) stative verbs and predicates like *Nigel cough-* and *Nigel vanish-* pattern alike with respect to the compatibility with time point PPs.

Section 5.2.2 showed that the Duration Principle offers an explanation for these data that extends to the problems noted in this subsection (and is even better in that in can take into account that the acceptability of these data may vary with the context).

Causativity

Dowty (1979) explains and motivates a feature of punctuality that accounts for the distinction of accomplishments and achievements in that he analyzes accomplishments but not achievements in terms of semantic decompositions that involve the causative operator CAUSE (see section 2.4.2). This operator has two propositional arguments, which express cause and result, respectively. The second argument can be further decomposed into the change-of-state operator BECOME and its propositional argument. The semantics of achievements, in contrast, comprises only BECOME and its argument. The schemata for the decompositions are (446a) for accomplishments and (446b) for achievements, respectively. Here φ and ψ stand for propositions:

(446) a ψ CAUSE (BECOME(φ))

b BECOME(φ)

This account fits most telic predicates, but there are counterexamples: Causative predicates like *blow up the bridge* pattern like 'punctual' predicates in that they, e.g., cannot be modified by time frame adverbs or be the argument of the progressive without reinterpretation:

(447) # The soldiers blew up the bridge in five hours

(448) # The soldiers were blowing up the bridge

The TFA and the progressive operator pertain to a preparatory eventuality of the blowing up in (447) and in (448), which is characterized as having a length of five hours and as ongoing, respectively. The semantic area 'kill' comprises many more examples of this type, e.g., *shoot*.

In contrast, some non-causative telic predicates like *leak out* show the reverse pattern and behave like 'non-punctual' predicates. E.g., both (449) and (450) can be understood literally:

(449) The water leaked out in five hours

(450) The water was leaking out

What is more, Dowty's analysis cannot be extended to a distinction of punctual and non-punctual predicates in the domain of the atelic yet bounded predicates. There is no causation involved in their semantics. For instance, the semantics of *Amélie play- a sonata* cannot be analyzed in terms of a causative decomposition, see the discussion on Dowty's (1979) attempts in this direction in Egg (1994). This is problematic for Dowty's correlation, since the distinction between predicates like *Amélie play- a sonata* on the one hand and predicates like *Max cough-* (the 'point' class of Moens and Steedman) on the other hand can be described equally well as the distinction between 'achievement' and 'accomplishment' predicates by tests like the combination with time frame adverbials or the progressive.

To sum up, the correlation of punctuality and non-causativity is a rather weak one, which does not provide additional support for an aspectual feature of punctuality.

Completion

The next kind of test adduced for a punctuality feature turns on the issue of *completion*. Two instances of this test are the modification with adverbs that refer to (non-)completion (Piñón, 1997) or the compatibility with *finish* (Dowty, 1979):

(451) (#) Max coughed halfway

(452) (#) Max finished coughing

(453) Max played the song halfway

(454) Max finished playing the song

The claim is that the first two sentences cannot be understood literally. (451) gets no interpretation at all while (452) can only be understood as referring to the end of a whole series of coughs. In contrast, replacing the punctual predicates by non-punctual ones returns sentences with literal readings, as illustrated by (453) and (454).

While there is a contrast in acceptability there, once again it depends on the context, hence the bracketing of the hashes in the above examples: These judgements hold good for a normal context. But in a slow-motion context, (451) and (452) receive a natural interpretation as referring to an initial and a final part, respectively, of an extended eventuality of Max coughing. I.e., one can assign expressions that introduce the notion of completion a DP selection restriction in terms of the sort **≥1**, exactly as in the case of the progressive operator.

Intentionality

Finally, *intentionality* has been adduced as an argument for a punctuality feature. E.g., the contrast in acceptability between (455) and (456) would be attributed to a classification of *Ariadne notice- Nigel* as punctual, and of *Ariadne insult- Nigel*, as non-punctual by researchers like Dowty (1979) and Piñón (1997).

(455) * Ariadne noticed Nigel intentionally/unintentionally

(456) Ariadne insulted Nigel intentionally/unintentionally

But this correlation does not hold for all predicates. The first exception is causative predicates that are associated with an extremely short typical duration (like *shoot*). These predicates have already been mentioned in the discussion of a potential relation between causativity and 'punctuality'. They are directly compatible with *(un-)intentionally*. The majority of atelic predicates which would be classified as punctual (like *cough*, *knock*, or *click one's tongue*), are compatible with *(un-)intentionally*, too.

In sum, once the Duration Principle and its influence on the acceptability of aspectually relevant data have been recognized, there is no need to assume an aspectual feature of punctuality: The Duration Principle provides alternative explanations for the data that are often attributed to a punctuality feature, and, what is more, these explanations are even better suited to account for the data than such a feature.

5.4.3 Problems for an aspectual feature of punctuality

In this section, two global problems will be discussed that arise as soon as one assumes an aspectual feature of punctuality, viz., its context-dependence and vagueness of predicates with respect to this feature.

Context-dependence

A striking common denominator of many phenomena that are cited as evidence for an aspectual feature of punctuality is their context-dependence. E.g., predicates may be compatible with the progressive or with time point PPs in some, but not in all contexts. Since this context-dependence appears so often, it cannot be explained away as an idiosyncrasy of some linguistic expression or other. Therefore the definition of punctuality in this book reflected this dependence on the context.

But the use of such a context-dependent definition for the characterisation of an aspectual feature of 'punctuality' would make it radically different from all other aspectual features in that it can only be assigned to predicates relative to a context. All other features (e.g., boundedness) are assigned to predicates once and for all – either in the semantic lexicon or through processes of semantic construction (for the issue of polysemous predicates whose readings belong to different aspectual classes, see below). Thus, I conclude that even though it is possible to define a notion of punctuality in the presented analysis of the Duration Principle, this notion should not be used as an aspectual feature that is on a par with context-independent features like boundedness.

Vagueness

The second problem for aspectual theories that include a feature of punctuality is the fact that for many predicates there is a certain leeway in classifying them with respect to punctuality even in a *fixed context*. As an example, consider *close the door*. It is compatible (in a single context and without reinterpretation) with both the progressive operator and time point PPs, although these two should be mutually exclusive from the viewpoint of punctuality:

(457) Max was closing the door

(458) At twelve o' clock sharp, Max closed the door

Other predicates that are ambiguous in this way are *realize*, *recognize*, *create*, *destroy*, *convince*, and *die*.

Now ambiguity of predicates across aspectual boundaries is in itself no counterargument to these boundaries. E.g., even an aspectual boundary as fundamental and well-established as that of boundedness can be bridged by lexical ambiguity. Two well-known groups of predicates that exhibit such an ambiguity are exemplified by *comb one's hair* or *heat the soup* on the one hand, and by *see*, *realize*, and *recognize* on the other hand.[75]

The members of the first group are ambiguous between a (process predicate) reading where a continuous rise along a given scale (here, orderliness and temperature, respectively) is at stake, and another (change predicate) reading where this rise reaches a (contextually supplied) endpoint (when the hair is 'combed' or the soup is 'hot'). In the second group, there is an ambiguity between a reading that denotes a change of state (for the three examples, roughly, 'becoming aware of something') and a reading that represents only the aftermath of this change (roughly, 'being aware of something' for the examples).

But these ambiguities differ fundamentally from the ambiguities with respect to punctuality as sketched above: They are instances of *polysemy*, while ambiguities with respect to punctuality instantiate *vagueness*. Readings of a polysemous expression are clearly separated (though related), whereas the (in principle infinite) readings of a vague expression form a continuum (Pinkal, 1991). Vagueness surfaces, e.g., in ellipsis and negation:

(459) Max closed the door and Nigel did, too

(460) Max did not close the door

(459) is appropriate even if Max closed the door slowly while Nigel closed it in an instant. There is no zeugmatic effect in this ellipsis (see Zwicky and Sadock 1975).

For vague expressions, negation rules out the whole range of their readings, hence, negating *Max close- the door* rules out both its 'punctual' and 'non-punctual' interpretations. Thus, (460) means that Max did not close the door at all, neither did he close it slowly, nor did he close it in an instant.

The distinction between polysemy and vagueness is relevant for aspectual semantics: If the continuum of readings of a vague expression extends over two different postulated aspectual classes, this ensues a rather weak boundary between the two classes. In contrast, it does not indicate weakness of a boundary between two postulated classes if readings of one polysemous

[75] See Rothstein (2004) for an alternative analysis of the first group that does not regard them as polysemous.

expression occur in both classes. This reasoning shows that the boundary between punctual and non-punctual predicates would be rather weak. This is in conflict especially with Piñón's analysis, which assigns to punctual and non-punctual predicates fundamentally different denotations. No such argument can be formulated against the other aspectual classes, which strongly suggests not treating punctuality on a par with aspectual features like boundedness.

I conclude this section with the observation that vagueness with respect to duration as encountered in predicates like *close the door* can be represented rather straightforwardly in the DP approach. The representation only requires that one associates with predicates a typical duration in terms of a set of absolute granularities that comprises $\frac{sec}{10}$ and at least one larger granularity. This duration constraint expresses the fact that, in a normal context, the main eventuality involved in the semantics of the predicate may have a duration of an instant, or a duration that is longer than an instant. I.e., again a DP analysis fares better with the data than assuming an aspectual feature of punctuality, since it is not affected by the fact that predicates may be vague with respect to (non-)instantaneous duration even in a fixed context.

The result of the discussion on the motivation for an aspectual feature of 'punctuality' in this section is therefore that it seems adequate to substitute the Duration Principle for it.

As a conclusion to this chapter on the Duration Principle, I will briefly summarize the results of the discussion in this chapter.

- Duration information that is associated with predicates is an important factor of conceptual knowledge.
- The Duration Principle instantiates the general rule that incompatibility of an expression with conceptual knowledge may give rise to reinterpretation, too. I.e., the DP is not a semantic phenomenon, in particular, it does not belong to the realm of aspect.
- In terms of the DP one can explain a number of non-aspectual reinterpretations as well as the phenomenon of semelfactive eventualities.
- For cases of aspectual reinterpretation the Duration Principle was shown to act as an additional constraint on the range of potentially applicable reinterpretations.
- The formalization of the DP in terms of sorts that model duration constraints can easily be integrated with the proposed approach to reinterpretation. In this way, one can describe how the DP triggers its own reinterpretations, or acts as an additional constraint on other reinterpretations.
- The arguments that are adduced as evidence for an aspectual feature of 'punctuality' can be explained even better in terms of the DP than by assuming an aspectual feature. This confirms the decision not to include such a feature in the aspectual classification in this book.

6

Conclusion

I conclude with a brief recapitulation of the work presented in this book. First, reinterpretation was shown to be a pervasive and eventually pragmatically motivated factor in natural language that cannot be captured fully in a framework of compositional semantic construction.

In reinterpretation, contributions of linguistic and extralinguistic sources together determine the meaning of an utterance. I.e., semantic construction cannot fully determine the meaning of reinterpretation candidates, which are thus semantically *underspecified*. Reinterpretation processes are *monotonic* in that no results of semantic construction are undone during reinterpretation. Thus, reinterpretation is not a repair mechanism that steps in for results of semantic construction that turn out to be ill-formed and must hence be undone.

The discussion of previous work on reinterpretation identified a number of requirements for analyses of the semantics of reinterpretation cases. First, representations of reinterpretation candidates that exhibit semantic mismatches between their constituents must at the same time model these mismatches and still be well-formed. This requirement can then be generalised to reinterpretation candidates without such mismatches, whose literal interpretation would be in conflict with the context or conceptual knowledge: Their semantic representation may not be fully specified, to allow the integration of additional information that makes them compatible with conceptual knowledge or the context.

Second, the analysis must distinguish the different parts of the meaning of reinterpretation candidates, those that stem from their syntax and semantics, and those that are contributed by other knowledge sources, in particular, by conceptual knowledge. In addition, it has to account for the interaction of these knowledge sources during reinterpretation. It should also be capable of describing different patterns of reinterpretation, and of attributing reinterpretation potential to expressions in a controlled fashion.

To meet these demands on the analysis of reinterpretation, the proposed account was cast in an *underspecification formalism*. In these formalisms, semantic representations are *descriptions* of meanings, here, constraints in a metalanguage, the language *Constraint Language for Lambda Structures* (CLLS). These constraints describe expressions in an object language, here, the λ-calculus. CLLS was augmented with information for linguistically relevant sorts, in particular, for sorts that model aspectual classes. Next, I provided a grammar fragment that allows the derivation of the semantic representations presented in this book on the basis of a simple phrase structure grammar and an appropriate syntax-semantics interface.

Formally, the reinterpretation potential of expressions is modelled by assigning them only a partial semantic description. Extralinguistically derived reinterpretation operators can then complement this partial description and thus determine the meaning of the expression fully. I.e., in an underspecified treatment of reinterpretation the readings that are compatible with a description are not merely derived by arranging the material of the description into a well-formed semantic representation: For reinterpretation cases, it is characteristic that they call for the integration of additional material into semantic representations.

The underspecification of a semantic representation that is crucial for reinterpretation cases is introduced in the syntax-semantics interface or in the lexicon. Lexemes may also specify that they do *not* participate in specific reinterpretation patterns, which allows one to exert a very fine-grained control on the reinterpretation potential of an expression. My strategy is to provide reinterpretation potential for certain constituent structures and/or lexemes, irrespective of the question of whether there is actually an impending semantic mismatch. This strategy is justified by the observation that reinterpretation may affect semantically well-formed expressions, too.

I then presented in detail two patterns of reinterpretation, *type coercion* and *landing site coercion*. Both patterns appear in the nominal as well as in the aspectual domain. Type coercion means that semantic mismatches between a functor and its argument are buffered by an intervening operator. This reinterpretation pattern is familiar from the literature. Next, the additional reinterpretation pattern of landing site coercion was identified. In this case, semantic mismatches between a functor and its argument are mediated differently: Reinterpretation proceeds by augmenting the argument so that it comprises a part (the new 'landing site') to which the functor can be applied. I.e., in landing site coercion, the functor is applied not to its argument as a whole, but only to a suitable part of it.

With this machinery, a wide range of phenomena in the nominal and aspectual domain were described in a uniform way. In particular, I covered the aspectual reinterpretation options as spelt out in Moens and Steedman's work, and data that are discussed in the work of Pustejovsky's 'Generative Lexicon'. It was shown that the reinterpretation patterns are the same for both the nominal and the aspectual domain. The proposed analysis also highlighted the common ground between reinterpretation and related phenomena like the ambiguity that arises in the modification of agentive nouns like *beautiful dancer* or like the repetitive/restitutive ambiguity of sentences in which telic predicates (those that denote a change of state) are modified by *again*.

While the book focused on the syntactic and semantic aspects of reinterpretation, it expounded at least one extralinguistic phenomenon that is crucial for reinterpretation in greater detail, viz., the duration information that is associated with (though not a part of the semantics of) predicates. It was shown that the need to keep the duration information that is involved in an expression non-contradictory triggers some reinterpretations on its own and, in case there are several semantically feasible reinterpretation options for an expression, it acts as an important guiding factor for the choice among these options. The proposed approach turned out to be capable of integrating an analysis of this phenomenon in a straightforward fashion.

In sum, I see the contribution of this book in its comprehensive analysis of the syntax and semantics of reinterpretation that brings together different currents of research on reinterpretation. Reinterpretation candidates were established as expressions that can be assigned a (partial) semantic representation by semantic construction as in any other semantically underspecified expression. In this way, the boundaries of semantic construction for reinterpretation candidates were demarcated.

These results are an intermediate step in a larger enterprise of fully determining the meaning of reinterpretation candidates. Since syntax and semantics of reinterpretation candidates can provide only part of this meaning, the analyses in this book need to be complemented by investigations into the other sources of knowledge that are relevant for reinterpretation. In this way, I hope that the results of this book will eventually contribute to a global and unified approach to the meaning of reinterpretation candidates in that it defines a module for the syntactic and semantic processing of reinterpretation candidates.

Glossary

This glossary mainly lists the technical terms and abbreviations that are introduced in this book. Terms from other sources are also included if they play a prominent role in the discussion of the book.

* indicates that an example is inacceptable

# indicates that an example is in need of reinterpretation

(#) indicates that an example may undergo reinterpretation

? indicates that an example is of dubious acceptability

accomplishment Vendler's term for bounded and non-punctual$_1$ predicates

achievement Vendler's term for bounded and punctual$_1$ predicates

aftermath the state that follows a change of state and is immediately adjacent to it (Moens and Steedman's *consequent state*)

aftermath modification modification of change-of-state verbs where the modifier pertains semantically only to the aftermath

aftermath proposition that part of the semantics of a change-of-state verb that specifies the aftermath of the change of state

agentive modification modification of agentive nouns like in *fast typist* that introduces ambiguity because the modifier may semantically pertain to the modified expression as a whole or to its stem only

agentive quale in the Generative Lexicon theory, that part of the semantic representation where the origin of an item is specified

atelicity the property of introducing no change of state, a property of predicates

begin-relation relation between an individual x, a property P, and an eventuality e iff $\lambda e'.P(x)(e')$ is true for an initial part of e

boundedness a property of predicates; no proper part of an eventuality in the extension of a bounded predicate P is likewise in the extension of P (Krifka)

box representation of a hole in the shorthand notation for constraints

change predicate in the proposed aspectual classification, predicates that introduce a change of state (and characterise the aftermath of elements in their extension)

CLLS Constraint Language for Lambda Structures, the underspecification formalism used in this book

connector Fauconnier's term for reinterpretation operators

consequent state Moens and Steedman's term for *aftermath*

constraint an expression of the language CLLS which describes semantic representations (in this book, λ-structures); if it is underspecified, it can capture a whole set of fully specified semantic representations

constraint graph two-dimensional visualisation of a constraint

constructive solution λ-structure that is described by a constraint in such a way that each node in the λ-structure is denoted by a node variable in the constraint (i.e., the λ-structure comprises no new material)

culmination that part of a nucleus where a change of state takes place (Moens and Steedman)

culminative event my term for Moens and Steedman's *culmination*, which also stands for an aspectual class in their system

cumulativity a property of predicates; two entities in the extension of a culminative predicate P that are joined by a suitable join operator belong likewise to the extension of P

DA durative adverbial (e.g., *for five hours*)

daughter (node) ν_1 is the daughter node of ν_2 iff ν_2 immediately dominates ν_1; formally, if the path of ν_2 is α, then the path of ν_2 is αi, for $i \in \boldsymbol{N}$

divisivity a property of predicates; a predicate P is divisive iff $P(e)$ entails that P holds for all proper parts of e, too

dominance relation between two nodes X_1 and X_2 in a tree: X_1 dominates X_2 iff X_1 lies on the path from the highest node (the root node) of the tree to X_2

dominance diamond a constraint structure that characteristically emerges as semantic description for scopally underspecified expression; in such a diamond, a top hole dominates two fragments (whose mutual scope is open), and the fragments both dominate a third fragment at the bottom

duration sort a subsort of the sort EV[entuality] that models duration information associated with predicates and expressions that modify or subcategorise for them; it corresponds to convex sets of relative temporal granularities

Duration Principle (DP) the principle that states that semantic construction may only combine expressions if they do not introduce conflicting information on the duration of an eventuality

event predicate bounded predicate

eventuality state of affairs of any kind

experiental perfect the experiental perfect of an expression P is true in case there is at least one P-eventuality in the past

extended change predicate non-punctual$_1$ and telic predicate

fragment in a constraint C, a maximal set of node variables such that all its elements X_1, X_2 are pairwise connected ($X_1{:}f(\ldots X_2 \ldots)$ is a conjunct of C, where f is a label for X_1 and the arguments of f are node variables immediately dominated by X_2)

gap a position between two fragments F_1 and F_2 in a constraint, formally, a dominance relation between a hole of F_1 and F_2's root

Generative Lexicon (GL) Pustejovsky's theory of the lexicon, which regards it not as static but as a part of linguistic competence that allows the flexible yet compositional derivation of meanings

granularity set convex sets of temporal granularities that model the typical duration associated with a predicate

ham sandwich examples cases of NP-coercion that are typical for professional jargons, e.g., in restaurants, hospitals, or among musicians

hole node variable in a constraint that is not labelled

immediate change predicate punctual$_1$ and telic predicate

immediate dominance relation between nodes X_1 and X_2: X_1 dominates X_2 and every other node dominated by X_1 is also dominated by X_2 (no node may intervene between X_1 and X_2)

indefinite pronoun pronoun that introduces a quantifier in its semantics, e.g., *someone* or *everything*

instant depending on the context, the smallest possible duration, formally modelled by the smallest relative temporal granularity 0

intergressive predicate in the proposed aspectual classification, the class of bounded yet atelic predicates

interval-basedness a property of predicates, the property of being not stative

intnode root of a fragment that may serve as a landing site for a functor, it is made available in the syntax-semantics interface as the value of the CONT|INTNODE feature

iterative an expression that denotes the repetition of a certain type of eventuality

IP individual-level predicate

label symbol for a function; it is associated with a node in a tree structure and determines the number of the nodes that are immediately dominated by the node

lambda structure (λ-structure) an extension of a tree structure that corresponds to λ-terms (modulo α-equivalence)

landing site fragment in the constraint of an argument to which a functor may pertain (which its fragment may dominate immediately)

landing site coercion (LSC) the type of reinterpretation that introduces additional landing sites

maximality operator operator that introduces maximal phases for which an unbounded predicate holds

m-expression expression that exhibits semantic mismatches between its immediate constituents

N-fragment fragment that comprises the semantic representation of an NP except the variable that is bound by the quantifier as introduced by the NP's determiner

node start- and endpoints of branches in a tree structure, formalised as paths

node variable the variables in constraints on λ-structures that refer to nodes of these λ-structures

NP-coercion case of sortal type coercion that coerces $\bar{N}$ constituents of NPs into expressions that fit in with the sortal restrictions introduced by the verb of which the NP is an argument

nucleus eventuality consisting of preparatory phase, culminative event, and consequent state in Moens and Steedman's approach; in my approach, an eventuality with its preparatory eventuality and aftermath (their preparatory phase and culminative event together correspond to the culminative event in my sense, see chapter 1.6.3.)

path sequences of natural numbers that uniquely identify tree nodes, e.g., in a tree with two branches whose first branch branches again, the path for the root node is the empty sequence ε, its daughters have the paths 1 and 2, and the daughters of 1, the paths 11 and 12

point predicate punctual_1 atelic predicate

poststate another term for *aftermath*

pragmatic reinterpretation reinterpretation that is triggered by the incompatibility of the (semantically well-formed) literal reading of an expression with conceptual knowledge

predicate verbs, their projections and larger constituents that contain verbal projections on the condition that these constituents do not include tense and sentence mood (except for embedded sentences)

preparatory eventuality eventuality that precedes another one and is conceptually linked to it (not identical to the *preparatory phase* of Moens and Steedman, see chapter 1.6.3)

preparatory phase the part of an nucleus that precedes the culminative event in Moens and Steedman's notion of nucleus

pre-reading interpretation of an expression where a TFA modifies a sentence radical in the sense that the TFA refers to a preparatory eventuality of the eventuality to which the sentence radical refers

process predicate in the proposed aspectual classification, the class of unbounded interval-based predicates (for Moens and Steedman, the class of atelic non-punctual$_1$ predicates)

proposition property (or a set) of eventualities

punctuality$_1$ in some other aspectual classifications, the property (of predicates) of referring to temporal entities that are extremely short or have no inner structure

punctuality$_2$ in this book, the (context-dependent) property of being associated with the set of relative temporal granularities $\{0\}$, which is not an aspectual feature but interacts with aspectual reinterpretation

Qualia Structure (QS) in the GL theory that part of a lexical entry that specifies additional information on essential properties of its main argument (see agentive and telic quale)

quantised predicate bounded, atelic, and non-punctual$_1$ expression

reinterpretation candidate expression that must undergo reinterpretation

reinterpretation operator material from extralinguistic sources that is integrated with the result of semantic construction for reinterpretation candidates to obtain a well-formed, fully specified interpretation for the reinterpretation candidate

R-free an expression that does not need to undergo reinterpretation because of impending semantic mismatches between its constituents (as opposed to an m-expression)

root that node variable in a fragment that dominates all others

R-position syntactically determined position in a reinterpretation candidate where reinterpretation may take place

scopenode node variable in a constraint that models the scope domain of a sentence; for scope islands it indicates the maximal scope domain of their quantifiers (except of those introduced by an indefinite article), it is made available in the syntax-semantics interface by the CONT|SCOPENODE feature

semantic underspecification partial description of the meaning of a linguistic item, in particular, for cases of structural ambiguity

semelfactive the property of referring to eventualities that may occur only once, a property of predicates

sentence radical specific predicates, viz., sentences without tense and sentence mood, whose semantics is a proposition

SLP stage-level predicate

sortal type coercion kind of type coercion where a reinterpretation operator affects the sort of the argument

stative predicate in the proposed aspectual classification, the class of predicates that introduce no change of state, neither explicitly, i.e., by the operator BECOME and its argument, nor implicitly (as opposed to process predicates, which refer to a continuous change of state)

ST semantic composition semantically transparent semantic composition

telic quale in the theory of the Generative Lexicon, that part of the semantic representation where the purpose of an item is specified

telicity the property of introducing a change of state, a property of predicates

template abstract reinterpretation operator in the analyses of Dölling

temporal granularity convex sets of absolute temporal granularities (e.g., *min, hour, week*) model the typical duration associated with predicates, absolute temporal granularities are mapped onto relative ones by a context-dependent function f; convex sets of relative temporal granularities correspond to duration sorts, the formalisation of duration information in this book

TFA time frame adverbial (e.g., *in five hours*)

top hole hole that makes up a fragment of its own, characteristic for dominance diamonds, where it occurs as the fragment that dominates everything else

topnode root of a fragment for a syntactic constituent, made available in the syntax-semantics interface by the CONT|TOPNODE feature

tree domain a way of specifying trees; a finite nonempty set S of nodes (formalised as paths) that is prefix-closed (every node in S [except the root node] is the daughter of another node in S) and closed under left siblings (if $\alpha i \in S$, then $\alpha j \in S$, too, for $1 \leq j \leq i$)

tree structure a tree domain with an appropriate labelling function from labels to nodes

type coercion (TC) the type of reinterpretation that introduces additional material between a functor and an argument

underspecification formalism a language of expressions that serve the purpose of semantic underspecification

verbal nucleus that part of a predicate that is made up by the verb relation or property plus its arguments, except the main eventuality argument

VP-coercion the standard case of sortal type coercion that coerces verbs or prepositions to make them compatible with the sortal restrictions introduced by their arguments

References

Abney, Steve. 1987. *The English noun phrase in its sentential aspect*. Ph.D. thesis, MIT.

Alshawi, Hiyan, ed. 1992. *The Core Language Engine*. Cambridge: MIT Press.

Asher, Nicholas. 1992. A default truth-conditional semantics for the progressive. *Linguistics & Philosophy* 15:463–508.

Bäuerle, Rainer. 1987. Ereignisse und Repräsentationen. LILOG-Report 43, IBM Deutschland.

Bierwisch, Manfred. 1983. Semantische und konzeptionelle Repräsentation lexikalischer Einheiten. In R. Růžička and W. Motsch, eds., *Untersuchungen zur Semantik*, pages 61–99. Berlin: Akademie-Verlag.

Blau, Ulrich. 1978. *Die dreiwertige Logik der Sprache. Ihre Syntax, Semantik und Anwendung in der Sprachanalyse*. Berlin: de Gruyter.

Blutner, R. and G. Jäger. 2000. Against lexical decomposition in syntax. In *Proceedings of IATL 15*.

Blutner, Reinhard and Gerhard Jäger. 2003. Competition and interpretation: the German adverb wieder ("again"). In E. Lang, C. Maienborn, and C. Fabricius-Hansen, eds., *Modifying adjuncts*, pages 393–416. Berlin: Mouton de Gruyter.

Bodirsky, Manuel, Katrin Erk, Alexander Koller, and Joachim Niehren. 2001. Underspecified beta reduction. In *Proceedings of the 39th ACL*. Toulouse.

Bonomi, Andrea. 1997. The progressive and the structure of events. *Journal of Semantics* 14:173–205.

Bos, Johan. 1996. Predicate logic unplugged. In P. Dekker and M. Stokhof, eds., *Proceedings of the 10th Amsterdam Colloquium*, pages 133–142. ILLC.

Chomsky, Noam. 1995. *The minimalist program*. Cambridge: MIT Press.

Cooper, Robin. 1983. *Quantification and syntactic theory*. Dordrecht: Reidel.

Copestake, Ann. 2002. *Implementing Typed Feature Structure Grammars*. Stanford: CSLI Publications.

Copestake, Ann and Ted Briscoe. 1995. Semi-productive polysemy and sense extension. *Journal of Semantics* 12:15–67.

Copestake, Ann, Daniel Flickinger, Carl Pollard, and Ivan Sag. to appear. Minimal Recursion Semantics. An introduction. *Research on Language and Computation* .

Dalrymple, Mary, John Lamping, Fernando Pereira, and Vijay Saraswat. 1997. Quantifiers, anaphora, and intensionality. *Journal of Logic, Language, and Information* 6:219–273.

Dalrymple, Mary, Stuart Shieber, and Fernando Pereira. 1991. Ellipsis and higher-order unification. *Linguistics & Philosophy* 14:399–452.

Davidson, Donald. 1967. The logical form of action sentences. In N. Rescher, ed., *The logic of decision and action*, pages 81–95. Pittsburgh: Pittsburgh University Press.

de Swart, Henriette. 1998. Aspect shift and coercion. *Natural Language and Linguistic Theory* 16:347–385.

Depratere, Ilse. 1998. On the resultative character of present perfect sentences. *Journal of Pragmatics* 29:597–613.

Diesing, Molly. 1992. *Indefinites*. Cambridge: MIT Press.

Dölling, Johannes. 1992. Flexible Interpretation durch Sortenverschiebung. In I. Zimmermann and A. Strigin, eds., *Fügungspotenzen*, pages 23–62. Berlin: Akademie-Verlag.

Dölling, Johannes. 1993. Polysemy and sort coercion in semantic representations. In P. Bosch and P. Gerstl, eds., *Discourse and lexical meaning*, Arbeitspapiere des SFB 340, Nr. 30, pages 61–78.

Dölling, Johannes. 1995. Ontological domains, semantic sorts and systematic ambiguity. *International Journal of Human-Computer Studies* 43:785–807.

Dölling, Johannes. 1998. Modifikation von Resultatszuständen und lexikalisch-semantischen Repräsentationen. In P. Ludewig and B. Geurts, eds., *Lexikalische Semantik aus kognitiver Sicht*, pages 173–206. Tübingen: Narr.

Dölling, Johannes. 1999. Kopulasätze als Zustandsbeschreibungen. *ZAS Papers in Linguistics* 14:95–122.

Dölling, Johannes. 2000. Formale Analyse von Metonymie und Metapher. In R. Eckardt and K. v.Heusinger, eds., *Meaning Change - Meaning Variation*, Arbeitspapiere der FG Sprachwissenschaft, Universität Konstanz, pages 31–53.

Dowty, David. 1979. *Word meaning and Montague grammar*. Dordrecht: Reidel.

Egg, Markus. 1994. *Aktionsart und Kompositionalität*. Berlin: Akademie-Verlag.

Egg, Markus. 1995. The intergressive as a new category of verbal aktionsart. *Journal of Semantics* 12:311–356.

Egg, Markus. 1999. Derivation and resolution of ambiguities in *wieder*-sentences. In P. Dekker, ed., *Proceedings of the 12th Amsterdam Colloquium*, pages 109–114. ILLC, Amsterdam.

Egg, Markus and Michael Herweg. 1994. A type hierarchy for aspectual classification. In H. Trost, ed., *KONVENS '94, Verarbeitung natürlicher Sprache*, pages 92–101. Springer.

Egg, Markus, Alexander Koller, and Joachim Niehren. 2001. The constraint language for lambda-structures. *Journal of Logic, Language, and Information* 10:457–485.

Egg, Markus, Joachim Niehren, Peter Ruhrberg, and Feiyu Xu. 1998. Constraints over lambda-structures in semantic underspecification. In *Proceedings of ACL/COLING '98*, pages 353–359. Montreal, Canada.

van Eijck, Jan and Manfred Pinkal. 1996. What do underspecified expressions mean? In R. Cooper et al., eds., *Building the framework*, FraCaS Deliverable D 15, section 10.1, pages 264–266.

Fabricius-Hansen, Catherine. 1983. Wieder éin *wieder*? Zur Semantik von *wieder*. In R. Bäuerle, C. Schwarze, and v. Stechow. A., eds., *Meaning, use, and the interpretation of language*, pages 97–120. Berlin: de Gruyter.

Fauconnier, Gilles. 1985. *Mental Spaces. Aspects of meaning construction in natural language*. MIT Press.

Fodor, Jerry and Ernie Lepore. 1998. The emptiness of the lexicon: Reflections on James Pustejovsky's The Generative Lexicon. *Linguistic Inquiry* 29:269–288.

Galton, Anthony. 1984. *The logic of aspect*. Oxford: Clarendon Press.

Gardent, Claire and Michael Kohlhase. 1996. Higher-order coloured unification and natural language semantics. In *Proceedings of the 34th Annual Meeting of the ACL*. Santa Cruz.

Godard, Danièle and Jacques Jayez. 1993. Towards a proper treatment of coercion phenomena. In *Proceedings of the Sixth Conference of the EACL*, pages 168–177. Utrecht.

Grice, Paul. 1975. Logic and conversation. In P. Cole and J. Morgan, eds., *Syntax and semantics 3: Speech acts*, pages 41–58. New York: Academic Press.

Grimshaw, Jane. 1982. On the lexical representation of Romance reflexive clitics. In J. Bresnan, ed., *The mental representation of grammatical relations*, pages 86–148. Cambridge: MIT Press.

Herweg, Michael. 1990. *Zeitaspekte*. Wiesbaden: Deutscher Universitäts-Verlag.

Herweg, Michael. 1991a. A critical examination of two classical approaches to aspect. *Journal of Semantics* 8:363–402.

Herweg, Michael. 1991b. Temporale Konjunktionen und Aspekt. *Kognitionswissenschaft* 2:51–90.

Hitzeman, Janet. 1993. *Temporal adverbials and the syntax-semantics interface*. Ph.D. thesis, University of Rochester.

Hitzeman, Janet. 1997. Semantic partition and the ambiguity of sentences containint temporal adverbials. *Natural Language Semantics* 5:87–100.

Jackendoff, Ray. 1997. *The architecture of the language faculty*. Cambridge: MIT Press.

Jaspars, Jan and Jan van Eijck. 1996. Underspecification and reasoning. In R. Cooper et al., eds., *Building the framework*, FraCaS Deliverable D 15, section 10.2, pages 266–287.

Kager, René. 1999. *Optimality theory*. Cambridge: Cambridge University Press.

Kamp, Hans and Antje Roßdeutscher. 1994. DRS-construction and lexically driven inference. *Theoretical Linguistics* 20:165–235.

Kamp, Hans and Uwe Reyle. 1993. *From Discourse to Logic*. Dordrecht: Kluwer.

Karttunen, Lauri and Stanley Peters. 1980. Interrogative quantifiers. In C. Rohrer, ed., *Time, tense, and quantifiers*, pages 181–205. Tübingen: Niemeyer.

Koenig, Jean-Pierre and Nuttanart Muansuwan. 2000. How to end without ever finishing: Thai semi-perfective markers. *Journal of Semantics* 17:147–18.

Koller, Alexander. 1998. Evaluating context unification for semantic underspecification. In I. Kruijff-Korbayová, ed., *Proceedings of the Third Student Session of the ESSLLI*, pages 188–199. Saarbrücken.

Koller, Alexander, Kurt Mehlhorn, and Joachim Niehren. 2000a. A polynomial-time fragment of dominance constraints. In *Proceedings of the 38th ACL*. Hong Kong.

Koller, Alexander and Joachim Niehren. 2000. On underspecified processing of dynamic semantics. In *Proceedings of COLING-2000*. Saarbrücken.

Koller, Alexander, Joachim Niehren, and Kristina Striegnitz. 2000b. Relaxing underspecified semantic representations for reinterpretation. *Grammars* 3:217–241.

Kratzer, Angelika. 1995. Stage-level and individual-level predicates. In G. Carlson and F. Pelletier, eds., *The generic book*, pages 125–175. University of Chicago Press.

Krifka, Manfred. 1989. *Nominalreferenz und Zeitkonstitution*. München: Fink.

Krifka, Manfred. 1992. Thematic roles as links between nominal reference and temporal constitution. In I. Sag and A. Sabolcsi, eds., *Lexical matters*, pages 29–53. Stanford: CSLI.

Krifka, Manfred. 1995. Telicity in movement. In *Proceedings of the Fifth Conference on Time, Space and Movement*. Université le Mirail, Toulouse.

Krifka, Manfred. 1998. The origins of telicity. In S. Rothstein, ed., *Events and grammar*, pages 197–235. Dordrecht: Kluwer.

Krifka, Manfred, Francis Pelletier, Gergory Carlson, Alice ter Meulen, Gennaro Chierchia, and Godehard Link. 1995. Genericity: an introduction. In G. Carlson and F. Pelletier, eds., *The generic book*, pages 1–124. Chicago: University of Chicago Press.

Lakoff, George. 1971. On generative semantics. In D. Steinberg and L. Jakobovits, eds., *Semantics: An Interdisciplinary Reader in Philosophy, Linguistics and Psychology*, pages 232–296. Cambridge: Cambridge University Press.

Landman, Fred. 1992. The progressive. *Natural Language Semantics* 1:1–32.

Landman, Fred. 2000. *Events and plurality. The Jerusalem lectures*. Dordrecht: Kluwer.

Larson, Richard. 1998. Events and modification in nominals. In D. Strolovitch and A. Lawson, eds., *Proceedings from SALT VIII*, pages 145–168. Cornell University, Ithaca.

Lascarides, Alex and Ann Copestake. 1998. Pragmatics and word meaning. *Journal of Linguistics* 34:387–414.

Markert, Katja and Udo Hahn. 1997. On the interaction of metonymies and anaphora. In *Proceedings of IJCAI 15*, pages 1010–1015. Nagoya, Japan.

Markert, Katja and Udo Hahn. 2002. Metonymies in discourse. *Artificial Intelligence* 135:145–198.

May, Robert. 1985. *Logical Form. Its structure and derivation*. Cambridge: MIT Press.

McCawley, James. 1971. Pre-lexical syntax. In J. O'Brien, ed., *Report of the 22nd Roundtable Meeting on Linguistics and Language Studies*, pages 19–33. Washington: Georgetown University Press.

Moens, Marc. 1987. *Tense, aspect, and temporal reference*. Ph.D. thesis, Centre for Cognitive Science, University of Edinburgh.

Moens, Marc and Mark Steedman. 1986. Temporal information and natural language processing. Tech. Rep. Research Paper RP-2, CCS, University of Edinburgh.

Moens, Marc and Mark Steedman. 1988. Temporal ontology and temporal reference. *Computational Linguistics* 14:3–14.

Naumann, Ralf and Rainer Osswald. 1999. Aspects of 'until'. In *Proceedings of the 3rd International Workshop on Computational Semantics (IWCS-3)*, pages 191–203. Tilburg.

Niehren, Joachim, Manfred Pinkal, and Peter Ruhrberg. 1997. A uniform approach to underspecification and parallelism. In *Proceedings of ACL'97*, pages 410–417. Madrid, Spain.

Nunberg, Geoffrey. 1977. *The pragmatics of reference*. Ph.D. thesis, City University of New York.

Nunberg, Geoffrey. 1979. The non-uniqueness of semantic solutions: polysemy. *Linguistics & Philosophy* 3:143–184.

Nunberg, Geoffrey. 1993. Indexicality and deixis. *Linguistics & Philosophy* 16:1–43.

Parsons, Terence. 1990. *Events in the semantics of English*. Cambridge: MIT Press.

Partee, Barbara. 1986. Noun phrase interpretation and type-shifting principles. In J. Groenendijk, D. de Jong, and M. Stokhof, eds., *Studies in Discourse Representation Theory and the theory of Generalized Quantifiers*, pages 115–143. Dordrecht: Foris.

Piñón, Christopher. 1997. Achievements in event semantics. In A. Lawson, ed., *Proceedings of SALT VII*. Cornell: CLC Publications.

Pianesi, Fabio and Achille Varzi. 1994. The mereo-topology of event structures. In P. Dekker and M. Stokhof, eds., *Proceedings of the 9th Amsterdam Colloquium*, pages 527–546. Amsterdam: ILLC.

Pinkal, Manfred. 1991. Vagheit und Ambiguität. In A. von Stechow and D. Wunderlich, eds., *Semantik: Internationales Handbuch der zeitgenössischen Forschung*, pages 250–269. Berlin: de Gruyter.

Pinkal, Manfred. 1996. Radical underspecification. In P. Dekker and M. Stokhof, eds., *Proceedings of the 10th Amsterdam Colloquium*, pages 587–606. ILLC, Amsterdam.

Pollard, Carl and Ivan Sag. 1994. *Head-driven Phrase Structure Grammar*. CSLI and University of Chicago Press.

Prince, Alan and Paul Smolensky. 2004. *Optimality theory. Constraint interaction in generative grammar*. Cambridge: MIT Press. to appear.

Pulman, Steve. 1997. Aspectual shift as type coercion. *Transactions of the Philological Society* 95:279–317.

Pustejovsky, James. 1991. The Generative Lexicon. *Computational Linguistics* 17:409–441.

Pustejovsky, James. 1993. Type coercion and lexical selection. In J. Pustejovsky, ed., *Semantics and the lexicon*, pages 73–94. Dordrecht: Kluwer.

Pustejovsky, James. 1995. *The Generative Lexicon*. Cambridge: MIT Press.

Pustejovsky, James. 1998. Generative explanation in semantics: A reply to Fodor and Lepore. *Linguistic Inquiry* 29:289–311.

Ramsay, Allan. 1996. Aspekt and aktionsart: fighting or cooperating? In *Proceedings of COLING 1996*, pages 889–894.

Reyle, Uwe. 1993. Dealing with ambiguities by underspecification: construction, representation, and deduction. *Journal of Semantics* 10:123–179.

Richter, Frank and Manfred Sailer. 2003. Basic concepts of Lexical Resource Semantics. Lecture notes for the course on Constraint-based Combinatorial Semantics at ESSLLI 2003, Vienna.

Rooth, Mats and Barbara Partee. 1982. Conjunction type ambiguity and wide scope "or". In *Proceedings of the First West Coast Conference on Formal Linguistics*, pages 353–362. Stanford University.

Rothstein, Susan. 2004. *Structuring events: an essay on the semantics of lexical aspect*. Oxford: Blackwell.

Sadock, Jerrold. 1991. *Autolexical syntax. A theory of parallel grammatical representations*. Chicago: University of Chicago Press.

Sag, Ivan. 1976. *Deletion and logical form*. Ph.D. thesis, MIT, Cambridge.

Sag, Ivan. 1981. Formal semantics and extralinguistic content. In P. Cole, ed., *Radical pragmatics*, pages 273–294. New York: Academic Press.

Sag, Ivan. 1997. English relative clause constructions. *Journal of Linguistics* 33:431–484.

Smith, Carlota. 1991. *The parameter of aspect*. Dordrecht: Reidel.

von Stechow, Arnim. 1996. The different readings of 'Wieder': A structural account. *Journal of Semantics* 13:87–138.

von Stechow, Arnim. 2003. How are results represented and modified? Remarks on Jäger & Blutner's anti-decomposition. In E. Lang, C. Maienborn, and C. Fabricius-Hansen, eds., *Modifying adjuncts*, pages 417–454. Berlin: Mouton de Gruyter.

Steedman, Mark. 1997. Temporality. In J. van Benthem and A. ter Meulen, eds., *Handbook of logic and language*, pages 895–938. Amsterdam: Elsevier.

Taylor, Barry. 1977. Tense and continuity. *Linguistics & Philosophy* 1:199–220.

Vendler, Zeno. 1967. Verbs and times. In Z. Vendler, ed., *Linguistics in philosophy*, pages 97–121. New York: Cornell University Press.

Verkuyl, Henk. 1989. Aspectual classes and aspectual composition. *Linguistics & Philosophy* 12:39–94.

Verkuyl, Henk. 1993. *A theory of aspectuality*. Cambridge: Cambridge University Press.

Wahlster, Wolfgang, ed. 2000. *Verbmobil: Foundations of speech-to-speech translation*. Heidelberg: Springer.

Worm, Karsten. 1994. *Interpretation und Uminterpretation natürlichsprachlicher Beschreibungen von Zeitobjekten: Repräsentationen und Inferenzen*. Diplomarbeit, Universität Hamburg, Fachbereich Informatik. Available from `http://www.coli.uni-sb.de/~worm/arbeit.ps.gz`.

Wunderlich, Dieter. 1997. Cause and the structure of verbs. *Linguistic Inquiry* 28:27–68.

Zimmermann, Thomas. 1993. Zu Risiken und Nebenwirkungen von Bedeutungspostulaten. *Linguistische Berichte* 146:263–282.

Zwicky, Arnold and Jerrold Sadock. 1975. Ambiguity tests and how to fail them. In J. Kimball, ed., *Syntax and Semantics*, vol. 4, pages 1–36. New York: Academic Press.

Index

accomplishments, 4, 62, 208–210, 213
achievements, 4, 62, 79, 208–210, 213
aftermath, xvii, 3, 7, 8, 49, 59, 61, 96, 131–136, 158, 162, 203
aftermath modification, xvii, 3, 42–47, 49, 59, 142, 159–166
aftermath proposition, 49, 131–133, 174
agentive modification, 48, 51, 144–152
α-equivalence, 6
aspect, *see also* punctuality
  and quantifier scope, 19–21
  classification, 1–5, 7, 11, 58–64
  implementation in CLLS, 78–79
  tests, 1–4, 60
aspectual coercion, vii, 7–12, 37–40, 42–47, 128–137, 158–172
Autolexical Syntax, 54

β-equivalence, 6
boundedness, xi, 3, 7, 11, 58, 60, 160, 208, 209

causation, 96, 132, 133, 174, 177, 179
causativity, 213–215
change of state, 22, 59, 60, 62
change predicates, 4, 49, 58, 62, 96, 207, 208

conceptual knowledge, xiii, xv, 16, 109, 132, 145, 169, 207
  see also typical duration, 189
  difference to semantic knowledge, 25–30
connectors, 35, 126
consequent state, *see* aftermath
Constraint Language for Lambda Structures, 68–81
constraints on λ-structures, 69–71, 73–81, 94, 157
  capturing problem, 70
  construction, 91–93, 102–105
  constructive solution, 70
conversational maxims, ix, 209
cumulativity, 2

Davidsonian eventuality arguments, 55
divisivity, 2, 58
dominance diamonds, 80, 91, 105, 142, 147–155, 186
DRT, 11
Duration Principle, 34, 63, 189–219
durative adverbials, vii, xi, xv, 2, 21, 30, 42, 44, 97, 130, 159–166

enriched semantic composition, 25
η-equivalence, 6

garden path effect, xiv
Generalised conjunction, 57
Generative Grammar, 50–54, 175

Generative Lexicon, xiii, 7, 15–21
Generative Semantics, 174
genericity, 51, 96, 146, 150

ham sandwich cases, 33–34, 120–123

imperfective paradox, 95, 199
intergressive predicates, 58, 208, 209
interval-basedness, 58–60, 201
intnode, 149
intrinsic clitics, 179
iterative, vii, xii, xv, xvi, 3, 8, 10, 21–23, 34, 38, 97, 136, 166, 190, 193, 196, 199, 203, 204, 206

λ-structures, 68–73, 94
  fragment, 73
  gap, 74
landing site coercion, xvi–xviii, 41–55, 141–188, 196

Mapping Hypothesis, 51
maximality, 95, 130
metonymy, vii
modification of indefinite pronouns, 185–186

nucleus structure, xvii, 8, 43, 61, 158

Optimality Theory, 183–184

P-quantity, 97, 160
perfect, 3, 11, 59, 96, 131–136
  experiental, 3, 9, 135
point predicates, 3, 7, 21–23, 209
poststate, *see* aftermath
predicate, 1, 8, 189
preparatory eventuality, xvii, 8, 59, 61, 97, 158, 164, 167, 169, 170, 199, 203
preparatory phase, *see* preparatory eventuality
process predicates, 2, 5, 11, 58, 61, 209, 213
progressive, 2, 5, 11, 12, 21, 30, 37, 58, 94, 128–130, 193, 198–200, 204, 210
propositions, 5, 56
punctuality, 3, 7, 21, 58, 62, 193, 208–218
  context-dependence of, 216
  vagueness of, 216

Qualia Structure, 15–18, 47–50, 109
quantifier scope, 86, 91–93
quickly, 172

R-positions, 10, 12, 31–35, 39, 91, 107, 114, 115, 120, 126, 143
reinterpretation
  and anaphoric reference, 27–30, 35–36, 122–127
  danger of overgeneration, 31–33, 37–40, 45, 48, 114, 116, 143, 155, 156, 164–166
  interaction with Duration Principle, 204–207
  introduction, vii–xix
  pragmatic motivation, ix–x
  pragmatic reinterpretation, viii, 124–126, 134–136, 156
  sources for, xiii
  vs. polysemy and homonymy, xviii
repetivite/restitutive ambiguity of *wieder*-sentences, 173–185

scopenode, 84, 86–88
selective binding, 47–50
semantic decomposition, 60, 79, 174, 178–179, 213
semantic underspecification, xv, 9–11, 19, 65
semelfactive, 203–204, 206
sentence radical, 1, 55, 56
sorts, 6, 10, 11, 13, 195
  implementation in CLLS, 76–78
stative predicates, 2, 7, 11, 58, 61, 153, 160, 201, 209
suddenly, 202
syntactic decomposition, 175
syntactically transparent semantic composition, 25

syntax-semantics interface, 10, 12, 19, 24, 31–35, 50–54, 103, 111, 117
  implementation in an HPSG grammar, 83–93

telicity, 4, 7, 58–60, 132, 162, 173, 174, 209, 214
temporal conjunctions, 136
temporal granularities, 192
time frame adverbials, 3, 30, 63, 131, 167–171, 211
time point PPs, 2, 200–202, 213
topnode, 84, 86–88, 149
type coercion, viii–ix, 99–140, 166, 170–171, 196
  for type-theoretic mismatches, 101–110
  previous approaches, 6–41
  sortal type coercion, 13–15, 43–47, 110–122
types, 5, 24
  implementation in CLLS, 74–76
typical duration, xiv, xvi, 63, 189
  formalisation, 192–194
  implementation in CLLS, 194–197

underspecification formalisms, 65–68

verbal nucleus, 87